THE FORMS OF THE OLD TESTAMENT LITERATURE

Editors

ROLF P. KNIERIM • GENE M. TUCKER • MARVIN A. SWEENEY

*Published

2 SAMUEL

ANTONY F. CAMPBELL, S.J.

The Forms of the Old Testament Literature

VOLUME VIII

WILLIAM B. EERDMANS PUBLISHING COMPANY
GRAND RAPIDS, MICHIGAN / CAMBRIDGE, U.K.

To

Rolf and Hildegard

without whom

these volumes

would not have happened

Wm. B. Eerdmans Publishing Co.
255 Jefferson Ave. S.E., Grand Rapids, Michigan 49503 /
P.O. Box 163, Cambridge CB3 9PU U.K.

Printed in the United States of America

10 09 08 07 06 05   7 6 5 4 3 2 1

Library of Congress Cataloging-in-Publication Data

Campbell, Antony F.
2 Samuel / Antony F. Campbell.
p.   cm.   — (The forms of the Old Testament literature; v. 8)
Includes bibliographical references (p.   ).
ISBN 0-8028-2813-2 (pbk.: alk. paper)
1. Bible. O.T. Samuel, 2nd — Commentaries. 2. Bible. O.T. Samuel, 2nd — Criticism, Form.
I. Title: Second Samuel.   II. Title.   III. Series.

BS1325.53.C37   2005
222'.4407 — dc22
                                        2004061979

www.eerdmans.com

CONTENTS

CONTENTS

ABBREVIATIONS

4QSam	Samuel material from Cave 4 at Qumran
BHS	*Biblica Hebraica Stuttgartensia*
DH	Deuteronomistic History
DH	in lieu of short title for the book, *The Deuteronomistic History,* by M. Noth
dtr	deuteronomistic; when needed, "deuteronomic" will be written in full
GKC	Gesenius-Kautzsch-Cowley, *Gesenius' Hebrew Grammar.* Edited by E. Kautzsch. Translated by A. E. Cowley. 2d ed. Oxford: Clarendon Press, 1910
LXX	Septuagint (= Greek)
LXX^A	Septuagint: Codex Alexandrinus
LXX^B	Septuagint: Codex Vaticanus
LXX^L	Septuagint: Lucianic recension (often equivalent to the MSS. group boc^{2}e^2)
MT	Masoretic Text (= Hebrew)
NAB	New American Bible
NJPS	New Jewish Publication Society version of the Tanakh, the Holy Scriptures
NRSV	New Revised Standard Version
OL	Old Latin
PR	Prophetic Record
RSV	Revised Standard Version
UBS	United Bible Societies

NB. The asterisk (*) is used throughout this volume to indicate that only the relevant parts of the verse or verses so marked are referred to. In other words, the asterisk (*) is a signal that a part or parts of the text involved are excluded from the reference.

Biblical references are given to the chapter and verse numbering of the Hebrew text and (where different) of the NRSV, thus covering the two sets of numbering in current use. Which set is employed by a given translation will be quickly recognized.

Editors' Foreword

With this volume, Professor Antony F. Campbell, S.J., presents the second of his two-partite commentary on the books of Samuel in the commentary series of The Forms of the Old Testament Literature. The rapid appearance of this part after the publication of Professor Campbell's volume on 1 Samuel is thereby particularly fortunate.

For a variety of reasons that need not be demonstrated, it is a matter of practicality rather than of principle that Campbell's commentary appears in two volumes. Nevertheless, it is inevitable that the two parts of his commentary are kept and read together. They represent one coherently conceived interpretation of the books of Samuel, just as these books themselves are one literary work. As much as the reader will benefit from studying the individual *Chapters* of the commentary, her/his understanding of any *Chapter* in either volume depends very much on Campbell's discussion of the imbeddedness of each of his *Chapters* in the total biblical work. Thus, it is self-evident that *"Chapter 1: The Overall Shape and Scope of 1-2 Samuel,"* on pages 23-33 of his first volume, Campbell's interpretation of the macrostructure of the books of Samuel, shows the conceptual basis on which each individual *Chapter* about the biblical text rests.

The reader will find that the numbering of the *Chapters* starts in each of the two volumes anew with *"Chapter 1."* One can see that the author has had reasons for this arrangement, and that it does not point to a self-contradiction in his view of the uninterrupted continuation of the individual units within the unity of the books of Samuel. Regardless of the count which those *Chapters* that treat the units of the biblical text have been given in the two volumes, all those *Chapters* in both volumes must be read in the light of their consecutive arrangement in the one work of 1 and 2 Samuel. It is important to note that what has been said in the *Editor's Foreword* and the *Author's Preface* and his *Introduction* in the volume on 1 Samuel also applies to this second volume, and therefore need not be repeated. Still, careful reading is recommended of Professor Campbell's additional statements in both his *Preface* in this volume, and also in his *Introduction* to it in which he especially expands on the discussion of the nature of the macrostructure of texts. Again, as in *Chapter 10* of his first volume, the author discusses in *Chapter 12 the "Diachronic Dimension: From Past Texts to Present Text."* And his *Afterword: The Bible's Basic Role,* represents a unique addition to the commentary series, which deserves to be noticed specifically.

The editors cannot but continue to be deeply appreciative of the cooperation of Eerdmans Publishing Company, and the continuing vital support by the Institute for Antiquity and Christianity at Claremont Graduate University, including the Institute's support by its Board of Trustees under the leadership of its chairperson, the Hon. Attorney at Law Mr. Rafael Chodos.

Last but not least, Ms. Janice Bakke, senior Ph.D. candidate in Hebrew Bible at Claremont Graduate University, deserves admiration and gratitude for the extent and quality of her work in the FOTL project generally, and on the present volume specifically.

ROLF P. KNIERIM
MARVIN A. SWEENEY

Bibliography of
Frequently Cited Works

In the text that follows, the works below will be cited by author's name only; bibliographical details provided here will not be repeated within the relevant sections. Other studies by these scholars will be referenced in the usual way.

Anderson, A. A. *2 Samuel.* WBC 11. Waco: Word Books, 1989.

Barthélemy, Dominique. *Critique textuelle de l'Ancien Testament.* Vol. 1. OBO 50/1. Fribourg, Switzerland: Éditions Universitaires, 1982.

Brueggemann, Walter. *First and Second Samuel.* Interpretation. Louisville: John Knox, 1990.

Driver, S. R. *Notes on the Hebrew Text and the Topography of the Books of Samuel.* 2nd ed. Oxford: Clarendon, 1913.

Hertzberg, Hans Wilhelm. *I & II Samuel.* OTL. London: SCM, 1964.

McCarter, P. Kyle, Jr. *II Samuel.* AB 9. Garden City: Doubleday, 1984.

Pisano, Stephen, S.J. *Additions or Omissions in the Books of Samuel: The Significant Pluses and Minuses in the Massoretic, LXX and Qumran Texts.* OBO 57. Freiburg, Switzerland: Universitätsverlag, 1984.

Stoebe, Hans Joachim. *Das zweite Buch Samuelis.* KAT VIII/2. Gütersloh: Mohn, 1994.

Ulrich, Eugene Charles, Jr. *The Qumran Text of Samuel and Josephus.* HSM 19. Missoula, MT: Scholars Press, 1978.

AUTHOR'S PREFACE

Much of what was said in the Preface to *1 Samuel* remains valid here. The invitation to contribute 1-2 Samuel within this series, The Forms of the Old Testament Literature, was accepted long ago in 1976, following on the grave ill-health of the late Fr. Dennis McCarthy, S.J. The writing was begun with an extensive handwritten draft in 1977 (that was in pre-computer days). Since then, much has happened for me, some directly affecting this Samuel volume. *Of Prophets and Kings* was published in 1986, followed by *The Study Companion to Old Testament Literature* in 1989; articles after that included "1 Samuel" for *The New Jerome Biblical Commentary* in 1990 and, with Mark O'Brien, O.P., "Samuel–Kings" in *The International Bible Commentary* in 1998. Perhaps most significant for the present work was the publication, again with Mark O'Brien, of *Unfolding the Deuteronomistic History* in 2000. This was the story up to *1 Samuel,* but the beat goes on, so *Joshua to Chronicles* was written in between the final versions of *1 Samuel* and *2 Samuel.* Around the same time, I wrote the article "Form Criticism's Future" in *The Changing Face of Form Criticism,* which gave me the opportunity to assess the whole movement, from its beginnings with Gunkel and Gressmann. I admit to being proud of the article's last sentence: "It [modern form criticism] has a future — if its past is allowed a decent burial." As a result of all this, instead of these Samuel volumes being the start of a young man's publishing career they are far closer to an older man's retirement years.

Since this work began, major developments have occurred in understanding the task of interpreting biblical literature. The uncertainty and infertility of some biblical analysis have been more widely recognized; the final text has come to be more appropriately valued. Two convictions have come to the fore for me. First, in matters of biblical analysis, what is possible need not be necessary; if some editorial activity is merely possible, it need not have happened. Second, experience of the biblical text has led to the conviction that it has been produced by skilled and intelligent editors, rather than the "inept redactors" often assumed in the past. The first of these views may argue against implausible fragmentation of the text. The second puts a premium on the issue of meaning

xi

in the final text. Analysis that does not generate meaning is unlikely to have lasting impact. At the same time, the text on occasion reveals that skilled editors and copyists can sometimes act like collection-building librarians rather than unity-creating authors.

Over recent years it has become clear that the range of biblical interpreters is spread across a spectrum that extends from "process" people at one end to "product" people at the other — and the range will remain (see, for example, Mowinckel, who in his 1946 *Prophecy and Tradition* laid out views clearly and with compelling logic — views that, to this day, many do not accept). Process people prefer to, or are disposed to, or find themselves compelled by the present biblical text as end product to explore the process of the text's production. Product people prefer to, or are disposed to, or find themselves compelled to stay with the present biblical text as end product and to explore the meaning a dialogue with it may generate. Both process and product readings are legitimate and both are necessary (see *Unfolding,* 4-7); neither reading ought be presented as though the other was not part of a legitimate reading of the Bible. A treatment of the product that is incompatible with the nature of the process is likely to be flawed. A treatment of the process that invalidates the product is equally suspect. For many people, what might be called an elevated view of biblical text can be helpfully modified by reflection on the process that produced the text. For many others, the meaning and significance generated by reflection on the text as it now stands needs to be given a priority. History and present reality indicate that not only is the range or spectrum with us but it will and should stay with us.

Some find more meaning and satisfaction in exploring the process that produced the text while others find more meaning and satisfaction in engaging with the final product. Among the many influences that bear on the choice of approaches to the text, the possibility exists of favor toward incarnation or fear of it. To simplify outrageously — and with strong emphasis on the "some" and "others" in what follows, which means "by no means all" — for some, the "this-worldliness" of the process producing the biblical text is important, for it may point to the incarnation of the divine and the ambiguity of the human; for others, the "other-worldliness" of the final biblical text is important, for it may point to the revelation of the divine and a clarity in the human. To each their needs.

An important civilizing and uplifting activity, whether intellectual or emotional, needs to be distinguished from both these. It is the weaving of a discourse that takes as its point of departure aspects of the biblical text, and that may integrate further aspects of the text into the discourse, but that is focused on the meaning of the discourse itself rather than on the meaning of the biblical text. The worth of what is said is derived from or measured against the value of the discourse as a whole and not by the light it throws on the understanding of the text. Many a sermon and many a literary piece fan the spark of spirit for their hearers or their readers. Rather than as an exacting interpretation of this particular biblical text, the value of the discourse is to be found in itself, as an interpretation of life or an unfolding of thought.

What is sought here is an understanding of the present biblical text that takes into account a couple of centuries of scholarship that, for all its errors, has succeeded in making the case that the biblical text has a history of past development. Not all present-text interpretation makes appropriate allowance for this past development. If, in the practicalities of interpretation, the history of past development is to all intents and purposes denied, then the flat surface of the present text becomes a hypothesis — odd though that may sound. The hypothesis: this present text is of such a nature that it can be interpreted as though it did not have a history of development — as though the text were somehow "disinherited," artificially rootless, without forebears we may call upon (characterized and castigated by K. Noll as "either impervious to, or antithetical to, historical considerations," *Faces of David,* 12). Such a text is one-dimensional; the multi-dimensional past is excluded. Such a "flat text" is a hypothesis, as is a "flat earth"; in the light of the evidence, both are unacceptable. If the biblical text is treated in this fashion, some present-text interpretation may be reduced to a certain kind of reader response. It may not hold the interest of adherents to the biblical tradition who place a high value on the humanness of the text in its past history — the "incarnational" aspect of the biblical word.

Some yearn for simplicity in their Scriptures. Alas, that yearning has to go unsatisfied. The Scriptures are no less complex than most of us human beings.

Interpretation is a work of art. Art seeks to be expressive, not definitive. It is beyond the reach of a Michelangelo to sculpt the definitive David or of a Fra Angelico to paint the definitive Madonna. There is often more than one way in which a text may be structured and named. The definitive interpretation of a text is out of reach because interpretation needs to take account of the experience of each generation and engage with the needs of particular individuals. It is unhelpful to ask whether an interpretation is the right one; it is usually helpful to ask whether an interpretation is adequate and responsible. Responsible: an interpretation that pays attention to the signals in the text that need to be interpreted. Adequate: an interpretation that integrates all or most of these signals into a single interpretative horizon.

With the passing years, the practice of noting scholarly argument has been subordinated here to the need for an uncluttered text. As a result, academic references have been severely restricted in this final version of the book. The aim has been to let the text tell its story. The inclusion or omission of a reference has often been judged in this light. If any feel overlooked, I offer my regrets and apologies.

Bibliography of Works Cited Above

Campbell, Antony F. *Of Prophets and Kings: A Late Ninth-Century Document (1 Samuel 1–2 Kings 10).* CBQMS 17. Washington, DC: Catholic Biblical Association of America, 1986.

————. *The Study Companion to Old Testament Literature: An Approach to the Writings of Pre-Exilic and Exilic Israel.* Wilmington: Glazier, 1989; Collegeville: The Liturgical Press, 1992.

————. "1 Samuel" in *The New Jerome Biblical Commentary.* Edited by R. E. Brown, J. A. Fitzmyer, and R. E. Murphy. Englewood Cliffs, NJ: Prentice Hall, 1990.

————. "Form Criticism's Future." In *The Changing Face of Form Criticism for the Twenty-First Century.* Edited by M. A. Sweeney and E. Ben Zvi. Grand Rapids: Eerdmans, 2003.

————. *Joshua to Chronicles: An Introduction.* Louisville: Westminster John Knox, 2004.

Campbell, Antony F., and Mark A. O'Brien. "1-2 Samuel" in *The International Bible Commentary.* Collegeville: The Liturgical Press, 1998.

————. *Unfolding the Deuteronomistic History: Origins, Upgrades, Present Text.* Minneapolis: Fortress, 2000.

Mowinckel, Sigmund. *Prophecy and Tradition: The Prophetic Books in the Light of the Study of the Growth and History of the Tradition.* Oslo: Jacob Dybwad, 1946; cf. Mowinckel/Hanson. *The Spirit and the Word: Prophecy and Tradition in Ancient Israel.* Minneapolis: Fortress, 2002.

Noll, K. L. *The Faces of David.* JSOTSup 242. Sheffield: Sheffield Academic Press, 1997.

INTRODUCTION

Like its predecessor on First Samuel, this volume on Second Samuel sets out to build on some of the best insights from recent biblical interpretation. These show up in the concern for close attention to the present text, in the concern to show due respect for the text's past, and in the concern to focus on the fundamental questions of the text's form and meaning.

At present, we can no longer be satisfied with the old patterns of biblical exegesis. Ways are needed to combine appropriately the insights of literary analysis with those of developmental analysis in the service of meaning. Like its companion volume on 1 Samuel this book, coming out of the form-critical stable, is an attempt to explore new patterns. Two aspects facilitate the literary process. First, the text is not atomized. It is dealt with in its larger units, whether of sense or story, where meaning is to be found. Second, the text is not fragmented into a hypothetical past. It is dealt with substantially as it now exists, as present text. At the same time, a couple of centuries of modern research are not ignored; they have uncovered a history of the text that no postmodern should want to claim as non-existent. The opening to union between present and past is the recognition of the high level of intelligence and skill used by the editors who shaped the past traditions into the present text. Finally, the two basic questions of form criticism are constantly asked: What sort of a text is this? What does it mean?

1–2 Samuel

In the experience of many, no narrative texts in the Older Testament are more stirring and more challenging than those in the books of Samuel.

In the person of Samuel, they deal with the emergence of the figure of the prophet, so significant in the religion, politics, and literature of Israel. In the person of David, they deal with the emergence of the figure of the king, the head of central government in ancient Israel, both north and south.

1

The overall structure of the books is centered in the monarchy, begun with Saul and established with David. The role of the prophet is central to the establishment of the monarchy; but the prophetic role goes beyond establishment, claiming the right not only to designate and dismiss certain kings but also to exercise ultimate control over the conscience of the king. The preeminent prophetic figures in these books are Samuel and Nathan.

Without question, kings are of central importance in the text of Deuteronomy through Second Kings; and for the most part, later in the text, they are not looked on kindly. Almost all kings are judged as doing what was right or doing what was evil "in the sight of the LORD." Solomon set Israel on a downward course (1 Kgs 11:9-13, esp. when read in the light of 1 Kgs 9:1-9). Jeroboam caused northern Israel to sin (1 Kgs 12:30; 13:34); all the northern kings from Jehu to Hoshea are noted as not departing "from the sins of Jeroboam the son of Nebat." Manasseh in his turn "caused Judah to sin" (2 Kgs 21:16). Only three are noted without reserve as doing what was right in the sight of the LORD: David, Hezekiah, and Josiah. Chronicles gives a similar accolade to Jehoshaphat (2 Chr 17); it may not be surprising that the Josianic DH omitted reference to Jehoshaphat's reform — a much earlier reform that had, alas, so evidently not borne lasting fruit. In the present text Samuel's role is viewed as both crucial and complex: to resist the monarchy at first; to yield when appropriate and inaugurate the monarchy; finally to give the guidelines by which monarchy could function positively in Israel (1 Sam 12:14-15, 20-24) and to warn against the dangers of infidelity (12:25). The attention given to Saul's kingship and Samuel's initial resistance to it can easily be allowed undue importance, once this monitory role is highlighted for Samuel.

The perception of a Josianic Deuteronomistic History, followed in the time of exile by a fully revised version, changes much for both 1 and 2 Samuel (see Campbell and O'Brien, *Unfolding*). A positive attitude toward the monarchy is not at odds with a Josianic DH; the History, after all, is understood to have been put together initially in support of King Josiah's reform. In a Josianic DH, the role of Samuel in establishing the kingship begins with 1 Sam 9:1–10:16. Attention is freed to focus on the enormous importance of David for Israel's future. A reading becomes possible, even reasonable, in which — despite 1 Sam 7–8 and 10:17-27, as well as 1 Sam 12 — the *prophetic* moves in 1 Sam 1:1–16:13 are seen as directed toward establishing David as king, followed then by the *political* moves to establish David as king (1 Sam 16:14–2 Sam 8:18). This cannot be claimed as a mandatory reading; it can be claimed as a reasonable one. This reading facilitates understanding the texts as efforts to articulate the experience of the institution of monarchy among God's people.

As to the origin of our texts, we may assume that many of them began as stories and that storytellers were often singers, that stories were often sung rather than prosaically narrated. Three obscure references to both male and female court singers — not to be confused with temple singers (in Hebrew, a different word) — allow us to assume that both men and women functioned ordinarily as storytellers in ancient Israel. These three are Barzillai's comment in 2 Sam 19:36 (NRSV, 19:35), Qohelet's in Qoh 2:8, and finally the narrator's in 2 Chr 35:25.

It is important to be aware that stories do not necessarily provide us with accurate information about details of life in ancient Israel. Then as now, we may assume, stories needed to be plausible; they did not need to be accurate in detail. A story of a legal action does not tell us with a lawyer's accuracy how such actions proceeded. It tells us what a storyteller considered an audience would find plausible. A story of behavior in the royal court does not tell us with accuracy about royal protocol. It tells us what an audience could be expected to find plausible.

The form-critical analysis of stories is extremely valuable. The emphasis on story as story brings an appropriate focus to bear on meaning, why the story was told, and the how of the telling. It was once all too easy to assume that stories recounted what happened, with the result that from stories the sequence of events could be recovered. Even today, scholars involved in biblical interpretation will be well aware of the popular passion for explaining details of the text by recourse to what might have happened — the often supposed events. Stories are not driven by what happened, but by the plot around which the storyteller has chosen to weave the story. The task of form-critical interpretation, in recognizing a story, is to focus on how the story is told so as to squeeze from the text its meaning — the light with which the story illuminates human experience.

Form Criticism

Form criticism is for many a "red rag" word. "Red rag" words bring with them an association of universes of ideas, strong emotions, deeply felt experiences. For many Americans, "socialized medicine" is a red rag word. For many biblical scholars, form criticism is another.

Ironically, form criticism is as unavoidable as breathing. We practice both all the time. Clearly there are connotations to form criticism that turn an essential human activity into a red rag word. These issues — and the associated ones of genre, setting, and meaning — have been discussed in the Introduction to *1 Samuel;* the discussion need not be repeated here.

New Perceptions Embodied Here

These matters were discussed more fully in the final chapter of *1 Samuel,* concerning the diachronic dimension of the texts. The new perceptions most relevant here relate to the understanding of the texts of the so-called Story of David's Rise and what is most neutrally termed the Stories of David's Middle Years. A brief summary of the new in each case will be helpful here.

Story of David's Rise

Two insights are significant for the Story of David's Rise, which has been one of biblical scholarship's unsolved mysteries for some time.

First, the narrative is made up of a multitude of fundamentally independent stories. Some of these belong in series, but the series are relatively short. So, there is not one definitive Story of David's Rise; there are many stories that can be combined in various ways to provide various portrayals of David's rise to power. Whether the text we have comprises all the stories we do not know. The present text probably originates from the Prophetic Record, but that is no guarantee that it is exhaustive. A corollary of this understanding, based on the independent nature of most of the stories, is that the much-disputed beginning and ending of the Story of David's Rise may be a non-issue. Different portrayals may very well have begun in different places and ended in different places. Where 2 Samuel is concerned, a classic ending has been with the Davidic capture of Jerusalem. It is very possible. It is equally possible that a version of the Story of David's Rise went further to include the coming of the ark to Jerusalem, the promise to David of a dynasty, and even some report of David's position as more than a mere king in Jerusalem but master of an empire — in other words, parts at least of 2 Sam 6, 7, and 8.

Second, if the texts we have are reported stories or the outlines of stories, then allowance has to be made for the skill of storytellers in presenting their stories. Minor details that have demanded scholarly attention for decades may have been precisely the details that storytellers either developed or ignored. We would be unwise to proclaim what might or might not have been part of the Story of David's Rise; wisdom suggests a degree of caution in hypothesizing about the past.

Stories of David's Middle Years

Where the Stories of David's Middle Years are concerned, again two insights are involved.

- First, to forget the issue of succession, based on one miserable verse (1 Kgs 1:48), and let the identification of the text be based on its peculiar qualities — with its interpretation to proceed from there.
- Second, to limit the text to 2 Sam 11–20, where these "peculiar qualities" are to the fore and where meaning may be discernible.

The outcome of this is significant at both ends of the story. 1 Kgs 1–2, in itself, forms a satisfactory story of the succession to David's throne; it does not require literary antecedents. The self-contained story of 2 Sam 11–12 is a satisfactory beginning to the Stories of David's Middle Years; it does not need to be traced back into 2 Sam 9 or 10 or earlier material about the succession to David's throne.

Issues of the genre, setting, and meaning of this text will be dealt with in their place. It is important to recognize the neutrality and appropriateness of the title, Stories of David's Middle Years. David's eldest sons, Amnon and Absalom, are old enough to commit rape and murder respectively. While the unfolding of time is not specified, Solomon is born in 2 Sam 12. By the time of David's old age, as in 1 Kgs 1-2, he needs to be old enough to reign without a regent. "Middle Years" is accurate and does not prejudge the purpose of some superb literature.

Finally, the issue of "modeling" needs a word. It is in no way a claim that the text presents David as a model king. It is rather that David's behavior, as portrayed in the story of 2 Sam 11-12, provides a model, conscious or unconscious, for the behavior in the stories that follow. David wants Bathsheba and takes her; David wants his tracks covered and kills to achieve it. What Amnon or Absalom or Sheba want they move to take. Absalom wanted Amnon dead; David should have (and may have) wanted Absalom dead; David certainly wanted Sheba dead. There may not be conscious modeling here, but Nathan's words are prophetically right. "The sword shall never depart from your house . . . you did it secretly but I will do this thing before all Israel" (2 Sam 12:10-12).

Nature of the Bible

One paradigm for Bible users is rapidly losing favor as experience of the text overhauls tradition. The evident disparity of biblical witness argues against use of the Bible for the direct establishment of doctrine or policy. While, in theory, few might admit to this practice, in practice many still do it. Most biblical text may well be a participant in dialogue that establishes doctrine or policy; but it participates, it does not establish.

The Bible is more important than the doctrine or policy that might be discussed today. It is needed by the biblical faith community. The nature of the need is, alas, not always luminously clear and is often clouded by areas of significant misuse.

The Bible is evidently enough the collection of texts associated with the development of faith communities. Whether Jewish or Christian, it is their foundation document. The Older Testament emerged along with the faith community of Israel; building on it, the Newer Testament did the same with the Christian community of faith. Some have quarried these foundational texts not so much for a rumor of angels but for the reality of God. Others have quarried them for history or piety. Fuller scrutiny of the text often provides little support for such quarrying — apart altogether from the significant roles of arousing feeling, fueling faith, and firing imagination.

The Bible can function as a mysterious glass, occasionally allowing its users glimpses of God. The Bible can function as a reflective glass, often allowing its users to see images of themselves. The modern scholar, within a faith community, may go further: the Bible can function as a pointer to the nature of part at least of God's communication with us and to the struggle of human faith to find expression. Articulating two extremes may help focus reflection. Faith may be understood as enlightenment to which God invites. Knowledge may be understood as enlightenment that God reveals and, to that extent, imposes. Any position taken on the range between faith and knowledge needs ultimately to be based on experience of the biblical text. Minimal reflection is needed to realize that God can invite to faith and God can impose knowledge. At issue is not the source of either; at issue is the nature of the biblical text. Ultimately a faith position needs to be founded on experience of the biblical text. In my experience of the biblical text, the invitation to faith predominates.

Signposts may be vital to travelers on a journey. A single signpost that is pointing in the right direction and has not been tampered with can be invaluable. Several signposts, pointing in different directions to the same destination, invite reflection. Some may be misleading or have been interfered with by vandals, but it is not necessarily so. Several routes can lead to the same goal; on occasion, the longest way round (in distance) is the shortest way there (in time or effort). Reflection is invited. Experience of the biblical text suggests that reflection is being invited constantly (see the Afterword below).

It is above all at the level of invitation, response, and the communication of thought and faith that my passion for the Bible, and the books of Samuel, is engaged. In these texts, God is constantly affirmed in events; events are constantly portrayed unfolding at an earthly level. The tension of theological affirmation and human experience is intensified by the multiplication of affirmations and the plurality of experiences — in the plurality of interpretations. In the process, God may be glimpsed. In the process, the images of humankind may be more deeply etched. But it is the process itself that speaks of the communication between God and humankind: affirmed, uncertain, in tension, and manifestly manifold. A researcher's paradise and a seedbed for faith.

Another aspect of the scrutiny of biblical texts that fascinates me is the discovery in them of what can attract or repel me in much modern society. In the composition of the text, there is the attraction of intelligence and integrity, of faith and skepticism. In the roles portrayed, there is much that can repel. For example: the arrogant claims of faith supporting self-righteousness or worse; the confident certainty that success denotes God's favor; the seesaw of motivation from self-interest to superstition.

In this context, Brueggemann's comment on the texts of Samuel is to be heard.

> A "religious" reading is tempted to make the story of Israel in the books of Samuel excessively pious, to overlook the tension of factions, the reality of power, the seduction of sex, the temptation to alliances, the ignobility of motivations, and the reliance on brutality. . . . There is a long-established practice of an "innocent" religious reading of the Samuel narrative. These elements of power, seduction, brutality, and ignobility, however, are all there in the text. (p. 2)

The reality of life and politics, often sordid enough, needs to be balanced by awareness of the place of God in it all. Brueggemann again:

If we try to reconstruct the transformation of Israel without serious reference to Yahweh, to Yahweh's words, deeds and purpose, we will have constructed a telling of the transformation that decisively departs from Israel's own recitation. (p. 3)

All of which leads directly to the issue of theology and history.

Theological Writing or Historiography

It was vigorously argued in *1 Samuel* (FOTL 7) that these books are closer to theology than history. To show that the primary concern was an understanding of what was happening rather than a presentation of its unfolding, three areas were singled out: (1) the existence of significant and unacknowledged leaps; (2) the presence of divine intervention, both highly visible and scarcely visible; (3) the frequent practice in the biblical text of amalgamating conflicting evidence rather than offering any assessment of it. The examples were taken primarily from 1 Samuel. Without slavishly reviewing the same areas, it is evident that 2 Samuel also scarcely comes under the category of ancient historiography (see the wide-ranging collection of essays in Long, *Israel's Past*).

It has been said that, for a wide constituency of scholars and students, "the appeal of the Hebrew Bible/Old Testament . . . lies pre-eminently in its link with history and archaeology" (Davies, "Introduction," 14). I trust that is not the case, especially not "pre-eminently." A regrettable prejudice is betrayed by one participant in the dialogue: "What is the early Jewish historiography that we call the Bible about?" (Thompson, "Historiography," 39). Students of ancient history have to make use of the Bible, most cautiously; "early Jewish historiography" it is not. Students of the Bible have to be aware of the influences that bear on their studies. "Biblical narratives make very different kinds of claims . . . from biblical scholarship. . . . The ambition of 'higher criticism' was to construct a metanarrative, a privileged metadiscourse capable of offering eventually the Truth about the history of the Bible's composition and hence necessarily about ancient Israelite history" (Schwartz, "Adultery," 335). The practice of the Bible is generally to amalgamate competing traditions rather than to adjudicate between them. History as a rendering of account about the past tends to adjudicate rather than amalgamate; amalgamation without evaluation is an abdication of the historian's role.

First Samuel ends with a major confrontation between the Philistines and Israel, to the north in the valley of Esdraelon. Israel is defeated, Saul and three of his sons are killed, their bodies fastened to the wall of Beth-shan (1 Sam 31). 2 Samuel opens without a word on the consequences of the Philistine victory. Ishbaal, Saul's son, succeeded to his father's throne, and Abner based Ishbaal's kingdom across the Jordan, at Mahanaim. Not a word of explanation is given in the text.

As will be noted in the treatment of 2 Sam 2:8–4:12, the text of Samuel allocates seven and a half years to David's rule over Judah at Hebron, and reports events that would occupy about four days; the text of Chronicles, on the other hand, has David move immediately to kingship over all Israel and the capture of Jerusalem, with numerous warriors flocking to his side. Biased motivation is available for both presentations. The biblical text does not decide between them.

David is portrayed in 2 Sam 8 as administering justice and equity to all his people and achieving victory over a wide range of neighboring peoples. In what precedes, after the capture of Jerusalem and a couple of victories over the Philistines, the coming of the ark to Jerusalem is presented and Nathan's word is reported, promising to David a secure dynasty and a son to build the temple. In what follows, almost nothing is added of David's subjection of the neighboring peoples. Overwhelming emphasis on empire it is not.

Three accounts are given of the sparing of Mephibosheth, Jonathan's son (2 Sam 9:1-13; 19:25-31 [Heb.; NRSV, 19:24-30]; 21:7); the three are not compatible. What follows in the Stories of David's Middle Years does not fall into the category of ancient historiography. Where David and Bathsheba are concerned, one extra-marital affair, one judicial murder, two pregnancies and two births, and one prophetic confrontation may allow for the weaving of a fascinating story — it is hardly to be adjudged the writing of history. The details of Amnon's rape of Tamar and the folly of David's handling of the affair are hardly the stuff of history. Even less so the details of David's retreat from Jerusalem and return there. Sheba's rebellion is not reported in terms of its significance for David's kingdom (whatever David may think — cf. 2 Sam 20:6); more to the point are its implications for Joab's power in David's kingdom, implications that are left safely between the lines.

Within 2 Sam 21–24, there are traditions of David's military organization that are at odds with the picture of David, the guerrilla leader, in 1 Samuel. This is not a matter of the preservation of variant traditions. It is as if an account of the U.S. military in the twentieth century made no mention of the Pentagon or the Marine Corps, West Point or Annapolis. This is a classic example of amalgamation without evaluation.

Much biblical narrative is written to articulate experience. It may be the historian's role to identify or date the experience; it is the interpreter's role to explore the articulation. Much articulation is not naive reporting of experience; much experience is not easily identified within the articulation. When all of this is placed in the context of faith in the involvement of God with human experience, the result is much more theology than history.

The biblical text that engages with these issues situates itself at the beginning of a fragilely and temporarily united kingdom. What happens if the historian insists that the experiences generating these texts belong in a later and much different time? The experience changes; the articulation may remain much the same. The portrayal of Samuel can serve as a model. The articulation is set in the time of Shiloh, Saul, and David, i.e., in the tenth century; the experience that triggered this particular articulation may well be the interpretation of Jehu's coup in the late ninth century. Once we have realized that 1–2 Samuel are not history and do not serve historiographical purposes, the questions that must be addressed are: What is the nature of 1–2 Samuel and what purpose does it serve?

Approached as neutrally as possible, the articulation of experience is a good model for understanding religious texts like 1–2 Samuel (I owe the model to Luke Timothy Johnson, *Writings,* esp. 10-16). Something triggers the drive to create what becomes text, whether remembered or written. Underlying that "something" may be found an experience. For stories of David's rise to power, the experience may be that David emerged as king — and an interpretation needed to be found to account for this emergence. God is appealed to in the interpretation; the text becomes theological. If ambition or the exercise of power or the issue of popular support was primary in the interpretation, it might well become political — and so on. It is possible that the historical reality of David's kingship was different from that portrayed in the text. The interpreter's challenge remains the same: to explore the articulation of the experience offered by the text.

What is the experience that provided the stimulus for 1–2 Samuel? At face value, it is that David has emerged as king in Israel, established in place by the institution of the monarchy. David's kingship was not an aberrant moment as might be said of any claim regarding Ahimelech. David's kingship is portrayed as successful in the establishment of a monarchic institution in a way that Saul's was not.

As is evident from the biblical text, this new state of affairs demanded interpretation. For some voices, whether early or late, this action — the experience — was akin to apostasy: "they have rejected me [YHWH] from being king over them" (1 Sam 8:7); "how can this man save us?" (1 Sam 10:27). Clearly, for these, the development is not of God. For David's supporters — the originators, at one time or another, of the bulk of 1–2 Samuel — their interpretation of the experience was far from one of apostasy. It was indeed of God. For them, God was with David, and his kingship was God's will and God's doing. God was with him. Of course the working out of the divine will in the reality of human politics had to be done by David. David may have been far from perfect, but he ended up being Israel's model for God's ideal of a king.

If the overwriting of the image and activity of Samuel owes something to the prophetic circles associated with the legitimacy of Jehu's coup, it is appropriate to identify the earlier (i.e., pre-PR) evidence on which belief in God's endorsement of David's kingship might have been based. Samuel's anointing of Saul (to be differentiated from Saul's commissioning by an anonymous prophet) as well as aspects of Saul's rejection and the anointing of David are all attributed to the Prophetic Record, the work of the late-ninth-century prophetic circles associated to some degree with Jehu's coup. Some prophetic endorsement of Saul seems to have been in the tradition, along with some rebuke. The prophetic anointing of David (1 Sam 16:1-13) is attributed entirely to prophetic writing. In a pre-PR text, the suggestion that Saul is in trouble with God would come first with 1 Sam 16:14-23.

At this early stage, then, the belief that God is with David is founded on David's victory over the Philistine champion (cf. 1 Sam 17:47) and David's sustained success (1 Sam 18:14-16; 2 Sam 5:2). According to the text, the Philistines posed a serious threat to Israel's independence. David's leadership and command, institutionalized in the monarchy, eliminated the threat and secured the independence. It must be of God. There is even a hint of this in David's comment on Solomon's accession: "Blessed be the LORD, the God of Israel, who today has granted one of my offspring to sit on my throne and permitted me to witness it" (1 Kgs 1:48). David gives twofold thanks to God. At a later stage (late ninth century), the belief in divine favor for David's kingship was expressed in terms of the prophetic endorsement and anointing.

In modern democracies, inundated by the media, subjected to the efforts of "spin doctors," we can become cynical about the interpretation put on events. We need to distinguish the inner-oriented from the outer-oriented. When interpretation is for the benefit of the inner being of those involved, whether as individuals or group, it can be a matter of conviction, morale, or indeed theology. When interpretation is oriented outward toward others, it can be concerned with persuasion, propaganda, or vindication (cf. Whitelam, "Defence of David," esp. 61-71). All theology that moves from the inner toward the outer becomes involved in the justification and/or propagation of the faith.

The conviction maintained here is that the origin of the bulk of the Davidic traditions is to be attributed to the interpretation of the experience of David's kingship. Such interpretation involves rehearsing the traditions of what David did; otherwise the experience would be a void. It involves an understanding of David's activity such that it is not believed to be in conflict with the will of God or, in Israel's case, that it does not demean the sovereignty of God. David is to be seen not as replacing God in Israel but as being God's instrument in assuring Israel's defense and independence. This is a theological endeavor; it is not history writing.

If "the origin of the bulk of the Davidic traditions is to be attributed to the interpretation of the experience of David's kingship," we need to be aware of the subsequent experiences that demanded understanding and articulation and that are largely situated within the wider context of the DH. A full exploration is not possible in this Introduction, but an indication can be given as to where such an exploration might need to go. Its fragility and its hypothetical quality go without saying. The Prophetic Record, for example, presumably responds to the threat posed by Baalism, especially Baalism of foreign origin. The articulation of a response appeals to the guidance from God's prophets. The Josianic DH is a manifesto for reform. Presumably, elements in the context of its experience include the fall of the north, Sennacherib's siege of Jerusalem, and increasing anxiety in the face of imperial power. The response looks over the wider range of Israel's experience and concludes that fidelity to God will bring life and prosperity. The revised DH faces the experience that Josiah's fidelity, and that of his generation, did not bring life and prosperity. The articulation of this required revision of the Josianic texts, the introduction of threats and warnings, and so on. To sum up: Israel's experience that surfaces in one way or another in the books of Samuel and Kings runs the gamut from the emergence of prophets and kings in the mainstream of Israel's national structures through to the end of Israel's national independence. A lot of articulating needed to be done.

How to Read This Book

The structure analyses that are so central to this book and to this series are not glorified tables of contents. They bear a similar relation to the literary text as flow charts bear to projects or organizations: they seek to identify the component elements of the text and to indicate the interrelationships between them.

Good biblical commentaries invariably tempt their readers to succumb to reading the commentary rather than the biblical text. Precisely because it is good, the commentary is eminently readable and the biblical text can be bypassed — especially if found to be difficult. To benefit from both the structure analyses and the discussion in this book, the following steps are recommended.

- The first step has to be to read the biblical text under consideration. All too often, people pass this by, thinking they know the text or finding it too opaque and difficult. No commentary can open up a text for a reader if the text has not been read. It is rather like shaking hands with a person who is not there.
- The second step is basically to contemplate the structure analysis. What does it identify as major blocks in the text? How does it relate them to each other? How do the details fit in? What perception of the text — what grasp of what it is doing and what understanding of its meaning — does the structure analysis reveal?
- The third step is to read the text again in the light of the analysis, to see whether one finds the analysis verified in the text, i.e., whether the analysis is putting forward a reasonable possibility.
- The fourth step depends on whether the reader finds the structure analysis helpful or not. It involves reading the discussion in the commentary, with the reflections on genre, setting, and meaning. If the reader is in instinctive agreement with the analysis of the text, the discussion can be read for understanding and verification. If the reader disagrees with the analysis, then this fourth step is the time for comparing the text and the structure and evaluating them in the light of the discussion.
- As a fifth step, when all this has been done, readers are in a position to proceed to their own interpretation, for their own times, their own lives.

Ideally, interpretation proceeds from the signals in the text. Ideally, the structure analysis should articulate a perception of these signals that organizes them as coherently as the text allows or suggests. Assessing the perception of the text given in the structure analysis against the text itself and again in the light of the discussion should give as good grounds for the text's interpretation as a commentary can offer.

Finally, a particular methodological aspect needs to be underlined. For analysis, the text has been broken into larger narrative units. These are structural sections within the telling of the narrative; they do not constitute literary genres in themselves. No treatment is given of their genre, setting, and meaning. It is appropriate that this treatment should be found in the section on the diachronic dimension; in this way, it has been possible to stay close to present-text analysis. Often enough, even within component elements of these larger narrative units more than one genre has been used to compile the narrative. For that reason, genre terms are not normally used in the superscriptions of units. Where, as often, a unit comprises several genres — for example, a story, a report or an account, and a notice or two — any overarching genre would be out of place in the unit's title. The text is narrative. The function that the various larger narratives perform is discussed under the rubric, Diachronic Dimension.

Avowal

An avowal such as this should be taken for granted throughout biblical scholarship. But since it is not taken for granted, it needs to be said; it was said about 1 Samuel and can be repeated for 2 Samuel. The avowal is this: the interpretation of 2 Samuel presented in this volume is no more than that — an interpretation. It is not and does not attempt to be the definitive interpretation, simply because interpretation is an art and art does not attempt the definitive. The interpretation of 2 Samuel presented in this volume attempts to be both adequate and responsible. Adequate: accounting for as many of the signals seen in the text as possible within a coherent horizon. Responsible: alert to the claims of the text, proposing interpretations that are plausible within the canons of Israelite literature as we know it, and not passing over signals simply because they do not fit the presentation.

Two scholars do not have the place in this volume that the extent of their work would suggest. They are Jan Fokkelman and Robert Polzin. Fokkelman's study of the narrative art and poetry in the books of Samuel runs to four volumes (2,403 pages). Polzin has so far devoted three volumes to a literary study of the Deuteronomic History, with Part Three given to 2 Samuel. I have learned greatly from Polzin's concern for the present text, especially given his acceptance of the traditional processes belonging within the text. I disagree often enough with his conclusions about the present text. A thorough discussion of Polzin's work would need a book-length study. Scattered comments along the way would not do justice to his undertaking. So I have chosen to make this tribute and as a rule refrain from the scattered comments. However, his remark about Jeffrey Tigay's work might be turned back on his own: "both important and trivial" (*Samuel,* 229) — important for its emphasis on the present text; trivial, alas, for aspects of its interpretation of the same present text, despite many valuable insights. Fokkelman's aims in his massive study are significantly different from mine in this one. Again, scattered comments would not do justice to the matter, while a thorough discussion is out of the question in a study of this kind.

It will be easily understood that the aim here of *1 Samuel* and *2 Samuel* (FOTL 7 and 8) is quite different from that of Steven McKenzie's *King David: A Biography.* These two FOTL volumes explore the text of 1–2 Samuel for its meaning. *King David: A Biography* remodels the text rather too freely and quarries it for details regarded as relevant for the biography of an imagined figure of David. We need not argue.

This volume, as its predecessor on 1 Samuel in this FOTL series, owes much to the inspiration of Rolf Knierim and to the hospitality offered me over the years by the parish of Our Lady of the Assumption, by Claremont Graduate University's Institute for Antiquity and Christianity, and the Claremont School of Theology, with especial thanks to its library staff. I am deeply grateful. Acknowledgment and profound gratitude are also due to my home institution, Jesuit Theological College, within the United Faculty of Theology, Parkville, and to its associated Joint Theological Library.

Finally, my gratitude to Allen Myers and his colleagues at Eerdmans for their care and competence in producing what I consider to be another splendid volume.

Bibliography of Works Cited Above

Campbell, Antony F., and Mark A. O'Brien. *Unfolding the Deuteronomistic History: Origins, Upgrades, Present Text.* Minneapolis: Fortress, 2000.

Davies, P. R. "Introduction." Pages 11-21 of *The Origins of the Ancient Israelite States.* Edited by V. Fritz and P. R. Davies. JSOTSup 228. Sheffield: Sheffield Academic Press, 1996.

Fokkelman, J. P. *Narrative Art and Poetry in the Books of Samuel: A Full Interpretation Based on Stylistic and Structural Analyses.* Vol. I: *King David (II Sam. 9–20 & I Kings 1–2).* Vol. II: *The Crossing Fates (I Sam. 13–31 & II Sam. 1).* Vol. III: *Throne and City (II Sam. 2–8 & 21–24).* Vol. IV: *Vow and Desire (I Sam. 1–12).* Assen/Maastricht, The Netherlands: Van Gorcum, 1981-93.

Johnson, Luke Timothy. *The Writings of the New Testament: An Interpretation.* Revised edition. Minneapolis: Fortress, 1999.

Long, V. Philips, ed. *Israel's Past in Present Research: Essays on Ancient Israelite Historiography.* Winona Lake, IN: Eisenbrauns, 1999.

McKenzie, Steven L. *King David: A Biography.* New York: Oxford, 2000.

Polzin, Robert. *A Literary Study of the Deuteronomic History.* Part One: *Moses and the Deuteronomist.* New York: Seabury, 1980. Part Two: *Samuel and the Deuteronomist.* San Francisco: Harper & Row, 1989. Part Three: *David and the Deuteronomist.* Bloomington: Indiana University Press, 1993.

Schwartz, Regina M. "Adultery in the House of David: The Metanarrative of Biblical Scholarship and the Narratives of the Bible." Pages 335-65 in *Women in the Hebrew Bible: A Reader.* Edited by A. Bach. New York: Routledge, 1999.

Thompson, T. L. "Historiography of Ancient Palestine and Early Jewish Historiography: W. G. Dever and the Not So New Biblical Archaeology." Pages 26-43 of *The Origins of the Ancient Israelite States,* edited by V. Fritz and P. R. Davies. JSOTSup 228. Sheffield: Sheffield Academic Press, 1996.

Whitelam, Keith W. "The Defence of David." *JSOT* 29 (1984) 61-87.

Chapter 1

DAVID'S KINGSHIP OVER JUDAH
(2 SAM 1:1–2:7)

The division into books for Israel's great narrative texts is often a late and relatively artificial operation. The death of Saul is an appropriate point for the book to stop; however, the story of Israel goes on (and that already begun with David — despite Stoebe, 23-24). The king and his heir presumptive, Jonathan, have died. The biblical text turns to the issue of succession. David is presented assuming the throne of Judah at Hebron. The commander of Saul's army was Abner (cf. 1 Sam 14:50). He was last sighted in 1 Sam 26, was not mentioned in ch. 31, and will resurface in 2 Sam 2–3. Two sons of Saul are also named in 2 Sam who were not listed in 1 Sam 14:49; three sons died with Saul on Mount Gilboa. The two survivors are Ishbaal and Meribaal (also referred to as Ishbosheth and Mephibosheth, substituting the noun "shame" for the name of the god "Baal").

Abner brought Saul's son, Ishbaal, to Transjordan (Mahanaim). Why Mahanaim we do not know. It may have been a safe place for a capital, but other reasons are likely to have been involved. As the text expresses it, Abner made Ishbaal king over all of Israel that did not belong to Judah (cf. 2 Sam 2:8-10). A long civil war ensued between Saul's followers and those of David (cf. 2 Sam 3:1). With the deaths of Abner (3:27) and Ishbaal (4:6-7), the war ended in David's favor and he is reported becoming king over both Israel and Judah at Hebron. David's first reported action is to capture Jerusalem as his own city and his capital. The text then deals with the establishment of David's power and the remarkable narrative of his middle years.

At this point, as we approach these chapters, it is worth noting that Chronicles tells a quite different story: "The LORD [Heb.: he] put him [Saul] to death and turned the kingdom over to David son of Jesse. Then all Israel gathered together to David at Hebron . . . and they anointed David king over Israel" (1 Chr 10:14–11:3). Where Chronicles admits of no significant passage of time, 2 Samuel allows for seven and a half years — and fills the time with some four days' worth of protestation of David's innocence of bloodshed. We can see the

15

interests possibly at work on either side. 1–2 Chronicles needed an Israel unified under the temple's founder, David. 1–2 Samuel needed a founder of Israel's first and only lasting dynasty to be free of the taint of murder. It would be naive to believe we know which of these versions is historically the more accurate.

Looked at from the point of view of literary narrative, the Samuel text first tells of David's kingship over Judah and then opens what appears to be a new unit on the civil war with Ishbaal, heir to Saul's kingdom. Signals for the structuring of the text are not strong. 2:12 presupposes v. 8; their association within one block is appropriate. From the point of view of David's defenders, the first block of text makes clear both David's innocence and his feelings over the deaths of Saul and Jonathan (2 Sam 1:1–2:7); the second block makes the same claim for David in relation to the murders of Abner and Ishbaal (2 Sam 2:8–4:12). After these two blocks, the text moves on to the establishment of David's kingdom. The overall movement of the book is: David's grieving and kingship over Judah; civil war between the house of Saul and the house of David; David's establishment of the kingdom of all Israel.

The first section of text has the following structure.

David's grieving and his kingship over Judah	**2 Sam 1:1–2:7**
I. Announcement to David of the death of Saul	1:1-16
A. Reception of the news	2-10
B. Reaction to the news	11-16
II. David's lamentation for Saul and Jonathan	1:17-27
A. Basic lament	19
B. Against foes and field	20-22
C. Eulogy of the fallen	23-27
III. David's establishment as king of Judah	2:1-7
A. Move to Hebron from exile	1-3
B. Anointing as king	4a
C. Announcement to Jabesh-gilead	4b-7

Within this, three units can be examined more closely: David's grieving, his lamentation, and his anointment as king of Judah.

The announcement to David of the death of Saul	**1:1-16**
I. Introduction: link to preceding	1
II. Announcement of Saul's death	2-16
A. Reception of the news	2-10
1. Arrival of a man from Saul's camp	2
2. Interrogation by David	3-10
a. Concerning the general situation: defeat	3-4
b. Concerning the death of Saul	5-10
1) Encounter with harried Saul	5-6
2) Request from Saul	7-9
3) Death of Saul	10
a) Killed by the Amalekite	10a

Textual Issues

As all OT scholars know, the text of 1–2 Samuel is poorly preserved. Careful attention to its correction and emendation is most important. At the same time Shemaryahu Talmon's comment, following analysis of the texts from Qumran, can be generalized and must be kept in mind: "The variance of the Greek traditions among themselves, and vis-à-vis the Hebrew, appears to preclude a systematic collation of these widely divergent texts" ("Textual Studies," 327). The comment is relevant to more than simply Jeremiah and Esther. It is certainly applicable here in Samuel. Eugene Ulrich makes much the same point: "The Scriptures were pluriform . . . until at least 70 CE, probably until 100, and quite possibly as late as 135 or beyond. Thus we must revise our imaginations and our explanations . . . we can see now more clearly that there were multiple literary editions of many of the biblical books" ("Bible in the Making," 92).

Ideally, before a change is made to any of the ancient texts in the light of one of the other versions (e.g., MT or LXX, etc.) — or indeed in the light of other occurrences — both need to have been thoroughly understood. They may be telling a story differently or telling a different story (e.g., the story of Hannah or Anna in 1 Sam 1 which is told so differently in MT and LXX as to be almost a different story [see Walters, "Hannah and Anna"]). We need to be well informed and appropriately cautious.

Discussion

The introduction to the account situates it in relation to what has already been narrated — [= Structure Analysis: I]. After Saul's death, when David had returned from his pursuit of the Amalekites, he remained at Ziklag and on the third day the man came from Saul's camp. The introduction picks up the preceding two chapters (the reference to Saul's death is not necessarily obtrusive, against Smith, *Samuel,* 256). The repetition of the necessary background information would permit this to be an independent story. On the other hand, these details allow the narrator to integrate this episode with what has gone before. The time lapse, three days, corresponds well enough with 1 Sam 30:1, presuming that a single soldier would be thought to travel faster than an armed band of some six hundred men.

The appearance of the man and the initial stages of the exchange follow closely the pattern we find traditional for the bringer of bad tidings (cf. 1 Sam 4:12-18) — [II.A.1 and 2.a]. As in 1 Sam 4, there is here a slow though less pronounced build-up in the narrative. The condition of the messenger — torn garments and earth on his head — already presages bad news. His first reply to David intensifies the visual symbols: from the camp of Israel "I have escaped" (1:3). His reply to David's second question spells out the details: flight and heavy casualties for the army; death for Saul and Jonathan.

The classic difficulty of this passage emerges with the details of Saul's death (vv. 5-10) — [II.A.2.b]. Karl Budde's discussion may be summarized in five points (cf. *Samuel,* 193-94).

1. In v. 5, David asks about both Saul and Jonathan, while vv. 6-10 concern Saul alone.
2. In v. 8, a question is answered which is asked again in v. 13.
3. In vv. 6-10, the details of Saul's death are not in harmony with the account in ch. 31.
4. It is inappropriate to assume the Amalekite is a liar, since the text does not note this.
5. There is some conflict with 2 Sam 4:10-11, where David claims to have killed the messenger himself (v. 10) and, according to Budde, David does not attribute Saul's death to the Amalekite.

As a result, Budde attributes vv. 6-10 and 14-16 to his E source (noting their intention to free Saul of the shame of suicide and David of the killing of an innocent), while vv. 5 and 13 are classified as redactional links (Budde, *Samuel,* 193). What is not explained in such an attribution to different origins is why the allegedly redactional vv. 5 and 13 should be so apparently clumsy.

There is some conflict with 2 Sam 4:10-11; there is more with 1 Sam 31. The former is scarcely grave. David's statement in 4:10 is not necessarily in opposition to 1:15. In 1:15, David gives the order which is executed by the young soldier; 4:10 does not go into detail about the "how" of the execution. There is even less tension with 4:11. It does not acquit the Amalekite of Saul's death; it simply does not equate his deed with the cold-blooded killing of an innocent man in his bed. That the killers of Ishbaal were "wicked men" (4:11) does not imply that the Amalekite was righteous.

The more evident difficulty arises from the conflict with the account in 1 Sam 31. One approach to resolution is to consider the Amalekite a liar, but nowhere does the text stigmatize him as such. I cannot share Robert Polzin's confidence in "the convention of the narrator's omniscience and reliability" (*David and the Deuteronomist,* 3). From the outset, we must remember that the judgment to be passed is not one of historical fact but one of plausibility within the horizon of the narrative. We may assume, although we need not, that the content of ch. 31 is known to the narrator and to the audience — as it is to us; in the narrative, this content is not known to David. David is portrayed as accepting the man's story and acting accordingly. Whether the different formulation in 4:10-11 is intended to reflect the passage of time and the possibility of David's there being better informed as to the actual truth of the matter is a question that can hardly be answered with any certainty.

Whether the compiled stories present us with an understanding of the Amalekite as liar is not easily decided. The juxtaposition of 1 Sam 31 and 2 Sam 1 suggests that the Amalekite is to be understood as a liar. But differing traditions can be juxtaposed without our knowing whether either reflects reality. Differing views can be brought to expression at different times (cf. Smith, *Samuel,* 251, 54, 56, for whom ch. 31 could be a secondary addition). The most that can be said without doubt is that 2 Sam 1:10 and 16 portray a different understanding of the manner of Saul's death than that given in 1 Sam 31. According to ch. 31, Saul fell on his own sword (31:4). According to the Amalekite, acceding to Saul's request, he killed him (1:9-10). According to the narrative, David explicitly rests the Amalekite's fate upon his own testimony, "for your own mouth has testified against you" (1:16).

The tensions alleged around vv. 5 and 13 may be largely illusory. Verse 5's inquiry about the death of Saul and Jonathan follows naturally enough on the reference to both in v. 4. The query, "How do you know?" may be understood as inviting the disclosure that follows. That it is simply a neutral question is suggested by the answer that applies only to Saul — I know because I killed him. The narrative cannot allow David to know already what vv. 6-10 will disclose; once disclosed, David's concern has to be with avenging the king. For apologists of David's party, this would make eminent sense; in their eyes, Saul was David's rival, not Jonathan. The innocence of David's attitude to Saul needed to be established; the same need did not exist in relation to Jonathan.

The alleged tension between vv. 8 and 13 needs to be viewed in the light of the two questions asked and their different implications. In v. 8, Saul asks: "Who are you?"; in v. 13, David asks: "Where do you come from?" The first is a question of identity; "I am an Amalekite." The second is a question of social belonging; "I am the son of a resident alien." Whatever of the former, for the latter David's indignation is given grounds: "Were you not afraid to lift your hand to destroy the LORD's anointed?" (v. 14). For the son of a sojourner, respect for the anointed king is demanded in a way that might not have been judged so appropriate for a foreigner.

The upshot of this discussion is that we are able to treat 2 Sam 1:1-16 as a unity. We, the audience, are aware of ch. 31 and we are free to regard the Amalekite as an opportunistic liar or to regard his story as a different tradition of Saul's end. David, however, is presented as unaware of ch. 31 (hence the importance of the chronological details in 1:1) and as accepting of the Amalekite's story. It is intriguing to notice how scholars' pursuit of the historical event bedevils their interpretation of storytelling.

The Amalekite claimed that he just happened by chance to be, in his eyes, in the right place at the right time *(niqro' niqrêtî běhar haggilboa' wěhinnēh . . .).* Given that he removed the royal crown and armlet (v. 10), any claim to disinterested honesty is open to suspicion. Doubts have also been raised about the military accuracy of the portrayal, in its reference to "the chariots and the horsemen" pressing on Saul (v. 6). The use of chariots in the hill country has been claimed as a late element (cf. Grønbaek, *Aufstieg Davids,* 217;

Nowack, *Bücher Samuelis,* 150). However, we know too little of military tactics, especially in the pursuit of the defeated, to be able to place much weight on this. The two words designating horsemen *(ba'ălê happārāšîm)* are used only here (cf. Driver, 232). The second word alone *(happārāšîm)* is used of both charioteers and horsemen; further specification is possible enough. Wellhausen's suggestion of a marginal gloss having been inserted in the wrong column has become less likely in the light of the dimensions of the scrolls now known from Qumran (cf. Wellhausen, *Bücher Samuelis,* 151; also, Driver, 232-34).

David's grief and that of his men is reported immediately following the final disclosure of Saul's death — [II.B.1]. The mourning is continued until evening. The report is a natural sequence to the news of Saul's death, but is not to be dissociated from the fate of the Amalekite (with Hertzberg, 237-38). The sequence of the text need not be taken to imply that the judgment of the Amalekite was delayed a day.

David's final judicial pronouncement has occasioned considerable debate — [II.B.2.c]. The clause, "Your blood be on your head," has been understood in the light of Lev 20:9 as proof of a crime worthy of death (cf. Boecker, *Redeformen,* 135-43). In that case, "your blood" is to be understood as the blood of the one killed. Alternatively, a more satisfactory explanation is offered by Klaus Koch to the effect that the formula is used in the execution of blood vengeance to ensure that bloodguilt from the slaying of the killer should not pass to the avenger (cf. Koch, "Der Spruch"; also Liedke, *Rechtssätze,* 134, n. 1). In this case, "your blood" is to be understood as the blood of the killer. This alternative makes particularly good sense in the context of the concern often present in these texts to shield David from bloodguilt.

Genre

The genre here may be characterized as (→) account, relating how the news of Saul's death was brought to David and how he reacted to it, but it clearly has the potential for a (→) story, presenting and resolving the tension of how David would react to the news of Saul's death and the offer of his crown. The passage, as it stands, tends to convey information about David's attitudes and actions, rather than explicitly arousing interest and resolving narrative tension.

Setting

The setting for this material, as we have it now, was most probably the compiled narrative of the stories and traditions of David's rise to power in Israel. The component elements — the reception of the news, the mourning for Saul, the execution of the Amalekite — might be expected to have circulated at David's court, both at Hebron and later in Jerusalem. Concerns about responsibility for Saul's death and about David's attitudes toward the succession were both likely to have been live issues in the power struggles of the civil war and later, especially while adherents of Saul were around to remember his reign (cf. Shimei in 2 Sam 16:5-13).

Meaning

The meaning of the passage emerges primarily from the dual reaction to the news, as reflected in the structure analysis. It would not be unnatural to expect that David would receive the news of Saul's death with something akin to satisfaction. Saul's constant pursuit that ultimately drove David into exile, as it is portrayed in the narrative, would provide reason enough. David's own comment on Saul's fate in 1 Sam 26:10 (cf. also vv. 18-20) might lead one to expect at least relief. Instead, the text indubitably counters this expectation (so Hertzberg, 237).

The news brought to David contains two elements: the fact of Saul's death and the manner of it. David's reaction to both is portrayed. The fact of Saul's death ignites the public demonstration of grief, the tearing of clothes and the weeping and fasting until evening. The manner of Saul's death, dispatched by the Amalekite according to his story, costs the man his life. The twofold reaction reported reflects the concern to present David's grief as real and not figured (Hertzberg, 237).

This emphasis makes the chapter most appropriate to open what is the final stage of a presentation of David's rise to power, his winning the civil war against Saul's supporters. Despite the elegy (which serves on an emotional rather than an intellectual level to reinforce the reality of David's grief), this is not the end of the Saul-David complex (against Hertzberg, 236). It is part of a skillful presentation of David's coming to kingship, according to which David did not grasp the kingship — it was brought to him. The bulk of this presentation is given over to demonstrating that not only was David not responsible for eliminating the obstacles that stood between him and the crown, but even his inner attitude was one of profound grief at the death of these who stood in his way.

This is the meaning of the mourning for Saul. This is also the meaning of the execution of the Amalekite, bringer of Saul's crown and armlet. These are not used to depict David as Saul's legitimate heir (against Grønbaek, *Aufstieg Davids,* 219-20). Quite the contrary! By ordering the Amalekite executed, David rejects the man's insinuation that he should be eager to accept the crown. Interestingly, nothing more is heard of it. As the narrative unfolds, it is not until the men of Judah anoint him that David becomes their king (2:4); it is not until the tribes and elders of Israel come to him that David becomes king in Saul's place (5:1-3). At the same time, of course, the episode of the Amalekite serves the compiler of the narrative well. Despite David's reaction, the passage still conveys the impression that David was the obvious person to succeed Saul.

What we do not and cannot know is whether this presentation is a reasonable reflection of reality or is heavily biased in favor of David. We know that, according to the Samuel text, there was a long civil war between the supporters of David and the supporters of Saul. We have stories of two revolts in David's lifetime, apparently along tribal lines, one led by Absalom (2 Sam 15–19) and the other by Sheba ben Bichri (2 Sam 20). Both were suppressed. The later revolt of the people against Rehoboam, Solomon's son, again apparently along tribal lines, was successful. We have on record the views of Shimei ben Gera, "a man of the family of the house of Saul" (2 Sam 16:7-8). On these grounds, we are forced to assume, with no room for doubt, that radically diverging understandings of the respective behavior of Saul and David existed in early Israel. Given that David was the victor, we assume that the normative version of these traditions comes from David's party. How extensively they may have been slanted we cannot know. The historical question must be left open. The theological viewpoint of the narrative is clear: David did not seize power; it was thrust upon him. The leitmotif from beginning to end has been: David succeeded because the LORD was with him (cf. 1 Sam 18:14; 2 Sam 5:10).

Textual Issues

1:18 Plumb in the middle of the verse is the Hebrew noun for "bow" *(qāšet)*, without so much as a definite article. Three approaches dominate: (a) it is ignored (e.g., LXX; McCarter, 67); (b) it is construed in terms of military policy (e.g., Barthélemy, 226; Stoebe, 94); (c) it is construed as song, in terms of the immediate context (e.g., Hertzberg, 238; NRSV, NJPS). One further suggestion is taken up by Driver (233-34), following Wellhausen; another is offered in Anderson, rendering "[A Lament called] Bow" (15). As it stands, the phrase is unintelligible. The NJPS use of brackets is as good an approach as any: "to be taught [The Song of the] Bow."

1:21 Numerous proposals have been made for the end of the first verset. Some balance the mountains (e.g., "mountain slopes," Anderson, 18); others balance the aspect of fertility, rendering along the lines of "fertile fields" (e.g., Barthélemy, 227-28).

Discussion

As a general methodological rule, the restoration of a text and the analysis of its structure should go hand in hand. The structuring of a corrupted text will make no sense; the restoration of a text without attention to its structure will not be helpful. Here, however, given the clarity of the structure, any future restoration of what is a difficult text is unlikely to have substantial impact.

The structure emerging from the analysis of the lament is a clear one: there is the basic utterance of lament — [II.A]; the utterances against the foe and the battlefield — [II.B]; and finally the eulogy, of both men together and of each separately — [II.C]. Whatever traditional materials a poet may draw on, such a lament is likely to have been composed orally. Oral composition is helped by envisaging the structural frame around which the poem will be built.

The introduction describes the poem as a lament *(qînâ)*, uttered by David over Saul and Jonathan — [I]. The poem, however, does not have the metrical structure typical of the later laments; metrically, it is similar to the victory songs of early Israelite poetry (cf. Cross and Freedman, *Studies,* 6). Verse 18 may be an editorial note about the poem, giving the instructions associated with it and the source where it could be found. The Book of Jashar is thought to be an ancient collection of Israel's poems or songs (another occurrence is in Josh 10:13; cf. Budde, *Samuel,* 196-97; Hertzberg, 238-39).

The lament begins with the basic statement of its theme: The splendor, O Israel, is slain upon your heights — [II.A.1]. Both "the splendor" (NRSV, your glory) and "the gazelle" are possible translations; they are probably complementary in sense (cf. Driver, 234-35; Freedman, "Refrain"). The reference to persons of exalted station by metaphors from the animal world is well known in Ugaritic poetry and not unknown in Hebrew (cf. Amos 4:1). The potential reference of the different associations of the word is debated; the issue is not of moment here (cf. among others, Stuart, *Studies,* 193; Freedman, "Refrain," 120; Driver, 234). This basic expression of Israel's loss, which is the core of the lament, is followed by an exclamatory expression of grief that becomes what might be called the refrain of the poem.

The utterance against the foe is a prohibition against communicating what would have been good news to the Philistines — [II.B.1]. In its own way, it is an expression of sorrow at the realization that the Philistine women will be singing in joy, as did the women of Israel when the situation was reversed (cf.

1 Sam 18:6-7). The utterance against the mountains of Gilboa is also in the form of a prohibition, calling down the penalty of drought and infertility upon the place where the tragedy occurred (cf. Fenton, "Ugaritica-Biblica," 67-68) — [II.B.2]. The motivating clause makes the reason explicit: for there the shield of Saul was defiled, the shield that will no longer receive its due care (Freedman renders differently). The emphasis on Saul in this verse suggests that, for all David's friendship with Jonathan, the primary subject of the lament (and therefore of v. 19) is Saul, the LORD's anointed and Israel's fallen king (see now Barrick, "Saul's Demise").

This motivating clause has however referred to the king's shield as "defiled," strong language, even in the emotion associated with defeat. Such language is counterbalanced by the praise in v. 22. There both Jonathan and Saul are celebrated in the images of those who fought as warriors and fell as heroes. Neither had flinched from the battle. This counterbalancing emphasis ties v. 22 to what precedes. The eulogy itself begins with the apostrophe in v. 23 (against Budde, *Samuel,* 196, whose assessment is otherwise in full agreement with the analysis here).

The eulogy of the fallen begins with Saul and Jonathan together — [II.C.1]. Particularly in the light of what has passed, the sentiments given David are strong and noble. Given the estrangement that David introduced between Saul and Jonathan (cf. 1 Sam 20:30-34; 22:6-8), these lines almost constitute restitution and reconciliation. "In life and in death they were not divided" reads in Hebrew as a sonorous and duly solemn line *(bĕhayêhem ûbmôtām lo' niprādû);* the adjectives "beloved and lovely" (with the NRSV catching something of the Hebrew assonance, *hanne'ĕhābîm wĕhannĕ'îmim)* and the similes ("eagles," "lions") are expressive of high praise and deep emotion.

The eulogy then turns to Saul, calling on the women of Israel to lament for him — [II.C.2]. He is eulogized as the one who has provided their prosperity. There are associations here with the spoils of war (cf. the hopes of Sisera's mother in Judg 5:30) as well as with the ancient Near Eastern understanding in which the king was held responsible for the prosperity and fertility of his realm. The eulogy of Saul concluded with the refrain, expanded by the reference to battle. It would be a mistake to see the refrain introducing the eulogy of Jonathan and acting as an inclusion for vv. 25-27 (with Budde, *Samuel,* 196; and against Freedman, "Refrain," 125; S. Talmon, "Textual Study," 365; and most commentators). In v. 19, the refrain follows the basic expression of lament; in vv. 25a and 27 it follows the eulogies of Saul and Jonathan respectively. A progressive intensity is given to it by the expansions — the first of two words, the second of three.

Finally, the eulogy of Jonathan is permitted to express all the deep emotion of David's feeling for his friend — [II.C.3]. The initial expression of lament (v. 25b) resumes the words of v. 19a. Then, in the eulogy proper, David gives expression to his sorrow at the loss of his brother Jonathan and to the power of the friendship between them. With the final repetition of the refrain, the lament is concluded. With the passing of Saul and Jonathan, the weapons of war are broken, "and the weapons of war perished" (v. 27b). It is an ironical statement so close to the outbreak of civil war.

Genre

The poem is a (→) lament, bewailing the loss of Saul and Jonathan, eulogizing their merits. The "how" *('êk)* of the refrain and the call to the women of Israel to "weep" *(bĕkeynâ)* are typical features of the lament. As a funeral song for an individual, such a lament is not to be confused with the lamentation in which an individual or a community bewails their fate, especially after a catastrophe or in time of oppression, danger, or ill-health. Eulogy, speaking well of the dead, is of course part of the lament.

Setting

The natural setting for a lament of this kind is within the mourning rites for the dead, including especially the burial rites. While it is possible for a lament to be a literary creation from a later date, the probable time for its composition would be in relation to mourning rites held in Saul's honor or, alternatively, in relation to a need to clear David of any suspicion of complicity or satisfaction in the death of Saul. Possible settings for the former possibility are offered by 2 Sam 1:11-12 and also 21:12-14. The reference to "the people of Judah" in v. 18 is a possible pointer to the early years of David's reign.

Meaning

Within the context of its own horizon as an independent composition, a (→) lament's meaning is to give expression to grief and sorrow. It may be a constrained and formal piece; it may, as here, be filled with personal feeling and emotion.

However, within the context of the Davidic narratives, the lament has further implications that cannot be overlooked. It purports to indicate the reality of David's grief at the passing of Saul. The reports of the mourning (vv. 11-12) and the execution of the Amalekite (vv. 13-16) express on an intellectual level that David's attitude is not one of relief and satisfaction, but one of grief. In the lament, this is given expression on an emotional level; the communication is all the more effective.

From this point of view, v. 18 is not unimportant. The lament is to be taught to the people of Judah; yet Saul was a Benjaminite. Within the context of the narrative, the conclusion has to be an emphasis that neither David nor even Judah rejoiced at the death of Saul.

David's establishment as king of Judah	**2:1-7**
I. Move to Hebron from exile	1-3
A. Consultation of YHWH	1
B. The move	2-3

Textual Issues

2:3 "the towns of Hebron": most probably the undefended settlements or villages associated with walled towns and cities (cf. Anderson, 24; Stoebe, 98).

    2:6 The MT has "this which," rather stretched to render "because" (although Hertzberg maintains it is a possibility, p. 245; cf. Stoebe, 98). Driver embraces Wellhausen's emendation, reading *taḥat 'ăšer* (p. 240); not supported by the ancient versions, but used in Deut 28:47 and 1 Sam 26:21.

Discussion

The report of David's return from Ziklag to Hebron is told with remarkable brevity and an almost total lack of circumstantial detail — [I]. It is introduced by the editorial link, "And after this" (*wayhî 'aḥărê kēn;* cf. 2 Sam 8:1; 10:1; 13:1; 15:1; 21:18; and also Judg 16:4; 1 Sam 24:6; 2 Kgs 6:24; Joel 3:1; 1 Chr 18:1; 19:1; 20:4; 2 Chr 20:1). Although there is a concentration in 2 Samuel, a particular significance is not evident; the shorter phrase *(wayhî 'aḥărê)* is more widely attested.

    The treatment of this significant major move is remarkably succinct. There is no reference whatsoever to David's relations with the Philistines, nor to any negotiations with Judah or any contact with the rest of Israel. There is simply the consultation with YHWH. Even that is reported in abbreviated form. The yes/no answers of such an inquiry do not allow for a direct response such as "To Hebron" (2:1). The process involved in reaching the result is not reported (cf. Hertzberg, 248).

    The report gives special emphasis to David's two wives (v. 2). The "there" of v. 2 suggests that David and his immediate entourage moved to Hebron itself; v. 3, despite its difficulties, indicates that his troops were quartered in its dependent villages. The mention of wives (v. 2) and households (v. 3) points to a permanent relocation of David's forces rather than to a temporary strategic move.

    The report of David's anointing by the men of Judah is baldly stated — [II]. The only link to Hebron is the verse's "there." No motivation is expressed;

there is no reference to past or present or YHWH. 2 Sam 5:13 is also short but, in comparison, it is far fuller. We can only conjecture as to possible reasons for so jejune a notice. Given David's standing in Judah by that time, readers might be expected to take it for granted as natural. Alternatively, if the march on Hebron was viewed as a naked power play, discretion might have deemed it best passed over in comparative silence. We do not know and have no way of penetrating the veil with any certainty.

The communication concerning the embassy to Jabesh-gilead — [III] — is linked to the preceding by its final reference to David's having been anointed as king over the house of Judah (v. 7). The message is densely structured in terms of loyalty. Its structure may be filled out slightly, beyond what has just been given above.

a.	Prayerful greetings	5b-6
	1) With regard to the past: their loyalty to Saul in death	5b
	2) With regard to the future	6
	a) YHWH's loyalty to them	6a
	b) David's benevolence to them	6b
b.	Veiled appeal for their allegiance	7
	1) Exhortation to valor, now that Saul is dead	7a
	2) Announcement that he, David, is now king	7b

The message rings the changes of the revolving of epochs and the realities of loyalty. The people of Jabesh-gilead have shown laudatory loyalty to Saul in death. Now it is David's prayer that God will show faithful loyalty to them and David's promise that he, David, will similarly show them appropriate gratitude. Now times have changed; Saul is dead, as they well know, and it is a time for valor. David has been anointed king by the men of Judah. The undercurrent of the message is that now David expects their loyalty and the exercise of their valor.

Genre

The present composition consists of a series of (→) short communications, vv. 1-3, 4a, 4b-7. Verses 1-4a are bound together as a unity; the link with vv. 4b-7 is looser. Rendtorff suggests that vv. 4b-7 are the continuation of 1 Sam 31:11-13 ("Beobachtungen," 435). The sequence is perfectly possible, but v. 7 is a reminder that at least the events of vv. 1-4a, and possibly more, would have been a necessary part of the context.

Setting

The original setting for the short communication is the activity of creating a narrative of substantial length, requiring particular information as a frame for its component elements. This is the case for vv. 1-3, although they could derive equally from investigation, common knowledge, or informed supposition — especially given the later traditions.

The phrasing of v. 4a does not point to its being drawn from any form of official record. Rather, it suggests a similar kind of information-gathering activity. The possibility has been mentioned of vv. 4b-7 belonging with 31:11-13. The report in 1 Sam 31:1-13 is composed of a series of short communications, including vv. 11-13. A similar setting may therefore be assumed. As it stands now, the short communication of vv. 4b-7 has been incorporated into the larger narrative.

Meaning

The burden of the first communication is transparent: it was by YHWH's direction that David returned to Judah and to Hebron. His departure was not explicitly related to any divine guidance (cf. 1 Sam 27:1); his return is. As noted, the mention of David's wives and his men's families makes clear that this is no passing expedition — after all, the language of v. 1 could be the language of attack. Instead, at God's command, David's seat has been transferred from non-Israelite Ziklag to ancestral Hebron.

The plain sense of v. 4a is to report the fact of David's kingship in relation to Judah; the men of Judah came to Hebron to make him their king. At the same time, v. 1 is not far away. Nothing is made explicit, but the association within the text gives the whole process the aura of YHWH's will. It may serve as a counterbalance to the potential political realities.

The communication regarding the embassy to Jabesh-gilead serves a twofold function. First, it reiterates the positions of ch. 1 concerning David's attitude to the death of Saul. While he may have moved fast in returning to Judah and assuming power in the vacuum left by Saul's death, David is here portrayed as having a right attitude toward Saul and, perhaps more important at this stage, a right attitude toward those who were loyal to Saul. Second, it presents David's first action as king of Judah as one which reaches well beyond the boundaries of Judah. In the assurance of David's benevolence to them, and in the close connection of Saul's death with David's own kingship (v. 7), the narrative has David serve notice that his kingdom is not expected to be restricted to Judah.

An aspect of this embassy that is completely passed over by the text is whether Gilead was already under Ishbaal's control and, consequently, what sort of a reception the messengers were accorded. Their reception is not mentioned and the issue of political control is passed over in silence. This silence may be a pointer to the independence of original traditions. Alternatively, with the close juxtaposition of 2:8-9, it may be a pointer to the complexity of the political situation. As the stories of revolution will show later in 2 Samuel, political loyalties were capable of violent fluctuation.

Clearly, Abner did not organize a kingdom in a day. Equally clearly, David's transfer to Hebron and his anointing there did not happen in a day either.

Such an embassy may have been meant to forestall Abner; an invitation to break away from Abner and Ishbaal would be geographically unlikely. We cannot know. Politically, however, the long-term response is present in 2:8-9 (so Budde, *Samuel,* 202-3).

Bibliography of Works Cited Above

Barrick, W. Boyd. "Saul's Demise, David's Lament, and Custer's Last Stand." *JSOT* 73 (1997) 25-41.

Boecker, Hans Jochen. *Redeformen des Rechtslebens im Alten Testament.* Neukirchen-Vluyn: Neukirchener, 1970.

Budde, Karl. *Die Bücher Samuel.* KHC 8. Tübingen: Mohr, 1902.

Cross, Frank Moore, Jr., and David Noel Freedman. *Studies in Ancient Yahwistic Poetry.* Original edition, 1950. Reprinted as SBLDS 21. Missoula, MT: Scholars Press, 1975.

Fenton, T. L. "Ugaritica-Biblica." *Ugarit-Forschungen* 1 (1969) 65-70.

Freedman, D. N. "The Refrain in David's Lament over Saul and Jonathan." Pp. 115-26 in *Ex Orbe Religionum: Studia Geo Widengren.* Studies in the History of Religions 21. Part I. Leiden: Brill, 1972.

Grønbaek, Jakob H. *Die Geschichte vom Aufstieg Davids (1. Sam. 15–2. Sam. 5): Tradition und Komposition.* Copenhagen: Munksgaard, 1971.

Koch, Klaus. "Der Spruch 'Sein Blut bleibe auf seinem Haupt . . .'." *VT* 12 (1962) 396-416.

Liedke, Gerhard. *Gestalt und Bezeichnung alttestamentlicher Rechtssätze.* WMANT 39. Neukirchen: Neukirchener Verlag, 1971.

Nowack, W. *Die Bücher Samuelis.* HAT. Göttingen: Vandenhoeck & Ruprecht, 1902.

Polzin, Robert. *David and the Deuteronomist: A Literary Study of the Deuteronomic History.* Part Three: 2 Samuel. Bloomington, IN: Indiana University Press, 1993.

Rendtorff, Rolf. "Beobachtungen zur altisraelitischen Geschichtsschreibung anhand der Geschichte vom Aufstieg Davids." Pages 428-39 in *Probleme biblischer Theologie: Gerhard von Rad zum 70. Geburtstag.* Edited by H. W. Wolff. Munich: Chr. Kaiser, 1971.

Smith, Henry Preserved. *Samuel.* ICC. Edinburgh: T. & T. Clark, 1898.

Stuart, Douglas K. *Studies in Early Hebrew Meter.* HSM 13. Missoula, MT: Scholars Press, 1976.

Talmon, Shemaryahu. "The Textual Study of the Bible — A New Outlook." Pages 321-81 in *Qumran and the History of the Biblical Text.* Edited by F. M. Cross Jr. and S. Talmon. Cambridge, MA: Harvard University Press, 1975.

Ulrich, Eugene. "The Bible in the Making: The Scriptures at Qumran." Pages 77-93 in The Community of the Renewed Covenant: The Notre Dame Symposium on the Dead Sea Scrolls. Edited by E. Ulrich and J. VanderKam. Notre Dame: University of Notre Dame, 1994.

Walters, Stanley D. "Hannah and Anna: The Greek and Hebrew Texts of 1 Samuel 1." *JBL* 107 (1988) 385-412.

Wellhausen, Julius. *Der Text der Bücher Samuelis.* Göttingen: Vandenhoeck & Ruprecht, 1871.

Chapter 2

CIVIL WAR
(2 SAM 2:8–4:12)

There is conceptual unity in the MT that extends from 2 Sam 2:8 to 4:12. In 2:8, Abner establishes Ishbaal, one of Saul's surviving sons, as king over territory in the north. War drags on between the house of David and the house of Saul. 2:12-32 depicts one significant episode from this war. In ch. 3, Abner is portrayed as willing to arrange a peace in David's favor; he is assassinated by Joab. In ch. 4, Ishbaal is assassinated and David's innocence proclaimed. It is a moot point whether the conceptualization of the narrative extends further, to include David's accession to power over all Israel as well as his conquest of Jerusalem and victory over the Philistines. Aesthetically, it is probably more appropriate to treat chs. 5–6 separately, focused as they are on David's conquest of Jerusalem and the consolidation of his power there.

For Chronicles, this civil war did not happen. Chronicles moves from the genealogies of 1 Chr 1–9 to the death of Saul in 1 Chr 10. A huge sweep of Israel's story is passed over (the ancestors, Moses, Joshua, Judges, Samuel, Saul). For Chronicles, "Saul died for his unfaithfulness . . . the LORD put him to death and turned the kingdom over to David son of Jesse" (1 Chr 10:13-14). In the Chronicles account, all Israel gathered to David at Hebron "and they anointed David king over Israel" (11:3). In 2 Samuel, this does not happen until ch. 5. Again according to Chronicles, David and all Israel marched on Jerusalem, captured it, and "it was called the city of David" (11:7). In the DH, David reigned over Judah at Hebron for seven years and six months and "at Jerusalem he reigned over all Israel and Judah thirty-three years" (2 Sam 5:5). In Chronicles, David's reign began with "all Israel" (1 Chr 11:1) to be followed immediately by the capture of Jerusalem.

At this point, Chronicles gives the traditions about David's troops that Samuel sets apart in 2 Sam 21–24 (specifically, 23:8-39, with some pluses and minuses). Chronicles follows this with a chapter listing both the warriors who joined David at Ziklag while he was still in conflict with Saul (1 Chr 12:1-23 [Heb.; NRSV, 12:1-22]) and the leaders and tribal contingents that came to David at Hebron "to turn the kingdom of Saul over to him" (12:24-41 [Heb.; NRSV, 12:23-40]). In other words, for Chronicles there is no rump kingdom of Saul's and no civil war.

Naturally, most biblical scholars would be surprised if Chronicles were proved to be right. The motivation is there. Chronicles portrays David as the great motivating figure behind the construction of the Jerusalem temple. It is fitting for such a figure to be the unifying ruler of all Israel from the outset. But motivation is there for the DH version as well. David, as we have noted, is given a seven-and-a-half-year rule over Judah; yet the Samuel text details events that would occupy about four days and that are all told in such a way as to exonerate David of any bloodshed. Within one day, David mourns for Saul and Jonathan and has the messenger executed who had brought Saul's crown to him. In a one-day battle, Abner earns Joab's undying enmity by killing his brother Asahel. In due course, on another day Joab kills Abner. Finally, two rogue military officers brought Ishbaal's head to David and were executed for it on the spot. All that has been left out is the march on Hebron and the period of negotiations between David and Abner. This has to be as suspect as the Chronicles account. The two versions are incompatible. We have no way of demonstrating which is right. The present commentary concerns the text of Samuel and will follow that, but we are well advised to be aware of the variant preserved in Chronicles.

The structure of 2 Sam 2:8–4:12 can be briefly represented.

Civil war between the house of Saul and the house of David	**2:8–4:12**
I. The division of Saul's kingdom between David and Ishbaal	2:8-11
A. Concerning the kingdom of Ishbaal	8-10a
B. Concerning the kingdom of David	10b-11
II. A story of the enmity between Abner and Joab	2:12-32
A. The opening battle	12-17
B. The pursuit by Asahel and his killing by Abner	18-24
C. The conclusion	25-32
III. The deaths of Abner and Ishbaal	3:1–4:12
A. Death of Abner	3:1-39
1. Introductory	1-5
a. The state of war: David's ascendancy	1
b. The sons born to David at Hebron	2-5
2. Concerning Abner's death	6-39
a. The killing of Abner	6-30
b. The mourning for Abner	31-39
B. Death of Ishbaal	4:1-12
1. Introductory	1-4
a. Concerning Ishbaal and all Israel	1
b. Concerning Baanah and Rechab	2-3
c. Concerning Saul's grandson, Mephibosheth	4
2. Concerning Ishbaal's death	5-12
a. The killing of Ishbaal	5-8
b. The retribution for Ishbaal	9-12

The first of these blocks is structured as follows:

The division of Saul's kingdom between David and Ishbaal   **2:8-11**

  I. Concerning the kingdom of Ishbaal   8-10a
    A. Abner's initiative in moving to Mahanaim   8
    B. Abner's installation of Ishbaal as king   9
    C. Accession formula for Ishbaal   10a
      1. Ishbaal's age on becoming king
      2. Length of Ishbaal's reign
  II. Concerning the kingdom of David   10b-11
    A. The loyalty of Judah to David   10b
    B. Length of David's reign over Judah   11

Textual Issues

2:8 The MT in this verse names Saul's son *ʾîš bōšet* (man of shame); other texts (e.g., 1 Chr 8:33) suggest the name was originally *ʾîš baʿal,* Ish-baal or Esh-baal (interpreted "man of Baal"; cf. Driver, 240, 253-55). The issue is further discussed below. The text-critical concerns are discussed at length in Barthélemy, 228-30, and, along with other issues, by McCarter, 85-87; Anderson, 32.

    2:9 The MT's "Ashurites" is unsatisfactory; a change to "Geshur" (McCarter, 82-83) has its problems (cf. Driver, 241). What was meant remains uncertain.

Discussion

The major narrative traditions in this context relate to David's behavior on hearing of Saul's death (2 Sam 1:1-27) and to Abner's actions after Saul's death (2:12–4:12). If the narrative was to relate a civil war between the house of David and the house of Saul, in between these blocks of tradition both David and Ishbaal had to be established on rival thrones. 2:1-4a and probably 4b-7 does that for David; 2:8-10a does it for Ishbaal, with a note concerning David (vv. 10b-11). When looking for the literary shape that has been given to the narrative text, we have to ask whether these intermediary steps are noted in a separate transition passage or whether, in the present text, it is more appropriate to hold David's together with the traditions of 1:1-27 and Ishbaal's together with what follows (see, for example, Budde, *Samuel,* 200-204; Gunn, *King David,* 75-78). Clearly, views can differ and the matter is not of great importance. In my judgment, certain aspects of the text send signals favorable to Gunn's position, which regards 2:8-11 as introductory to what follows. Three may be noted.

    First, in what follows, Abner is the major figure in the narrative. After vv. 8-10, Ishbaal is not mentioned until 3:7-11; there, Abner wields the power and

Ishbaal is explicitly said to be afraid of him (v. 11). When Abner's death is reported, Ishbaal's courage fails him (4:1). It is appropriate to open the narrative with 2:8, where Abner's identity is established and where it is on his initiative that Saul's son moves to Transjordan; just as, according to the text, it was God's directive that moved David to Hebron. The contrast has potential for meaning: God directed David but Abner directed Ishbaal.

Second, 2:8 is to be preferred over 2:12 as the opening for a major narrative sequence. Not only is the syntax better, but v. 12 assumes both the position of Ishbaal (with its reference to "the servants of Ishbaal," i.e., those loyal to him) and the location of his forces at Mahanaim — information given in 2:8-9.

Third, the fleeting reference to David in 2:10b resumes what has been narrated in 2:1-4b. If, conceptually, these intermediary steps were noted in a separate transition passage (i.e., 2:1-11), there would be no need to come back to David a second time. If, on the other hand, 2:8 is a beginning, a brief reference to David's position as king of Judah is fully in order. The understanding of vv. 10a and 11 will be treated in due course.

So, while being clear that these are not momentous issues, it seems more appropriate to treat the text in two parts — as we have done — from 1:1–2:7 and 2:8–4:12.

It is appropriate at this point to clarify the choice of names being used for Saul's son and grandson, here named Ishbaal and Mephibosheth. The NRSV regularly footnotes Ishbaal to note that the Hebrew has Ish-bosheth; on Mephibosheth, in 4:4, it notes that 1 Chr 8:34 and 9:40 have Merib-baal. Our text in this volume will follow the NRSV, using Ishbaal and Mephibosheth. Religiously, what has happened appears to be that the so-called theophoric element, the name of the god "Baal" within the proper name, has been replaced by the Hebrew word for "shame" (bosheth [= Heb.: *bōšet*]). It would seem that in Saul's judgment it was right and orthodox that some of his sons had names including the theophoric element *"ba'al"* (so, Ish-baal, quite conceivably understood as "man of Yahweh" [McCarter, 87]). Later, we will see David, on coming to Jerusalem, where the local god may have been El Elyon, giving some of his sons names using the element *"'el"* (cf. 2 Sam 5:13-16). Insight, or possibly misunderstanding, and consequent change may not have been effective until later, perhaps as late as the period depicted in the Elijah stories (cf. 1 Kgs 18 and 2 Kgs 9–10) and even in the prophet Hosea. At depth, the naming of God is no simple matter. The fact that the NRSV uses one of each (i.e., Ishbaal and Mephibosheth) may well be text-based; it also helps to keep the issue alive. The different usages within the MT are noted: cf. 1 Sam 14:49 (for Ishvi); 1 Chr 8:33 and 9:39 (for Esh-baal); 1 Chr 8:34 and 9:4 (for Merib-baal). For extensive details, see Barthélemy, 228-30 (note that the UBS committee set itself the goal of ascertaining what is most likely to have been the "earliest attested text" — whether attested directly or indirectly); for the Qumran evidence, see Ulrich, 45-49.

Abner's role in the northern kingdom is glimpsed in 2:8-9; it will be unfolded as the story progresses. Just as David's move from Ziklag to Hebron is reported with an almost total lack of circumstantial detail, so here important political circumstances are passed over in equally frustrating silence. It has to be significant that in both cases no mention is made of the victorious Philistines.

Nothing is said of the severing of David's ties to Achish, king of Gath, who had "given" Ziklag to David his servant (cf. 1 Sam 27:1-7). Nothing is said of whether Ishbaal was at the battle of Gilboa nor of his survival nor of the choice of Mahanaim; no account is given of the Philistine control of the valley of Esdraelon (cf. 1 Sam 31:7).

The text speaks twice of the "war between the house of Saul and the house of David" (3:1, 6). However, the narrative itself is not about the broader scope of this war, hugely significant though it may have been; it is about the narrower power struggle between two men, Abner and Joab. It is Abner and Joab who propose the combat at the pool of Gibeon; it is Abner and Joab who are the chief figures in the wrap-up of the battle; it is Abner who kills Joab's brother, Asahel, and it is Joab who kills Abner at the point where Abner is negotiating to transfer the kingdom from the house of Saul to David. The focus is on power in Israel, not political relations with the Philistines. In the narrative, it is Abner and Joab, the military commanders, who determine the extent of David's power. Even the final episode, the death of Ishbaal, is played out by two military captains. This is skilled and detailed storytelling. It is concerned with the personalities wielding power; it is not concerned with any broader political picture, not with the Philistines, not with the people of Judah or Israel (except for 3:17, reminding us there were undercurrents we know nothing of).

Abner is named as commander of Saul's army; Ishbaal is named as Saul's son. Nothing is said of the role of either in the battle of Gilboa. The move is to Mahanaim, across the Jordan. Again no reasons are given. Presumably, after their military success, the Philistines controlled the great fertile valley of Esdraelon (cf. 1 Sam 31:7). When Abner and his troops return to Mahanaim after the battle of Gibeon, they use a southern route ("through the Arabah," 2:29). There may be more to it than simply issues of access. When David needed to regroup against Absalom's revolt, he went to Mahanaim (cf. 2 Sam 17:24a). Evidently he had supporters there (cf. 17:27-29). Nothing is said in the text to justify the choice for either Abner or David. Significantly, no mention is made of the two and a half tribes settled east of the Jordan.

Abner makes Ishbaal king (literally: "and he made him king"). This in itself is a remarkable statement. Nowhere else in the Hebrew Bible does an army commander elevate another man to the throne. As prophet, Samuel anoints Saul and David; the people make both king (cf. 1 Sam 10:24b and 11:15; 2 Sam 2:4a and 5:3). David orders Solomon's coronation (1 Kgs 1:32-40). Later kings tend to succeed their fathers, with no details given. Jehu is an army commander who is himself acclaimed by his fellow officers, after anointing by Elisha's disciple. The priest Jehoiada does the honors for Jehoash, but even there the verbs for making king and anointing (in the MT, at least), and for clapping and shouting, have plural subjects, presumably the captains and the temple guard (cf. 2 Kgs 11:12). So, Abner alone makes Ishbaal king; it is an isolated instance, and we do not know what to make of it. One thing at least is clear: in this kingdom of Ishbaal's, the power behind the throne is unquestionably Abner. The observation raises thoughts about the role of Joab in David's kingdom.

Ishbaal's kingdom is described in a verse, moving from north to south: Gilead, the Ashurites (cf. Judg 1:31-32 and the textual comment above),

Jezreel, Ephraim, Benjamin, and all Israel. Nothing is said about the political developments that made this possible. When last heard of, the Philistines occupied the valley of Esdraelon (1 Sam 31:7). Did they pull back entirely or leave garrisons in specific towns? We are told nothing. We have no evidence for Philistine imperialism. So does 2:9 describe an ambit claim or progressive realism or symbolic aspiration? We are left to wonder or to speculate.

David's kingdom is mentioned in half a verse: "the house of Judah followed David" (2:10b). His anointing by the people and his kingship over Judah have been mentioned already in 2:4a. The loyalty of Judah needs only to be confirmed.

Verses 10a and 11 are recognized by almost all commentators as later additions. They can be attributed to those responsible for the Deuteronomistic History (cf. Noth, *DH*, 34 and 101, n. 4). Both verses reflect the accession formula for the kings of Judah, extended back to include Saul; for David, only the second part of the formula is given, perhaps because his accession had occurred earlier (2:4a; although cf. 5:4). The formula notes the age of the king at his succession to the throne and the duration of his reign; in the books of Kings, the name of the queen mother is often given (cf. 1 Sam 13:1; 2 Sam 5:4; 1 Kgs 14:21; 22:42; 2 Kgs 8:17, 26; 12:1-2 [Heb.; NRSV, 11:21–12:1]; 14:2; 15:2, 33; 16:2; 18:2; 21:1, 19; 22:1; 23:31, 36; 24:8, 18).

It is puzzling that editors with a clear concern for chronology should have placed so close together but without any comment a reign of two years for Ishbaal and a reign of seven and a half years for David. Dependence on a source (e.g., 5:5) does not explain why the tension has been introduced here (Hertzberg, following Thenius, has v. 10a originally introducing v. 12 [p. 250] — i.e., a reign of two years before Abner's move). Alternatively, it is possible that only Ishbaal's reign "over all Israel" (v. 9) is being reckoned. This reign of Ishbaal's is not coextensive with David's, whether at its beginning or at its end. We know nothing of the context and we do not know why no mention is made of it. The various conjectures made do not help. One assumption is safe: a veil of discreet silence has been drawn over a great deal of political and military activity in this period that must have had considerable impact on the events to follow.

Genre

Verses 8-9 and 10b are (→) short communications. They are excellent examples of the kind. See above on 2 Sam 2:1-4a. Verses 10a and 11 contain elements of the (→) regnal resumé.

Setting

As noted above, the original setting for the short communication is the activity of creating a narrative of substantial length, requiring particular information as a frame for its component elements. The regnal resumés come from those responsible for the Deuteronomistic History.

Meaning

Verses 8-9 and 10b set the scene for what is to come. The bitter enmity between Abner and Joab, which will end with Abner's death (3:27), belongs within the context of the "war between the house of Saul and the house of David" (3:1, 6). For this, it is important to have both established as rival kings and to emphasize Abner's role.

At one level, the contrast between Ishbaal's extensive kingdom and David's Judah makes David's final rise to power in Israel all the more remarkable and all the more evidently YHWH's doing. At another level, this utterly barebones sketch of the political situation allows the narrator to note the existence of war between David and Ishbaal, while giving it almost no place among the factors that brought David to power. Whether such silence constitutes a delicate falsification of history is an issue we have to leave open. It depends largely on what in fact David's activities were during this period — and that, precisely, we do not know. The text is not history. The text to come is less concerned with how David came to power than with his innocence of the deaths of Abner and Ishbaal. That will emerge in due course.

A story of the enmity between Abner and Joab	2:12-32
I. The opening battle	12-17
A. The confrontation of forces	12-13
1. The leaders and their forces	12-13a
2. Their disposition	13b
B. The specialist combat	14-16
1. The proposal	14
2. The combat	15-16a
3 The etiology	16b
C. The generalized battle	17
1. Its condition: very fierce	17a
2. Its outcome: Abner and Israel beaten	17b
II. The pursuit by Asahel and his killing by Abner	18-24
A. Identification of Asahel	18
B. Asahel's pursuit of Abner	19-22
1. Unswerving pursuit by Asahel	19
2. Attempts at dissuasion by Abner	20-22
C. Outcome	23-24
1. Abner's killing of Asahel	23
2. Pursuit of Abner by Joab and Abishai	24
III. The conclusion	25-32
A. Cessation of hostilities	25-28
B. Aftermath of the engagement	29-32

Textual Issues

2:13   The LXX has "went out from Hebron." According to Ulrich, the spacing in 4QSam^a requires this inclusion (p. 54); but, as Smith noted long ago, "the insertion is more likely than the omission" (*Samuel,* 270).

2:15, 25, 31   The text has "Benjamin" in all three places, yet it is "the servants of Ish-baal" that Abner led out from Mahanaim (2:12). The Benjaminites are also significant in 3:19. Their role as Saul's tribe can be assumed; their role in this narrative, at some point, is uncertain (cf. Anderson, 43).

2:29   The MT has Bithron *(bitrôn),* a word that is unknown to us. It can be rendered in terms of locality (NJPS: through all of Bithron) or time (NRSV: the whole forenoon). Fully discussed by Driver, 245.

Discussion

This is a vivid story of four men, two of whom will die, one in this chapter and one in the next. Bit players in the story are two dozen young men who die, two armies that fight a battle, and two peoples apparently at war. In the background are two kings. To add spice to the interpretation, aspects of the story are puzzling.

The four men are Abner, on one side, and three brothers on the other side, Joab, Abishai, and Asahel. In this story, Abner will be forced to kill Asahel; in the next, Joab will kill Abner. Abner has been familiar as Saul's army commander (cf. 1 Sam 14:50); from the preceding verses we know him as the one who made Ishbaal king. Joab was obliquely mentioned in 1 Sam 26:6, where Abishai is described as "Joab's brother." Joab is a shadowy figure. His position as David's army commander is tenuous (cf. 2 Sam 8:16; 19:14 [Heb.; NRSV, 19:13]; 20:13; and 1 Kgs 2:5-6). His brother Abishai is listed as chief of the Thirty, but not one of the Three (2 Sam 23:18-19, with NRSV). His brother Asahel is listed as one of the Thirty (23:24). Joab is not listed at all.

There may well have been political reasons why Abner and Joab should fight a long war on behalf of their respective kings. What this story does is shift the focus from the political to the personal. Within the Davidic tradition, it is valuable. The political necessarily involves David as king; a personal vendetta is not of David's doing.

The story opens with the confrontation of the two men, Abner and Joab, at the head of the forces of their respective kings — [I.A]. The location at Gibeon is puzzling; it is not immediately evident that forces from Mahanaim and Hebron would meet at Gibeon. Abner's route from Transjordan is not specified; he will return home "through the Arabah" (2:29). "Arabah" usually means plain or desert; here it is west of the Jordan. There are plenty of plains and deserts, so the term does not specify the route. It is likely, however, that Abner and his force are portrayed crossing the Jordan just north of the Dead Sea, as did David in flight from Jerusalem on his way to Mahanaim (cf. 2 Sam 15:28; 17:16; note also Josh 8:14; 1 Sam 23:24; 2 Sam 4:7; 2 Kgs 25:4-5 etc.). There is no passage across the hill country of Ephraim that it would make sense to call the Arabah. Why, then, should Abner's forces have swung south and then north to fight a battle around Gibeon? Verse 15 lists twelve combatants for Benjamin and Ishbaal (cf. also vv. 25 and 31). That Benjaminites should fight at Gibeon makes good sense; it is their territory, in southern Benjamin. Has a localized story been expanded to incorporate Ishbaal's forces? It is possible, but we do not know. The text gives hints; it does not allow of reconstruction. More is needed than suggesting Gibeon as an appropriate place for Joab to block a move against Judah (despite Keil, *Bücher Samuels,* 234; Löhr, *Bücher Samuels,* 128; Nowack, *Bücher Samuelis,* 156; Thenius, *Bücher Samuels,* 133; and also Josephus, *Antiq.* VII/10). The balanced disposition of the two groups, on either side of "the pool of Gibeon," is too tidy to reflect campaign conditions. Something special is going on; we are not told the details of precisely what.

Without any details being specified, Abner proposes that two groups of soldiers join in combat and Joab agrees — [I.B]. It is reminiscent of David's combat with Goliath, although no equivalent to Goliath's conditions is mentioned (1 Sam 17:9) — in the Goliath story, the conditions were not observed. Two aspects of this combat puzzle interpreters. First, was it a display of martial arts or was it serious warfare (cf. Hertzberg, 251: "some sort of 'mock duel' with definite rules"; to the contrary, de Vaux, "Combats Singuliers," 225-26 — citing in support also Sukenik, "Let the young men," and Eissfeldt, "Ein gescheiterter Versuch" and "Noch Einmal: Ein gescheiterter Versuch")? Second, did all the participants die or did an equal number on each side die (all: de Vaux, "Combats Singuliers," 225; an equal number: Sukenik)? Some such form of combat is portrayed in reliefs from Tell Halaf (see de Vaux, "Combats Singuliers," 226). It is clear from the text that generalized war developed from this engagement, perhaps inevitably or perhaps indicating that it did not produce a clearcut outcome. (For possible understandings of the name given to the place, "Helkath-hazzurim," see Driver, 242-43.)

The specialized combat turns into a generalized battle, noted as particularly savage, and one in which Abner and "the men of Israel" were beaten — [I.C]. This is a battle; the war is mentioned only in 3:1 and 6. This is a story of battle that leads to Abner's death in the next story; there is no account of the war.

The modulation from defeat to pursuit is sudden; there is no statement of a general pursuit. If necessary, a storyteller would have no trouble smoothing out the abruptnesses. Without introduction and without reference to Joab's earlier presence, three brothers are named as there: Joab, Abishai, and Asahel. Asahel is singled out as fleet of foot (v. 18). Asahel is identified by two factors: his brothers and his speed. His speed kills Asahel; in due course, one of his brothers kills Abner.

The text has Asahel pursue Abner unswervingly — [II.A and B]. Twice Abner tries to talk him out of it. The reason is clear in the text; in one word, Joab. In the first attempt at dissuasion, Abner identifies his pursuer. It is Asahel. We already know that Asahel is Joab's brother. In the second attempt, Abner is explicit: If I kill you, how "could I show my face to your brother Joab?" (vv. 20-22). At this point, there is no mention of Abishai (by contrast with v. 24). The focus is tightly drawn on Joab and Abner. Asahel will not give up; Abner is left with no choice but to kill him — [II.C.1]. The "butt of his spear" suggests a sudden prop and a backward thrust of the spear, probably the cunning move of a veteran warrior. It would not come as a surprise if the butt of Abner's spear was sharpened with some such a situation in mind (differently: Schulz ["Narrative Art," 131-32] and Hertzberg [252] suggest Abner's action may have been intended to stun and disable rather than to kill; if so, fate overtook him). The text notes a mark of respect paid the dead Asahel by his fellow soldiers (v. 23b; cf. 2 Sam 20:12). The pursuit of Abner is taken up by Joab and Abishai — [II.C.2]. The verb of pursuit in v. 24 may well indicate that what Asahel began in v. 19 Joab and Abishai will finish in due course.

Whenever this "in due course" is to be, it is not on this day of battle — [III]. "The Benjaminites" rally to Abner on a hilltop. The pursuit and the precisely located hill of Ammah are mentioned almost in passing. Ironically, both Abner and Joab acknowledge the bitterness of fratricidal strife, and hostilities are terminated. What Asahel denied Abner Joab grants him — and Joab will kill him. What is puzzling within this text, with its principal focus on the conflict between two powerful rivals (Joab and Abner), is the discussion of the fratricidal quality of civil strife in vv. 26-28. What may be true of strife between peoples is not a lesson that is going to be taken to heart by Joab in this narrative. Abner's end will be bitter.

Abner and his men return to Mahanaim by way of the Arabah (see above), in what has all the appearances of a forced march (all night and the whole forenoon). Joab and his men marched all night to regain Hebron. The urgencies are not explained. Sandwiched in between are the report of Joab's people regrouping, the casualty count, and the burial of Asahel in Bethlehem. The figures of 360 and 20 suggest a stunning victory for David's people, indicative of the outcome ahead. Puzzling is the description of the 360 as Benjaminites. The significance of Asahel is underscored by the particular mention of his burial in his ancestral tomb at Bethlehem.

Genre

As the text stands, it is best described as a (→) reported story, combining perhaps more than one (→) reported story. Rendtorff wants to describe it as a (→) historical story ("Beobachtungen," 432). The focus on Abner and Joab, the disjunctions in the narrative, and the puzzling features all caution against too ready an identification with history.

Setting

The original setting for these traditions is most likely to be sought in the military circles so long dominated by Joab. It is worth noting that Joab's troops are referred to throughout as "the servants of David" (cf. vv. 13, 15, 17, 30, 31); Abner's troops, on the other hand, are referred to by a variety of designations (cf. "the servants of Ishbaal," v. 12; "Benjamin and Ishbaal," v. 15; "the men of Israel," v. 17; "the Benjaminites," vv. 25 and 31; "Israel," v. 28; and "his men," v. 29). Some explanations are possible; the variation remains striking. That the stories may have circulated among "the servants of David" with whom it identifies is likely. The variety of designations for the other side remains unexplained.

The present form of the text, with the exception of vv. 10a and 11, would derive from the compilation of traditions in support of David's rise to power over all Israel. The sustained storytelling power present in chs. 2–4 of 2 Samuel has led David Gunn to claim them for the so-called Succession Narrative (associated with 2 Sam 11–20; cf. Gunn, *King David,* 66-84; applauded by Flanagan, *David's Social Drama,* 37-40). The disjunctions and puzzling aspects of this block militate against the attribution. More significantly, these traditions belong within the horizon of David's rise to political power in Israel. The horizon and concern of the later chapters in Samuel are different (see below). The similarities in skill, however, caution against any attempt to drive too much of a chronological wedge between these Davidic texts.

Meaning

The narrative is rich in meaning. Originally, whether taken together or told as isolated elements, the happenings would have been of special interest among David's forces; there are several aspects of instructional value in military tactics, and there is the personal interest associated with the rivalry of Abner and Joab.

As part of a compilation reflecting on David's rise to power in Israel, it takes on new contours. David is king of Judah; Ishbaal has been made king in the north. Yet here the aggression comes from Abner and, more remotely, Ishbaal. The compilers of these traditions have steadfastly avoided having David grasp for the crown. While civil war is present in this story (cf. 2:26-28), the reality of a state of war is mentioned only in 3:1 and 6. Within that war, this battle associated with Gibeon is the only battle described, and, from the Davidic point of view, the initiative in it was taken by the other side.

Furthermore, within the narrative now, the story suggests that the balance of power has swung markedly in David's direction. The "servants of David" had the better of the battle (v. 17); the casualty figures are overwhelmingly in David's favor (vv. 30-31).

The story provides the overt motive for Joab's killing of Abner (cf. 3:27, 30) and thus tends to confirm David's claim to innocence. Without being overly

Macchiavellian, it also gives Abner a more substantial motif for coming over to David than an angry tiff over a "concubine" (secondary wife). The text of ch. 3 hints at a groundswell toward David among the elders of Israel (cf. 3:17). This story of ch. 2 portrays David as the power figure on the scene. The suspicion is there that Abner may be portrayed as having recognized reality and been preparing his place alongside the future victor. Small wonder Joab killed him.

Textual Issues

3:2-5 Driver notes Wellhausen's observation that v. 6b is a continuation of v. 1 and therefore vv. 2-5 may be an insertion in an earlier text, with v. 6a concealing the juncture (p. 246).

3:3 4QSamᵃ and the LXX have Dalouia in place of Chileab and omit mention of Nabal (Ulrich, 64, 81); cf. McCarter, 101. Driver, 246, is surely right: "it is impossible to say what the original form of the name was."

3:5 "David's wife": Driver, 246, comments, "by analogy (see v. 3a) the name of 'Eglah's first husband would be expected." He suggests a slip of the pen or transcriptional corruption; nothing more helpful has been forthcoming.

3:7 The MT has no subject for the verb; 4QSamᵃ and the LXX (most witnesses) have Mephibosheth (cf. Ulrich, 55, for the Qumran character count). The phenomenon recurs in 4:1-2 (Ulrich, 42-45). See McCarter, 106. The LXX repeats Mephibosheth at 3:8, 11, 14, 15 as well as 4:1, 2, 5, 7, 8 (2x), 12 — (the NRSV footnoting Ish-bosheth in these areas is misleading). Sustained error is unlikely; differences of tradition are more probable. The LXX may well be revealing to us glimpses of what we do not see. The MT has Ish-bosheth at 3:8, 14, 15, no subject at 3:11, and no personal name at 4:1, 2.

3:12 Instead of the NRSV's to David "at Hebron," Anderson, 51, 53, translates "instead of going himself"; as Stoebe's second option, this is described as "not elegant but possible" (p. 125).

3:24-29 The variety of minor agreements and disagreements among the witnesses points to the probable fluidity of the text traditions.

3:39 The NRSV's "even though anointed king" brings out a contrast that is expressed in Hebrew simply by the copula; much must be understood from the context (see Driver, 252; McCarter, 111-12).

4:4 The issue of Merib-baal/Mephibosheth is largely akin to that discussed above at 2:8 for Ishbaal/Ishbosheth. As noted there, see Driver, 253-54; Barthélemy, 228-30; McCarter, 85-87, 124-25.

4:6-7 Two options are to the fore. With Anderson, the possibility of two versions (70; also Stoebe, 151-52); with Barthélemy, 237-40, the likelihood of a high level of complexity. The presence of alternative accounts is not unusual in the Samuel narrative.

Discussion

Although this will be a lengthy analysis, it cannot represent the finer details in depth. Three factors suggest that the text is best reflected by keeping the deaths of Abner and Ishbaal together — [I and II]. First, how Abner's power was exercised and how it was frustrated is the leitmotiv from v. 6 on. It is brought to closure by the burial of Ishbaal's head in Abner's tomb. In death as in life, Abner was the leading figure. Second, the beginning of the account of Ishbaal's death is hardly the way that a new section is introduced in Hebrew narrative (cf. 4:1). Third, Abner's tomb at Hebron is referred to (in 4:12) without any comment as to his death or his burial at Hebron — both explained in the preceding. In this understanding, the compositional arrangement of the present text moves in three stages. The first concludes with David's anointing as king of Judah. The second concerns the elimination of Ishbaal and the northern kingdom as an obstacle to David's kingship over all Israel. The death of Abner, on the other hand, is the elimination of an obstacle to Joab's power, not to David's kingship. The third stage is, then, the establishment of David's kingship over all Israel.

With the claim that David was responsible for Abner's murder — "a crafty and unctuous David lured Abner to Hebron for a peace conference . . . turned on him and killed him" (*Secret Demons,* 83-84) — Baruch Halpern is overzealous in his denigration of David. Abner is portrayed as a serious threat to Joab, not to David.

A new beginning is marked in 3:1 and 3:6 with the emphasis on the house of Saul and the house of David (against Hertzberg, 253). What preceded intensified the enmity between Abner and Joab; it will reemerge in what follows. But the night marches, with both armies returning to Mahanaim and Hebron, respectively, are so structured as to conclude the story that began at the pool of Gibeon. Reference to the "house of Saul" is relatively rare (cf. 2 Sam 3:1, 6, 8, 10; 9:1-3; 16:5, 8 [Shimei]; 19:18 [Heb.; NRSV, 19:17 = Ziba]). It is appropriate to the context; it is also indicative of the context.

While there is obvious repetition within 3:1 and 3:6, there is an even more obvious shift in emphasis that betrays the movement in the events to be narrated. Both verses mention the war between the two groups. According to 3:1, David's forces were in the ascendancy in the war and Ishbaal's forces (the house of Saul) were in decline. David is looking like a winner. According to 3:6, while this war is going on, Abner was growing more powerful in Ishbaal's camp. What will unfold in the narrative is here available for any cynical political analyst: David is on the winning side; Abner is the powerbroker on the other side; Abner will switch allegiance to David. Once this has been said, something else becomes obvious: if Abner switches allegiance, he will be a rival to Joab. There is not room for both Abner and Joab in David's camp; one or the other must die.

Between these two verses, a list or register appears naming the sons born to David in Hebron — [I.A.2]. At first view, it seems clumsily out of place; on further reflection, it is most appropriate and skillfully inserted; Driver notes Wellhausen's observation that 3:6b is the logical continuation of 3:1 (p. 246). The language is of "the house" of David or Saul. Here is palpable evidence that David is founder of a dynasty. Saul's sons have died with him in battle; the surviving Ishbaal is a shadowy figure. David's sons are being born to him at Hebron.

As such lists go, this is a strange one and different from its companion piece in 2 Sam 5:13-15 (cf. 1 Chr 3:1-9, with slight expansions in both 2 Sam 3:5 and 1 Chr 3:5; also for Jerusalem only, 1 Chr 14:3-7 [without the expansion]). In 2 Sam 3:2-5, one son only is named for each wife, and yet the sons are numbered from first to sixth. Particular attention is given to the identification of the mothers; but there is no mention of daughters. Three of these six sons — Amnon, Absalom, and Adonijah — are central to later texts as potential heirs to David's throne. Of Chileab (Dalouia/Daniel), Shephatiah, and Ithream nothing more is heard; death in infancy is not unlikely. It is possible that the list was maintained with a view to the dynastic succession. It is improbable that David had only one son from each wife over these seven and a half years. The numbering here and the apparent order of succession from Amnon to Absalom to Adonijah suggest that, at least at the time of this list, the firstborn of each wife may have had a privileged position in the order of succession. Beyond this text, we are unaware of any such privilege. Independently of this aspect of succession, it is noteworthy that the name of the king's mother is normally a feature of the accession formula for the kings of Judah.

With v. 7, the narrative takes up the implications of vv. 1 and 6 — [I.B.1.a.2)]. Abner is the power figure in Ishbaal's kingdom, David is emerging as the victor in the struggle of kings, and Abner needs to be given reason for distance from Ishbaal. The text is odd on two grounds: the initiative in the quarrel is given to Ishbaal not Abner, but Ishbaal is not named as the opening speaker — the MT has just "and he said to Abner" (v. 7; the name is explicit in the following verse). The same phenomenon occurs at the end of the passage (v. 11). Beyond Ishbaal's accusation, Abner's crime is not reported. The text focuses on Abner's reaction, the rift with Ishbaal. Whether the episode is told to justify the rift, with the real reason lying in the tilt of the balance of power to David, we do not know. The text is suitably silent.

Abner's angry response gives a clear indication of the realities of power in Ishbaal's kingdom. The presentation of Abner openly averring to Ishbaal his intention to transfer the kingdom to David (vv. 9-10) would be implausible and unthinkable if the subsequent narrative did not confirm it (Driver, 246, speaks of undue power and presumption; the narrative does not bear him out). Abner's confident supremacy is borne out in v. 11; Ishbaal was afraid.

Abner's speech refers to a sworn promise to David of which we have no trace in the tradition (cf. v. 9; it scarcely reflects the story of David's anointing, against Hertzberg, 258). It is an interesting example of what we might term "vulgar theology," reflecting the interplay between God's will and human politics — constant in these texts. Abner vows to bring about what God has promised; God promises it and Abner does it. It is the opposite of the stance given David in 1 Sam 26:10. In the light of Abner's imminent fate, it is not without a certain irony. Commentators have been understandably troubled by these verses, along with vv. 17-19, 28-29, 38-39 (cf. for example, McCarter, 113-20; Veijola, *Ewige Dynastie,* 30-32, 59-63; comprehensively, Haelewyck, "Mort d'Abner"). Editorial interventions are clearly possible; given the compiled nature of these texts at their origins, however, and the pro-Davidic stance already evident in this material, the further evidence adduced is not strong enough to claim more than the clearly possible.

Once the rift with Ishbaal has been established, the narrative can turn to Abner's opening of negotiations with David to effect the transfer of power from Ishbaal to David. With 3:12, we have one of those verses — they are many — where the meaning is clear enough and how it is to be derived from the words of the text is highly unclear. Abner sends messengers to David, the NRSV says "at Hebron," with a note saying it is following the Greek and giving the Hebrew as "where he was." The NRSV is following the Greek's best attempt to make sense of the dubious Hebrew; that is probably enough for us. It is possible that the Hebrew word *(tahtāw)* might refer not to David ("where he was") but to Abner and mean something like "in his place" — i.e, at this preliminary stage of negotiations, Abner sent messengers; later he will come himself (cf. McCarter, 107). The second difficulty offered by the Hebrew is the repetition of the word, "saying" *(lē'mor)*. It would be easy enough to see this as introducing two alternative clauses or a second clause that unfolds the first (cf. Talmon, "Textual Study," 344-57), if the first clause were not problematic — but it is. Literally, it reads: "to whom a land?" If we read "the land," it would be so much easier, meaning on Abner's lips, "whose is the land?" — who has the power around here, with the evident answer, "I do" (cf. Driver, 247-48). Barthélemy (233-34) points to 1 Sam 9:20, refers to David rather than Abner, and understands, "who has a land" — with a meaning such as "what is the point of being king without possession of a land" (possession that Abner can deliver). In Barthélemy's understanding, David was a king without a land and Abner controlled a land without a king (p. 234). Attractive, but difficult to squeeze from the Hebrew. Anderson probably says it best: "In view of the textual uncertainty and in absence of any generally accepted solution, we retain the MT even though it may not preserve the original reading" (p. 53). The sense is clear: commit to me and I'm your man and I'll bring all Israel into your camp. David's acceptance is prompt but conditional; the condition is the return of Michal. Most probably, what is at stake is a demonstration of Abner's ability to deliver (against Hertzberg, 258-59). In this understanding, David's embassy to Ishbaal is appropriate and proper. David's request is properly addressed to Ishbaal, as reigning monarch and brother of Michal. Abner's claim implies that he can deliver the kingdom because he controls the king. The proof of Abner's power becomes evident when the king delivers Michal. As a final crushing touch, the narrative brings Abner on the scene to order Paltiel, her husband, bluntly to go back (v. 16b). The terseness of the command is brutal *(lēk šûb)*, the equivalent of "Get lost!"

With Abner's control of Ishbaal demonstrated, the narrative turns to the negotiations that assure the broader political basis for the transfer of political allegiance. Two items are reported that were unknown to us. First, there has been a groundswell in David's favor; according to the narrative, for some time the elders of Israel have been seeking David as king over them (v. 17). We are left to wonder whether Abner is controlling or adroitly anticipating the shifting balance of power. Second, there is another promise of God to David that is unknown to us (v. 18). Its reference to the Philistines has echoes of the anointing of Saul (1 Sam 9:16). We are reminded of just how much may have existed in Israel's traditions that we do not know about. Of course, retrojection of later belief is always possible and seldom demonstrable. Other occurrences of "my servant David," at least, are late; an exception is possible, but not evident (of vv. 17-18, McCarter gives at least v. 18b to the Deuteronomist, p. 116; Veijola attributes 3:9-10, 17-19, 28-29, and 38-39 to his Deuteronomistic Historian, *Ewige Dynastie,* 31-32, 59-63). It must be remembered that most of these narratives can safely be assumed to have been composed well after the events they retail. They have the benefit of hindsight. Beyond the elders of Israel, Abner is reported to have negotiated with Benjamin, Saul's tribe (v. 19). Any special role for Benjamin in all this is unknown to us, but needs to be noted. However, in noting Abner's departure for Hebron to speak to David, the text specifically refers to Israel and "the whole house of Benjamin" (v. 19b).

The final negotiations with David involve a delegation of twenty with Abner and are highlighted by the solemnity of a banquet. Abner's confident power is evident in the three first-person verbs of v. 21a; small wonder Joab was threatened. Abner promises that David will "reign over all that your heart desires"; the same promise is made by Ahijah, YHWH's prophet, to Jeroboam in 1 Kgs 11:37, perhaps echoing Abner here. The phrase is common enough; these are the only two occurrences referring to kingdoms.

The theology of the text needs noting; all the elements in play are listed and among them is God's promise. In 2 Sam 5:2, historical reality and divine utterance are set side by side. In this text a similar delicate interplay of factors is present. Abner's exercise of power is there, along with the weakness of Ishbaal, the political will expressed by the elders of Israel, also that of Benjamin, and in due course Joab's drives (v. 23ff). David's attitudes are in the background. God's promise is affirmed. There is no ranking or coordination; the factors simply surface at different points. In this, they mirror the complexity of human life and caution us against reading Israel's interpretation of its own history in too superficial a fashion. Israel's biblical texts hold together the various aspects of political negotiation and divine determination.

With v. 22, a new force is introduced: David's men and Joab — [I.B.1.b]. The balance of power shifts once again. Abner had had twenty men with him; Joab arrives with David's troops, back from a raid, "bringing much spoil with them" (v. 22). Joab is fresh from war; Abner has been sent away in peace. Three times it is mentioned that Abner had gone away in peace (vv. 21, 22, 23); it will not last for long. Joab immediately reproaches David (vv. 24-25). The tone of the exchange is blunt, as between equals; for all that we know little of Joab, this exchange gives him a tone of intimacy with David. On David's side, there is no trace of Ishbaal's fear. On Joab's side, we do not know whether his reproach was based on a genuine suspicion of Abner's motives or was an insidious pretext to cover his own. The narrative does not tell us; we are also not told what was known or unknown to Joab of what the narrative has recounted.

Joab may be a familiar of David's; in the narrative, he is a shadowy figure. He is central to 2 Sam 2–3; he is listed as David's army commander in 2 Sam 8:16; he does not feature in between. He has a clear role as faithful commander in chs. 10–12 and is broker for Absalom in ch. 14. In 2 Sam 17:25, Absalom gives Amasa Joab's job. In 2 Sam 18, Joab kills Absalom; he is significant in chs. 19–20. He is absent from the lists of the Three and the Thirty from David's early traditions (cf. ch. 23); he figures in ch. 24. In the factions around

David's succession, along with the priest Abiathar, Joab supported Adonijah; it cost him his life. When he heard that Solomon had banished Abiathar, he fled to the sanctuary and "grasped the horns of the altar" (1 Kgs 2:28). Solomon had Benaiah kill him there. He had lived by the sword; he died by the sword. He remains an enigma.

Whatever his motivation here, Joab wasted no time in recalling Abner before he was too far from Hebron. Abner may have been shrewd enough to kill Asahel with the reverse end of his spear; he was not shrewd enough to escape from Joab's sword, or rather Joab's relentless blood-vengeance.

The text twice says that Abner died for killing Asahel. The first time, Joab did the killing and Asahel is described as "Joab's brother" (3:27); the second time, Joab and Abishai are termed the killers and Asahel described as "their brother" (3:30). Sandwiched between the two is David's protestation of his innocence. It will be manifested in the mourning for Abner to follow (vv. 31-39). We have seen enough reason to query whether some of these Davidic texts were slanted to exonerate David from the guilt that Shimei, for example, accused him of. The question can be asked of vv. 28-29. However, the whole tenor of the story from the outset strongly suggests that it would have been in David's interest to keep Abner alive, at least until the merger of the kingdoms was effected. If David was a far-sighted and ambitious politician, the elimination of his middleman on the eve of the successful consummation of favorable negotiations would appear an incredibly inept blunder. At this point, David's ambitions were not threatened by Abner; Joab's were (against Halpern).

According to the text, David ordered Joab to participate in the mourning rites for Abner — a small penalty for a murderer — [I.B.2.a]. The lament for Abner does not spare Joab: "as one falls before the wicked you have fallen" (v. 34). There is an insistence on the lamentation of all the people (cf. vv. 32-33); king and people are innocent. The fasting till evening that was observed for Saul and Jonathan (1:12) is observed by David for Abner too, with special notice of its being against the people's urging (v. 35). Attention is drawn to the popular approval of David's attitude and the recognition of David's innocence by the people and by all Israel. We are entitled to wonder whether the text protests too much; it may well, but, as noted above, it seems unlikely that the protestation involved a cover-up of David's wrongdoing.

David is given a final address to his own — [I.B.2.b.2)]. His praise of Abner as "a prince and a great man" agrees well enough with the picture of Abner given earlier in the story. The open reference to the difficulty that the sons of Zeruiah present to David is puzzling. Does it indicate why Joab and Abishai did not meet the fate of the Amalekite or of Rechab and Baanah? Is it to be dismissed as part of the extravagance of funerary rhetoric? Or is it a pointer to some deep-seated tension between David and his chief lieutenant, contributing perhaps to his later brief replacement (19:14 [Heb.; NRSV, 19:13]) and the subsequent attribution of his death to David's command (1 Kgs 2:5-6)? As with so much of the relationships of those around David, and the inner working of the Davidic court, we are left in the dark.

Another aspect is seriously puzzling, needs discussion, and can be dealt with here as well as anywhere. Biblically, it is extremely rare for men to be named with a matronymic, an identification including the mother's name, as here. The ancient Israelite custom was to use patronymics (son of X, the father). Three significant military figures — Joab, Abishai, and Asahel (cf. 2 Sam 2:18; 1 Chr 2:16) — are all referred to as "son of Zeruiah," their mother. Chronicles lists her as a sister of David (2:16). The identification has proved a puzzle. Joseph Auneau suggests the possibility of a clan name, later interpreted as a matronymic ("Çeruya"); Ronald Simkins comments: "It is uncertain why these men are always identified by the name of their mother. Zeruiah may have been a prominent woman, eclipsing her husband, or possibly was named in order to connect her sons to David's family. . . . Zeruiah might have been the half sister of David" ("Zeruiah"). In certain segments of modern society, one option to explain the identification of three brothers by their mother's name would certainly be that the father or fathers was or were unknown. Such a possibility cannot be excluded from the ancient world (cf. Abimelech and Jephthah, whose mothers were unnamed [cf. Judg 8:31 *(pîlegeš)* and 9:18 *('āmâ);* 11:1 *(zônâ)*]; note also Edmund's lines, with their culmination: "Now, gods, stand up for bastards" [*King Lear,* act 1, sc. 2, lines 1-22] — Abimelech was not one, Jephthah was; Abimelech failed, Jephthah succeeded). A husband for Zeruiah is never named. She seems likely to have been a formidable woman. For the narrative use of the characterization of the three as "sons of Zeruiah," equivalent to "hard men," see Gunn, *Story of King David,* 39-40.

Concerning Ishbaal and all Israel, Ishbaal's fear is well founded — [II]. He was already afraid of Abner (3:11). With power now unquestionably in the hands of David and Joab, Ishbaal has little future to look forward to. The "dismay" of all Israel may seem strange following 3:37's assertion that "all Israel" understood that David "had no part in the killing of Abner." But there had been negotiations with Abner, and Abner they knew; Joab they did not know. Uncertainty begets fear.

The two assassins are presented in 4:2. Two factors are specifically mentioned that militate against David's complicity: they are Ishbaal's own captains; they are members of his own tribe of Benjamin. Some note about the people of Beeroth may have been felt necessary (4:3; cf. Josh 9:17); possibly, it is a later update or a marginal note that has moved into the text (cf. Hertzberg, 263-64).

The note concerning Mephibosheth may well serve a couple of purposes here. He is Jonathan's son, to our knowledge next in line for the throne after Ishbaal. Lamed at the time of Saul's death, he is scarcely a suitable candidate for Saul's throne (cf. tentatively, Hertzberg, 264). Alternatively, the note may explain Mephibosheth's absence and how he did not, therefore, share Ishbaal's fate. We have traditions about Mephibosheth's survival under David at 2 Sam 9, 19, and 21; they are not in complete harmony. The existence of varying traditions serving varying purposes is hardly surprising.

The account of Ishbaal's murder has caused textual confusion (the RSV follows the LXX for v. 6; the NRSV notes that the meaning of the Hebrew of v. 6 is uncertain). Verse 6 has both captains enter the house, kill Ishbaal, and escape. Verse 7 goes into greater detail: Ishbaal was having an afternoon nap; after killing him, the murderers cut off his head and traveled through the night with it. Verse 6 is needed for the entry into the house; v. 7 is needed for the gruesome beheading. Clarity on the details is not needed for the impact of the story (for further references, see above under "textual issues").

What the two captains say to David — [II.B.1.b] — is in line with what Shimei ben Gera might have been expected to have thought: David considered his enemy was Saul; with Ishbaal's death, David could consider himself avenged "on Saul and on his offspring" (4:8). The only detail that reflects Davidic tradition is the description of Saul as one "who sought your life." Davidic apologists could not allow such a presentation to pass unchallenged. It is promptly met with David's speech, his order for Baanah and Rechab's execution, and the burial of Ishbaal's head in Abner's tomb — [II.B.2]. Much is conveyed in a short space; the narrative technique is good. Not only is David seen as punishing the assassins of Ishbaal, but his righteous actions in the case of Saul are also felicitously recalled.

It is worth noting that the emphasis in these traditions on David's innocence of bloodguilt puts them in a different category from the stories of David's middle years (2 Sam 12–20) where that emphasis is lacking.

Genre

The passage is described by Rendtorff as (→) historical story, a narrative that is almost history-writing ("Beobachtungen," 432). A better genre description is probably (→) reported story. Too much demands unfolding, especially the Ishbaal-Abner relationship; the storyteller's role would be significant. The moment concerned is one of importance for the history of the people; it opens the way to a united kingdom. The narrative details the negotiations involved and portrays the deaths of two of the central figures, Abner and Ishbaal. The tension of a storyline is more possible than actual. The opening tension created is between Abner and Ishbaal. The dénouement of the narrative is not the resolution of this tension; nor does it deal with Abner's transferring the kingdom to David. The plot of a story is not developed; instead, there is a concern with the events, their interaction, and the motivations for them.

Setting

The principal beneficiary is David; the original setting could well have been in Davidic circles. A couple of periods would have been particularly appropriate. Immediately following the two deaths, of Abner and Ishbaal, it would clearly have been in David's interest to have an account circulated of how Ishbaal and Abner met their deaths. The other side would surely have had other views and let them be known. Later, during the period of unrest that culminated in the rebellions of Absalom and Sheba ben Bichri, accusations similar to those of Shimei ben Gera (cf. 2 Sam 16:7-8) can be expected to have circulated. A rebuttal of Shimei's charge, "you are a man of blood," would have been required.

Later again, these traditions took their place in the compositions of Israel's narratives where we have them now. It is usually taken for granted that this particular narrative portrays the build-up to a unified kingdom and David's ultimate power. As noted earlier, the capacity for sustained narrative has led David Gunn to compare 2 Sam 2–4 with the narrative dealing with David's middle years, often called the Succession Narrative (2 Sam 9–20 and 1 Kgs 1–2; for Gunn, see above and *King David,* 65-84).

Some reflection is in order. First, Gunn has valuably shown the similarities of style between the two sections of narrative. While there has been brilliant storytelling earlier in the Davidic traditions, what is presented in chs. 2–4 contains a sustained portrayal of the chain of causality that led almost inevitably to the final outcome. Gunn's position is a healthy warning to those who want to drive a wedge between the sacral stories of early on and the secular stories of later texts. Not too much can be built on style alone here. A methodological point needs noting: similarities of style may point to the same circle of authorship, perhaps even to the same hand, but they do not constitute literary unity. One author can create two works; similar style may be found in different creations.

Second, any suggestion that 2 Sam 2–4 belongs with chs. 9–20 etc. faces the task of tracing something of a continuous text from ch. 4 to ch. 9. The simple association of 9:1 with 4:12 is scarcely plausible (but cf. Gunn, *King David,* 68-70) and, in my judgment, Gunn's case for it does not carry conviction. Too much of significance has to be assumed.

Third, the claim on this material of a story of David's rise to power has to be taken into account. With the coming of David to Saul's court (1 Sam 16:14–18:13), a story has begun that has as its theme David's replacement of Saul, on the battlefield and ultimately on the throne. The issues of replacement and rivalry are present throughout the subsequent material. A process has been set in motion that cannot be allowed to end with David's anointing as king of Judah. In 1 Sam 18:16, "all Israel and Judah loved David"; the narrative will scarcely stop until David is king over all Israel and Judah.

Meaning

The meaning of the narrative lies in the information provided on the events that led up to the deaths of Abner and Ishbaal. It cannot be separated from the illustration of David's attitude to the elimination of the final obstacles that stood between him and ultimate power, kingship over all Israel.

The narrative makes clear — and, as we have seen, probably correctly — that, in the case of Abner, his death was not intended by David as a stepping-stone toward the throne. It resulted from a combination of Joab's vengeance and suspicion. In the case of Ishbaal, it is true that his death was directly intended to clear David's way to the throne, but in the narrative the intention was not David's but came from the side of Ishbaal's own captains. In both cases, far from rejoicing at his political good fortune, David is portrayed as saddened and grieving (3:37; 4:10-11).

For later compilers, the narrative admirably suited the overall theme that David, like the earlier deliverer-judges, did not force his way to leadership but was brought to it by a chain of events that was revelatory of YHWH's will. The interaction of YHWH's will and the human factors of politics and power is, as we have noted, avowedly complex. David, for example, is shown negotiating with Abner, but it is not through these negotiations that he comes to power. At the same time, Abner's negotiations with the elders of Israel and with Benjamin portray the popular feeling that will eventually make David king (cf. 5:1-3).

There is a three-stage movement in the narrative which, like that of ocean waves, on the surface looks simple, clear, and beautiful. Stage one: David is there when the Philistine makes his challenge and, under the power of God's spirit, David acts as Israel's deliverer and Saul's replacement. Stage two: under the power of God's direction, David moves to Hebron and the people of Judah come there and anoint him their king. Stage three: Abner, powerbroker over Saul's kingdom, incurs Joab's hatred and rivalry; Joab kills him and subsequently two northern captains kill Ishbaal, hoping to curry favor with David; the coast is clear for David to step into the vacuum that gapes before him.

As with oceans, the currents beneath the waves are sometimes fierce and usually complex.

It may seem out of keeping with this overall theme to have 3:1 and 3:6 as a constituent part of the text. The reference to a long war between the house of Saul and the house of David leaves open the possibility that, as Shimei thought, David did claw and fight his way to power. Two considerations may have made this aspect more acceptable to Davidic supporters. First, despite the fact that there was war, about which almost nothing is said, it is not directly by means of war that David is propelled to the throne. Second, while David has been consistently portrayed as respectful of YHWH's anointed, that situation no longer exists. Neither Abner nor Ishbaal has any apparent claim to be the anointed of YHWH. If anything, the narrative tends to discredit Ishbaal's kingdom; it was not the creation of YHWH but of Abner. Ishbaal is not presented as the anointed of YHWH; instead, he is portrayed as the puppet of Abner.

Bibliography of Works Cited Above

Auneau, Joseph. "Çeruya." Page 252 in *Dictionnaire encyclopédique de la Bible*. Edited by P-M. Bogaert et al. N.p.: Brepols, 1987.

Budde, Karl. *Die Bücher Samuel*. KHC 8. Tübingen: Mohr, 1902.

Eissfeldt, O. "Ein geschciterter Versuch der Wiedervereinigung Israels." *La Nouvelle Clio* 3 (1951) 110-27,

———. "Noch Einmal: Ein gescheiterter Versuch der Wiedervereinigung Israels." *La Nouvelle Clio* 4 (1952) 55-59.

Flanagan, James W. *David's Social Drama: A Hologram of Israel's Early Iron Age*. JSOTSup 73. Sheffield: Almond, 1988.

Gunn, D. M. *The Story of King David: Genre and Interpretation*. JSOTSup 6. Sheffield: JSOT, 1978.

Haelewyck, Jean-Claude. "La Mort d'Abner: *2 Sam* 3,1-39. Etude littéraire et historique." *RB* 102 (1995) 161-92.

Halpern, Baruch. *David's Secret Demons: Messiah, Murderer, Traitor, King.* Grand Rapids: Eerdmans, 2001.

Josephus, Flavius, *Jewish Antiquities,* Books V-VIII. The Loeb Classical Library. London: Heinemann, 1934.

Keil, Carl Friedrich. *Die Bücher Samuels.* 2d ed. Leipzig: Dörffling und Franke, 1875.

Löhr, Max. See under Thenius and Löhr.

Nowack, W. *Die Bücher Samuelis.* HAT. Göttingen: Vandenhoeck & Ruprecht, 1902.

Rendtorff, Rolf. "Beobachtungen zur altisraelitischen Geschichtsschreibung anhand der Geschichte vom Aufstieg Davids." Pages 428-39 in *Probleme biblischer Theologie.* Edited by H. W. Wolff. Munich: Chr. Kaiser, 1971.

Schulz, Alfons. "Narrative Art in the Books of Samuel." Pages 119-70 in *Narrative and Novella in Samuel: Studies by Hugo Gressmann and Other Scholars, 1906-1923.* Edited by David M. Gunn. JSOTSup 116. Sheffield: Almond, 1991. German original, 1923.

Simkins, Ronald A. "Zeruiah." Page 1419 in *Eerdmans Dictionary of the Bible.* Edited by D. N. Freedman et al. Grand Rapids: Eerdmans, 2000.

Smith, Henry Preserved. *Samuel.* ICC. Edinburgh: T. & T. Clark, 1898.

Sukenik, Y. "Let the young men, I pray thee, arise and play before us!" *JPOS* 21 (1948) 110-16.

Talmon, Shemaryahu. "The Textual Study of the Bible — A New Outlook." Pages 321-81 in *Qumran and the History of the Biblical Text.* Edited by F. M. Cross Jr. and S. Talmon. Cambridge, MA: Harvard University Press, 1975.

Thenius, Otto. *Die Bücher Samuels.* KeHAT. Leipzig: Hirzel, 1842.

Thenius, Otto, and Max Löhr. *Die Bücher Samuels.* 3d ed. KeHAT. Leipzig: Weidmann, 1898.

Vaux, Roland de. "Les Combats Singuliers dans l'Ancien Testament." Pages 217-30 in *Bible et Orient.* Paris: Cerf, 1967. Repr. from *Bib* 40 (1959) 495-508.

Veijola, Timo. *Die Ewige Dynastie: David und die Entstehung seiner Dynastie nach der deuteronomistischen Darstellung.* AASF B 193. Helsinki: Suomalainen Tiedeakatemia, 1975.

Chapter 3

THE ESTABLISHMENT OF DAVID AS KING OF ALL ISRAEL (2 SAM 5–8)

The texts concerning David's establishment as king of all Israel, with his capital in Jerusalem, can be studied as individual units. It would be willful, however, to ignore the thematic unity that holds together the arc from David's anointing as king by all the tribes of Israel (5:1-3) to David's administering "justice and equity to all his people" (8:15). A brief structure analysis will represent the movement of the text.

David's establishment as king of all Israel	2 Sam 5:1–8:18
I. David established as king	5:1-25
A. His crown	1-5
B. His capital	6-10
C. His palace	11-12
D. His children	13-16
E. His security	17-25
II. David's kingdom securely established	6:1–8:18
A. Religiously: the coming of the ark	6:1-23
B. Dynastically: the promise of Nathan	7:1-29
C. Politically: the conquest of empire	8:1-18

Once we have seen the overall concern that holds these traditions together, it is appropriate to look at each block more closely.

David established as king	5:1-25
I. Installation of David as king over Israel	1-5
A. Offer of the kingship from "all the tribes of Israel"	1-2
B. Installation of David as king by "all the elders of Israel"	3
C. Accession formula	4-5

53

Textual Issues

5:4-5 4QSam[a] lacks these verses (Ulrich, 60-62; cf. Pisano, 98-101); the LXX supports the MT.

    5:8 The MT (Qere) can be understood as "those whom David hates"; the LXX (and MT Kethib), on the contrary, read as "those who hate David." "Those who hate David" would refer to the defenders' boast of v. 6; Barthélemy considers it likely to have been the original reading (p. 239). For Barthélemy, both the MT (Qere) and further the reading of 4QSam[a] are to be understood as euphemisms, formulated to avoid "David's soul" being the object of the verb "to hate" (p. 240). Ulrich, however, understands the 4QSam[a] reading as "David's soul hating the blind and the lame" (pp. 136, 148).

Discussion

The report of David's establishment as king over Israel is skillfully told — [I]. 5:1 opens with "all the tribes of Israel" coming to David at Hebron; 5:3 opens with "all the elders of Israel" coming to the king, also at Hebron. In between, the reasons are given that are alleged for David's kingship of Israel. They fall into three categories: ethnic (kinship), political (recent history), and theological (YHWH's utterance). Following the coming of the elders, two aspects of ritual are reported. King David made a covenant with the elders at Hebron before YHWH; they anointed David king over Israel. Twice in v. 3 David is named as king before his anointing by the elders of Israel: the elders come to the king at Hebron; King David made a covenant with them. Both references can be accounted for by his being king over Judah (but 5:1 has simply "to David"); both give a tone of inevitability to the proceedings.

The repetition in vv. 1 and 3 may point to two sources of origin or it may indicate popular support and official action (cf. advocating unity: Hertzberg, 266-67, and Carlson, *Chosen King,* 55; with vv. 1-2 as an addition: Veijola, *Ewige Dynastie,* 63-66; with the start of v. 3 as an addition: Budde, *Samuel,* 218, and Eissfeldt, *Komposition,* 28). We do not and cannot know. Given the earlier texts (3:10 [Israel and Judah]; 3:21 [all Israel]; 4:1 [all Israel]), a broad representation is legitimately envisaged.

The reasons alleged for allegiance to David raise questions. There is no mention of negotiations with Abner; that might be a matter of political discretion. The kinship claim, "we are your bone and flesh," is not immediately evident. In Gen 29:14, the phrase is used for Laban and Jacob, as uncle and nephew; in Judg 9:2, by Abimelech to the burghers of Shechem; and in 2 Sam 19:13-14 (Heb.; NRSV, 19:12-13) by David to Judah and Amasa. Amasa may provide the clue. He was the son of an Ishmaelite (according to 1 Chr 2:17), and was related by marriage to Joab's family. So here David's marriage to Michal may legitimate the claim. The political grounds, "it was you who led out Israel and brought it in," reflects especially 1 Sam 18:16 (cf. also 18:13b; 29:6); it reflects the claim of earlier texts regarding David's constant success. The originality of the theological claim has been disputed (= v. 2b; cf. Schmidt, *Jahwes Initiative,* 124-26; also: Veijola, *Ewige Dynastie,* 65; Alt, "Staatenbildung," 42; Fohrer notes that v. 2b's YHWH-oracle had been referred to several times [1 Sam 20:15-16; 24:5, 21-22; 25:28, 30; 2 Sam 3:18] as if commonly known and suggests it most likely is to be traced back to the inquiry referred to in 1 Sam 22:13, "Vertrag," 2). However, it is clear that if this promise to be "ruler [*nāgîd*] over Israel" (5:2b) derives from the later prophetic editing, the claim here is later than David's time. Once, however, the promise is seen as future, "you shall be ruler," a clear difference can be seen from the usage of the prophetic editing where the *nāgîd*-role is present, not future (cf. 1 Sam 9:16; 10:1; etc.). In the context, the Davidic anointing spoken of in 1 Sam 13:14 has to be that of 1 Sam 16:13, not 2 Sam 5:3 (note that 1 Sam 16:1 is discreetly reticent and that 1 Chr 11:3 harmonizes erroneously). It is clear from 1 Sam 9:16 and 10:1, that an office is promised for Saul (9:16) and conferred on him with immediate effect (10:1) that prepares the way for his future elevation to the role of king. It is also clear that in later texts, the word of a prophet or the anointing of a prophet constitutes a man king (cf. 1 Kgs 14:7 [Jeroboam: the prophetic word] and 2 Kgs 9:6 [Jehu: the prophetic anointing]). 2 Sam 7:8, looking back on David's early years, might mean either king-designate or king; however, because David left the flock in 1 Sam 16 and because 2 Sam 7:9a points to David's time when Saul was king, king-designate is the more probable understanding for *nāgîd* in 7:8.

This leaves three cases in the early traditions of David where *nāgîd* cannot mean king-designate: 1 Sam 25:30; 2 Sam 5:2; and 6:21. In 1 Sam 25:30, Abigail's flattery points to a future time when David will have the top job. Courtly flattery does not stop short at the lesser role of king-designate. In

2 Sam 6:21, David does not assert his superiority over King Saul by claiming the mere status of king-designate. In both cases, *nāgîd* has to have the meaning of actual leader in Israel (cf. the excursus on *nāgîd* in Campbell, *Of Prophets and Kings,* 47-61). That same early meaning is possible in 2 Sam 5:2. The later prophetic usage, with its aspect of present designation *(nāgîd)* for a future role (king), is out of place here and, therefore, unlikely. Once again, we need to keep in mind the assumption that these Davidic traditions were not given anything like final formulation until well into David's established reign at the earliest. It is unlikely that David's people refrained from claiming YHWH's explicit backing for David's ultimate success.

Two elements are noted in relation to David's establishment as king: covenant and anointing. David makes a covenant with the elders of Israel and they anoint David king (5:3). Covenants are familiar to us from David's relations with Jonathan (1 Sam 18:3; 23:18) and from Abner's negotiations with David (2 Sam 3:12-13, 21). Covenants are explicitly associated with Jehoash's establishment as king (2 Kgs 11:17; cf. v. 4) but are otherwise unmentioned in accounts of coronation. In Jehoash's case, the covenant making appears to have followed his establishment as king (cf. 2 Kgs 11:12 and 17); in David's case, it may have preceded the anointing (2 Sam 5:3). In both cases, the covenant making appears to be associated with the establishment of the king rather than an integral part of the ritual involved.

David is anointed by the elders (the verb is plural). It is worth noting that anointing by a prophet is restricted to three occurrences: two by Samuel (of Saul in 1 Sam 10:1 and of David in 1 Sam 16:13) and one by Elisha's disciple (of Jehu in 2 Kgs 9:6).

The accession formula (vv. 4-5) gives the usual information for a king of Judah — age at accession and length of reign, but here not the name of the queen mother (cf. 2:10a, 11). The specification of the length of a king's reign makes clear that such information was provided after the completion of the reign. These regnal frameworks are attributed to the compositional activity of the Deuteronomist (cf. Noth, *DH,* 34 and 101, n. 4; also Campbell and O'Brien, *Unfolding,* 283, 287, 382, n. 80). Verse 5 repeats and completes 2:11. The capture of Jerusalem is anticipated; the formula is simply given its normal place (however, as noted, vv. 4-5 are lacking in 4QSam^a).

With the issue of kingship established, located in Hebron, the narrative turns to the capture of a capital for the king — [II]. My impression, gained from a survey of the literature on 2 Sam, is that few verses in the book have attracted the attention given to 5:6-8. As so often happens when texts are impossible to render with accuracy, immense attention is given to their possible meaning. At the end of it all, the answer may be that we do not know the details; the outcome however is clear. David captured Jerusalem. The problems arise around the mode of capture and the references to the blind and lame.

The primary difficulty with the Samuel text on the capture of Jerusalem revolves around two words: one is a noun, *ṣinnôr,* and the other a verb, *yigga'* (we will deal with the text from Chronicles shortly; for the linguistic issues, see Driver, 258-62). In the context, we are not certain of the meaning of either word. The noun, *ṣinnôr,* occurs only twice in the Hebrew Scriptures, here and

Ps 42:8 (Heb.; NRSV, 42:7). In the psalm, it is between deep calling to deep on one side and waves and billows on the other. So something to do with water is likely; anything else is uncertain. The verb, *yigga'* (root: *n-g-'*), normally means to touch or strike. Since C. H. Warren's 1867 discovery of the water supply system and tunnels under Jerusalem, it has been common to identify the *ṣinnôr* with the thirteen-meter vertical Jebusite water shaft. Unfortunately, *yigga'* does not mean to climb but to strike or touch — not particularly appropriate to climbing a water shaft. All of this and more are discussed by Hugues Vincent, whose delicate jousting as he rebuts Dalman (*ṣinnôr* = canal in general, penis in particular) and Albright (joint, articulation) raises a wry smile ("Prise de Jérusalem").

Stoebe's comments are worth recording: the identification of *ṣinnôr* with the Jebusite water shaft is very probable (sehr wahrscheinlich); the idea of climbing the water shaft to penetrate the city is romantic and most improbable (romantisch aber auch recht unwahrscheinlich, p. 168; cf. "Einnahme" — despite being a feat achieved in under half an hour by a young British army officer during the Parker expedition [Vincent, *Underground Jerusalem,* 33-37; "Prise de Jérusalem," 365]). Stoebe rightly notes that the Jebusites would have been fools not to have guarded such an obvious weakness in their defenses and that shaft-climbing assailants would have been easily repulsed. What Stoebe, sympathetic to a damming or diversion of the water supply at the spring itself, fails to note is that any attempt to interfere with the water supply — involving an approach under the precipitous slopes of the Jebusite hillside — could have been equally easily repulsed. The Jebusite leaders may have indulged complacent folly; civic leaders can. In legend, Troy fell to the stratagem of the Trojan horse, the city's defenders ignoring the elementary precaution of checking the thing for content; Jebusite Jerusalem might well have fallen to a combination of Joab and the water supply. Much is possible; little is sure. In this case, we simply do not know. We are probably justified in making an association with the water supply; as so often, we are unwise to go further (see also Holm-Nielsen, "Warren's Shaft"; Kleven, "Use"; Dever, "Israelite Monarchy," 188).

McCarter understands *ṣinnôr* as throat or gullet, and combines this with the reference to the blind and lame (pp. 139-40). A colloquial rendering would be: go for the jugular and leave no wounded. Two factors, in particular, militate against an otherwise attractive proposal: how did David's troops get into the town to go for the jugular; the lame may be understandable but a reference to the blind is not particularly appropriate within the context. Beyond these factors, we may add that no OT references to killing use this language.

Reference to the lame and the blind occurs three times (5:6, 8 [2x]). Three possibilities have been advanced: i) the complacency of the Jebusite defenders; ii) a phobia of David's court; iii) the purity of Jerusalem's temple (cf. Olyan, "Anyone Blind or Lame"). The first is appropriate for v. 6. The two occurrences in v. 8 are more likely to be appropriate to the second or third. In the case of the third, in particular, the placement here would lend Davidic weight to the injunction. In truth, we cannot be certain. Ceresko extends the saying (v. 8b) to "the larger story of the monarchy," foreshadowing failure — "the lame," Mephibosheth/Saul; "the blind," Zedekiah/David ("Identity").

The text of Chronicles (1 Chr 11:4-9) is slightly different and does not help greatly. The references to the blind and the lame do not occur (compare 2 Sam 5:6 with 1 Chr 11:5). 2 Samuel 5:8 is practically replaced by 1 Chr 11:6, referring to Joab's role in leading the attack ("going up first") and so becoming chief and commander. Whether Chronicles is better informed or is attempting to make a better fist of a difficult tradition we do not know.

The outcome, at least, is clear: David took the city and occupied it. Brueggemann: "The main point of the text is clear enough. David captures the ancient city of Jerusalem, which has been in the hands of the Canaanites. He captures it with 'his men' (v. 6); . . . It [the city] is David's personal property and the seat of his unfettered autonomy" (pp. 239-40).

Beyond the report of capture is the observation that David occupied the city, claimed it as his own by naming it, and reinforced its defenses. Verse 10 offers the narrative comment that David went from strength to strength and "the LORD, the God of hosts, was with him." The language of v. 10a is slightly different from 3:1; the sentiment is the same. The language of v. 10b is slightly more formal than 1 Sam 18:14; the sentiment is the same. 5:10 sums up what the Davidic traditions have been expressing in story after story: David is succeeding for the LORD is with him. The narrative is putting the finishing touches on this aspect of David's success story; a summary statement is appropriate. As noted earlier, some versions of the Story of David's Rise need not have ended here (despite McCarter, 142-43).

Once a king has his capital city, he needs a palace in it — [III]. Verse 11 states succinctly that Hiram of Tyre sent messengers to David, along with timber, carpenters, and masons or stonecutters, and they built a palace for David. It is striking that the initiative is given to Hiram; no negotiations are mentioned. Later, when it is a question of Solomon's temple building, the negotiations include such aspects as work practices and price (cf. 1 Kgs 5:15-26 [Heb.; NRSV, 5:1-12]; also 9:10-14). The biblical tradition of Hiram's relationship with David is clear (cf. 1 Kgs 5:15 [Heb.; NRSV, 5:1]). However, the Phoenician kinglist quoted by Josephus places Hiram's reign from 970/69 to 936 or 926 (cf. Soggin, "Davidic-Solomonic Kingdom," 351). The chronology casts doubt on whether the building of the palace took place as early in David's reign as 2 Sam 5:11 suggests. It is quite possible that the presence of v. 11 here is governed by thematic rather than chronological considerations. Interestingly, Solomon must have found the palace unsatisfactory enough that he spent thirteen years replacing it (cf. 1 Kgs 7:1).

For many interpreters, the Story of David's Rise ends at this point, if not earlier. This cannot be taken for granted. The existence of a narrative compilation, quite possibly in various versions, that can well be called the Story of David's Rise is likely. Its beginnings, as we have seen, may be as far back as 1 Sam 9. The narrative about God's choice and dismissal of Saul, before being heightened by any prophetic editing, is suitable as a lead-in to the stories of David's struggles. Two elements are important in the background to these stories: first, the legitimacy of a king in Israel; second, the discrediting of the incumbent, to whom David appears as a rival. The early stories of Saul would have provided a desirable background for the Davidic traditions. At the other end, the conclusion of a Story of David's Rise need not end with the capture of Jerusalem and the building of a palace there. The coming of the ark to Jerusalem is important to securing David's position. Nathan's promise of a Davidic dynasty, also precluding David from building a temple, is another major element in securing David's position. Finally, David's military and political (or administrative) successes listed in 2 Sam 8 put the seal on his establishment as ruler over Israel.

What cannot be forgotten is that we are dealing with narrative traditions from Israel's past. A compilation of these individual stories to form a more extensive narrative is, of course, possible; there is no hard and fast evidence to guarantee the enduring existence of such a compilation. There is no superscription, such as we find in the prophetic books. There is no statement of conclusion, claiming that the compilation has reached its end. As with so many of the extended narratives of the Older Testament (Yahwist, Priestly Document, Story of David's Middle Years, Prophetic Record, for example), we are confronted with issues of likelihood and probability. The structuring of certain parts of the text we now have (for example, 1 Sam 17–18, 23–26, and 28–31) suggests that there was a Story of David's Rise. We are invited to that conclusion; it is not imposed on us. That there are stories and traditions about the period of David's rise to power is certain. That they were at some time brought together as a compilation we can call the Story of David's Rise is certainly possible, may indeed be probable. The circumstances of such a compilation are open to discussion and opinion: How long it existed? Where it circulated? Where at any point in its existence it began and ended? And so on. Wisdom urges caution. Cautiously, we may note that a Story of David's Rise that began with 1 Sam 9:1 and ended with 2 Sam 8:15 must be reckoned as at least one of the possibilities.

The comment in v. 12 says about David what significant others have said earlier (e.g., Jonathan, 1 Sam 23:17; Abigail, 25:28-31; Saul, 26:25; Abner, 2 Sam 3:9-10, 18); here, for the first time, it is attributed to David's own awareness. The reference to Israel must include north and south, by contrast with 5:1-3 (cf. Noth, *DH,* 88, n. 4). Given the fragility of David's kingdom, it is not easy to assess when such a comment might have been made. Attribution to a Deuteronomist is far from certain (against Carlson, *Chosen King,* 57; Veijola, *Ewige Dynastie,* 98-99; Grønbaek, *Aufstieg Davids,* 257-58). Establishment of the king or the kingdom has parallels in 1 Sam 13:13, 2 Sam 7:12, and most closely in 1 Kgs 2:24; none need be dtr. The clause, "exalted his kingdom," occurs only here.

If weight is given to the first half of the verse, to "king" rather than "kingdom," the statement is timely. According to the preceding traditions, David has indeed been led by YHWH to become king over the people of Israel. The secure establishment of his kingdom (its consolidation) lies ahead. If weight is placed on the motivation expressed, "for the sake of his people Israel," the statement is appropriately located in relation to the people of Judah (2:4a) and the people of Israel (5:1-3). Attribution of this to the benevolence of YHWH is, of course, at best a statement of faith and at worst a piece of royal propaganda. Given this balance of king and kingdom in 5:12, if the emphasis is laid on the exaltation of the kingdom, it would be difficult to stop short of an early version of 2 Sam 7.

Defeating one's enemies, unifying one's people around a rallying point, and securing one's dynastic succession are all essential steps for a successful monarchy. Here they lie ahead.

This is as good a place as any to note the observations coming from an archaeological base. Israel Finkelstein comments: "Many of the archaeological props that once bolstered the historical basis of the David and Solomon narratives have recently been called into question [p. 124]. . . . The image of Jerusalem in the time of David, and even more so in the time of his son Solomon, has for centuries been a subject of mythmaking and romance [p. 132]. . . . There is hardly a reason to doubt the historicity of David and Solomon. Yet there are plenty of reasons to question the extent and splendor of their realm [p. 142]. . . . At first, in the tenth century, their rule extended over no empire, no palatial cities, no spectacular capital. Archeologically we can say no more about David and Solomon except that they existed — and that their legend endured [p. 143]" (*Bible Unearthed,* cf. pp. 123-45). Much more will surely be said, but such observations are to be heeded. A balancing view can be Dever's: "Few 10th-century archaeological levels have been *exposed* in the deeply stratified and largely inaccessible ruins of ancient Jerusalem, so the paucity of finds means nothing. Yet there is growing evidence of extensive occupation" (*Biblical Writers,* 131). With little "exposed," skeptics may smile and the wise may say little.

In the text as it now stands vv. 13-16 and vv. 17-25 function as appendixes, sandwiched between David's capture of Jerusalem and the coming of the ark there. Both the note of family building and the list of sons are a pointer to the duration of Davidic presence in Jerusalem — [IV]. The defeat of the Philistines makes it safe for the ark to come to Jerusalem — [V]. The seal is gradually being set on Davidic power there. It is appropriate that a text that has given David kingship and capital should go on to the immediate basic consolidation of what has been achieved. Any observer of dynasties knows that the generation of children is essential; any Israelite knew that subjugation of the Philistines was critical to Israel's existence.

The list in vv. 13-16 — [IV] — has a general introduction, signaling an extensive, new Jerusalem household: more "concubines" (secondary wives) and wives; more sons and daughters. It is followed by a list of the sons' names. The introduction (v. 13) is careful to make clear that it refers to the new situation in Jerusalem. It reports that David took more "concubines" and wives. We cannot know if there is any significance attached to the mention of "concubines" first (omitted in 1 Chr 14:3); we notice that no names are given for these Jerusalem women. David had "more sons and daughters" (v. 13); the daughters are not named in what follows. Even the sons' names differ slightly between 2 Samuel and 1 Chronicles (cf. 14:4-7). The list here is not a continuation of the list in 3:2-5; the form is quite different (against Hertzberg, 271). There is no ranking in explicit order; the mothers are unnamed.

Names are sometimes revelatory of historical context. According to the Samuel text, four of David's Jerusalem-born sons had names that included the theophoric element of the god El, generally accepted as god of Jerusalem (they are Elishua, Elishama, Eliada, and Eliphelet; cf. Noth, *Personennamen,* passim, esp. pp. 82-99). The YHWH names evident at Hebron (Adonijah and Shephatiah, 3:4) are not evident at Jerusalem. The Chronicles text replaces Eliada with Beeliada; the theophoric element of the god Baal is likely. As was noted earlier, it is highly unlikely that Saul intended anything unorthodox in giving two of his sons Baal names. It appears that David, too, may have given a Baal name to one of his sons. Again as noted earlier, the suppression of Baal in favor of YHWH is associated with the later time of Elijah and Jehu (1 Kgs 18; 2 Kgs 9–10). In Israel's religious history, the same fate did not befall the god El.

The reports of the Philistine defeats in the second appendix (vv. 17-25) fall into the category of battle reports in which a consultation of God is involved — [V]. In fact, this concern with the consultation is predominant, especially in vv. 22-25. This observation should give us pause before taking for granted that the text's concern is with military history. The precise historical situation of the two battles escapes us. The present text situates them after the capture of Jerusalem and the building of a palace there. Verse 17's comment that David "went down to the stronghold" may militate against this. The term "stronghold" has just been used of David's city (cf. 5:7, 9); but if Zion is meant, why should David "go down to" it (discussed in Garsiel, "David's Warfare")?

According to the text, the first Philistine initiative is related to the anointing of David as king over Israel (v. 17a) — [V.A]. This happened at Hebron (v. 3). The "valley of Rephaim" is not a great help as a geographical locator. Boundary lists in Joshua put it in the close vicinity of Jerusalem (cf. Josh 15:8; 18:16); elsewhere, the location is less precise. 2 Sam 23:13-14 has David at the cave of Adullam and the Philistines at the valley of Rephaim in v. 13, with David in "the stronghold" and a Philistine garrison in Bethlehem in v. 14. The repetition enhances the geographical uncertainty. It is probably unwise to try to remove the uncertainty. Somewhere in the vicinity, south of Jerusalem, accessible from Jerusalem or Hebron, is enough. What the two passages convey is adequately expressed by David: "The LORD has burst forth against my enemies before me, like a bursting flood" (5:20). YHWH has enabled David to eliminate the Philistine threat that menaced Israel's existence.

David's consultation of the LORD is probably to be understood as having been carried out through the lot; only, in the narrative, the two questions and the two answers have been telescoped into one consultation. No details of the victory are recorded; its significance is preserved in the etiology of Baal-perazim. Nothing is said of the fate of the Philistine idols. Victory is in the sphere of the divine; YHWH has conquered and the enemy idols have been abandoned.

The second report is almost completely concerned with the consultation — [V.B]. The tactics are dictated by God and are changed from the first encounter. According to v. 23, unlike v. 19b, David is not to "go up" (assuming a frontal attack) but to move to the Philistine rear. The action expected of David is expressed by an unusual verb *(ḥāraṣ);* in a dozen occurrences, there is not a context that is parallel to this one (Chronicles, reporting the same event, has David commanded to "go out to battle" — 1 Chr 14:15). The sense here is unmistakable; YHWH is the instigator of the victorious action and David complies by striking down the Philistines from Geba to Gezer, from the Judean hills to the Mediterranean littoral. YHWH goes out before David; the battle and the victory are YHWH's. David's role is merely to comply. With the rout reaching to

Gezer in the coastal plain, the Philistine threat is reported as substantially diminished (cf. 1 Chr 20:4).

Genre

A number of genres are represented in this passage. The (→) account of David's installation as king over Israel is probably based on a (→) short notice (v. 3), expanded by the narrator's introductory interpretation of the basis for it (vv. 1-2; cf. Rendtorff, "Beobachtungen," 435; Grønbaek, *Aufstieg Davids,* 248-50). Verses 6-9 and v. 11 may perhaps be best classified as (→) short notice (cf. Rendtorff, "Beobachtungen," 435-36). Verses 4-5, on the other hand, are (→) accession formulas from the dtr compilers. Verses 10 and 12 are interpretative (→) comment from the narrator/compiler (cf. Rendtorff, "Beobachtungen," 435). Verses 13-16 are a (→) list, with the appropriate superscription and introduction. Verses 17-25 are formally (→) battle reports; as noted, the concern with God's will and action, visible in the emphasis on the consultation of YHWH, has practically speaking replaced the content of battle.

Setting

The setting in which these traditions have been brought together is most simply explained as the compilation of a Story of David's Rise. Alternatives may be envisaged. Some of the short notices might derive from royal archives (e.g., vv. 3, 9, 11, 13-16). The uncertainties of vv. 6-9 are appropriately reflected in uncertainty about their setting. The basic information of vv. 17-25 may have begun in military circles; a likely source for the emphasis on divine consultation cannot be pinned down. Prophetic circles are possible (cf. 1 Kgs 20).

Meaning

For all the difficulties associated with these traditions, their meaning is not in doubt. The kingship was offered to David by all the tribes (5:1) and elders (5:3) of Israel and was duly solemnized with covenant and anointing. It can be represented as the logical working out of YHWH's will in Israel's history (v. 2). The acquisition of a capital and a palace bring to an end David's guerrilla days in the wilderness and with the Philistines. Sons were born to David in Hebron; no other claim is made. The claim made for Jerusalem is given a definitiveness by its being "the city of David" (5:9), by the palace built there by Hiram (5:11), and by David's extensive household there (5:13-16). That this is portrayed as God's will is evident from vv. 10, 12, and 17-25.

    According to the narrative, what Saul could not deliver (despite 1 Sam

9:16) God has achieved through David, for the sake of God's people Israel (5:12). The narrative ahead gives full emphasis to the permanence of this situation in three moves: the coming of the ark to Jerusalem; the dynastic security of David in Jerusalem; David's military power over the surrounding peoples and his political administration domestically.

Textual Issues

6:2 Anderson's note sums up the options: "the MT reading מבעלי יהודה could be translated as 'from the citizens of Judah' . . . or 'from Baale (or Baal of) Judah.' . . . We follow 4QSam^a (and 1 Chr 13:6) reading [בעלה היא קרי]ת] to Baalah which is Kiria[th-jearim]' " (p. 97). Details in McCarter, 162-63, and Pisano, 101-4. See the discussion below.

6:3-4   There is a reduplicated phrase in the MT, omitted by the LXX and the NRSV. A dittography is likely (cf. Barthélemy, 242; Pisano, 272-77). The sense is not affected.

6:5   Anderson, with many, reads with 1 Chr 13:8, while acknowledging that the MT could be paraphrased "with all manner of instruments of cypress wood" (p. 98). For the detailed argumentation, see Barthélemy, 242-43; also McCarter, 163-64.

6:7   The NRSV notes: "meaning of Heb uncertain." It is; it may point to the mysterious; it should not be demythologized. See discussion below; also Anderson, 103-4. Stoebe: "alles bleibt unsicher" (p. 190).

6:19   The Hebrew word, *'ešpār,* is "quite unknown" (Driver, 270). The best options are "a date cake" (probable) or "a choice cut of meat" (possible; see McCarter, 173).

6:22   The MT has "abased in my eyes" with one Hebrew manuscript having "in his eyes"; the LXX has "in your eyes." Stoebe, opting for "my eyes," comments of the LXX reading that it is smoother but not necessarily better (p. 203). Anderson's "in our view . . . provides a better contrast" (p. 99) is indicative of the subjectivity that is unavoidable here.

Discussion

This is one of those texts where it is particularly important to differentiate between what might have happened and what the text narrates. Probably quite rightly, most readers and commentators take for granted that David brought the ark to Jerusalem. They assess it as a brilliant move, politically and religiously, uniting the nation around a traditional cultic symbol in a non-traditional capital city. That is probably an appropriate assessment of what might have happened. On the other hand, however, it is emphatically not what the text narrates. The text tells a story of an attempt to bring the ark to Jerusalem by David that was abandoned. David was angry at what happened, afraid to bring the ark into Jerusalem, and he abandoned the expedition. The text then goes on to tell of a successful expedition to bring the ark to Jerusalem, again led by David, but this time triggered by the news that the ark was generating blessing from YHWH. Event and text should not be confused. In the event, for most interpreters, David in a brilliant move consolidated his position by bringing the ark to Jerusalem. In the text, David plays a subordinate role to YHWH; he is God's instrument in the coming of the ark to Jerusalem, inaugurating a new epoch in Israel.

The opening sentences are puzzling and have attracted attention — [I.A]. 6:1 has David "again" gather all the chosen men of Israel. Other issues apart, we have no notice of a previous gathering to justify the "again" (Alt wanted to relocate the verse to 8:1 — cf. "II Samuel 8:1"). The literal reading of 6:2 has David rise and go and all the people *(hā'ām)* who were with him from the citizens of Judah. The two components can be harmonized along the lines of soldiers and civilians; the two sentences are not so easily harmonized. Ideally, from a religious and political point of view, representatives of Israel and Judah should have been involved. A second difficulty is presented by 6:2's phrase, "from there." If the Hebrew is understood as citizens of Judah (cf. the usage *ba'ălê* in Judg 9 for citizens of Shechem — NRSV, lords), the geographical referent for "from there" has to be traced back to faraway Kiriath-jearim in 1 Sam 6:21–7:1. While this would be acceptable in the text of a four-chapter ark narrative (1 Sam 4–6; 2 Sam 6), it would be unusual for so significant a reference to have been left unchanged in the present extended narrative. This has led to understanding the Hebrew as a place name, identifying the Hebrew *"ba'ălê yĕhûdâ"* with the town Baalah, noted as an alternative name for Kiriath-jearim (Josh 15:9). It should be noted that the other occurrences for Baalah appear to be somewhere else (cf. Josh 15:10, 11, 29). Kiriath-jearim is also known by the name Kiriath-baal (Josh 15:60; 18:14). 1 Chr 13:5-6 has a repetition similar to that of 2 Sam 6:1-2 and has David and all Israel go up "to Baalah, that is to Kiriath-jearim, which belongs to Judah" (1 Chr 13:6; so 4QSam^a). This looks like an attempt to make the best of a difficult text. The text-critical situation is complex and is summed up by Pisano: "it may be said at least that there is no *textual* basis for correcting the MT reading, which is surely an old one" (p. 104; see pp. 101-4).

Whatever the uncertainties of the text, what happened is clear: David and his followers went to bring up the ark from Kiriath-jearim to Jerusalem.

The ark is named as "the ark of God, which is called by the name of the LORD of hosts who is enthroned on the cherubim" (6:2). This precise naming of the ark is unique. In 1 Sam 4:4, the ark is named as "the ark of the covenant of the LORD of hosts, who is enthroned on the cherubim." These two are the only references to the ark in connection with the God who is "enthroned on the cherubim." Even the reference in 1 Sam 4:3 does not have it. 1 Chr 13:6 has all the elements of 2 Sam 6:2 and has trouble with them. 2 Sam 6:2 has "the ark of God" in conjunction with the God who is "enthroned on the cherubim." The term "the ark of God" is in common usage (see, for example 2 Sam 6:3, 4, 6, 7, 12; 7:2); also in common usage are the terms "ark of the LORD" and "ark of the covenant of the LORD." "The ark of God" and "the ark of the LORD" may be indicators of redactional activity or they may be interchangeable (cf. 1 Chr 15:2; also, potentially redactional, 2 Sam 6:9, 10, 11). The description of Israel's God as "enthroned upon the cherubim" occurs once in Hezekiah's prayer (2 Kgs 19:15 = Isa 37:16) and twice in the psalms (80:2 [Heb.; NRSV, 80:1]; 99:1). Dating of such a title is almost impossible; its solemn use at 1 Sam 4:4 and 2 Sam 6:2 is not surprising. There may be no more significance than this (cf. Campbell, *1 Samuel,* esp. pp. 302-9). We may note that in Solomon's temple the ark is described as "underneath the wings of the cherubim" (1 Kgs 8:6); the ark made by Moses had two cherubim facing each other on its lid and God met with Moses "above" the cover, between the two cherubim (Exod 25:22; Heb., *kappōret;* NRSV, mercy seat or cover; literal: lid). The hint of a throne is given in Ezek 10:1.

The ark was transported on a new cart, as the Philistines were instructed to do (cf. 1 Sam 6:7) — [I.B]. Sacred objects are given the newest and best; grotty farm wagons will not do. Two men, the sons of Abinadab, drove the cart. According to 1 Sam 7:1, Abinadab's son, Eleazar, was consecrated to have charge of the ark. Here, the two sons mentioned are named Uzzah and Ahio (i.e., *'aḥyô* or "his brother" i.e., *'āḥîw*). The variation in the names has engendered considerable scholarly discussion (e.g., Anderson, 99-100; Budde, *Samuel,* 47; Campbell, *Ark Narrative,* 129, 171; McCarter, 163, 169; Stoebe, 189, 192; Wellhausen, *Bücher Samuelis,* 167). The names are not of great importance; both men are described as sons of Abinadab, in whose house the ark has rested for a goodly period of time (cf. 1 Sam 7:2). What matters, therefore, is that both were as well qualified as any in Israel to journey with the ark. If vv. 3 and 4 are held together, it is likely that Uzzah drove the wagon (v. 3) and his brother Ahio walked in front of it (v. 4). Meanwhile, David and the Israelites with him danced and sang and celebrated. This was a great liturgical occasion; the ark of the LORD, long absent from Israel's life, was coming home. (Note: the phrase "all the house of Israel" is likely to be late, suggesting that vv. 5 and 15 are expansions of the text; if so, they simply emphasize what is evident: this was party-time in liturgical Israel [cf. vv. 12-14].)

A joyful liturgical celebration is in full swing — and suddenly it is spoiled — [I.C]. It is stopped dead; on the ark's wagon, Uzzah dropped dead. The text is unclear as to what happened, apart from the fact that he dropped dead. In 1 Sam 6:19, too, the text is far from clear as to what action caused a slaughter. Here it says that Uzzah took hold of the ark (v. 6) and God struck him dead (v. 7). What actually happened and what reason is alleged for God's striking Uzzah dead are not clear; guesses are hazarded. As usual, the text matters more than the event. The following text is about David and it is explicit: "David was angry" (v. 8), "David was afraid of the LORD" (v. 9), "David was unwilling to take the ark of the LORD into his care in the city of David" (v. 10). Polzin is right: "David's question, therefore, initiates a fearful stutter that interrupts the ark's joyful journey toward Jerusalem" (*David and the Deuteronomist,* 63).

Chronicles says Uzzah was struck down "because he put out his hand to the ark" (1 Chr 13:10). In Samuel, the Greek does not have the phrase; the two words in the Hebrew (*'al haššal*) may evoke the explanation in Chronicles. It is probably a guess and not a very good one. As a son of Abinadab, no one was better qualified than Uzzah to touch the ark. If a reason is sought, it must lie deeper. The text does not explore the death; instead, it unfolds the attitudes of David: anger, fear, and unwillingness to have the ark come into Jerusalem. Working on the puzzle of Uzzah's death can lead to avoidance of the core message of the text: David's attempt to bring the ark to his city, Jerusalem, was a deathly failure and was abandoned. The ark was shunted off to a foreigner's, the house of Obed-edom the Gittite (6:10).

If the text ended here, that is where the ark would have ended up, in the house of Obed-edom the Gittite, until some future time. Instead, according to the text, during the ark's three-month stay Obed-edom and his house were blessed (6:11) — [II]. David was told. The text in the telling makes the causal link explicit: "the LORD has blessed the household of Obed-edom . . . *because of the ark of God"* (6:12). The ark is no longer a source of death, but a source of blessing. "So David went and brought up the ark of God from the house of Obed-edom to the city of David with rejoicing" (6:12).

The text portrays David as theologian enough to read the signs — [III.A].

If the LORD is bestowing blessing because of the ark, the LORD may be understood to be ready to have the ark move on into David's city. This time, no cultic details are mentioned, no new wagon, no names, just "the bearers of the ark" apparently on foot ("six paces," 6:13). The mood is signaled from the outset as being one of rejoicing (v. 12). The issue has been raised whether an ox and a fatling were sacrificed once at the beginning or were repeatedly sacrificed every sixth step (initially: Anderson, 105; Hertzberg, 279; Stoebe, 195, 197; repeatedly: Carlson, *Chosen King*, 88; McCarter, 167, 171; Miller and Roberts, *Hand of the Lord*, 16-17, 96). Syntax favors the once-only initial offering (Driver, 269). This initial sacrifice acknowledges God's favor (cf. v. 12), does not imply that the first procession may have been cultically defective, does not raise problems over the altars needed (cf. 1 Sam 14:33-35), and does not run the risk of creating the impression that the many sacrifices of the procession (every sixth pace) were on a par with the final celebration of arrival (cf. vv. 17-18; totals are not given, in contrast to 1 Kgs 3:4; 8:63). As so often, central is whether the passage is the basis for a story interpreting events or is a report recording them. The mention carries symbolic weight; it brings "the rejoicing" to the fore.

Elements foreshadowed in the journey will be expanded on its accomplishment: sacrifice, dancing, celebration, and contempt — [III.B]. David's dancing reflects the aspect of rejoicing. Verse 15, whether later or not, emphasizes the communal aspect of the celebration. Verse 16, on the other hand, brings out Michal's self-imposed exclusion; she despised David in her heart (6:16). The note prepares for the exchange in vv. 20-23, to be discussed below. It signals from the outset, however, as the ark of YHWH was entering David's city, that the last significant representative of the old era held herself apart from the inauguration of a momentous new epoch in the story of Israel.

"The inauguration of a momentous new epoch in the story of Israel" may sound overdrawn and is certainly not made explicit in the text. It is there nonetheless — [III.C]. The ark is set in its place. David sacrifices before the LORD, blesses the people, and distributes three portions of food to all the people (vv. 17-19). That is no ordinary event. When Solomon consecrates the temple, there is much about his sacrifices, but nothing about a distribution to the people; it may be assumed, but it is not said (cf. 1 Kgs 8:62-66). Interestingly, in 1 Kgs 8:66 the people blessed the king; in 2 Sam 6:18 the king blessed the people. It is treated as a great occasion. With it, something definitive is achieved; "then all the people went back to their homes" (v. 19b).

The exchange between David and Michal, Saul's daughter, is all the more pointed, given the occasion — [III.C.3]. Michal comes out to express her disdain for David's lack of decorum. David goes for the political and theological jugular: the LORD "chose me in place of your father and all his household" (v. 21); "I danced before the LORD." David is the chosen of YHWH and a populist politician; Michal is a king's daughter and where Saul's royal line will end. The old has no future; the new is begun.

Note: David is presented referring to himself as *nāgîd* over Israel (NRSV, "prince over Israel"). As discussed earlier, this cannot be the prophetic usage of *nāgîd*, meaning king-designate and expressing a present state that relates to a future role. As in 1 Sam 25:30 and 2 Sam 5:2, the meaning here has to be that of actual leader in Israel. David's superiority over King Saul is hardly asserted by claiming the mere status of king-designate — a role that was his while Saul was king. The *nāgîd* designation did not affect Saul's house; the royal office certainly did (v. 21: your father and all his house). See on 2 Sam 5:2, above, and the excursus on *nāgîd* in Campbell, *Of Prophets and Kings,* 47-61.

Genre

The genre for the chapter is → theological narrative. It is a good example of narrative traditions being used to communicate theological conviction. It is storytelling. Interest is artfully aroused in the opening verses by the expectation that the ark will at long last return to the mainstream of Israel's life, now in Jerusalem. The expectation is suddenly shattered by the death of Uzzah and David's anger and fear. The shattered expectation is equally suddenly resurrected and the ark is safely in Jerusalem. As theological narrative, it seeks to present events in Israel's history in such a way as to communicate an interpretation of them in terms of God's dealings with God's people, in terms of God's rejection of an old order and election of a new.

The rejection of the old order is most sharply expressed in the exchange initiated by Michal. It may have begun as a remembered tradition. Crystallized in written form, it becomes a (→) notice. Taken into the larger story, it has become part of a theological narrative. The theology: "Do not remember the former things. . . . I am about to do a new thing" (Isa 43:18-19). It is claimed here; Isaiah has theological forebears.

Setting

It is tempting to imagine an early form of the text that reported the bringing of the ark to Jerusalem, using only the title "ark of God" (*'ărôn ha'ĕlōhîm;* cf. Fohrer, "Ladeerzählung"). The alternation of the titles "ark of God" and "ark of YHWH" is most noticeable. The title, "ark of God," is used in vv. 2-7 and in v. 12. Verse 12 refers to the house of Obed-edom. In order to assume a complete early form of the text, it must be assumed that vv. 10-11 have totally replaced an earlier mention of a sojourn in the house of Obed-edom. That is, of course, possible (see the discussion in *1 Samuel,* FOTL 7, ch. 10, "Diachronic Dimension"). It remains an assumption.

A second assumption postulates an early text of the ark narrative that ended with 1 Sam 7:1 (e.g., Miller and Roberts, *Hand of the Lord*). Such a text would necessarily be early; its composition after the move of the ark to Jerusalem would make little sense. It is possible; it too remains an assumption.

Other assumptions must be at least listed, even if not entertained. There is the assumption of an ark narrative, existing independently of other texts about these early Davidic times. Associated with it is Fohrer's assumption of an early "ark of God" text, later expanded. There is the assumption that any narrative of David's rise to power in Israel began no earlier than 1 Sam 9:1 and, therefore, would not have included the early section of the ark stories (1 Sam 4–6). There is also the assumption that the Prophetic Record did not include the ark narrative traditions (1 Sam 4–6; 2 Sam 6), because Samuel is singularly absent from them. Further discussion of these may be found in *1 Samuel*, FOTL 7, ch. 10, "Diachronic Dimension."

Among these assumptions, we have to find a setting for 2 Sam 6. As is sketched a little more fully in the section on the diachronic dimension, it seems reasonable to assume a brief account of the coming of the ark to David's Jerusalem, giving the locals credit for knowing where the ark had been for the last twenty years or so. Once the ark had been settled in its sanctuary in Jerusalem — and later in Solomon's temple — some account of its significance and its coming to Jerusalem might have been expected (hence the Ark Narrative, in whatever stages). Finally this narrative would have been taken over for the composition of the Deuteronomistic History, the text we now have. Coupled with the emergence of Samuel as prophet to all Israel, the departure of the ark from Shiloh creates an expectation that something in Israel is about to change. The arrival of the ark in Jerusalem indicates that what God has been doing through the prophets is confirmed by the blessing that the ark brings to Jerusalem.

Meaning

As interpreted here, 2 Sam 6 communicates God's blessing on David's choice of Jerusalem as his city and the capital of all Israel and Judah. Appended to it is a notice that points starkly to this meaning: the old regime represented by Saul and his family is barren, and the rule of David, the chosen king, will be Israel's future.

The story starts with a straightforward expedition by the king to bring the symbol of God's cultic presence to the newly acquired capital, Jerusalem. The usual cultic respect is shown — a new cart, and so on. The expedition is stopped by the royal reaction to Uzzah's death at God's hand. David was angry, afraid, and unwilling to bring the ark into Jerusalem. Without YHWH's blessing, David's expedition was not going anywhere. The reversal, from death to blessing, changes everything. David is told of YHWH's blessing. Cultic care need not be emphasized; the expedition is under YHWH's auspices.

Put in the terms of the text, it is God's will that David should be king in Jerusalem and, with God's blessing, Israel's central cult object will reside in Jerusalem and bring God's blessing there. This is a huge statement. It is also a faith statement. The act of bringing the ark to Jerusalem is one thing. It is a stroke of Davidic genius to wed the religious to the political. What will be David's undisputed capital will be home to Israel's undisputed symbol of God's presence and favor. The text, however, goes beyond the act. The text places David's act of genius firmly under YHWH's will. Just as the slaughter at Beth-shemesh had put a stop to the ark's going anywhere more significant than Kiriath-jearim (1 Sam 6:19-21), so Uzzah's death put a stop to the ark's going to Jerusalem. It is YHWH's blessing that causes the journey to be resumed and the ark to be set up in its place in Jerusalem.

The rather unseemly exchange between Michal and David highlights, in a different mode, what has been signaled by the coming of the ark. A new epoch has begun with the reign of David; all that Saul stood for is relegated to the unfruitful past.

Textual Issues

7:7 With few exceptions, interpreters used to opt for "judges" here; with one exception (the MT of 1 Chr 17:6), the manuscript evidence supports "tribes." The following clause, "whom I commanded to shepherd my people Israel," points to a responsibility not entrusted to any tribe. Verse 11 speaks of some responsibility entrusted to judges (whatever we may think of that today). It is likely that at some point the MT of Chronicles opted for the easier text (against both the MT and LXX of Samuel and the LXX of Chronicles). Some form of office is appropriate (cf. McCarter, 192; Barthélemy, 245-46; also Reid, "2 Samuel 7:7"). NJPS and NRSV translate "tribal leaders," which catches the meaning well enough.

7:11b Three different versions of this half verse exist, meaning three different things.

The MT: the LORD will make a house for you.
The LXX^B: you shall build a house for him.
The LXX^L: he will build a house for himself.

The Chronicles text (1 Chr 17:10) expresses the same meaning as the MT of 2 Sam 7:11b. "A house for you" (MT) is understood as a dynasty; "a house for him" (LXX^B) would be understood as a temple and could be understood in terms of beginning the project, but it is Solomon who completed it; "a house for himself" (LXX^L) looks like an attempt to improve a difficult text. This and a number of lesser divergences among these ancient versions here bear witness to the theological activity focused on this important passage (see Lust, "David dans la Septante"). For more detailed textual discussion, see McCarter, 193-94; also Stoebe, 221.

7:16 The MT and the Vulgate have "before you" (so NJPS); the LXX has "before me" (so NRSV). Most commentators opt for the LXX (cf. McCarter, 195). Barthélemy points to 3rd person suffixes in the LXX instead of the 2nd person of the MT and sees these referring to a future messiah; he advocates retaining the MT, confirming David's kingdom, rather than risk endorsing a move toward the messianic (pp. 246-47; cf. 1 Chr 17:14, where any reference to future failure is absent — according to Barthélemy, due to messianic concern).

7:23 Several textual difficulties are evident in this complex verse (cf. Driver, 277-78; McCarter, 234-35; Barthélemy, 247-49). "Another nation" may be preferable (with LXX), although "one nation" can be retained (with Hertzberg, Anderson, NJPS); the NRSV makes acceptable sense with "doing great and awesome deeds for them" (the MT has "doing a great deed and awesome deeds for you"); "by driving out" (LXX) is preferable to "for your land" (MT; cf. Barthélemy, 248); the end of the verse can be retained, although reading the MT (and the Vulgate) as "a nation and its god(s)" (cf. McCarter, 235; see also Barthélemy, 249; Ulrich, 71).

Discussion

Seventeen verses of this much-worked-over Samuel chapter are devoted to God's promise to David. A dozen are devoted to David's gratitude to God. Most commentaries give more space to the promise than to the gratitude. This one will be no different, but at least we can confess the failing.

The literature dealing with this chapter has been boundless (cf. Campbell,

Of Prophets and Kings, 72, n. 19). This is hardly surprising since in it God is presented making an indissoluble commitment to David: "your house and your kingdom shall be made sure forever before me" (7:16). If the house of David rather dropped the baton in the person of King Jehoiachin, whom we may assume died in Babylon, the succession was taken up in Christian eyes by Jesus Christ. This is ground enough for limitless scholarship. When studying such a text, we must never forget in faith that it was written by theologians on behalf of God. As a matter of fact, down the track Israel's theologians felt free to modify the promise they had articulated on God's behalf (cf., for example, 1 Kgs 2:4; 8:25; 9:4-5). The text is hugely important; it should not become an idol.

The text of 2 Sam 7 articulates God's promise to David; the word "covenant" is not mentioned. The absence of the word does not diminish the importance of the concept, but it does give desirable clarity of focus. "Covenant" is a way of articulating the relationship between God and David (as between God and Israel); it is not the relationship itself. Other texts speak of God's covenant with David (e.g., Ps 89:4-5 [Heb.; NRSV, 89:3-4; cf. also "sure oath," Ps 132:11-12]; Jer 33:21; 2 Chr 21:7). The Hebrew text articulates faith in God's commitment to the Davidic dynasty in Jerusalem. In Israel's political and religious history, this dynasty is of central significance (for ancient Near Eastern aspects, see Laato, "Second Samuel 7").

David's proposal is reported discreetly — which is just as well as the text is about to reject it — [I.A]. David, referring to his palace (reputedly just built for him by Hiram of Tyre), remarks to Nathan that he, David, is living in a house of cedar and God's ark is in a tent. Nathan, ever the diplomat, gives his approval: "do all that you have in mind" (v. 3). According to the text, Nathan adds "for the LORD is with you" — perhaps a trace presumptuously. In the preceding texts, this has traditionally been true of David; Nathan is about to discover that God is a God of surprises. We are not told what Nathan said when the word of the LORD came to him that night; he would hardly have been happy. The approval he had given was turned down flat, reversed, overturned. Nothing doing.

The promise to David is articulated in what may be aptly described as unpromising circumstances: the rejection of a proposal by the king — [I.B]. This is well caught in the often-used summary of the promise: you will not build a house for me; I will build a house for you. Of course, David had a temple in mind and God was speaking of a dynasty. No matter. Most kings would gladly trade a temple for a dynasty.

The text at this point is prolix — not so much unclear as diplomatically indirect — [I.B.1.b]. It is noteworthy that to David's suggestion of temple building God never actually says "No, I don't want one." Naturally, one would expect Nathan to be presented putting the divine negative to his king as delicately as possible. Furthermore, the text will go on to say that God will have Solomon build the temple. So it might appear to be not so much that God does not want a temple as that God does not want David to be its builder. Not surprisingly, Solomon had no problem with this (to judge from the text of 1 Kgs 8:19); David might be expected to have felt rather differently about it — if the text addressed such issues. The temple does not rate a mention in David's thanksgiving (vv. 18-29). The NRSV does not spare David's sensitivities: "Are you the one to build me a house to live in?" (v. 5). The finger is pointed directly at David. This may be fine if Solomon's view is accepted: "my father David could not build a house . . . because of the warfare with which his enemies surrounded him" (1 Kgs 5:17 [Heb.; NRSV, 5:3]; cf. 1 Chr 22:8; 28:3). In the light of 2 Sam 8:1-15, this is suspiciously like special pleading. The literal Hebrew does not need to be read as pointing the finger at David; it can be simply: "Are you going to build me a house to live in?" It is a question; it is not answered. A second question follows it: Did I ever ask for a temple? (cf. the bulk of v. 7). That is not answered either. So two questions are asked; neither is openly answered.

Verse 6 does not ask a question but makes a statement: I have not lived in a house from the exodus until today, but I have moved about in a tent and a tabernacle in all my moving about with all the people of Israel. Note that the NRSV, with other translations, breaks this sentence differently, ending the first sentence with "a tent and a tabernacle." Either version is possible. The rendering given above has two advantages. First, by holding within one sentence the repetition of "moving about," it gives emphasis to the idea of God's moving about with the people. In this view, God is not to be pinned down to any one place or any immobile temple. Second, leaving the repetition with the sentence begun in v. 6, the second question is brought to the fore. Both questions then begin with the usual Hebrew interrogative particle. These advantages are real but are not of great moment. In both renderings, vv. 5 and 7 contain questions that are left unanswered. In both renderings, v. 6 introduces a statement that, without due explanation as to what has changed, appears negative to both David's proposal and Solomon's temple. According to v. 6, it is not a matter of proposing to do the right thing at the wrong time; it is a matter of principle, the wrong thing, and the wrong idea of God. It raises the question of God's relationship with Israel. In the past, the localization of God's presence has been symbolically fluid. Is it appropriate for that now to change?

The text wisely does not become entrapped in these issues — [I.B.1.c]. Instead, Nathan's instructions are to deliver a word to David that promises, first and foremost, dynastic security for his kingdom. Before that, however, God's word takes a swing through recent past history ("I took you from the pasture, etc.") and looks into the near future ("I will make for you . . ."). Then comes the promise: "the LORD will make you a house" (v. 11). The promise goes on to Solomon, whose kingdom will be established and who will build the house for God's name (vv. 12-15). Finally, the divine promise returns to David: "Your house and your kingdom shall be made sure forever before me; your throne shall be established forever" (v. 16).

The recent past is well known to us from the Davidic traditions. David was summoned from his father's Bethlehem farm to join Saul's court; the shepherd role is present in 1 Sam 16:11; 17:15, 34. The reference to being "prince" (nāgîd) over God's people looks back to 1 Sam 16:1-13. The avowal that the LORD was with David in all his success has been a mark of the narrative since 1 Sam 18:14. The look into the near future may require us to reevaluate our image of David at this moment and the meaning of v. 1b. David is promised a great name (v. 9b); a place is promised for Israel (v. 10a; cf., as implying permanence and security, Murray, *"MQWM"*); a line is drawn between the period of the deliverer-judges and the new institution of the monarchy, in favor of the monarchy, and David is promised rest from his enemies (vv. 10b-11a). Then comes the core of the promise to David (v. 11b).

We can be led astray by 7:1 and our awareness of David's name and power. In the light of vv. 9b-11a, the content of 7:1 can mean no more than that David had his capital, his palace, and his victory over the Philistines. What lay ahead was empire and renown (cf. 2 Sam 8). At the core of that was the promise of dynasty and security.

Nathan told David the whole of his communication from God. David went and "sat before the LORD," and gave thanks — [II]. What is remarkable in this report of David's prayer of thanksgiving is the absence of any mention of Solomon or the temple that Solomon was to build; nothing particularly explicit about David's great name or the place for Israel where their enemies might not disturb them either. As reported, God's promise can be reduced for David to three Hebrew words: a house I will build for you *(bayit 'ebneh lāk)* — that is what gave David the courage to pray his prayer (7:27). It is a beautiful prayer, expressing gratitude and extolling God; its silences are surprising.

The prayer begins with the expression of David's gratitude, but formulated in abstract generalities — [II.A]. You have brought us so far . . . you have done all this greatness (vv. 18-21); nothing as concrete as the pasture, the throne, the name, the place, the enemies, and the rest. Verse 18 is focused on David and his dynasty: "who am I . . . and what is my house that you have brought me thus far?" Verse 19 is one of those verses that we know what it has to mean without being sure how it means it. It has to mean that in God's eyes what has been done seems small in comparison with what is yet to come, and this is the way it is in human affairs. The phrase "for a great while to come" *(lĕmērāḥôq)* is rare; it is used only eight times, usually in relation to the past or to distance. This and 1 Chr 17:17 are the only references to the future, but the future is what it must mean (for the others, see 2 Kgs 19:25 and Isa 37:26; Job 36:3; 39:29; Ezra 3:13; 2 Chr 26:15). The NRSV's "instruction for the people" translates a not uncommon phrase, usually rendered "this is the ritual" or "this is the law," followed by some specification of the people or situation where the law applies (e.g., "this is the law for the nazirites," Num 6:13, 21). "This is the way it is in human affairs" may catch what is meant. There is nothing left for David to say (v. 20). What God has done has been done in accord with God's word and God's heart (v. 21). So David is duly grateful.

The emphasis of the prayer then moves from what God has done for David and his house to focus first on God and then on God's people, Israel. There is none like God (v. 22). Who is like Israel? (v. 23). The passage ends with an echo of Deut 26:17-18, with Israel as God's people and YHWH as Israel's God (v. 24).

The focus of the prayer comes back to David and his house to ask that what God has promised God may do (vv. 25-29) — [II.B]. There is more than a hint that the greatness of God's name will be dependent on God's ability to produce what God has promised (cf. v. 26).

A great deal of scholarly energy has been expended on discussing both the analysis and the development of the promise and the prayer. Here we can point only to one possibility; readers need to know that there are others. The literature is vast and will not be examined in detail.

The syntactical signals are not obtrusive; there are three. First, in v. 4, the Hebrew verb *wayhî,* loosely meaning "and it happened," occurs twice where once would have been quite enough. Literally: and it happened that night, and it happened that the word of the LORD came to Nathan. Second, the statement in v. 6, coming between two questions and preempting the answer to the second, is odd. Not impossible, naturally, but odd. Third, the transition within v. 11 is somewhat abrupt, from future to present and from 1st person address (v. 11a: I will give you) to 3rd person address (v. 11b: the LORD declares to you; cf. 1 Chr 17:10). Not impossible, but abrupt.

The thematic signals are clearer to identify and more ambiguous to interpret. Basically, there are two. First, and most easily identified, are three occurrences of dtr terminology (contrary to McCarter's "the present form of the text is built largely of Deuteronomistic rhetoric . . . touched almost everywhere by a Deuteronomistic hand," p. 221): the description of the early deliverer figures as "judges" (v. 11a); God's granting David "rest" from his enemies (vv. 1b, 11a); and the reference to the temple as a house "for my name" (i.e., for God's name; v. 13a). Less easily identified are the references that are probably associated with the concerns of the Prophetic Record. These would include the survey of the recent past. Taken by YHWH from the pasture, from the sheep, can clearly hark back to 1 Sam 16:1-13; the pre-PR Davidic traditions have David's role as shepherd, but they do not have so directly YHWH's role in taking David away from his flock. Made "prince" *(nāgîd)* over Israel is the prophetic usage of 1 Sam 9:1–10:16 etc., to be heard behind 1 Sam 16:1-13. The LORD's being with David flows easily as a consequence of his being "prince" *(nāgîd).*

The look into the near future does not affirm specific prophetic concerns but is consonant with them. It surprises us that Israel should be appointed a place to live in security and peace. It is less surprising set against advocacy of the monarchy as a new institution that will unite the people and provide a lasting tranquility that earlier structures did not (cf. above, Murray, *"MQWM").* This is in full harmony with the prophetic view of their responsibility, under YHWH, to designate and dismiss kings.

The material associated with Solomon is also only loosely associated with prophetic concerns, but again links are present. The punishment threatened for Solomon (human rod and human blows) is known to us only in the traditions about Hadad and Rezon (1 Kgs 11:14-25; cf. *Unfolding,* 369, n. 56). The steadfast love that was taken from Saul, "whom I put away from before you" (v. 15), is a direct reflection of the thinking of the Prophetic Record (cf. 1 Sam 15:1–16:13). For the editors of the Prophetic Record, such a promise would be coherent with the history they knew. Solomon remained on the throne for his lifetime and David's dynasty ruled in Jerusalem. It was after Solomon's death that what the prophets claimed to have given David they now claimed the right, speaking for God, to give to Jeroboam ("an enduring house," 1 Kgs 11:38).

Late composition that reflects prophetic theology and dtr language is possible, although the syntactical signals are not obtrusive. If an earlier beginning is postulated, then stages of later reflection are equally possible. Sketched briefly, an early core could have consisted of vv. 1a, 2, 4b-5, 7*, 11b, 16. This core contains David's proposal, the LORD's declining of it, and the LORD's promise of a dynasty to be sure forever. Prophetic material could consist of vv. 3-4a, 8-10, 12, 14-15, 17. This would insist on the prophet's subordination to the word of the LORD, pick up the prophetic theology of David's immediate past and future, expand the dynastic promise to be explicit for Solomon, anticipating his failings but providing the assurance that the dynasty will survive them. The dtr editing can be limited to vv. 1b, 11a, and 13. Such editing would have emphasized the conditions that allowed David to make his proposal, would have endorsed the move from deliverer-judges to kings, and would have given emphasis to Solomon's commission to build a temple for YHWH's name.

Only one verse (more or less) has been left out in this discussion. Verse 6 — with or without the following clause ("wherever I have moved about among all the people of Israel") — can be understood as a statement: I do not need a temple. It certainly says that God has not dwelt in one till now; it does not advert to any ground for changing that in the future. As such, it answers both the question that precedes and the one that follows. The answer is negative. The issue is not so much that David and other early leaders were warriors and shedders of blood. It is rather that YHWH as God of Israel moves about with the people in a tent and a tabernacle. We do not know precisely where this tradition, opposed to the fixity of a temple, might have come from. Situated between the questions, it negates what they leave open.

David's prayer, as we have seen, shows little interest in Solomon or the temple. The dynasty is everything. This points to its being either very early or quite late. The extent of the petition that what God has promised God may do (vv. 25-29) is almost unbecoming for one of David's faith. The language does not favor an early origin. The constant address, "Lord GOD" *('ădōnāy yhwh),* could be early, but the odds are against it. The term is common in Jeremiah, Ezekiel, and later Isaiah; it is relatively rare in the DH. Phrases of the type rendered "instruction for the people" are not found early (v. 19). In the same verse, the word rendered "for a great while to come" is not found early. Verses 22-24 closely resemble Deut 4:7-8, 34-39, secondary in Deuteronomy.

Genre

Nathan's communication to David is best termed, within the biblical horizon, a (→) prophetic announcement, concerning royal destiny. There are prophetic announcements to the people, whether of judgment or salvation. There are prophetic announcements to individuals, about themselves or the nation (cf. Isaiah to Ahaz about the people, Isa 7:14ff.). These announcements can have the solemn overtone of proclamation, appropriate for the prophetic declaration of God's intention for someone who usually is either king or about to become king-designate. Such an announcement can communicate good news or bad news to the recipient.

Examples of such announcements (often within a larger context) are: 1 Sam 10:1; 13:13-14; 15:26; 2 Sam 12:7-14; 1 Kgs 11:31-39; 14:7-16; 21:17-24; 2 Kgs 9:6-10; 22:18-20. Akin to this — and displaying a similar prophetic negativity toward royal behavior — are proclamations about kings and their houses (e.g., Jer 21:12-14; 22:6-8, 13-17, 18-19, 28-30). These are not addressed to the king but are proclamations about the king.

Such announcements are usually set within a story, sometimes part of a dialogue. They may retell recent royal behavior or the recent actions of YHWH. What is central to such proclamations is the expression of divine favor or disfavor, the designation of one to be king or the dismissal of one who is king, announcements that impinge on the destiny of the recipient.

It is worth noting that a majority of these prophetic announcements of royal destiny belong within the texts attributed to what we call the Prophetic Record. There are parallels alleged outside the biblical texts for divine affirmation of temple founders. Within the biblical texts, there is only one such document because Solomon was the sole builder of a temple in preexilic Israel. The Deuteronomistic Historians were certainly not going to give any credit to Jeroboam.

However, temple building is almost incidental to 2 Sam 7:1-17 (MT). It is David's dynasty that is central; the temple Solomon will build rates half a verse (v. 13a). Saul's dynastic hopes had been overthrown by Samuel; in the future, Ahijah would downsize Solomon's ambitions and dismiss Jeroboam's, while Elijah and Elisha's disciple put an end to any hopes entertained by the house of Ahab. We are not privy to the politics behind all of this; we know there were some (cf. 1 Kgs 12:1-15). What we can recognize is the extraordinary faith claim made on behalf of these prophets: to have in their power the hiring and firing of Israel's kings. If the core of the promise to David is found in 2 Sam 7:11b and 16, it may be that we have here the faith claim on which all that followed was based.

David's prayer is precisely that: a (→) prayer of thanksgiving. It notes the benefit received, although in general terms. It attributes that benefit gratefully to God. It hymns the greatness of God. In this case, because the benefit has taken the form of a promise, it goes on to pray that God will perform what God has promised.

Setting

The setting for the text of God's promise to David may be localized in stages or taken as a whole. Taken as a whole, it can hardly be earlier than the Deuteronomistic History, i.e., in the late seventh century, around the time of Josiah. The dtr editing may be restricted in quantity (vv. 1b, 11a, and 13); it is unmistakably recognizable as dtr.

If an early core is considered (vv. 1a, 2, 4b-5, 7*, 11b, 16), a setting cannot be determined with any certainty. It would have been earlier than the Prophetic Record, probably earlier than the division of the kingdom, probably then within Solomon's lifetime. More than that is speculation. Such a tradition could have existed on its own, fostered by David or Nathan or their supporters. Such a tradition could have been incorporated into versions of the composite narrative of David's rise to power. The ultimate highpoint of that rise would be the divine promise of a dynasty.

A version resulting from prophetic editing (vv. 3-4a, 8-10, 12, 14-15, 17) could have had its setting in the Prophetic Record. It is precisely the prophetic claim to have been God's mediators in the gift of a dynasty to David that gives legitimacy to their gift of a similar dynasty to Jeroboam (cf. 1 Kgs 11:38b). These three stages are substantially consonant with McCarter's outcome (pp. 223-24); for a visual presentation laying out these stages for vv. 1-17, see Campbell, *Of Prophets and Kings,* 76-77.

The setting for David's prayer, as noted, is likely to be late. It can scarcely be after the fall of Jerusalem and the collapse of the Davidic dynasty. Its focus on David and his succession suggests that it may reflect a text without the emphasis on Solomon's temple building, therefore earlier than the Deuteronomistic History. The theological activity around the time of Hezekiah is a possible setting. The precise literary shape that such a setting might have taken has to remain uncertain.

Meaning

The meaning of the promise to David is straightforward: he can claim divine backing for his crown and his capital. It is important for both. The monarchy is a relatively new institution in Israel. Its debut under Saul ended in a major defeat at the hands of the Philistines. While David has been God's instrument in redressing the balance (5:17-25), divine authorization for the permanence of the monarchy is a major step. Jerusalem, as a capital, is a Jebusite city with no roots in Israel's traditions. As has been widely observed, David's making Jerusalem his capital was a move of political genius. The text of 2 Sam 6 puts the coming of the ark to Jerusalem under YHWH's auspices, therefore expresses YHWH's approval of the city. The event of the move may not have been so clear. The promise to David of a dynasty and the added promise that his son would build a temple for God's name are, therefore, a major expression of approval for what David has achieved.

It would be dishonest not to note that had David known the whole promise and the future history, it is unlikely that he would have been a happy man. A strict interpretation of the text allows for the promise to be kept intact: the Davidic dynasty continues; the temple is built by Solomon for God's name; Solomon's apostasy may be punished but he is not rejected as king. Were David informed that the continuation of his dynasty would cost the loss of ten tribes, he might well have thought that the promise was made by a legalistic mind rather than a loving God. Solomon may not have been put away as Saul was, but after him the realm of his rule was mightily diminished. This ambiguous aspect of the Davidic promise has to be borne in mind when reflecting on the potential growth of the text.

Whatever the tacit limitations in what might be called the "fine print" of the promise, God's promise communicated by Nathan to David is a massive endorsement in faith of the enormous social change that the Davidic monarchy involved. To paraphrase another's words, it is a statement not of what David might do for God but of what God would do for David. Its significance is not to be underestimated.

David's prayer of gratitude (vv. 18-29) does not underestimate the significance of what has been promised, but — as we have noted — is discreetly silent about what might not have been so greatly appreciated. David's prayer speaks of the king and his house having been brought "thus far" (v. 18). It speaks of the promise to David's house "for a great while to come" (v. 19). It says nothing of the temple; after all, David's proposal was not accepted. It says nothing of Solomon's apostasy and its divisive consequences. The prayer speaks of what is of enormous consequence to Davidic and later Israel: the continuance of a stable ruling dynasty, asking God, "therefore may it please you to bless the house of your servant, so that it may continue forever before you" (v. 29).

David's kingdom established, politically: the conquest of empire 8:1-18

Textual Issues

8:3   The Hebrew *"yād"* has the meaning of monument (cf. 1 Sam 15:12; 2 Sam 18:18). However, a different word is used *(šēm)* if a monument is to be understood at the beginning of 8:13. The MT Kethib has "the river," frequently specified as the Euphrates (so Qere and LXX); the Kethib may be acceptable here (cf. McCarter, 248; Stoebe, 243; also Halpern, see discussion below).

8:12   The MT has Aram here, retained by Hertzberg (p. 289) because of the Aramean presence in vv. 5-6; most emend to Edom in view of what is to come. Edom is absent from the preceding, so that Hertzberg may well be right.

8:13   Arameans can be retained here (with the MT; for the diversity of traditions, see McCarter, 246). While the Hebrew *"šēm"* can be understood as a monument (so McCarter, 251), Driver notes that "it is safest" to take it as "name" (p. 282).

8:17   "Zadok son of Ahitub and Ahimelech son of Abiathar": Barthélemy (pp. 252-53) and McCarter (pp. 253-54) offer differing accounts as to how this well-attested text might have arisen.

Discussion

It has been suggested that the beginning of v. 1 and the end of v. 14 have been added by an editor (Noth, *DH,* 89-90; cf. also Alt, "II Sam 8:1"). "And afterwards" (NRSV, "Some time afterward") is a standard way of linking in the next piece of tradition (cf. 10:1). More importantly, the variations of the items in vv. 1-14 suggest that they are not so much a single sketch of David's success as a collection of his achievements, noted at different times or in different ways. So, for example, while vv. 7-10 are focused on specific booty taken from the troops and towns of Hadadezer and the gifts given by King Toi of Hamath, no mention is made of the others listed in vv. 1-6a. Similarly the list in v. 12 goes beyond those listed in vv. 1-6a — which may, incidentally, account for the presence of the Arameans in v. 12. The disparate nature of these elements calls for caution.

Before the promise of a dynasty, 2 Sam 7 made three points about the immediate future: a great name for David, a place for the people, and freedom from oppression (7:9b-11a). Subsequent tradition gives David a great name. Monarchy freed Israel from the repetitive oppression characteristic of the period of the Judges. In the book of Joshua tradition has already dealt with the place where Israel might be planted. It is not directly taken up in what follows; instead, 8:1-14 offers a picture of Israel's security at the heart of a minor empire, with clear superiority over its surrounding neighbors.

Initially, a number of conquests are listed for David — [I.A.1]. Victory over the Philistines is reported, with no details beyond the taking of Methegammah, otherwise unknown to us (v. 1). The defeat of the Moabites is noted, with details of a life-or-death selection process and a pointer to vassal status (v. 2). Victory over Hadadezer of Zobah is recorded, with numbers for the horsemen and infantry captured (vv. 3-4). The defeat of the Arameans (Syrians) of Damascus who came to the aid of Hadadezer is noted, along with the Aramean losses, the setting up of garrisons on Aramean territory, and an indication of their vassal status (vv. 5-6a). At this point (v. 6b), the same narrative comment is made that recurs in v. 14b: "the LORD gave victory to David wherever he went." A way station has been reached in the listing — [I.A.2]. In the present text, weight has to be given to these two summary comments. Although the structuring as three sections is attractive, these two comments show that the whole first block — [I] — is to be understood as falling into two categories: the conquests and the consequences.

The first part of the next section is focused on David's booty, where it came from and where it went — [I.B.1.a]. The booty consists of gold, silver, and bronze; it is all dedicated to the LORD in Jerusalem. The precious metals are the central focus of vv. 7-10; the subdued peoples are the focus of v. 12. The various lists of conquered peoples (vv. 1-6a, 7-8 [9-10], 12) are by no means identical.

The second part of this section opens with v. 13 and opens rather oddly — [I.B.1.b]. The reference to David's making himself a name suggests a new and major section, yet it is hardly to be restricted to a successful campaign against Aram (Heb.; LXX, etc. and NRSV, Edom) "on his return." The reference to his return suggests some preceding text that we do not have. In v. 13, the Hebrew reports the killing of eighteen thousand Arameans in the Valley of Salt, associated with Edomite territory (cf. 2 Kgs 14:7; Ps 60's superscription [cf. 2 Chr 25:11]); v. 14 reports the stationing of garrisons in Edomite territory and the Edomites' vassal status. Given the geographical location, the reading Edom in v. 13 may well be correct (so the NRSV). The ancient translations appear to reflect trouble with the text. The superscription to Ps 60 attributes the military action to Joab.

The section concludes with the comment already made at v. 6b: "the LORD gave victory to David wherever he went" — [I.B.2]. Verse 15 adds a generalizing comment: "So David reigned over all Israel and David administered justice and equity to all his people." It is noteworthy that v. 15's comment refers to the internal affairs of Israel; the preceding verses, however (vv. 1-14), have been about David's international relations with Israel's neighbors. All in all, the chapter gives the impression of a collection of various traditions, brought together to provide a summary of David's success.

In modern non-academic terms, this chapter is close to a media release. We have learned — or should have — not to trust these too easily. Israel Finkelstein allows thoughts of a "Golden Age" to run away with him when he indulges in biblical overkill: "David now ruled over a vast territory, far more extensive even than the tribal inheritances of Israel" (*Bible Unearthed,* 127). A guiding principle for such claims is that they need keep no closer to observed reality than the "discoverable" facts require. So, for example, accuracy was not the hallmark of the daily figures given of planes downed during the Battle of Britain in World War II, nor for casualty counts in the Vietnam War, and certainly not for the success rate of "smart bombs" during the Gulf War. In more academic terms, Baruch Halpern draws the parallel with Near Eastern display inscriptions.

Halpern provides a mass of informative detail with regard to the issues of 2 Sam 8 (*Secret Demons,* 133-226). The reference to interpreting Davidic literature "in the light of the conventions of royal literature of the time" (ibid., 226) is fully legitimate. The attribution of authorial intention in the following, for example, is not: "The authors of 2 Samuel, and of its sources, *deliberately employed* writing techniques exhibiting a close kinship to those of Near Eastern display inscriptions. They *suggested, implied, insinuated* that David's achievements were a great deal more extensive than in reality they were. But they did not openly prevaricate, on this subject at least" (ibid., pp. 206-7; emphasis added).

Apart from the issue of authorial intention (and that in itself is a grave issue), it is unwise to speak of "the author of 2 Sam. 8 . . . [as] a highly skilled propagandist" (Halpern, *Secret Demons,* 158), without discussion of the complex and differing traditions incorporated into this compilation.

A summary passage (v. 15) is followed by a list of David's administrative officials (vv. 16-18) — [II]. As the text stands now, v. 15 functions as the general statement about David's administration, to be followed by the list of those who carried out the specific functions. This structural perception is reinforced by the two summary comments (vv. 6b and 14b). Without vv. 16-18, v. 15 might very well have served as a general statement about David's administration of "all his people," whether independently or as a conclusion to what precedes. As the text now stands, v. 15 is better understood as a prelude to the list of officials.

Such lists occur at three points: for David, here and at 2 Sam 20:23-26; for Solomon, at 1 Kgs 4:2-6. The positioning of the Davidic lists may not indicate where ancient documents ended. Such positioning does indicate where Israel's editors thought fit to locate these lists. There was a concern for the traditions of David's early years and for the traditions of David's middle years. The "early years" stop with 2 Sam 8.

The three lists may be compared (the numbers indicate the sequences).

2 Sam 8:16-18	2 Sam 20:23-26	1 Kgs 4:2-6	Office
1 Joab	1 Joab	4 Benaiah	Over the army
2 Jehoshaphat	4 Jehoshaphat	3 Jehoshaphat	Recorder
3 Zadok and	6 Zadok and	1 Azariah b. Zadok	Priests (I)
Ahimelech b. A.*	Abiathar		
4 Seraiah	5 Sheva	2 Elihoreph & Ahijah	Secretary
5 Benaiah	2 Benaiah		Over the mercenaries
6 David's sons			Priests (II)
	7 Ira		David's priest
		6 Zabud b. Nathan	(Priest) King's friend
	3 Adoram	8 Adoniram	Over the forced labor
		5 Azariah b. Nathan	Over the officials
		7 Ahishar	Over the palace

*The Syriac reading here is very attractive, reversing the names to read "Abiathar ben Ahimelech," in line with 1 Sam 23:6; 30:7 and in conformity with the Davidic traditions known to us.

Bureaucracies expanded in those days as now, but perhaps more slowly; six offices for early David, seven for later David, and eight for Solomon. Jehoshaphat holds his job in all three lists. Abiathar backed Adonijah and was banished; Joab too backed Adonijah and lost to Benaiah. Adoniram is noted in 1 Kgs 4:6 and 5:28 (Heb.; NRSV, 5:14) as over the forced labor; Adoram has that responsibility in 2 Sam 20:24 and the same name recurs in 1 Kgs 12:18. It is possible that both names denote the same individual. There is little to be said about the others. We assume such lists were taken from official records.

Genre

The chapter is made up of (→) notices, (→) comments, and (→) a list. The notices for the Moabites, Arameans, and the Edomites refer to these peoples becoming servants to David; vassal status is involved. Tribute is mentioned for the Moabites and Arameans; the stationing of garrisons on their territory for the Arameans and Edomites.

Comment occurs at vv. 6b, 14b, and 15. The beginning of v. 13 is looking in this direction but is too fragmentary for identification. The list, of course, is found in vv. 16-18. It is not a list of jobs and the people who filled them but of people and the jobs they filled.

Setting

The compilation of the notices is believed to have been the work of the Deuteronomists. Similarly, the list is thought to have been taken from official records by those responsible for the Deuteronomistic History.

There is not the slightest trace of deuteronomistic thought or language in these formulations — beyond, perhaps, the glorification of David and that is not specific to the Deuteronomists. What is accurate in this attribution is the realization that such traditions do not float about unattached. They are either archived in palace vaults or anchored in more extensive narratives. The Deuteronomistic History is such a narrative. If the traditions of David's rise to power were ever arranged as a structured composition, whether oral or written, the traditions of 2 Sam 8 would have formed a fitting conclusion.

Verse 15 is singled out as the possible ending to this section in the Prophetic Record. What would make this particularly fitting is the concern with the administration of "justice and equity" to all Israel. The concern of the prophetic texts associated with the Prophetic Record — with the possible exception of 1 Sam 9:16 — is not with the establishment of empires but with fidelity to the God of Israel and right government of God's people.

Meaning

The text of 2 Sam 7 places David in charge of Israel but promises him a greater future. The traditions noted in 2 Sam 8 flesh out that greater future.

Given friendly relations with Hiram of Tyre, in the northwest, the assembled traditions offer Davidic Israel what 2 Sam 7:10 promised, the security of living in their own place, undisturbed by the threat of enemies. The Philistines accounted for the southwest and west, the Arameans for the northeast, the Moabites for the east, and the Edomites for the southeast. South of Jerusalem was Judah and south of Judah was the desert. As a security package, 2 Sam 8:1-14 is near watertight.

No empire survives long without justice at home. That is the role of 8:15. Abroad, "the LORD gave victory to David wherever he went" (vv. 6b and 14b). At home, "David reigned over all Israel; and David administered justice and equity to all his people" (v. 15). Even the dry list of David's officeholders has its part to play here. Under the king, they were responsible for the administration of justice and equity as well as the maintenance of empire.

Bibliography of Works Cited Above

Alt, Albrecht. "Die Staatenbildung der Israeliten in Palästina." Pages 1-65 in *Kleine Schriften zur Geschichte des Volkes Israel*. Vol. 2. Munich: Beck, 1953. Original 1930.

————. "Zu II Samuel 8:1." *ZAW* 54 (1936) 149-52.

Budde, Karl. *Die Bücher Samuel*. KHC 8. Tübingen: Mohr, 1902.

Campbell, Antony F. *The Ark Narrative (1 Sam 4–6; 2 Sam 6): A Form-Critical and Traditio-Historical Study*. SBLDS 16. Missoula: Scholars Press, 1975.

————. *Of Prophets and Kings: A Late Ninth-Century Document (1 Samuel 1–2 Kings 10)*. CBQMS 17. Washington: CBA of America, 1986.

————. *1 Samuel*. FOTL 7. Grand Rapids: Eerdmans, 2003.

Campbell, Antony F., and Mark A. O'Brien. *Unfolding the Deuteronomistic History: Origins, Upgrades, Present Text*. Minneapolis: Fortress, 2000.

Carlson, R. A. *David, the Chosen King*. Stockholm: Almqvist & Wiksell, 1964.

Ceresko, Anthony R. "The Identity of 'the Blind and the Lame' (*'iwwēr ûpissēaḥ*) in 2 Samuel 5:8b." *CBQ* 63 (2001) 23-30.

Dever, William G. "Archaeology, the Israelite Monarchy, and the Solomonic Temple." Pages 186-206 in *The Blackwell Companion to the Hebrew Bible*. Edited by Leo G. Perdue. Oxford: Blackwell, 2001.

————. *What Did the Biblical Writers Know and When Did They Know It? What Archaeology Can Tell Us about the Reality of Ancient Israel*. Grand Rapids: Eerdmans, 2001.

Eissfeldt, Otto. Die *Komposition der Samuelisbücher*. Leipzig: Hinrich, 1931.

Finkelstein, Israel, and Noel Asher Silberman. *The Bible Unearthed: Archaeology's New Vision of Ancient Israel and the Origin of Its Sacred Texts*. New York: Free Press, 2001.

Fohrer, Georg. "Der Vertrag zwischen König und Volk in Israel." *ZAW* 71 (1959) 1-22.

————. "Die alttestamentliche Ladeerzählung." *Journal of Northwest Semitic Languages* 1 (1971) 23-31.

Garsiel, Moshe. "David's Warfare against the Philistines in the Vicinity of Jerusalem (2 Sam 5,17-25; 1 Chron 14,8-16)." Pages 150-64 in *Studies in Historical Geography and Biblical Historiography: Presented to Zecharia Kallai*. Edited by G. Galil and M. Weinfeld. VTSup 81. Leiden: Brill, 2000.

Grønbaek, Jakob H. *Die Geschichte vom Aufstieg Davids (1. Sam. 15–2. Sam. 5): Tradition und Komposition*. Copenhagen: Munksgaard, 1971.

Halpern, Baruch. *David's Secret Demons: Messiah, Murderer, Traitor, King*. Grand Rapids: Eerdmans, 2001.

Holm-Nielsen, Svend. "Did Joab Climb 'Warren's Shaft'?" Pages 38-49 in *History and Traditions of Early Israel: Studies Presented to Eduard Nielsen*. Edited by A. Lemaire and B. Otzen. Leiden: Brill, 1993.

Kleven, Terence. "The Use of *ṢNR* in Ugaritic and 2 Samuel V 8: Hebrew Usage and Comparative Philology." *VT* 44 (1994) 195-204.

Laato, Antti. "Second Samuel 7 and Ancient Near Eastern Royal Ideology." *CBQ* 59 (1997) 244-69.

Lust, J. "David dans la Septante." Pages 243-63 in *Figures de David à travers la Bible: XVIIᵉ congrès de l'ACFEB [= l'Association catholique française pour l'étude de la Bible] (Lille, 1ᵉʳ-5 septembre 1997)*. Edited by L. Desrousseaux and J. Vermeylen. Paris: Cerf, 1999.

Miller, Patrick D., Jr., and J. J. M. Roberts. *The Hand of the Lord: A Reassessment of the "Ark Narrative" of 1 Samuel*. Baltimore: The Johns Hopkins University Press, 1977.

Murray, D. F. "*MQWM* and the Future of Israel in 2 Samuel VII 10." *VT* 40 (1990) 298-320.

Noth, Martin. *Die israelitischen Personennamen im Rahmen der gemeinsemitischen Namengebung*. Stuttgart: Kohlhammer, 1928.

————. *The Deuteronomistic History*. 2d ed. JSOTSup 15. Sheffield: Sheffield Academic Press, 1991. German original: 1943.

Olyan, Saul M. "'Anyone Blind or Lame Shall Not Enter the House': On the Interpretation of Second Samuel 5:8b." *CBQ* 60 (1998) 218-27.

Polzin, Robert. *David and the Deuteronomist: A Literary Study of the Deuteronomic History.* Part Three: *2 Samuel.* Bloomington, IN: Indiana University Press, 1993.

Reid, Patrick V. "*šbty* in 2 Samuel 7:7." *CBQ* 37 (1975) 17-20.

Rendtorff, Rolf. "Beobachtungen zur altisraelitischen Geschichtsschreibung anhand der Geschichte vom Aufstieg Davids." Pages 428-39 in *Probleme biblischer Theologie.* Edited by H. W. Wolff. Munich: Chr. Kaiser, 1971.

Schmidt, Ludwig. *Menschlicher Erfolg und Jahwes Initiative: Studien zu Tradition, Interpretation und Historie in Überlieferungen von Gideon, Saul und David.* WMANT 38. Neukirchen: Neukirchener Verlag, 1970.

Soggin, J. Alberto. "The Davidic-Solomonic Kingdom." Pages 332-80 in *Israelite and Judaean History.* Edited by J. H. Hayes and J. M. Miller. Philadelphia: Westminster, 1977.

Stoebe, H.-J. "Die Einnahme Jerusalems und der Ṣinnôr." *ZDPV* 73 (1957) 73-99.

Veijola, Timo. *Die Ewige Dynastie: David und die Entstehung seiner Dynastie nach der deuteronomistischen Darstellung.* AASF B 193. Helsinki: Suomalainen Tiedeakatemia, 1975.

Vincent, L. H. (= H.V.). *Underground Jerusalem: Discoveries on the Hill of Ophel (1909-11).* London: Horace Cox, 1911.

———. "Le ṣinnôr dans la prise de Jérusalem (II Sam. v, 8)." *RB* 33 (1924) 357-70.

Wellhausen, Julius. *Der Text der Bücher Samuelis.* Göttingen: Vandenhoeck & Ruprecht, 1871.

Chapter 4

ANTICIPATORY APPENDICES
(2 SAM 9–10)

2 Samuel 9 and 10 are best described as anticipatory appendixes to the sustained narrative of 2 Sam 11–20. Mephibosheth's situation is background knowledge for two sections in chs. 11–20 (16:1-4 and 19:24-30; see below). The Ammonite war is the background for the story of David and Bathsheba in 2 Sam 11–12. Neither chapter is written with the same high literary style that graces the extensive narrative of 2 Sam 11–20. They both are situated after the narrative of David's early years is over; in their different ways, they both prepare for what is to come without being an integral part of it.

The sparing of Mephibosheth	**2 Sam 9:1-13**
I. The inquiry	1-5
A. David's question	1
B. Interrogation of Ziba	2-4
1. Presentation of Ziba before David	2
2. Interrogation proper	3-4
a. Existence of a descendant of Saul	3
b. Whereabouts of Jonathan's son	4
C. Bringing of Jonathan's son to David	5
II. The outcome	6-13
A. Mephibosheth's settlement	6-8
1. Presentation of Mephibosheth before David	6
2. Statement of David's provision for Mephibosheth	7
a. Life: assured of David's loyalty	
b. Land: granted the estates of Saul	
c. Liberty: security given or freedom restricted	
3. Acceptance by Mephibosheth	8
B. Ziba's duties	9-11a
1. General disposition of Saul's lands	9
2. Specific dispositions	10

Textual Issues

9:10 The LXX[L] has "so that your master's house may have food to eat," which makes good sense in the context (cf. Barthélemy, 254; McCarter, 259). Mephibosheth's food is provided at David's table.

9:11b The MT has "my table"; the LXX, "David's table"; and the Vulgate, "your table." McCarter notes how the MT reading might have arisen from vv. 7 and 10 (p. 259). The royal table must be meant (cf. Driver, 286-87).

Discussion

The text falls easily into its two parts: the inquiry — [I] and its outcome — [II]. David's question sets up the inquiry, giving the question and a reason for it. The question: Is there a survivor of the house of Saul? The reason for the question: to show kindness (*ḥesed:* loyalty) "for Jonathan's sake." Jerubbaal (Judg 9) and Jehu (2 Kgs 10) would have had doubts about the reason. Survivors from the old regime were a threat to the powers of the new regime, then as now. There is ambiguity here and it will not be removed.

David's question is general: "anyone left of the house of Saul" (v. 1). It is worth noting that in the chapter the name "Mephibosheth" occurs only once on David's lips (in the formal presentation in v. 6). That Mephibosheth has a son, Mica, and therefore a potential heir, is mentioned almost in passing, toward the end of the passage. A political adviser might recommend surveillance; the text says nothing.

The issue of loyalty to Jonathan is sidestepped when Ziba is brought before David. David speaks instead of "the kindness of God" (v. 3a). Jonathan is named by Ziba: "there remains a son of Jonathan; he is crippled in his feet" (v. 3b). Ziba knows exactly where he is: "in the house of Machir son of Ammiel, at Lo-debar" (v. 4). Machir reappears in 2 Sam 17:27 as one of David's east-of-Jordan supporters, with Shobi and Barzillai; presumably they were influential. Was Machir a committed supporter, waiting for David's bidding? Or was Machir a wise politician, waiting to see which way the wind might blow? We do not know and the text is careful not to tell us.

Mephibosheth's arrival at the court of David is given full formality: "son of Jonathan son of Saul" (v. 6) — [II]. David's words to him treat three issues: life, land, and liberty. First, Mephibosheth need not fear for his life — an assurance that is far from meaningless in the circumstances. He is assured of David's loyalty, for Jonathan's sake. Second, Saul's estates will be returned to him; surely not an insubstantial bequest. He will enjoy the economic benefits that befit his royal status. Third, he will dine at David's table; whether this is liberty given or withheld is not said. It may be the security of a royal pension; it may be the restriction of royal surveillance. Of his wife and son nothing is said.

Mephibosheth may be under house arrest till the end of his days or he may be an honored guest at the royal table, "like one of the king's sons" (v. 11 — also to be kept under surveillance by a cautious king). In either case, David has to make provision for the management of the estates granted to Mephibosheth. This responsibility is given to Ziba and his household, with the proviso noted that Mephibosheth will eat at David's table always (v. 10a). The legal status of Ziba's household, as servants of Mephibosheth, is noted at v. 12.

Verse 11b is difficult. Technically, it is part of Ziba's speech, accepting David's dispositions. But the reference is to "my table," implying that David is the speaker. The least obtrusive change would be to "your table," locating the clause within Ziba's speech: Mephibosheth will eat at your table. Alternatively, as in the NRSV, the clause is changed and given to the narrator, belonging with what follows: Mephibosheth ate at David's table.

Either way, the insistence on Mephibosheth's eating at David's table acts as an envelope around the mention of Mica, Mephibosheth's young son. Either David is genuinely generous, out of loyalty to Jonathan; or David is politically cautious, out of loyalty to David. Or both.

The Mephibosheth traditions surface in three areas: here (2 Sam 9:1-13), in the Stories of David's Middle Years (2 Sam 16:1-4 and 19:18, 25-31 [Heb.; NRSV, 19:17, 24-30]), and in the final collection of traditions (2 Sam 21:1-14). It has been proposed by McCarter that 2 Sam 21:1-14 and 9:1-13 "once stood in continuous narrative sequence," with 21:1-14 preceding 9:1-13 (p. 263). At first sight, this is plausible. If Jonathan is the sole survivor of Saul's house, clearly the slaughter of the other descendants is presumed — narrated in 21:1-14. On reflection, this rearrangement is highly problematic. In 9:1-13, David is portrayed as unaware of Mephibosheth's existence, a most unlikely picture to paint after noting royal awareness that Mephibosheth was around — the king spared Mephibosheth because of the oath of the LORD that was . . . between David and Jonathan son of Saul (cf. 21:7). To further complicate matters, 2 Sam 19:28 presupposes the scenario of 21:1-14; the other descendants have not yet been put to death. But it adds the reference to Mephibosheth's eating at the king's table, not given in 21:1-14 but prominent in 9:1-13, and no reference is made to David's loyalty to Jonathan. In all probability, three independent traditions are involved, reflecting different aspects of the same event.

Genre

The genre is that of (→) story, or probably more accurately (→) reported story. Narrative tension is established by David's question about the existence of a survivor. Subjacent to this is the tension about David's intentions. Is he really acting for Jonathan's sake or for his own sake?

The story unfolds, with the bringing of Mephibosheth from Transjordan to Jerusalem, the assurance that he will be shown kindness, the disposal of Saul's estate in his favor, the arrangements for its management, and the provision for Mephibosheth to eat at the royal table for the rest of his life. The basic tension is brought to equilibrium; a survivor exists and he is to be well cared for. The subjacent tension is left unresolved. Mephibosheth's life is spared, but he will always eat at David's table, "like one of the king's sons" — for Jonathan's sake or for David's sake, we are not told.

Copious information is provided on Ziba, his family, his slaves, their responsibilities, and their legal status. Minimal information is provided about David's bond to Jonathan, about Saul's estates, about Machir's status and loyalties, about the young son whose name was Mica, or about the implications of dining at the king's table. The extent of this "minimal information" suggests the probability that the text is a (→) reported story.

In the Deuteronomistic History, David's bond to Jonathan has long been narrated; the oath David swore (cf. 2 Sam 21:7) was reported back in 1 Sam 20 (vv. 15-17, 42). If the tradition here is independent, some development about the bond might be appropriate. Machir's status is not mentioned. Association with 2 Sam 17:27-29 would have indicated something of the man's standing. For an independent tradition, some development would be appropriate. Of Mephibosheth's young son, Mica, nothing is said; he is never heard of again. Silence about the implications of dining at the royal table invites the suspicions of a Jerubbaal or a Jehu. A Davidic propagandist might indicate the benefits and honors of such permanent presence at the royal court. Storytellers leave gaps; gaps should not always be filled. With too many gaps unfilled, there is almost no story.

Setting

The setting for the text, as we have it, is clearly the Deuteronomistic History. What remains open is whether there may have been an early documentary setting or a plausible social setting for the text as an independent tradition.

The event belongs relatively early in David's reign at Jerusalem. As an indication of David's political wisdom, it might seem inappropriate after the divine promise of a dynasty (2 Sam 7:1-17), although Davidic theology would probably not have objected to taking the steps necessary to ensure that God's will was done. As an indication of David's humane generosity, it would be appropriate to the tenor of the traditions of David's rise to power, but it is difficult to see where it might best fit. Certainly, in either case, it would have been more likely to precede 2 Sam 8 rather than follow it.

Association of 2 Sam 9:1-13 with the later chapters is unlikely. It does contribute to the theme of succession to David, but the theme of succession is subdued — if not absent — in 2 Sam 11–20. David's comment on the identity of his successor is about as bland as it is possible to imagine — "someone [Heb.]/one of my offspring [LXX]" (cf. 1 Kgs 1:48). So much for 2 Sam 7! There is a sharp conflict of content in the portrayal of David's attitude. 2 Sam 9:1-13 affirms that David did not know of Mephibosheth's existence; 2 Sam 19:29 (Heb.; NRSV, 19:28) affirms that David spared Mephibosheth, while the rest of his father's house "were doomed to death before my lord the king." Co-existence in the same document would raise a credibility issue for David. Intangible, but probably more important than anything else, 2 Sam 9 lacks the style that can be sensed throughout 2 Sam 11–20.

2 Sam 9 is acceptable as an independent tradition. It takes for granted the substantial background of the Davidic stories. It opens with David's question and closes with Mephibosheth's status. It reflects on David's treatment of Saul's heirs. In this, it is parallel to and quite different from the tradition in 2 Sam 21:1-14. Its function here, in the present text, is as an anticipatory appendix to 2 Sam 11–20. It provides supplementary detail of the background to the appearances of Ziba and Mephibosheth in these chapters. It is not only background that is not needed; as noted, it is background that is in conflict with the later story.

Meaning

At the overt level of the text, its meaning is to put on record how David's fidelity to Jonathan was reflected in his benign treatment of Mephibosheth. Even as the text stands, it is open to the suspicions of a disciple of Macchiavelli's school of political thought. What is said is clear: to show kindness "for Jonathan's sake" (9:1). What is done is less clear: "and you yourself shall eat at my table always" (9:7). The text does not tip its hand. As a final comment, it should be noted that David's oath to Jonathan is observed just as long as Mephibosheth is not put to death. From this point of view, the meaning of the text may be to report how David kept his oath — most wisely. Mephibosheth does not die, but Saul's royal line is dead.

Textual Issues

10:18 The differing numbers and categories of troops found in various ancient versions are tabled by McCarter (p. 269).

Discussion

The structure of the passage is clear and immediately visible in the structure analysis above. A new situation emerges with the death of the Ammonite king and the succession of his son — [I]. David sends an embassy to ensure the continuation of friendly relations — [II]. The embassy is rejected and the royal messengers humiliated. Aware that they had given David provocation for war, the Ammonites arranged a coalition in which the Arameans were the principal partners (with twenty thousand foot soldiers) — [III.A]. Joab defeated the coalition, putting the Arameans to flight. The Arameans regrouped and brought in reinforcements — [III.B]. This time, David led the attack and the Arameans were decisively defeated (losing seven hundred chariot teams and forty thousand horsemen [possibly forty thousand foot-soldiers, cf. 1 Chr 19:18] and their commander). The allies of the Arameans sued for peace and the Ammonites were left isolated — [III.C]. The stage is set for the story to come, dramatically located within Joab's siege of the Ammonite capital.

Without it being said explicitly in text, it is clear that the second Aramean campaign was on a far larger scale than their first participation in the coalition. The total for the mercenaries hired for the coalition is thirty-three thousand (v. 6). This total of the participating allied forces is substantially less than the casualty total given for the second campaign (however the forty thousand is read). A corollary of this observation is of interest: Joab led the Israelite forces in the lesser campaign; David led the Israelite forces in the major campaign. This ought give food for thought to those who quibble over David's staying in Jerusalem while Joab besieges the isolated Ammonite capital. Furthermore, no mention is made of the ark. It should be obvious — no matter what a Hittite might allege — that the ark did not always accompany Israel's armies (cf. for example, 1 Sam 4:3 [where bringing the ark to the army is associated with a more dramatic defeat, v. 10] or 2 Sam 15:25).

The function of this chapter in relation to the narrative that follows needs discussion. What follows in chs. 11–12 is a story about David's behavior with a woman and her husband and its implications for the future of David's family. This story is set within the parameters of a campaign against the Ammonites and a siege of their capital. 11:1 provides the opening: "they ravaged the Ammonites, and besieged Rabbah." Closure comes with the conclusion of the siege: "So David gathered all the people together and went to Rabbah, and fought against it and took it" (12:29). Within the story considerable time has passed; time enough for one child to have been conceived, born, and to have died, and time for a second child to have been conceived, born, and to have been named. Within the story, great issues are played out: a woman violated, a man murdered, a family tainted, a prayer unheard, and a child favored.

What 2 Sam 10 does is provide a context within which the siege of Rabbah, the chief city of the Ammonites, can be understood. Whether a listener or reader needs this understanding to engage with the story is doubtful. Nevertheless, it is there. The rejected and humiliated embassy renders war with the Ammonites more than mere imperial expansion. The nature of Joab's victory over the coalition makes a return engagement with a regrouped and reinforced Aramean army almost inevitable. The Israelite defeat of the Arameans leaves the Ammonites isolated and without allies. A siege of Rabbah can be conducted without fear of outside intervention generating a wider war.

For Rost, the account of the Ammonite war (2 Sam 10:6–11:1; 12:26-31) is a separate source utilized in the composition of the Succession Narrative. "We could well have a very short, independent source here" (*Succession*, 61). "The style is simple, concise and terse; the action pushes continually forward; there are speeches only at decisive points" (*Succession*, 62). As to the author, "it is quite clear that it was a soldier who wrote the report, perhaps even a general" (*Succession*, 64). The relegation of ch. 10 to the status of anticipatory appendix does no more than recognize a greater freedom in storytelling and literature than was allowed in Rost's time. With regard to style, content, and independence, Rost and the position advocated here are in accord. Gillian Keys takes 2 Sam 10–20 as the extent of the narrative, without notable discussion (beyond the elimination of 2 Sam 9 and 1 Kgs 1–2), probably for much the same reason (cf. Keys, *Wages of Sin;* cf. p. 79). Ironically, as with his "Succession Narrative" itself, Rost once again begins his analysis at the end of his narrative, here 2 Sam 12:26-31 (*Succession*, 57-58).

In 2 Sam 8:1-14, the Ammonites rate a mention in one verse (v. 12), along with Edom, Moab, the Philistines, Amalek, and the spoil taken from Hadadezer. Earlier in the chapter, a substantial notice is consecrated to David's conflict with Hadadezer (cf. vv. 3-8). No reference is made to any coalition with the Ammonites. A different campaign seems to be indicated (v. 3); when support was needed, it came from Damascus, not from beyond the Euphrates (v. 5). Among the Arameans of Damascus, David set up garrisons and established vassal status with them. From Hadadezer, David took considerable spoil.

It is not difficult to harmonize this information with what is given us in 2 Sam 10. A key is offered in 10:1. A change took place when an Ammonite king died and his son succeeded him. The ch. 8 campaigns against Hadadezer can be located earlier, in the reign of Hanun's father; the ch. 10 campaigns then belong later, in the reign of the son, King Hanun. The earlier defeats could even be alleged as reasons for Hadadezer to come to the aid of Hanun. It is not difficult to harmonize the two chapters. It needs to be noted that the biblical text does not make any such correlation.

Nahash is mentioned as Hanun's father in v. 2, not in v. 1. Nahash, king of the Ammonites, figures in 1 Sam 11 as a cruel threat to the townsfolk of Jabesh-gilead. He was soundly defeated by Saul. Given the brevity of Saul's reign, Saul's Nahash and David's Nahash could well have been the same king. Defeated by Saul, he might well have "dealt loyally" with David. Harmonization is possible. Again, the biblical text does not undertake it.

What these observations reveal to us is the likelihood of the transmission of tradition within circles that did not necessarily communicate much with each other. Here we have two sets of traditions about Hadadezer and, possibly, two sets about Nahash. Harmonization is not difficult; the biblical text does not even approach it. There is no evidence of contact between the transmitters of these traditions that might have suggested the desirability of a cross-referencing phrase or two. It is important to be aware of this as a possible element in the patterns of tradition in ancient Israel. It is also important to be aware that it should not come as a surprise. 2 Sam 21–24 is a collection of traditions that has had no impact on the Davidic traditions earlier in the books of Samuel — and vice versa. In the prophetic books, collections of prophetic sayings may coexist with minimal evidence of contact (e.g., Amos 1–2, 3–6, 7–9).

A few points may be raised about the content of the chapter. We know nothing to suggest that relations between David and the Ammonite king were not as portrayed (10:1-2). At the same time, there is nothing to suggest suspicion of ulterior motives on the part of the Ammonite princes in their distrust of David (10:3). A change of Ammonite ruler would be an appropriate moment for David to adopt a change in policy.

Joab's willingness to fight a battle on two fronts, even given his precautionary strategies (vv. 9-12), points to the relatively limited strengths of the forces opposing him. The outcome of the battle confirms this. While the Arameans flee, to return after regrouping, the Ammonites retire into their city. There they are left for Joab's campaign in chs. 11–12.

The reinforcement of the regrouped Arameans is organized by Hadadezer himself (v. 16a); the army is headed by Shobach, Hadadezer's commander (v. 16b). Neither man was mentioned in relation to the coalition (v. 6). For the coalition, the Ammonites had "hired" mercenaries from four towns; it would look as if, in this second campaign, the interests of the Arameans were more seriously at stake, with a correspondingly increased military commitment. As noted, the casualties listed are proportionately higher than the Aramean participants listed in the coalition (cf. v. 18; in excess of forty thousand casualties over against twenty thousand Aramean participants previously, v. 6); the commanding general, Shobach, is listed as killed.

Genre

The chapter is unusual in that it consists of a collection of traditions rather than being integrated into a text in its own right. David's embassy, in response to a new situation, is described in a (→) notice. The two campaigns are noted in what are basically (→) battle reports. The outcome is again given in a simple (→) notice.

The notice of David's embassy is brief and relatively unadorned. The changed situation and David's overture are noted; the Ammonite rejection of the embassy, the reasons for it, and the humiliation of David's envoys are listed, along with David's reaction. The final notice is even briefer: the vassals of Hadadezer switched allegiance to Israel; the Ammonites were on their own.

The two battle reports follow the basic structures determined by the subject matter. In the first case, there are a gathering of the coalition and a description of how they were arrayed for battle; in the second, there is a gathering of the Aramean forces. In the first, there is detail on Joab's strategy before the outcome of the battle; in the second, the outcome of the battle is followed by the casualty figures.

Setting

The setting for such a collection is difficult to determine. From a literary point of view, it is highly likely that this material was put together independently of the story of chs. 11–12; in all probability, in the present text it has its setting as part of the Deuteronomistic History.

A trace more detail is given than would be expected in official records. Preparatory information of this kind might have been prepared at any time in view of the story in chs. 11–12. The narrative of Chronicles shows how the text might have looked without any of the stories of David's middle years (compare 1 Chr 19:1-19 with 2 Sam 10:1-19; 1 Chr 20:1-3 with 2 Sam 11:1 and 12:26, 30-31; 1 Chr 20:4-8 with 2 Sam 21:15a, 18-22; 1 Chr 21:1-27 with 2 Sam 24:1-25; from here Chronicles proceeds to the building of the temple, David's preparations for it and Solomon's building of it). Several elements point to a substantial reticence in the Chronicles text rather than an addition made to the text of Samuel.

If the two notices and the two battle reports are not from official sources, a setting closer to the time of David has to be possible. It will be suggested below that the Stories of David's Middle Years might well have originated at Jeroboam's court, in the late ninth century. There is nothing to suggest that the traditions of 2 Sam 10 might not have been prefaced to 2 Sam 11–12 about this time.

Meaning

The meaning of the text needs to be distinguished from its function (discussed above). It functions as an anticipatory appendix, providing background for the following story in chs. 11–12.

Its meaning is straightforward. It accounts for the state of war between David and the Ammonites and the isolation of the Ammonites. It allows the listener or reader to realize that the siege of Rabbah was a relatively minor imperial campaign; it could be entrusted to Joab. The major battle had been with the assembled Aramean forces; that campaign had been led by David.

The text endorses the portrayal of David as the successful overlord of the area. Even Aramean forces from beyond the Euphrates succumb to David's military capability. According to 1 Sam 14:47, Saul fought against "all his enemies on every side — against Moab, against the Ammonites, against Edom, against the kings of Zobah, and against the Philistines; wherever he turned he routed them." The summary sounds overly optimistic and does not square with the texts we have; but the texts we have are from David's camp. According to 2 Sam 8 and 10, David not only exercised military superiority over his foes, but by setting up garrisons and establishing treaty relationships, he created a political dominance of significant proportions.

Bibliography of Works Cited Above

Keys, Gillian. *The Wages of Sin: A Reappraisal of the 'Succession Narrative.'* JSOTSup 221. Sheffield: Sheffield Academic Press, 1996.

Rost, Leonhard, *The Succession to the Throne of David.* Sheffield: Almond, 1982. German original: 1926.

Chapter 5

THE STORIES OF DAVID'S
MIDDLE YEARS: STRUCTURE
(2 SAM 11–20)

Probably the least prejudicial title for 2 Sam 11–20 is Stories of David's Middle Years. They are indeed middle years. Amnon and Absalom, born to David in Hebron, need to have grown to young adulthood; the stories have one commit rape and the other murder. The seven or so years at Hebron need to be extended. In order to succeed to David's throne, Solomon, born at the end of 2 Sam 12, needs to have grown to royal age. Despite the protests of Chronicles (cf. "young and inexperienced," 1 Chr 22:5; 29:1), Solomon was no raw juvenile when he took over from David. The narrative speaks of some eleven years between the rape of Tamar and Absalom's rebellion; Solomon's growth needs more time. "Middle years" is appropriate.

Study of the books of Samuel is immeasurably indebted to Leonhard Rost. He freed Samuel research from the conceptual shackles of pentateuchal sources and pointed the way to an understanding of the text of 1–2 Samuel based on narrative blocks rather than extensions of the sources (see Rost, *Succession*). Rost's influence popularized the idea of a Succession Narrative, incorporating 2 Sam 9–20 and 1 Kgs 1–2, concerned with the succession to the throne of David. It is clear that succession is not thematically irrelevant to passages such as 2 Sam 6:20-23, 2 Sam 7:1-17, and 2 Sam 9:1-13, as well as the texts describing the birth of Solomon, the murder of Amnon, the death of Absalom, and the accession of Solomon, before his elimination of Adonijah. Where this succession narrative began, as proposed by Rost, was unsatisfactory; its ending, however, was widely accepted to be found in 1 Kgs 1–2, either at 2:12 or 2:46.

Two arguments, above all, militate against this understanding of the text as including 2 Sam 9–20 and 1 Kgs 1–2 and focusing on the issue of succession. First, the characteristic qualities of sustained narrative found in 2 Sam 11–20 are not found to the same extent in the associated texts. Second, the issues that are central to 2 Sam 11–20 do not include the succession to David (for 2 Sam 13–20, see Conroy, *Absalom,* 101-5). As far as the second is concerned, without question, Solomon is born in ch. 12, Amnon is murdered in ch. 13, Absalom is killed in ch. 18, Solomon accedes to David's throne in 1 Kgs 1, and Adonijah is eliminated in 1 Kgs 2. On the other hand, we have no record of the deaths of David's other sons (cf. 2 Sam 3:2-5 [six]; 5:13-16 [eleven]). 1 Kgs 1–2 is adequate as an independent story of Solomon's accession to David's throne and his subsequent measures to assure his hold on power. The story of David and Bathsheba is centered on royal wrongdoing; the story of Amnon and Absalom begins with rape and ends with murder and has David give the permissions that allowed both events to happen; the story of Absalom and David is one of royal rebellion, with the flight and return of a sensitive and skilled politician; the story of Sheba's revolt reflects both the fragility of the kingdom and the role of power in holding it together. Succession is not central to the telling of these stories, although in them a future king is born to David and two crown princes die.

Charles Conroy remarks: "it is enough to have pointed out that the current state of research no longer justifies an automatic and uncritical acceptance of 2 Sam 9–20; 1 Kgs 1–2 as a fully rounded literary unity with a clearly defined theme" (*Absalom,* 3, following a summary of literature that need not be repeated here). In this context, two points need to be made from Rost's original study. First, "the beginning of the succession story is to be found in 2 Sam 6.16, 20-23" (*Succession,* 26; but as attached to the very different Ark Narrative cf. pp. 85-90). All things considered, the beginning suggested by Rost has to be regarded as unsatisfactory; it has not been to the fore in later work (e.g., Whybray: "probable that the beginning is missing," *Succession Narrative,* 8; Seiler: "its beginning is lost," *Geschichte von der Thronfolge,* 324, n. 8). Second, for Rost, "the account of the Ammonite wars is shown to be an independent source incorporating 10.6–11.1, 12.26-31" (*Succession,* 62). The listing of ch. 10 as an anticipatory appendix is in basic agreement with Rost's literary judgment (with appropriate adjustments). His view of 2 Sam 7 need not be explored. Regarding 1 Kgs 1–2, McCarter's views need to be heard: "the purpose of 1 Kings 1–2 is quite clearly to defend the legitimacy of Solomon's accession. . . . the accession of Solomon lies entirely outside the horizon of the Samuel materials, which are concerned with issues of David's reign" (pp. 12-13). Frolov's treatment of 2 Sam 1–1 Kgs 2, with a purported single author, is rather too fractured to generate fresh insight, but his quotation from Ackroyd on the Succession Narrative bears repeating (p. 394, below): "there are so many uncertainties — uncertainties of chronology, uncertainties about the nature of the narratives, uncertainties about their proper order" (Frolov, "Succession Narrative," 82; cf. further documentation and discussion in Bailey, *David in Love and War*). Stoebe's arguments may be uneven; his decision against a "succession narrative" is sound ("eigentlich überraschend," quite surprising that the designation has been kept alive in biblical scholarship, cf. pp. 32-34).

The issue of "the characteristic qualities of sustained narrative" (above) is difficult to pin down. Author Doris Lessing, who published *The Diaries of Jane Somers* under the name of Jane Somers and not her own, reflects on those few who recognized her hand in the work and the many who did not and she ponders: "This surely brings us back to the question: what is it that the perspicacious recognize, when they do?" (p. 7). An analytical answer is not easy. Yet generations of readers have recognized the qualities peculiar to 2 Sam 11–20. There is something close in the story of 2 Sam 2–4 (Gunn, *King David,* 65-84, 95-96); but its context is not the same. There is something near in 1 Kgs 1–2, but again the context is not the same; the focus of attention is different. Perhaps, beyond the narrative style, it is the capacity of the text of 2 Sam 11–20 to create space for so many questions and to answer so few. The possibilities and areas of interest associated with the so-called Succession Narrative are many and have been brought out well by Ackroyd (cf. "Succession Narrative"). What matters most and is central to the treatment here is "the characteristic qualities of sustained narrative" — the chapters where these are to be found and the meaning to be found in them.

This openness to questions makes 2 Sam 11–20 different from other narratives. The Ark Narrative (1 Sam 4–6; 2 Sam 6), for example, is no stranger to questions. It opens with one that it may take four chapters to answer. Each segment answers one question and raises another. In 1 Sam 4:3, the question is explicitly asked: Why did the LORD defeat us today? With the ark present, the second defeat answers that question: not because of the absence of the ark. With the anecdotes of Eli's death and Ichabod's death, the question is: Has God gone into exile from Israel? The episode in Dagon's temple gives one answer to that question: not involuntarily; YHWH is the superior power. Then has YHWH chosen to abandon Israel? The rest of 1 Sam 5 offers an answer to that question: certainly not; the ark is making the Philistines most uncomfortable. So the question arises: Where will the ark go? The answer is in 1 Sam 6: the ark will go back to Israel. The question is hardly necessary: So, is Israel back in favor? Unfortunately, the slaughter at Beth-shemesh raises the question by answering it: no, Israel is not back in favor. So the ark is sidelined at Kiriath-jearim. The question that lingers unanswered has to be: When will Israel be back in favor? The answer is given in 2 Sam 6: Israel is back in favor when the Davidic monarchy is established in Jerusalem. Only then can the opening question of 1 Sam 4:3 be answered. Why has God defeated us today? Because the era of God's presence at Shiloh is to cede to the era of God's presence in Jerusalem.

Plenty of questions here, but also plenty of answers. In 2 Sam 11–20, there are almost no answers. To sample a few questions, by way of example. Did Bathsheba consent to David's advances? We do not know. Was the murder of Uriah the most practical solution to David's problem? We do not know. Was David aware of the risk to which he was exposing Tamar in sending her unescorted to Amnon? We do not know. Was David aware of the risk to which he was exposing Amnon in allowing him to accept an invitation from Absalom? We do not know. Was David irresolute in his treatment of Absalom? We do not know. Why did David abandon Jerusalem without a fight? We do not know. Why was Ittai loyal to David? We do not know. Why did David send the ark back into Jerusalem? We do not know. Why did Ziba curry favor with David? We do not know. Did Joab kill Absalom on his own initiative? We do not know. Was Amasa delayed or disloyal? We do not know. Plenty of questions here, but scarcely any answers. We can speculate on answers to these questions, but we know the full answers are not given in the text and are not obtained by interpretation of the text. In the Ark Narrative, the answers are not given in the text, but they are obtainable by interpretation of the text.

Another example of narrative in these texts of the early monarchy is the Story of David's Rise to power in Israel. Here, questions can be asked about events, but the questions are not posed by the text itself. Very often, they are not answered by the text either. One question can be asked regularly: Why did David enjoy such success? The text has an equally regular answer: because the LORD was with him. We may ask why Saul behaved in such unkingly fashion in the face of Goliath's challenge. The text's answer has been given: "the spirit of the LORD departed from Saul" (1 Sam 16:14). We may ask why David met the challenge. The text has its answer: "for the LORD was with him" (18:14). We do not ask why Saul gave Merab to Adriel the Meholathite; it does not matter to the story. We may ask why Jonathan was committed to David; the text takes it as a given in the situation. We do not ask why David lied to Ahimelech; it is something the desperate have to do. We do not wonder why no one had told Saul of Jonathan's commitment to David; it is hardly critical to the narrative. And so on.

This is not the case for 2 Sam 11–20. Certain questions are almost invited by the text. For example, David's exchange with Absalom over the invitation to the sheep shearing is such that a listener or reader has to ask whether David knew what would happen. Most questions are not invited by the text, but the text is singularly open to them. Had David not defended Keilah (1 Sam 23:1-14), the narrative of David's rise would have unfolded anyway. Had David not violated Bathsheba, Uriah would not have been murdered and Nathan would not have been needed. Had David not sent Tamar unescorted to Amnon, Tamar would not have been raped, Amnon would not have been murdered, and Absalom's rebellion might well have been avoided. Had David chosen to defend Jerusalem, the story might have taken a totally different turn. Had Sheba ben Bichri's rebellion not occurred, Joab might not have regained his position of power. The text of 2 Sam 11–20 has an openness to questions it does not answer that is unprecedented in biblical narrative.

It may be this openness to unanswered questions that has made possible debate over whether the narrative itself or subsequent editing was favorable or unfavorable to the monarchy (beginning with the work of Delekat ["Tendenz"] and Würthwein [*Thronfolge Davids*]; see below chapter 12, "Diachronic Dimension"). Favorable and unfavorable elements can certainly be found in the text. No consensus has been reached that would recognize a narrative and its subsequent editing. The attitude of mind that allows conceptual doors to be opened without closing them may account for both the favorable and the unfavorable.

J. W. Flanagan, leaving aside 1 Kgs 1–2 from an original narrative, suggested the title Court History. While insightful and a move away from the unfortunate theme of succession, it falls short on two counts. First, the stories are not history; they are stories. Second, the bulk of the action in the narrative takes place outside the court. The narrative covers some fourteen years or more. We may assume that a great deal went on at the court of King David during this time; these stories convey revealing insight into only a fraction of that activity, although a central fraction. For a thoroughgoing analysis indicating that 1 Kgs 1–2 cannot be considered an original part of the preceding narrative, see Keys, *Wages of Sin,* 53-69.

It has been suggested that 2 Sam 10-12 should be seen as an insertion into the DH, with the result that "it becomes clear just how much they [chs. 10–12] have changed the tone and message of the subsequent material. The troubles . . . are now understood as punishments for, or at least consequences of his sins with Uriah and Bathsheba" (McKenzie, "So-called Succession Narrative," 135). Modeling implies consequences. The narrative in chs. 13–20 hardly needs David's initial modeling to raise questionable issues. The David of chs. 13–20 is far from being portrayed as a pious and gentle soul. In ch. 13, he delivers an unprotected Tamar to Amnon. In the same ch. 13, he allows Amnon to be put at Absalom's mercy. In ch. 14, he fails to act decisively. In chs. 15–19, he is brilliant, balancing piety and politics. In the handling of Absalom, the interplay of royal power (David) and military power (Joab) is evident. The same interplay is present in ch. 20. Chapters 11–12 emphasize David's wrongdoing and ruthlessness and allow a shift of emphasis from David's own behavior (chs. 13–20 alone) to David's impact on others (with chs. 11–12). The difference between the stories is not such as to require their separation without further substantial evidence.

In their comprehensive coverage of Western literature, the Chadwicks referred to these chapters as the Story of David's Later Years (cf. H. M. and N. K. Chadwick, *Growth of Literature,* II, 645). The title is appropriate and neutral; it does not claim that this is the Story of David's Final Years. However, if the association with 1 Kgs 1–2 needs to be severed, a clearer title is the Stories of David's Middle Years. The "expert in war" (2 Sam 17:8) is not yet an old man. The warrior king is not to go out with his troops because "you are worth ten thousand of us" (18:3). The independent collection of Davidic traditions in 2 Sam 21–24 had to be situated where it is, before David's evident age and death. The list of David's administrators (20:23-26) is appropriate after the return "to Jerusalem to the king" (20:22). Yet it is difficult not to see a balance with the list in 2 Sam 8:16-18, the one closing off the stories of David's early years and the other closing off the stories of the middle years.

These stories of David's middle years exhibit their independence and could each be told for their own sake. The essentials of plot are there for each. Only a minimal knowledge of Davidic background is presumed. As the present text stands, however, the beginnings and endings essential to independent stories are not there. 2 Sam 11:1 is a satisfactory beginning; 12:31 brings the campaign and the story to closure. The phrasing of 13:1 is not such as to suggest a satisfactory beginning to an independent story. A satisfactory separation between chs. 13 and 14 is difficult to achieve. If 14:33 was the end of an independent story, the impression of a successful reconciliation would be difficult to escape. 15:1 removes any such impression and is, on its own, too abrupt for the start of an independent story (cf. 1 Kgs 1:5a, lacking here). Once the story of Absalom's revolt has been begun, it runs through to the end of ch. 19. The debate there and the sequence of 20:1 (reversed in the NRSV) both demand the inclusion of ch. 20. We can conclude to independent stories, but in the present text they have been so woven together that they have lost their independence.

The structure of the narrative woven from these stories can be represented as follows.

Stories of David's middle years   **2 Sam 11–20**
  I. David: the modeling of a king   11–12
    A. Rabbah besieged: setting opened   11:1
    B. Story of David and Bathsheba   11:2–12:25
      1. Marriage to Bathsheba   11:2-27
      2. Confrontation with Nathan   12:1-15a
      3. Children of Bathsheba   12:15b-25
    C. Rabbah captured: setting closed   12:26-31
  II. The modeling within David's family   13–19
    A. Internal impact: without threat to David's rule   13–14
      1. Amnon and Absalom: rape and murder   13:1-36
      2. Transition   13:37-39
      3. Absalom and David: return and reunion   14:1-33
    B. External impact: a grave threat to David's rule   15–19
      1. Prelude: the gathering storm   15:1-12
      2. The drama: Absalom's rebellion   15:13–19:44 (NRSV, 43)
        a. David's flight from Jerusalem   15:13–16:14
        b. David's conflict with Absalom   16:15–19:9 (NRSV, 8)
        c. David's return to Jerusalem   19:10-44 (NRSV, 9-43)
 III. The modeling within David's kingdom   20
    A. Sheba's call to disunity   1-2 (3)
    B. Enforcement of unity   4-22a
      1. David's ordering of power   4-7
      2. Joab's reordering of power   8-13
      3. Joab's crushing of Sheba's revolt   14-22a
    C. Joab's return to David   22b

Discussion

There must be at least as many ways of structuring 2 Sam 11–20 as there are ways of looking at life. Structure analysis looks for insight; a literary masterpiece offers insight over and over again. What is offered above is undoubtedly possible; so are many other ways of looking at the text. As Brueggemann notes, questions have been raised "concerning where the literature begins, whether it is a unit, and what its purpose might be" (p. 265). Even more important than where it begins, for ascertaining "what its purpose might be," is the question as to where it ends.

For understanding the text in its own time, "modeling" as used here cannot be understood in any post-Freudian sense. This is not a post-Freudian text. "Modeling" here relates to the image David projected of his person and role; it relates to the pattern of attitudes and behaviors adopted by others under his influence. It is modeling as used, for example, by Nathan: "therefore the sword shall never depart from your house" (12:10); "I will take your wives before your eyes" (12:11). The first can be understood as act and consequence; the second is expressed as direct divine causation. Not far from this is the comment made about Adonijah's upbringing: "His father had never at any time displeased him by asking, 'Why have you done thus and so?'" (1 Kgs 1:6). In the formulation "as you have done to others, so it will be done to you," modeling becomes an extension of the *ius talionis*. A modern reader may want to reflect in terms of more recent understandings of modeling, but that is a modern reading.

That acts have their consequences is a strong element in ancient Hebrew thinking. Modeling such as we are discussing here is a facet of that understanding. One of the consequences of acts by significant figures is that, consciously or unconsciously, they may be imitated, replicated, rejected. To those around him, his children and his courtiers, David was a significant figure. Behaviors that he modeled — values that he externalized — were there to be absorbed by others. David's acts contributed to the consequences for David's kingdom.

Given David's status in tradition as Israel's model king, the use here of the phrase "David: the modeling of a king" is fraught with irony and ambiguity. For a narrative so filled with ambiguity and irony, it is suitable.

It has been a commonplace in biblical scholarship to contrast the secular context of these stories of David's middle years with the sacral context in which the stories of David's rise to power are steeped. In the latter, the LORD is constantly invoked as a force in the movement of the narrative. In the former, YHWH's impact on the narrative is noted only three times: the LORD's dispatch of Nathan (2 Sam 11:27–12:1); the LORD's love for Solomon (12:24-25); and the LORD's defeat of Ahithophel's good advice (15:31; 17:14; cf. von Rad, *Theology* 1.48-56, 314-17). It is worth pointing out also that Joab's influence impacts on the narrative significantly. He is active at Rabbah, modifying the king's stratagem for killing Uriah and summoning the king to take the glory for the capture of the city (2 Sam 11–12). He is active in having Absalom brought back from exile and finally admitted to the king's presence (2 Sam 14). He stiffens David's resolve, after the death of Absalom (2 Sam 19). He seizes the authority to crush Sheba's revolt that threatened David's kingdom and he returns to Jerusalem to the king (2 Sam 20). Joab's role in these stories is not to be neglected. The unfettered exercise of royal power is limited in these stories by Nathan (with reference to God), by Joab (with reference to military power), and by the people (with reference to popular support). All three — but Joab especially — are a reminder of the powerlessness of the powerful.

It has been traditional to charge David with adultery. It is important to recognize why this is unsatisfactory, inadequate, and nowadays unjust. In former times, the defining note concerning adultery related to marriage alone; adultery could be described as "violation of the marriage bed" (*Webster's New Twentieth Century,* second edition). More recently, the importance of consent has been made explicit; so the description becomes "voluntary sexual intercourse" where at least one partner is married *(Webster's New Collegiate)*. Linguistic patterns are rendered more complex by the note in the older *Webster's* that, in Scripture, adultery is used for "all manner of lewdness or unchastity" as well as idolatry or apostasy (cf. Stone, *Sex, Honor, and Power,* 94-95). In David's case, the biblical text is totally silent about Bathsheba's consent: "David sent messengers to get her, and she came to him, and he lay with her" (11:4). When this passage is compared with 1 Sam 25:39b-42, where consent is clear, and with 2 Sam 13:11-14, where consent is refused, its ambiguity is patent.

Two observations point to the description of David's behavior as rape. First, the principle of much law that a person is innocent until proven guilty. In the story, David is guilty of murder and sexual wrong, whether adultery or rape. In the story, Bathsheba is not reported to be consenting; she is innocent until alleged in the narrative to have consented, whether by word or act. Without consent on her part, the action is rape. Second, the Hebrew innocuously translated by the NRSV as "to get her" reads literally: and he took her (*wayyiqqāḥehā,* v. 4; the NRSV has softened this by integrating it with the messengers). The verb "to take" can be used in association with consent (cf. 1 Sam 25:40 above); the baldness of its use here does not suggest consent. The text could have read more ambiguously, omitting the verb of taking: David sent messengers to her, and she came to him, and he lay with her. However, it does not. Fidelity to the text suggests the charge should be rape (cf. Noll: "it must be labeled for what it is," *Faces of David,* 59-60, n. 81).

However, where royalty and rank are concerned (kings and presidents, for example), the accusation of rape is rare in either law or literature. The reasons for this are surely complex and are probably best not explored here. Given the centuries that have spoken of David's adultery, with its implicit condemnation of Bathsheba, and given the attitude found in so many places that somehow manages to blame Bathsheba, it is possible that "the rape of Bathsheba" as counterbalance to the past is indeed the appropriate terminology. It is certainly more appropriate than "David's adultery." On the other hand, given the non-use of rape where royalty and rank are concerned, it may not be appropriate for David and Bathsheba. Israel's traditions were not permissive in relation to the sexual behavior of those of rank, especially foreigners (e.g., the Pharaoh, Gen 12:17; the king of Gerar, Gen 20:3; the princely Shechem, Gen 34:6-7). What is beyond dispute, entirely independent of issues of consent, is that Bathsheba's person or her relationship to Uriah, and in the light of the text probably both, were violated. The "violation of Bathsheba" may be the least unsatisfactory terminology, especially given the ambivalence of the text's storytelling.

In this understanding, then, the story of David and Bathsheba has the king violate a woman, order her husband murdered, marry her, and face judgment from God's prophet. The stories that follow rehearse what Nathan's prophecy details: the sexual and homicidal violence that has begun with the king will not depart from the king's house. The more strongly future-oriented element of the prophecy (12:7b-12) is often seen as a later development. Even so, what it develops is already latent in the tradition. The analysis given is fully consonant with the tradition itself and also with the prophetic interpretation of it, if "the king's house" is understood broadly (i.e., the king's entourage). Independently of the formulation of Nathan's interpretation, the role of Joab in ch. 20 reflects his role in chs. 11–12; there, he was David's loyal hatchet man and, in ch. 20, he cannot be lightly set aside. David used him to kill Uriah and this violence returns to impact on David's destiny. For Keys, the theme of sin and punishment is to the fore in this narrative, without neglecting a focus on the character of David as well as on other minor themes (*Wages of Sin,* 123-55). The present treatment gives less emphasis to the issue of sin and punishment, but the issue has its place within the consequences of David's behavior that are part of what may be termed his royal "modeling."

David's treatment of Bathsheba is reflected in Amnon's rape of Tamar. Amnon is David's crown prince; Tamar is his half-sister, daughter to David and sister to Absalom. The murder of Uriah is reflected in the murder of Amnon. David's treatment of Uriah is reflected in Absalom's treatment of David. David owed fidelity to Uriah and instead used the sword against him. Absalom owed fidelity to David and instead used the sword against him. It is known to David: "my own son seeks my life" (2 Sam 16:11). It is known even more explicitly to the reader or listener. Ahithophel: "'I will strike down only the king.' . . . The advice pleased Absalom" (2 Sam 17:1-4). Joab's role as killer on David's behalf (in ch. 11) is reflected in ch. 20; Joab kills Amasa, crushes Sheba's revolt, and returns to David's employ. David was ruthless in getting his way; Joab was no less ruthless in getting his. At the beginning, he went out from Jerusalem on the king's service; at the end, he returns to Jerusalem, to the king's service.

The basic modeling provided by the opening story is that what you want you take by force. David took Bathsheba sexually; David took Uriah's life forcefully. Initially, his actions are duplicated by two of his sons: the rape of Tamar and the murder of Amnon. Subsequently, the narrative modulates from action to attitude, the attitude that generates the action: what you want you take by force. Thus, combining these, the narrative moves through three loose stages. First, David's deeds are replicated within his family, basically restricted to the palace — [II.A]. Amnon rapes Tamar and Absalom murders Amnon, after nursing his need for vengeance for two full years. Second, David's pattern of behavior, his attitude, is replicated within his family still, but extended to the larger sphere of the kingdom — [II.B]. Absalom turns to violence and the sword in his rebellion against David. Third, beyond his family, David's pattern of behavior, his attitude, is replicated within the kingdom — [III]. Joab is murderously ruthless in the reassertion of his power. Amasa went out; Joab came back.

As will emerge below, David's role in all this is left unclear in the narrative. To have sent a virgin princess unguarded to a besotted half-brother, to have allowed a hated rapist to attend his brother's party, to dither while a murderer's anger turned to a rebel's ambition, to have sought to spare the life of a murderous and rebellious son — much of this may cover what is murky. McCarter's comment that in chs. 13–20 "David is guilty of no more serious crime than excessive paternal affection (13:21)" (p. 289) is all-too-trustingly naive.

It should not come as a surprise to moderns that the appearance of power and the reality of power do not always coincide. It should not come as a surprise to us that it has been always so. Behind the royal figures of Saul, David, and Solomon, there are the figures of Abner, Joab, and Benaiah (cf. 1 Sam 14:50; 2 Sam 8:16 and 20:23a; 1 Kgs 4:4). The precise extent of their influence we shall never know. Abner was apparently able to broker kingdoms (2 Sam

3:12). Joab knew how to work his will (2 Sam 12:28; 14:18-19, 29-33; 19:6-9 [Heb.; NRSV, 19:5-8]; 20:10, 22). Benaiah took Joab's place under Solomon (1 Kgs 2:35). Behind these again, there is a world we hardly know existed; we get glimpses of it, no more. Apart from the legendary traditions of 2 Sam 21:15-22, there are the organizational structures and the military leaders we have never heard of (2 Sam 23:8-39) and the unknown elements in the faction disputing David's succession (1 Kgs 1:8 — Shimei, Rei, and David's own warriors [cf. 2 Sam 20:7; 23:8], who were with Benaiah not Joab). Power is seldom simple; these stories explore aspects of human complexity, opening up so many questions and answering so few.

Great literature can be read in many ways. This analysis is one possible reading of the Stories of David's Middle Years, one that is appropriate and responsible. It does not exhaust the possibilities. Before entering into close engagement with what is undoubtedly a great text (2 Sam 11–20), it is important to clarify the expectations we bring to it. After sustained and close reading, it will be just as important to reflect on how these expectations fared. A full and helpful review of relevant literature is given by Keys, *Wages of Sin,* 14-42.

Genre

These are (→) stories not history. An affair, a death in battle, and two pregnancies are not the stuff of courtly chronicles. A princely rape might precipitate fratricide; it would not make the chronicles in detail. A major rebellion might well be matter for a chronicler, but scarcely the details of David's flight and return. Sheba's revolt might be of interest, but not Joab's recovery of power, without appropriate follow-up.

We have spoken of the policy of unasked and unanswered questions visible in these stories. A course of action is taken from which the narrative develops. Spaces (gaps) are open throughout the stories; the narrative could have moved into one or another of these spaces and the outcome might have been so very different. The narrative did not and so the outcome is not. It will help to note some examples. Bathsheba's attitude toward David is left ambiguous. Was she willing or unwilling? Was she submissive, seductive, scheming, or victim? The text is silent. Various attempts to sketch a convincing plot fail to do so. The ambiguity here is not so much an unasked question as a background that reflects the complexity of human motivation every leader needs to be aware of.

Bathsheba's announcement of her pregnancy is given simply and briefly. No reflection or motivation is mentioned. David's action follows immediately on the news. The options open to him for her protection would certainly include bringing Uriah home to cover David's tracks for him and protect her from possible prosecution (cf. Josephus, *Antiquities,* 7, 131). The options open to him for his own protection are not canvassed, yet they are many. The least complicated would be to kill her; it would remove the evidence and the witness. A nocturnal break-in or a fatal accident could have been more easily arranged than the killing of Uriah. To pay for her silence would at least have gained time.

To brazen it out might not have been possible, but the option is not explored. A stay in the country might have led to a miscarriage or a fostering. Could Uriah have been ordered to a posting in Jerusalem? Were there other children? Why have Uriah brought home before having him killed? Once in Jerusalem, what did Uriah know and what did Uriah want? Had Uriah obeyed David's orders and gone to his house, what then? Was it an episode to be forgotten? Was passion to be denied its desire? Was some hope to be kept alive? The text is discreet. All of these are not so much doors that the narrative opens as doors that are open; in its silence, the narrative closes none of them.

Amnon wanted Tamar badly enough that Jonadab knew it and Absalom knew it. Did David know it? Should David have known it? Amnon asked for Tamar's physical presence. Should David have refused the request? Should David have arranged for a burly chaperon? David did nothing. What should he have done? What were his options and what were the possible consequences? Jonadab foresaw Amnon's murder by Absalom. Should David have foreseen it? Did he? Should David have stifled his human feelings and left Absalom in exile for life? Should he have forgiven him promptly? Brought about a reconciliation swiftly? What were the implications of David's emotional indecision? The narrative is silent.

Why did David flee the legendarily impregnable city at the first sign of rebellion? What is the import of the stories told of those David met in his flight and on his return? In killing Absalom, was Joab disloyal, politically astute, or doing the bidding of his king? Why was Joab dropped in favor of Amasa? Revenge or realpolitik or what else? Why did Amasa not return to Jerusalem in three days? Delayed or disloyal? Why did David entrust his troops to Abishai and not Joab? What was David's reaction when he discovered that Joab had reclaimed his place and power? We are not told.

Not all stories have this capacity to maneuver through a set of questionable human actions leaving so many questions unanswered. Other unanswered questions remain. Is this capacity peculiar to these stories? Does this capacity in some way specify these stories?

Setting

It would be the height of temerity to determine a setting for such elusive texts. A couple of reflections are not out of place. First, the stories show David sometimes in a good light (usually out of the city — crafty on campaign) and sometimes in a bad light (usually in the city — shady in the city). A setting too close to David's time or too far from David's time is unlikely. Too close to David would be likely to be dangerous. It is not usually wise to malign a ruling monarch. Settings in which this might be envisaged do not cohere well with the rest of the stories. Too far from David is unlikely. For the Deuteronomistic History, David was the ideal king of Israel. It is not usually wise to malign a national ideal. Again, settings in which this might be envisaged do not cohere well with the rest of the stories, where David is the decisive leader and able commander.

Second, the stories in the narrative have this peculiar capacity to leave space for questions that could be asked and to close off almost none. Central to the story of Absalom's rebellion is the scene where counsel is taken, pitting Ahithophel against Hushai (2 Sam 17:1-14). It has been prepared for in David's prayer (15:31) and his plans (15:32-37). It comes with the highest possible accolade for Ahithophel: "in those days the counsel that Ahithophel gave was as if one consulted the oracles of God; so all the counsel of Ahithophel was esteemed, both by David and by Absalom" (16:23). It is followed by the report of God's only intervention in the core of the narrative: "The LORD had ordained to defeat the good counsel of Ahithophel, so that the LORD might bring ruin on Absalom" (17:14b). Its outcome was fatal for Ahithophel; he took his life (17:23). If counsel given the king is esteemed so highly, might it say something about the open questions of these stories and something of their possible setting?

A serious contender in the possibility stakes is the court of Jeroboam, first king of northern Israel. With the court in late-tenth-century Shechem or Penuel, such a setting would be far enough away from David in time and space to be safe. It is early enough and northern enough that the ideal image of David would not have taken root. Many of Jeroboam's courtiers would have been at court in Jerusalem and been well aware of the Davidic traditions. With the establishment of a new kingdom and a new court, a high value would have been set on the availability of courtiers capable of giving counsel to the king.

Does this offer a possible setting in which these stories of David's middle years might have been given their particular form and taken a place in the history of Israel's literature — including in due course their place in the present text? Might these stories originally have been told for royal courtiers to explore the boundaries of counsel given the king? At what points in the stories would counsel have been desirable? What options might have been proposed and what consequences might have followed from them?

Such a setting would account for this peculiar capacity of the stories to leave space for questions that could be asked and to close off almost none. Such is the wisdom of a counselor: to open unthought-of options for reflection and to choose wisely. Given the court of Jeroboam, negative views of David would hardly have been out of place. Given Jeroboam's role as king, positive views of the king's leadership abilities and political astuteness might not have gone astray. It is a possibility that cannot be ignored.

Meaning

To nail down the meaning of a masterpiece would be impressive folly. A text of this quality may inspire as many meanings as there are approaches to a work of art. Emerging from what has been said above, however, it is possible and legitimate to focus on a particular meaning that can be seen in the text, without being so foolish as to make any claim to being exhaustive.

What these stories of David's middle years do is to lay out episodes of human behavior that have extreme consequences: rape, murder, rebellion. What these stories invite is reflection on courses of action that might have been taken and what might have happened had they been taken. Did Uriah have to die? Did Tamar have to be put at risk? Did Amnon have to be endangered? Did Absalom have to be alienated? Did rebellion have to be handled the way it was? Could royal power be separated from military allegiance?

One direction for meaning in these stories is the realization of how many avenues are open to human choice in various moments of life. Wisdom is needed to recognize choices. Wisdom is needed to make choices. Courage and ability may be needed to rise to the challenge posed by a choice. Wisdom is needed first to recognize the choice and then to make it. Is a meaning from these stories to be sought in the direction of this wisdom (cf. Whybray, *Succession Narrative,* 56-95)? It is possible.

Bibliography of Works Cited Above

Ackroyd, Peter R. "The Succession Narrative (so-called)." *Int* 35 (1981) 383-96.

Bailey, Randall C. *David in Love and War: The Pursuit of Power in 2 Samuel 10–12.* JSOTSup 75. Sheffield: Sheffield Academic Press, 1990.

Chadwick, H. Munro, and N. Kirshaw Chadwick. *The Growth of Literature.* Vols. 1-3. Cambridge: Cambridge University Press, 1932, 1936, 1940.

Conroy, Charles. *Absalom Absalom! Narrative and Language in 2 Sam 13–20.* AnBib 81. Rome: Biblical Institute, 1978.

Delekat, L. "Tendenz und Theologie der David-Salomo Erzählung." Pages 26-36 in *Das Ferne und Nahe Wort; Fs. L. Rost.* Edited by F. Maass. Berlin. Töpelmann, 1967.

Flanagan, James W. "Court History or Succession Document? A Study of 2 Samuel 9–20 and 1 Kings 1–2." *JBL* 91 (1972) 172-81.

Frolov, Serge. "Succession Narrative: A 'Document' or a Phantom?" *JBL* 121 (2002) 81-104.

Gunn, D. M. *The Story of King David: Genre and Interpretation.* JSOTSup 6. Sheffield: JSOT, 1978.

Josephus, Flavius, *Jewish Antiquities,* Books V-VIII. The Loeb Classical Library. London: Heinemann, 1934.

Keys, Gillian. *The Wages of Sin: A Reappraisal of the 'Succession Narrative.'* JSOTSup 221. Sheffield: Sheffield Academic Press, 1996.

Lessing, Doris, *The Diaries of Jane Somers.* Harmondsworth: Penguin, 1985.

McKenzie, Steven L. "The So-Called Succession Narrative in the Deuteronomistic History." Pages 123-35 in *Die sogenannte Thronfolgegeschichte Davids.* Edited by A. de Pury and T. Römer. OBO 176. Freiburg, Switzerland: Universtätsverlag, 2000.

Noll, K. L., *The Faces of David.* JSOTSup 242. Sheffield: Sheffield Academic Press, 1997.

Rad, Gerhard von. *Old Testament Theology.* 2 vols. Edinburgh: Oliver and Boyd, 1962-65.

Rost, Leonhard, *The Succession to the Throne of David.* Sheffield: Almond, 1982. German original: 1926.

Seiler, Stefan. *Die Geschichte von der Thronfolge Davids (2 Sam 9–20; 1 Kön 1–2).* BZAW 267. Berlin: de Gruyter, 1998.

Stone, Ken. *Sex, Honor, and Power in the Deuteronomistic History.* JSOTSup 234. Sheffield: Sheffield Academic Press, 1996.

Whybray, R. N. *The Succession Narrative: A Study of II Samuel 9–20; I Kings 1 and 2.* SBT 2/9. London: SCM, 1968.

Würthwein, Ernst. *Die Erzählung von der Thronfolge Davids — theologische oder politische Geschichtsschreibung?* TS 115. Zürich: Theologische Verlag, 1974.

Chapter 6

DAVID AND BATHSHEBA
(2 SAM 11–12)

The tone for these stories of David's middle years is set by this first one. There is royal wrongdoing, compounded by royal cover-up involving killing. There is confrontation with the prophet. There are the consequences for the royal family: death and new birth. The prophet will not be heard from again within 2 Sam 11–20, nor will there be another new birth. Acts have consequences. Forgiveness does not necessarily void such consequences. Favor need not override them either. Throughout the story, the decisiveness of human action is to the fore; the overwhelming uncertainty of human motivation is seldom absent.

3. Announcement of divine favor   25
III. Rabbah taken: setting closed   12:26-31

Textual Issues

11:1 The MT Kethib has המלאכים *(hammal'kîm)* messengers, instead of the expected המלכים *(hammĕlākîm)* for kings. Kings are clearly meant. With the extra aleph, the word spelled is equivalent to "messengers." The insertion of the aleph as an extra letter in a word is rare, but it does occur (cf. GKC, §72p); this case is the only certain example for the word "king" (but cf. 2 Kgs 6:33 and 1 Chr 21:20 where, however, the meaning is debated). It is noteworthy that Gesenius-Kautzsch regards "the messengers" in 2 Sam 11:1 as "the true reading" (GKC, §23g).

Whether it is an innocently happy fault or a sophisticated literary conceit, we do not know. The meaning "kings" is clear. Apart from the evidence of the ancient translations, messengers are "sent"; only kings "go out" in this sense (i.e., to war). Nevertheless, the pointer to messengers is most apt; their place and potential in the story are considerable. The presence of the word as spelled in 11:1 is an invitation to imaginative storytelling and literary reflection (cf. Polzin, "deliciously ambiguous," *David and the Deuteronomist,* 109-12; Alter, *David Story,* 249).

11:4 The MT has "and she came to him" as does the text of Rahlff's LXX, noting that LXX^B, LXX^A, and LXX^L have "and he came into her"; the Brooke-McLean edition of LXX^B, of course, has "and he came into her."

11:22 The LXX^B has a substantial "plus" in this verse, with a somewhat different plus occurring in LXX^L; basically, both have the exchange unfold more closely in line with Joab's prediction than is recorded in vv. 23-24 (for details, see Barthélemy, 257-61; McCarter, 282-83; Pisano, 49-54). Driver comments: "the text of LXX describes in detail how what Joab anticipated [in] vv. 21-22 [sic, but cf. vv. 20-21] took place. The addition is a necessary one . . ." (p. 290). The addition is necessary if the events are to be accurately reported. The addition is not necessary if a story is being told. The issue is uncertain (cf. Barthélemy), but it is legitimate to say that the text's portrayal assumes a messenger "intelligent enough to know how to avoid David's anger by getting right down to the information that he wanted, that Uriah had been killed" (Pisano, 54). Despite its literary caliber, if this is "reported story" the likelihood of the text's leaving expansion and elaboration to the storyteller is enhanced. While textual errors certainly occur, it is also important to allow different versions to reflect stories told in different ways.

12:14 The MT has "enemies of YHWH." While it is satisfactorily explained as a scribal correction to avoid the phrase "you have utterly scorned the LORD" (often referred to as *tiqqunê soferim* [cf. Tov, *Textual Criticism,* 64-67]), uncertainties remain; see McCarter, 296.

12:30 The absence of a referent for the plural suffix, "their kings," confirms reading *milkōm,* in line with 1 Kgs 11:5, 33 (cf. Barthélemy, 263; McCarter, 311-13).

Discussion

It takes a moment to realize what an artful piece of literature this story is. Between the opening and closing reports of a military campaign (11:1 and 12:26-31) are sandwiched a story about the evil of Israel's greatest king, David, and the birth of his son and successor, Solomon the wise. Narrated in the story are sexual wrongdoing, deceit, murder, two pregnancies separated by a marriage, a prophetic confrontation, a child's death and a child's birth, concluded by a reappearance of the same prophet with a totally different message. Questions abound; answers are largely absent. It is one of the Bible's great narrative texts. Polzin: "the story is filled with multiple gaps that force the wary reader to reflect upon what is supposed to be going on in the story" (*David and the Deuteronomist,* 113); cautions are expressed and insights offered by Garsiel ("Story of David and Bathsheba").

Any analysis of the story faces a dilemma. To name the major moments inevitably means bypassing much of the detail where the fascination is. To name the detail inevitably leads to baffling complexity and boredom. I have opted for naming the major moments in the structure analysis and unfolding the detail in the discussion.

It seems unjust to absorb the violation of Bathsheba into a section entitled "Marriage," but that is how the story ends. It seems even more unjust to bury her husband's murder under the rubric "Complication," but within the story it is the unfortunate means for resolving the complication of Bathsheba's pregnancy.

The beginning of the story is admirably appropriate to it — [I]. No other story in the Older Testament is so steeped in ambiguity. It is fitting that its opening clause might be said to be elusively and "deliciously" ambiguous (cf. above, under textual issues). Give or take a few manuscripts here and there, the Hebrew consonantal text has: "In the spring of the year, when messengers go out . . ."; pretty much unanimously, the ancient translations have: "In the spring of the year, when kings go out. . . ." The NRSV quite justifiably explains what kings go out for by expanding "when kings go out to battle" (so too the Vulgate: "ad bella"). The difference between the words for messengers and kings in Hebrew is one consonant, one aleph; the vocalization reflects age-old difficulty over the word (normally, kings: *mĕlākîm;* messengers: *mal'ākîm*). The richness of the ambiguity is its rightness. Messengers are not the primary actors in the story, but without them there would be no story. David sent messengers for Bathsheba (v. 4); Joab sent a messenger to David (vv. 19, 22, 23) who was sent back by David to Joab (v. 25); at the end, Joab sent messengers for David (12:27). Beyond that, there is a great deal of sending in the story, much of which involved messengers. David sent Joab to besiege Rabbah; no messenger needed there. David sent someone to inquire about Bathsheba; he sent messengers for Bathsheba; she sent the message: I am pregnant. David sent for Uriah; David sent a letter to Joab, carried by Uriah; Joab sent and told David of Uriah's death; and David sent for Bathsheba to make her his wife. YHWH sent Nathan to David; YHWH sent a message of favor for Solomon; Joab sent for David.

We need to allow the ambiguity of this beginning rather than erase it. It is worth noting that its appropriateness does not extend to the rest of the stories of David's middle years. The word *mal'āk* (as messenger) is not used in chs. 13–20 (despite 15:10, 13).

David sent Joab, with the royal troops (NRSV, "his officers"; literally: his servants) and the conscript army of Israel, to besiege Rabbah. "David remained at Jerusalem" (v. 1b). Without David's remaining in Jerusalem while the army was in the field, there would be no story — [II]. Moralizers often point an accusing finger at the indolent monarch who dallied in the city while his commander led the army in the field. This accusation is not made by the text and may be unjustified and unfair. As noted, in the preceding chapter Joab led the army against the initial coalition (10:7) and David took the lead when an apparently more major engagement loomed (10:17). It may therefore be quite appropriate for Joab to lead what may have been minor mopping-up operations. David's remaining in the city may be a sign of the administrative demands of a complex kingdom, coupled with the capacity to delegate authority. David's conduct with Bathsheba was wrong; moralizing is not needed.

Scapegoating is not needed either. It has long been a frequent tradition in Western art and interpretation to attach some deflected blame to Bathsheba. The biblical text provides nothing on which to hang such blame. Nothing is said about where Bathsheba was. David was on the roof and he saw her from there. (A Latin MS has "through a door"; even there, the reference is to David's seeing, not to Bathsheba's bathing.) Nothing is said about any indiscretion on Bathsheba's part. In the crowded conditions of David's Jerusalem, a basin would be more likely than a bath. The text later adds: "she was purifying herself after her period" (v. 4). While we do not know the rules and customs of that tenth-century time, it is likely that a basin would have been more than adequate. The text says that David saw her and "the woman was very beautiful" (v. 2b). No suggestion is made of immodesty or indiscretion. The equivalent of a camera's slow panning over "the length of her entire naked body at her bath" (Bach, "Signs of the Flesh," 75) is an excellent distillation of exactly what the narrative does not offer and does not invite to. Sternberg's treatment of the gaps in this story is classic (*Poetics,* 190-222); equally classic is the language he uses of Uriah's awareness of "his wife's adultery" or "his wife's infidelity" — neither of which suggests a gap allowing for the possibility of royal abuse.

It would have been a brave counselor who suggested to the king that he take his post-siesta stroll somewhere else; it would have been a wise king to have done so without waiting for advice. Instead, he sent someone "to inquire about the woman" (v. 3a — so certainly not a long-term infatuation). The inquiry turned up two danger signals and the king was foolish enough to ignore both. She is a married woman, the wife of one of his soldiers. We do not know Uriah's status, but living in Jerusalem he may well have been a member of David's officer corps (cf. 2 Sam 23:39). A wise king does not sleep with the wives of his troops while they are fighting his wars. Bathsheba is not only a married woman; she is the daughter of Eliam, himself one of David's Thirty (2 Sam 23:34), and granddaughter of Ahithophel, the most respected counselor in David's realm (cf. 2 Sam 16:23). A wise king does not alienate his best adviser. The treatment of Bathsheba may have been at least a contributing factor in

Ahithophel's switch of allegiance to Absalom (2 Sam 15:12; cf. Daube, "Absalom," 320-22). If morality was not influential for David, political prudence should have been.

At issue is whether the text portrays Bathsheba as consenting or as victim, whether the crime is portrayed as adultery or rape/violation — [II.A.1]; it has been discussed above. The key sentence would keep a modern court of law in lengthy session. Literally, the Hebrew reads: "And David sent messengers and he took her and she came to him (some major LXX MSS: he came into her) and he lay with her." The context is not decisive either. Nature abhors a vacuum; most humans abhor confusion and want a decision. But the narrative may not reveal an event or veil one either. The narrative may be structured to create an ambiguity. We recognize that we are interpreting a text; we have no independent access to reality. Attitudes to royal customs may affect reality; the text has nothing to say, beyond Nathan's savage condemnation. The conclusion Würthwein draws from a comparison with 2 Sam 13:12-13 is fallacious (*Thronfolge Davids*, 27-28). Tamar is portrayed protesting; Bathsheba is not portrayed protesting. The portrayal does not allow the conclusion that Bathsheba is, therefore, guilty; it does not allow the assumption that she is portrayed as consenting. The key form-critical issue here, as so often, is whether the text is a report reflecting an incident or whether it is a story that may have other aims. Is a report's ambiguity veiling an event or is a story crafting ambiguity? In my judgment, a story here is crafting ambiguity.

The reference to Bathsheba's "purifying herself after her period" (v. 4) interrupts the flow of action, but it sends two significant messages: she is likely to conceive and the child can only be David's. If later law is any guide (e.g., Lev 15:19), the lapse of time from the end of her period to her purification would mean that she was at peak fertility (so H. P. Smith: "that such a time was favourable to conception was known to the Arabs at an early day," *Samuel*, 318). Certainly, although only she and the text know this, the child is David's, beyond any possible doubt (cf. Sternberg, *Poetics*, 198). Neither matter is raised further in the text; the first allows for a speedy narrative and the second allows for no doubt as to paternity.

What calls for much reflection and receives none in the text is Bathsheba's announcement of her pregnancy. "She sent and told David, 'I am pregnant'" (v. 5). At opposite poles are two possibilities: "I am pregnant, my darling" or "I am pregnant, you bastard." In either case, why tell him? The text sheds no light. The several possibilities are not explored; there is her protection and there is his. If there is love, possibilities may have been adumbrated between the two. If there is hatred, the risk may be deemed worth running. The text is silent.

The next move calls for just as much reflection — [II.A.2]; the text gives it none. Immediately, David sends to Joab for Uriah (v. 6). The options open to David were many; they have been discussed above (cf. 2 Sam 11–20, under Genre). They are not discussed in the text. He sent for Uriah. What David hoped for from Uriah's coming to Jerusalem is not clear. Had Uriah followed his king's orders and gone down to his house (v. 8), David would have had a cover against any embarrassment from paternity. Was that all he wanted? We do not know and the text does not tell us.

Why did Uriah refuse royal orders, why did he sleep so publicly at the palace, and why does the story have this reported to David? Questions have to be asked as to who knew and what they knew. Inquiries had been made about Bathsheba, messengers had been sent for her, presumably she was escorted home, she sent a message in due course, a message was sent to Joab, and later a present was sent down to the house. From a narrative point of view, is it plausible to have all this activity occur without arousing some curiosity? Critical to an understanding of the story are the questions: What did Uriah know and what did Uriah want? Is the homespun secondhand piety of a non-Israelite plausible? David obviously had not expected his resistance and thought it could be overcome. Was Uriah too trusting, too angry, or too greedy and ambitious? Did he not think David capable of strategic killing? We do not know and the text does not tell us.

Joab knew what David wanted. He may not have known why but he knew what. He did not follow his instructions "to draw back from him, so that he may be struck down and die" (v. 15). There are good reasons to think David's plan impractical; too many had to be told. From a narrative point of view, Joab's plan has an unexpected advantage: David's ruthlessness is revealed. Some of David's troops die and with them Uriah (v. 17). David is told and his anger flares. With the news of Uriah's death, anger is replaced by ruthlessness: "Do not let this matter trouble you, for the sword devours now one and now another" (v. 25). What is it about this man that can inspire incredible loyalty (e.g., 2 Sam 23:15-17) and allow him to be so ruthlessly disloyal?

With Uriah dead, and out of the way, David moves to marriage with Bathsheba — [II.A.3]. The marriage does not decide between earlier options; issues of love, public image, and royal status are too intermingled to allow for clarity. With the marriage, one might expect the story to move to closure. A half-verse indicates that closure is not in reach: "the thing that David had done displeased the LORD" (v. 27b). Whoever chose to end ch. 11 with this half-verse, opening ch. 12 with YHWH's dispatch of Nathan, was probably right. Closure is not in reach. There is more to come and come it will. Kings have power and power has limits, whether in the eyes of God or the unfolding of history.

The brilliance of Nathan's parable is that its thinking is so lateral it almost misses the mark — and so takes David totally by surprise — [II.B.1]. David is guilty of sex with a married woman and of having her husband murdered. Nathan's parable is about sheep stealing in a particularly obnoxious set of circumstances. Sheep stealing in a farming community may be almost as close to the ultimate crime against humanity as one is likely to get. Throw in the pathos of the wealthy grazer with his flocks and the poor old man with his one pet lamb and the scene is set for outrage. David is outraged. Nathan has his man. A tiny signal was there for David — "it was like a daughter to him" (v. 3); as signals go, it is so small David can hardly be blamed for missing it.

David's outrage is explosive. The man is a *ben mawet* (literally: a son of death). The phrase is used twice elsewhere (1 Sam 20:31 and 26:16). In the first case, it could mean "doomed to die," but it need not; Saul had the power to execute David. In the second case, "doomed to die" is most unlikely; David had no power over Abner. So here, it is more expression of outrage than judicial sentence; the sentence is assessed as fourfold restitution (v. 6). The reference to David's life (v. 13) is probably more strongly in contrast with the death of the first child (v. 14).

The bulk of Nathan's speech is troubled Hebrew prose (cf. vv. 7b-12) — [II.B.3]. Introductions to divine speech and references to the sexual crime and to the murder all occur twice; the punishment for sex and for murder is referred to once for each. Two versions of the divine word are likely, with a couple of adjustments concerning the crimes; so accusation in v. 9 with its punishment in v. 10a and accusation in v. 10b with its punishment in vv. 11-12 (cf. Fokkelman, *King David,* 83-86). Sex and murder are both noted in v. 9a. Reference to the murder is made more precise by v. 9b; sex is referred to again in v. 10b. Twice, the concrete cases of sexual and homicidal crime are prefaced by abstract references to "despising" the word of the LORD (v. 9a) or the LORD (v. 10b). If this were all, it would be troubling enough. There is more.

Among the verbs, the "perfect" (or: qatal) form predominates with ten occurrences; the "imperfect" (or: yiqtol) form occurs six times. Three of these occur in 12:8, referring to a tradition that is otherwise unknown to us: "I gave you your master's house, and your master's wives into your bosom, and gave you the house of Israel and of Judah; and if that had been too little, I would have added as much more." "Your master" must refer to Saul; there is no other possibility. One could quibble over Saul's house. There is no reference in the tradition to David having been given Saul's wives. Merab and Michal were Saul's daughters; Merab was not given to David and Michal was taken from him and given to another. Only one wife is named for Saul, Ahinoam, daughter of Ahimaaz (1 Sam 14:50). David marries an Ahinoam, from Jezreel (1 Sam 25:43); she is referred to as the Jezreelite, with no reference to Ahimaaz or Saul, while Abigail from Carmel can be referred to as the widow of Nabal (cf. 1 Sam 27:3; 30:5; 2 Sam 2:2).

It is possible that this sentence (v. 8) — with its strange imperfects and its unique tradition — is a remnant of an original form of Nathan's speech. It is possible; and it is not possible to say more. For this to be the case, the original introduction has to be regarded as completely lost, replaced by v. 7b. It would fit well with the emphasis in Nathan's parable on the taking of the one lamb by the man with abundant flocks. It would lead into the crimes, specified in the latter part of v. 9a, without the abstract aspect of despising — i.e., "you have struck down Uriah the Hittite with the sword, and have taken his wife to be your wife." It is possible; it would require some modification of the text; it certainly cannot be considered demonstrable or necessary. It would leave an unexplained tradition still unexplained, but it would remove it from a context where it is unexpected.

Another observation is worth noting. Verse 10a operates in the sphere of act and consequence: "now therefore the sword shall never depart from your house." Verses 11-12, to the contrary, operate within the sphere of divine causation: "I will raise up trouble against you. . . . I will take your wives before your eyes. . . . I will give them to your neighbor. . . . I will do this before all Israel." Naturally, the two spheres need not be the least exclusive of each other. The two formulations, however, are different. They may reflect different emphases (cf. Campbell, *Study Companion,* 411-36).

For a number of reasons, it has been thought that vv. 7b-12 might be an expansion of Nathan's original speech, emphasizing what is latent in the sequence of the narrative. It is possible; it is not demonstrable. Without these verses, the movement would be significant in its conceptual abruptness.

> Nathan: You are the man (v. 7a)
> David: I have sinned (v. 13a)
> Nathan: The LORD has put away your sin (v. 13b)

The remote consequences of what David has done are not "put away" by the forgiveness of his sin. Tamar will be raped, Amnon will be murdered, women will be violated, and Absalom will die. Nathan's speech recalls all this before David's confession. The first person style of v. 7b and its reference to anointing echo later prophetic passages (cf. 1 Sam 9:16; 10:1; 15:1, 17; 16:3, 12-13). An expansion is possible, perhaps even likely; its necessity is not demonstrable. Whether Nathan's interpretation is original or later, what is stunning is the instant immediacy of forgiveness. In any reading of the text, David confesses in v. 13a and in v. 13b Nathan assures him that God has put away his sin. Though the Samuel text is more complicated, there is a certain resemblance with the final exchange of Saul and Samuel.

> Saul: I have sinned . . . return with me . . . that I may worship the LORD.
> (1 Sam 15:30)
> Samuel: Samuel turned back after Saul; and Saul worshiped the LORD. (15:31)

What troubles many readers is rather that while the sinful king lives, the innocent child dies — [II.C.1]. Casuistry has to be at its mind-numbing worst to offer a justification for the death of the first child and the favor shown the second. We do not have the right to declare v. 14 late because we disagree with its content; nevertheless, it would be a brave interpreter who would argue for its being demonstrably early. The suggestion that the dead child is a substitute for David may be morally objectionable; it is unsupported in the text — v. 14 portrays punishment not substitution (against Wénin, "David roi," 92).

The way that the conception and birth of the second child is portrayed in the story is an indicator that the first child had died before ever the story was told. To that degree, the storytellers were dealing with a reality that they could not change. We may dispute the link made between David's sin and the child's death; that is our freedom as readers. The formulation — "The LORD struck the child" — is harsh and rare; among others, it is used of Nabal (1 Sam 25:38), of Israel after the golden calf (Exod 32:35) and after a loss to the Philistines (1 Sam 4:3), and in 2 Chronicles it is used of Jeroboam (13:20) and Jehoram (21:18). The tradition of David's seven days of anguished prayer and fasting followed by a total change of attitude clearly exercised a fascination (cf. v. 21). It may be that the fate of the child was emphasized to accommodate this tradition. The law in Deuteronomy is clear: children shall not be put to death for their parents' crimes; only for their own crimes may persons be put to death (Deut 24:16). We do not know when this law was first formulated. The contrary statements, preserved in the self-description of God — "visiting the iniquity of the parents upon the children . . . to the third and fourth generation" (cf. Exod 20:5; 34:7; Num 14:18; Deut 5:9) — may refer rather to the long-term consequences of sin, as reflected in the stories that follow this one. Forgiveness of what has been done does not do away with the consequences of what has been done.

David's behavior in these circumstances clearly exercised a fascination (vv. 16-23). The child died on the seventh day (v. 18). We do not know the details of David's actions over this week, but the intensity of his intercession is evident and had his entourage worried (vv. 17-18). The change of attitude described in the activities of v. 20 had them surprised — he rose, washed, anointed himself, changed his clothes, worshiped, and called for food. The formulation may be anachronistic — "the house of the LORD"; it seems the behavior, the inner becoming outer, was of lasting interest. The tradition holds examples of an apparent fatalism or realism in David's faith (e.g., 1 Sam 26:10; 2 Sam 15:25-26; 16:10-12); it may be that this is a further case. The intensity of the prayer may have effectively expressed for David the feelings of his grieving and his mourning (exacerbated by his guilt?). The level of emotional involvement is evident.

The report of David's interaction with Bathsheba can also be read as expressive of genuine caring — [II.C.2]. In Hebrew, the verb comes first: "he consoled." Then follow "David" and "Bathsheba his wife." Only then is sexual expression given to his care: he came to her, he slept with her, and she bore a son. That God loved this son, Solomon (Jedidiah) — [II.C.3] — is as inexplicable as that God should have struck the other. The sentence communicating this is odd. It begins with Nathan being sent, we presume by YHWH; it ends with a reason for the naming, "because of YHWH" (v. 25). Odd. Nathan was sent "and he named him Jedidiah"; odd, because he was already named Solomon (v. 24) and the name Jedidiah is never mentioned again in the Bible. In the biblical text, this is the last we hear of Bathsheba or Solomon until 1 Kgs 1, where Nathan and Bathsheba are working together cooperatively. The understanding of the name Solomon as evoking a replacement of the dead child is possible (Jones, *Nathan Narratives,* 111-13). The attempt to attach the name Jedidiah to the symbolic *destitution* of David in favor of his son ("la destitution symbolique de David en faveur de son fils") involves an unacceptable distortion of 1 Kgs 1 (against Wénin, "David roi," 93).

The story of David and Bathsheba is encapsulated within the account of the campaign against Rabbah — [III]. The campaign has been in the background: it is where Uriah came from; it is the reason he gave for not going down to his house in Jerusalem; it is where Uriah died. It has been going on without intruding on the story's action. There have been two completed pregnancies; perhaps there were two seasons campaigning. Within the story it has not been important. Now, at the end, the campaign comes back to the foreground. Joab is on the point of completing the capture of the city. His message to David underscores either his utter loyalty or his not inconsiderable power — or both. He, Joab, could take the city and it would apparently be called by his name. The implications we do not know, but they might have included Joab's establishment of his own Transjordanian principality. Instead, David does what he is told and presides over the capture of the city and the attendant celebrations. What precisely the inhabitants of the city were set to do escapes us; we may assume some form of public works.

"David and all the people returned to Jerusalem" (v. 31). The theme has echoes. It recurs at the start of Absalom's rebellion (2 Sam 15:8). It recurs, for Joab, at the end of these stories of David's middle years (2 Sam 20:22). Oddly enough, it recurs almost at the end of the account of Josiah's reform (2 Kgs 23:20). These are totally natural movements (like, for example, 2 Sam 17:20); for all their naturalness, they generate a power of symbolism.

Genre

As we have seen, the text gives us a (→) story, set within the broader parameters of an (→) account. Within the story, there is also a (→) prophetic judgment speech, against an individual.

As expected of an account, the material on the campaign against Rabbah (11:1a and 12:26-31) provides the necessary information on the siege and capture of the city. Joab went out with the standing army and the conscript army, took control of the Ammonite countryside, and besieged the capital Rabbah. When it was time for the final stages of the capture, he sent word to David so that the king might preside over the final triumph. Nothing is said about the duration of the campaign and the maintenance of the siege. All that is needed for a framework to the story is the opening of the campaign and its conclusion. Taken on its own, the account could well be seen as the work of a single summer; taken in conjunction with the story, it has to occupy a couple of summers at least.

The story moves through a series of stages, with an initial disequilibrium arousing interest and tension and moving to the restoration of something like equilibrium at each stage, only to have the action or plot move on to a further stage where a similar process is repeated. So, for example, David's interest in Bathsheba flags a disequilibrium; her return home is an apparent restoration of equilibrium. Her announcement of pregnancy puts paid to that. Uriah is summoned to Jerusalem and the situation is again one of disequilibrium. His return to the front and to his death, followed by David's marriage to Bathsheba, is an apparent restoration of equilibrium. God's displeasure and Nathan's intervention puts paid to that. When Nathan has returned home, the short-term tension is focused on the dying child; a long-term tension is latent: What will be the outcome of Nathan's words for the house of David? With the child's death, David's reaction to it, and the birth of a second favored child, equilibrium is restored for the moment.

Nathan's speech has the classic marks of a prophetic judgment speech: the crimes are stated and the punishment announced, with the appropriate attribution to YHWH. As we have seen, both crimes are covered with their respective punishments; there might once have been two such speeches. As it is now, they are found within the one speech of Nathan, following the parable that brought out David's anger and Nathan's condemnation: "You are the man!"

If plot is seen as controlling a story's structure by moving from exposition through forms of complication to resolution, a series of complications move the action here through its various stages. First there is Bathsheba's pregnancy, then Uriah's non-cooperation, next Nathan's intervention, and finally the fate of their first child. Each of these "complications" drives the story's action forward to a new stage.

As an independent story, the long-term tensions implicit in Nathan's words can be left latent. What Nathan says is a statement about the situation that now exists in David's house (vv. 11-12 are the exception). This story does not need to pursue the implications of that situation. The short-term issue of the fate of the child is enough. The more extensive narrative formed by bringing together a series of these stories moves precisely to address the long-term implications of what David has done.

Setting

The present setting for the story of David and Bathsheba is clearly as the lead story in the narrative of the Stories of David's Middle Years. This has been discussed above.

It is to be expected that versions of the story were told before it came into its present form and setting. The difficulty of attributing a setting to the present text as an independent David and Bathsheba story can be approached by reflecting how this story might look in a couple of different settings.

If it were to be told at David's or Solomon's court, particularly in the presence of Bathsheba, some radical changes would be necessary. At Solomon's court, certainly, the recent deaths of Adonijah, Joab, and Shimei would have been reminders of the wisdom of remaining within the politically acceptable. A possible version might be imagined as follows:

> The exquisite beauty of the Lady Bathsheba attracted the attention of the enraptured all-conquering King David. His manliness was irresistible; his royal morality, however, unassailable. Her poor boring bumbling Uriah, on duty with the army at Rabbah, tripped while facing forward and at the same time strategically retreating backward; he fell and hit his head on a rock and died at the front, opening the way for her to a fated destiny. Their first royal prince died in early infancy. The prophet Nathan, a good man and such a darling prophet, brought God's greetings and blessing to the second child, none other than Solomon.

Or something like that!

Alternatively, as the aged Shimei, of the house of Saul, might have told the story to his grandchildren, on evenings at Bahurim on the Mount of Olives, across the valley from the flickering oil lamps of Davidic/Solomonic Jerusa-

121

lem. He had it from Mephibosheth, who had it from the palace-serving girl who applied salve to his feet, and she had it from a sergeant in the royal guard. So it was certainly authentic. It could have begun as follows:

> That lecherous rake of a king, the usurper David, was in the habit of spending his early evenings prowling the palace roof, scanning the dwellings in the city below, searching for any sign of an attractive woman who might be summoned to provide his sordid evening's entertainment. Etc.

The difference in the two versions brings out the surprising neutrality and openness to interpretation of the present text. Such openness would probably not have been appreciated at the Davidic/Solomonic court.

As presently formulated, the story fits remarkably well with a setting at Jeroboam's court in the north, with particular concern for the role of the counselor in royal affairs (see the discussion of the Stories of David's Middle Years, above). There is sufficient distance from Jerusalem for such a version to be completely safe. There is sufficient openness to interpretation to constitute a challenging exercise for would-be royal counselors or to provide for the entertainment of those already skilled in the arts of counseling kings.

Meaning

A well-told story like this one has a wealth of meaning locked into it, waiting to interact with the imaginations of readers or listeners. Major trouble spots of human experience are tapped into: sexual violence, homicidal violence, political roles, divine roles, etc. What is unlocked from the text will correlate in many ways with what is brought to it. Affecting the story's meaning is also the context within which it is read. Is it read in conjunction with the stories that follow? Is it read with Nathan's interpretation of it? Its meaning is a many-headed beast.

One aspect of the story that is difficult to escape is the impact of human passion on ordered living. Passion need not be sexual; there are others: for example, jealousy, greed, ambition, anger — to name but a few. In this story passion begins with the sexual; where it goes after that is left open. The impact on ordered living is more than just the loss of Uriah's life. In the story, the palace entourage is aware of Uriah's visit to Jerusalem and where he slept; aware too of his unexpected death. An instability has been thrust on the security of their lives. We do not know where things were between David and Joab before this story; after it, all we know is that Joab has been David's willing and aware hatchet man and that there will be a cost to be paid. Nathan is God's representative in the story. Whether we name it God or however we name it, the inner reality of a person is confronted by the actions that shape their being. David may have needed Nathan to bring him to think; his actions would have had their impact whether he thought about them or not. What the impact of these actions was on Bathsheba we do not know. We know it ended one marriage and began another for her, had her carry two pregnancies to term, and brought her to the royal court; how it impacted on her we are not told.

Another aspect of the story is the potential impact on the interaction in Israel's faith of its God with its people. Royal license finds itself limited by what Israelite society symbolized as God's displeasure. To some, it may seem unfairly ambivalent; one child dies and the other is favored. Others might attribute one outcome to David and the other to Bathsheba, but both children are David's. An opening is left for forgiveness. Is God's forgiveness of David exemplified in the favor shown the second child? Is the apparent inevitability of consequences adumbrated in the death of the first? Do such consequences flow on to the following stories?

A further aspect of the story is the effect of what we might call "act–consequence" thinking. It is a strong feature of Israel's understanding of its world. The acts that people performed wove a web of consequences within which they had to live (e.g., Ps 7:16-17 [Heb.; NRSV, 7:15-16]; Prov 26:27). The web woven by David has drawn him into sexual violence and homicidal violence. Its consequences within the action of the story are the death of his child. Its consequences sketched by Nathan will never leave his house. God's forgiveness can restore God's relationship with David. Forgiveness alone cannot unravel the web that has been woven.

Bibliography of Works Cited Above

Alter, Robert. *The David Story: A Translation with Commentary of 1 and 2 Samuel.* New York: Norton, 1999.

Bach, Alice. "Signs of the Flesh: Observations on Characterization in the Bible." *Semeia* 63 (1993) 61-79.

Campbell, Antony F. *The Study Companion to Old Testament Literature: An Approach to the Writings of Pre-Exilic and Exilic Israel.* Wilmington: Glazier, 1989; Collegeville: The Liturgical Press, 1992.

Daube, David, "Absalom and the Ideal King." *VT* 48 (1998) 315-25.

Fokkelman, J. *Narrative Art and Poetry in the Books of Samuel.* Vol. 1: *King David (II Sam. 9–20 & 1 Kings 1–2).* Studia Semitica Neerlandica 20. Assen: van Gorcum, 1981.

Garsiel, Moshe. "The Story of David and Bathsheba: A Different Approach." *CBQ* 55 (1993) 244-62.

Jones, G. H. *The Nathan Narratives.* JSOTSup 80. Sheffield: Sheffield Academic Press, 1990.

Polzin, Robert. *David and the Deuteronomist: A Literary Study of the Deuteronomic History.* Part Three: *2 Samuel.* Bloomington, IN: Indiana University Press, 1993.

Smith, Henry Preserved. *Samuel.* ICC. Edinburgh: T. & T. Clark, 1898.

Sternberg, Meir. *The Poetics of Biblical Narrative: Ideological Literature and the Drama of Reading.* Bloomington, IN: Indiana University Press, 1985.

Tov, Emanuel. *Textual Criticism of the Hebrew Bible.* Minneapolis: Fortress, 1992.

Wénin, A. "David roi, de Goliath à Bethsabée: La figure de David dans les livres de

Samuel." Pages 75-112 in *Figures de David à travers la Bible: XVIIᵉ congrès de l'ACFEB* [= *l'Association catholique française pour l'étude de la Bible*] *(Lille, 1ᵉʳ-5 septembre 1997)*. Edited by L. Desrousseaux and J. Vermeylen. Paris: Cerf, 1999.

Würthwein, Ernst. *Die Erzählung von der Thronfolge Davids — theologische oder politische Geschichtsschreibung?* TS 115. Zurich: Theologischer Verlag, 1974.

Chapter 7

AMNON–TAMAR–ABSALOM (2 SAM 13–14)

Textual Issues

13:16   The MT is described as "unintelligible" (McCarter, 318). Pisano points to the Antiochian (LXX^L) text, "No brother, for the last evil is greater than the first," as close to the MT, suggesting "a textual corruption . . . rather than an alternate reading" (see pp. 128-30; also Driver, 298-99).

13:18   "In earlier times" suggests a relatively late comment of antiquarian interest; the "in," however, is syntactically troublesome. Stoebe is respectful of McCarter's "from puberty" (pp. 318-19) but opts for regarding the final word, "robes," as a late and clumsy clarification ("als ungeschickte nachträgliche Erläuterung") to be ignored (p. 322).

13:21-22   Basically, the LXX and Qumran (cf. Ulrich, 84-85) provide an explanation for David's behavior. The additional clause is accepted by most commentators, including Barthélemy (p. 265). Pisano's conclusion, however, is the outcome of thorough discussion: "it is not possible here to determine, on the merits of the plus alone, whether it should be considered original to the narrative or not" (p. 223; see pp. 219-23; also Stoebe, 322). Given the occasional ambivalence of the Samuel text toward David, while a need for explanation is appropriately felt, it may well be unwise to supply it; other reasons are possible.

13:27   The LXX adds "Absalom made a feast like a king's feast"; Qumran has space for it (Ulrich, 85). Most commentators opt for it, including Barthélemy (p. 266). Again, Pisano is reserved: "it does not seem possible to determine which form, MT or LXX, contains the original reading" (p. 225). Stoebe considers a gloss probable (p. 328).

13:34   Here again, the LXX has an expansion that most commentators have adopted, including Barthélemy (pp. 266-67). The NRSV has adopted only the designation of the road. Pisano is again reserved; it is possible that the MT has been augmented (pp. 225-32). Stoebe is also cautious (pp. 330-31).

We have here three cases where a substantial text tradition went beyond the MT. Awareness of the existence of variant versions demands caution in emending the MT — above all where the nature of the text does not require it. Storytellers must be allowed their role (cf. Campbell, "Storyteller's Role").

13:39   The LXX and Qumran (Ulrich, 106-7) have "spirit of the king" for the MT's "David the king." The feminine verb and the word order favor "spirit" here. Driver understands the verb as "failed with longing" and translates: "the spirit of the king longed to go forth unto Absalom" (p. 305). Anderson understands "spirit" as "anger" (so *BDB,* etc.) and translates: "the king's anger ceased to be actively directed against Absalom" (pp. 182, 184). So McCarter: "The meaning is rather that David is no longer openly hostile to Abishalom and, therefore, ready to be prodded step by step towards a reconciliation" (p. 344).

14:14   Barthélemy argues that the king may be understood as subject of the verb "to devise" (pp. 268-69). McCarter obtains the same sense, emending the MT in line with the LXX (p. 341). McCarter then, following Budde and others, argues for placing vv. 15-17 between vv. 7 and 8 (cf. esp. pp. 345-47); Anderson makes the same move, without discussion (pp. 182-83). The sequence achieved makes good sense; but, as McCarter notes, there is no textual support from the MT or any of the versions. Stoebe argues against the move (pp. 346-47).

14:30 In my judgment, the text of LXX, found at Qumran (4QSam^c) and in OL manuscripts, offers a classic case of what may be regarded as a reminder to storytellers of the possibilities of the situation. It reads: "Joab's servants came to him with their clothes torn and said, 'The servants of Abishalom have set the property on fire!'" (McCarter, 337, who adopts it, p. 343). Pisano is against it: "it is the shorter text of MT which is the more original here" (p. 236, cf. pp. 232-36). It is important to be aware that the LXX in this tradition may be displaying what Pisano describes as a "penchant for filling in where MT leaves actions unsaid" (p. 234).

Discussion

Chapters 13–14 bear a remarkable similarity to chs. 11–12. In both, the first chapter of the pair contains a rape and a murder that are connected. In both, the second chapter of the pair begins with a parable to open the royal eyes and moves toward some form of equilibrium. Nathan is the bringer of awakening in ch. 12; in ch. 14, it is Joab. In ch. 12, God's forgiveness comes with surprising immediacy; to the contrary, David's forgiveness comes slowly in ch. 14 — and, as we learn from outside the story, probably too late, and certainly ineffectually. In terms of narrative resemblance, David's behavior has its impact within the royal family, an impact that is internal to the royal family and without threat to David's rule. In terms of narrative portrayal, it is probably right to say that things go from bad (David) to worse (Amnon). "Even though 2 Samuel 11 and 2 Samuel 13 tell not dissimilar tales of sexual acquisitiveness and violence, both of which ultimately lead to death, the latter, in its rhetorical presentation, is identified as the darker and more terrible" (Gray, "Rhetorical Strategy," 40).

As in the case of ch. 12, the story of rape and murder here is a unity — [I]. This is not simply an observation that the murder of Amnon was the result of his rape of Tamar. Amnon's encounter with Tamar was facilitated at the beginning by the advice of Jonadab (13:3-5), and his murder was interpreted at the end by the same Jonadab (13:32-33, 35). At the beginning of the story, both Absalom and Amnon are referred to by their patronymics: Absalom ben David and Amnon ben David. Near the end of the story, Amnon is dead (v. 33) and Absalom has fled (v. 34). There is a two-year transition period between the rape and the murder; there is no suggestion of a break in the storytelling.

In this story, Tamar is the only figure portrayed with any nobility. It is not inappropriate to the story that she is featured at the start sandwiched between the two men who will reduce her to the status of "a desolate woman" (13:20). The sequence of the literal text is as follows: to Absalom ben David there was a beautiful sister, and her name was Tamar; and loved her Amnon ben David (13:1). She is sandwiched between her brother the murderer and her half-brother the rapist. Her status is noted as Absalom's sister; it is Absalom who will enjoin her to silence after Amnon has raped her.

It is also worth noting that since both Absalom and Amnon are given their full names, "son of David," David is there in the context at the start of the story — as he should be. He is involved in what happens, and questions need to be asked. He sends Tamar to her fate; he allows Amnon to go to his death. At a subtle level, the issue is present from v. 2. Its third word (in Hebrew) is a big bulky polysyllabic infinitive, in the NRSV "that he made himself ill" (*lĕhithallôt*). The word itself is impossible to miss. Amnon's condition should have been impossible to miss. Jonadab did not miss it (v. 4). Absalom had not missed it (v. 20). It would seem that David missed it; whether he did is a question that needs to be asked.

After naming the participants, the story opens with Amnon sick from desire and facing the apparent impossibility of satisfying his desire — [I.A]. The reference to Tamar as a virgin (v. 2) alludes to the isolated and cloistered circumstances in which the virgin daughters of a king were raised. Amnon's lust similarly suggests early isolation. "Individuals reared in close domestic proximity during the first six years of life . . . are automatically inhibited from strong sexual attraction and bonding when they reach sexual maturity. . . . Those affected are usually quite unable to offer a rational explanation of why they have no attraction" (Wilson, "Religion and Evolutionary Theory," 85-86). The lust is there; so is the apparent impossibility.

Verse 3 introduces Amnon's friend, Jonadab, David's nephew, son of his brother. The NRSV describes him as "a very crafty man." This may accurately reflect reality; it is a most unfortunate translation of the Hebrew, "a very wise man" (*'îš hākām mĕ'ōd*). The infamous snake in the Garden is described in the NRSV as more "crafty" than any other wild animal; the Hebrew word is *'ārûm* (cf. also Job 5:12; 15:5. In wisdom literature, the word is also used for those who are the opposite of fools, cf. Prov 12:16, 23; 13:16; 14:8, 15, 18; 22:3; 27:12). Wise counselors and wise people are described in Hebrew as *hākām*. Wisdom can be used for good ends or bad. In this story, Jonadab is portrayed as very smart. His advice gets Tamar within Amnon's reach; according to Hugo Gressmann, in ancient custom "the sick may receive female visitors" (Gressmann, "Oldest History Writing," 32). What Amnon then does is not part of Jonadab's advice. Does that exculpate Jonadab? Whatever, the modeling from Amnon's father takes over and what ought be impossible is achieved by force: "being stronger than she, he forced her" (13:14).

An aspect of the story that cannot be ignored and cannot be adequately accounted for either is the failure to make Jonadab accountable. He gave Amnon the strategy for fooling David. Too late, he told David not to be fooled (13:32-33). He is portrayed knowing exactly what was going on and he is never brought to account for it. He comes on the scene unheralded and he departs from it, never to be heard of again. What does the mysterious figure of Jonadab represent? The unthinkable: Did David put him up to it?

Jonadab's advice is swiftly given and swiftly followed — [I.B.1]. The NRSV's "pretend" in vv. 5 and 6 is unfortunate. It was not deemed necessary in v. 2; it is not necessary here. Amnon is lovesick (Jonadab: "Why are you so haggard morning after morning?" v. 4); pretence is not needed. David visits his sick son and accedes to what is a very sick request.

Jonadab's advice was available to Amnon. Where was the advice that should have been available to David? To the best of our knowledge, reinforced by v. 2, the women of the royal palace were held in high security. Before the king breached this security, where was the royal counselor to suggest at least that a trusted soldier should accompany the princess — and never leave her. Perhaps this is hindsight. Good counselors were supposed to have foresight enough not to need hindsight later.

Tamar's first line of defense has been breached; the king has failed her. The second line of defense will prove as feeble. On her arrival and after the food preparation, Amnon orders everyone to leave: "Send out everyone from me" (v. 9). And they went; not a single demur among them. They left Tamar to her fate. Her second line of defense has been breached; the social fabric has failed her. Might David have relied on such social solidarity to shield Tamar from danger? We do not know.

There are clear parallels. In the story of Naboth (1 Kgs 21), where royal power — whether exercised by Ahab or Jezebel — is used to bring about murder in order to acquire property, the biblical text is emphatic that Jezebel's letters were sent to "the elders and the nobles who lived with Naboth *in his city*" (1 Kgs 21:8), and the stratagem was executed by "the men *of his city*, the elders and the nobles who lived *in his city*" (21:11). Social complicity is involved in both stories. The dual concern for royal and social responsibility is visible in the revision of the Deuteronomistic History (Deuteronomy–2 Kings). When with the death of Josiah things have gone radically wrong, one focus of the subsequent revision blames the kings of Israel. Another focus of the revision implicates the people; they did evil and failed in fidelity to the law. So here: David, the king, has exposed Tamar to danger; her society then withdraws the protection she had every right to expect. There was apparently an awareness in Israel's reflection that the freedom of kings to do evil was served or limited by the compliance of their people.

Jonadab's stratagem has brought Tamar within Amnon's reach. Social servility has abandoned her to Amnon's power. She is left with no defense but her own resources. The story portrays her as an eloquent and honorable woman, gifted with an agile mind. The first move given her is to name the deed for what it is: an outrage *(něbālâ)*, unacceptable in Israel (v. 12). The second move is to emphasize her own situation: "where could I carry my shame?" (v. 13a, first part). The third move is to highlight his future: "you would be as one of the scoundrels *(něbālîm)* in Israel" (v. 13a, second part). Finally, the text has her offer him a way out: "speak to the king; for he will not withhold me from you" (v. 13b). Amnon does not listen to her, uses force, and rapes her.

We are ignorant about the possibility (the "way out") that Tamar puts before Amnon. If it is out of the question, she is being portrayed as desperate and bereft of hope. If it is to be treated as a way out that he refuses, it must have some narrative plausibility. The law of Israel known to us forbids it (cf. Lev 18:6, 9, 11; 20:17; Deut 27:22). We do not know whether such laws in precisely such formulation were in force in David's time (note, for example, Smith, *Samuel,* 329; Hertzberg, 322-23; Mauchline, *1 and 2 Samuel,* 260, who argue that it was considered legal at the time; possible example, Abraham in Gen 20:12).

McCarter comments about the law: "we cannot be sure" (p. 323). We do not know what rights the king might have had to make special arrangements. We do know that Amnon would not listen.

Rape is vile. Ruthlessness compounds it. The previous story has already put David's ruthlessness on display (11:25). Now Amnon shows he is his father's son. Tamar is to be put out in the street. Her protest, which looks to her support and standing in Israelite society, is ignored. By the rape, her person has been violated; by her expulsion, the social structure is assaulted. The door is bolted behind her (vv. 17-18). Amnon's words mirror the awfulness of his action. The NRSV's "Put this woman out" is all that English can do; the Hebrew is more brutal, "Put this out" *(zō't).*

In the street, Tamar has a choice. She can be silent, a silence her brother Absalom will later enjoin on her (v. 20). She can cry out and make public the shame visited upon her. Characteristically, the text does not address the options. Her immediate response is to adopt the public gestures of mourning and to cry aloud. Absalom's immediate reaction is to identify Amnon and impose silence on Tamar. The narrative does not explore his motivation. Tamar's situation is stated bluntly: she remained "a desolate woman" in her brother's house (v. 20).

Time passes; two years need to be accounted for — [I.B.2]. Nothing is said of Amnon. Something is said of two people. Of David, that he heard about it and was very angry (v. 21). Of Absalom, that he silently hated Amnon (v. 22). As short-lived emotions, these might not matter. As long-term attitudes, they prove destructive.

Of the first of these, of King David, the Hebrew has merely that he heard about it all and was very angry. Qumran and some of the Greek MSS, followed by the NRSV, add an explanation. In the NRSV, "but he would not punish his son Amnon, because he loved him, for he was his firstborn" (v. 21; see above under textual issues). It may be that this is less a textual issue than a narrative one. The added explanation opts for the more benign option. The alternative is almost unthinkably harsh: that David in his anger did nothing because he left this for the boys to sort out and discover the man fit to be his successor as king; or, worse, that David smiled because his strategy was working well. We do not normally associate such thoughts with Israel's revered King David. We might have less hesitation over such associations where certain biblical figures and certain modern dictators are concerned. The silent ambiguity of the Hebrew text may be appropriate to the telling of this story.

What follows after two years, but immediately in the text, does not alleviate anxiety about David — [I.B.3]. The text gives an unusually expansive four verses (vv. 24-27) to the exchange between Absalom and David over the invitation to a shearing party. The passage may give us insight into royal landholdings or grazing practices. Absalom's people are shearing at Baal-hazor (not mentioned elsewhere), near Ephraim. Unfortunately, the passage may give us even more insight into royal character.

Looking back at the decisions of politicians on issues of war and peace, we must often ask the question whether they were shortsighted or ruthless. The same question must be asked of David here. Was he shortsighted or was he ruthless? Other descriptors might be found; "shortsighted" will do. According to the text, David knew about "all these things" (v. 21). So he knew that Amnon had raped Tamar. He may be assumed to have known that Absalom hated Amnon for it. When the invitation to the shearing party was made, did David not realize the danger that Amnon might be incurring, away from the structures of life at the palace? If David did not realize it, was he shortsighted? If he did realize it, was David ruthless? What is the point of consecrating four verses of the narrative to this decision if it is not fraught with the weightiest of consequences? Where were the counselors who could have reflected for the king on the risks involved? Jonadab claims later to have known (vv. 32-33). He was unlikely to have been alone in this knowledge. But, in the story, the king does not take counsel. Did he need it or did he know what he was doing? Shortsighted or ruthless?

Hebrew narrative could find a briefer sequence quite adequate. For example:

- Absalom invited all the king's sons. (cf. v. 23)
- Absalom commanded all his servants: . . . "when I say to you, 'Strike Amnon,' then kill him." (cf. v. 28)

An observant reader will notice shifts of emphasis as the present narrative unfolds. First the invitation is reported as to "all the king's sons" (v. 23). Then it is extended to the king and his entourage ("servants," v. 24). The king declines the invitation, at least partially: "let us not all go" (v. 25). This "all" might denote the royal entourage and might naturally include the king's sons. At this point, all that the text has the king grant Absalom is a refusal coupled with a blessing. Absalom then asks that Amnon might come (v. 26a). The king's response, "Why should he go with you?" (v. 26b), is read in the next verse as a negative. So Absalom presses the issue "until he [the king] let Amnon and all the king's sons go with him" (v. 27).

With the explicit mention of Amnon, the danger signals are set on red alert. The text has singled out the man who raped Absalom's sister, the brother Absalom hated. David's "Why should he go with you?" (v. 26b) is a wise refusal. That the refusal is not sustained raises the question: Shortsighted or ruthless? Did David believe that Absalom might have mellowed? Did David know there was not room for both sons in his kingdom?

When narrative suddenly becomes expansive, as here, there is always the possibility that added meaning is involved. With the expansion, the king is implicated and the invitation to Amnon is highlighted. The narrative could move from v. 23 to v. 28, without vv. 24-27. Protocol suggests that it should; the king is not invited after his sons have been. Do we have two traditions combined? One, the shorter, would leave the blame unambiguously with Absalom; the other, the expansion, would implicate David. A combination is possible, but it is not of great importance. The present text leaves open an embarrassing question. Was David shortsighted or was David ruthless? Whatever of motivations and machinations, the narrative promptly has Amnon dead and the king's sons in flight. Joab killed for David; his servants kill for Absalom.

Jonadab's omniscience could be passed over; the narrative does not need it, unless it is there with meaning — [I.C]. Its meaning: Jonadab has known this was coming for two years. If Jonadab, presumably anybody else with any insight. If Jonadab, why not David? Or did David know too? It is a fearful story. Nathan would have nodded. "All the king's sons" arrived at the royal court. Apart from Absalom, Adonijah, and Solomon, we never hear of them again. It is a reminder to us of how much is not told. A story might end with the flight of the crown prince into exile. Here, the next story needs this one; the present text is an interconnected narrative.

The two-year transition after Tamar's rape is followed by a three-year transition after Amnon's murder — [II]. The text is troubled; three times it is reported that Absalom fled (vv. 34, 37, 38), the first time perhaps by Jonadab (so Mauchline, *1 and 2 Samuel,* 263), the second time mentioning the king and his town, the third time simply mentioning the town and adding the three years Absalom stayed there. Talmai, king of Geshur, was Absalom's maternal grandfather (cf. 2 Sam 3:3); Geshur was in northern Transjordan (cf. Josh 13:11, 13).

It would be unwise to assume that we are told David's state of mind where Absalom is concerned. The Hebrew is tantalizingly ambiguous. According to 13:37, Absalom fled and David "mourned for his son" — but which son, Absalom or Amnon? According to 13:39 (which needs a feminine subject, David's spirit or heart; cf. textual issues), "[the heart of/spirit of] David ceased to go out to Absalom." The NRSV has "went out, yearning for Absalom" which is beautiful, but it is not the plain meaning of the Hebrew. It may resolve an issue that should be left open; it may also confuse the meaning of the story of ch. 14. David kept Absalom at bay for two full years. Was he yearning or was he ambivalent about his son? According to 13:39, David was consoled over Amnon because he was dead. The NRSV inserts a "now" that is not in the Hebrew and has David "consoled over the death of Amnon." This may be right, but it disregards the possibility that it did not take David three years to overcome his regret that Amnon had lost out to Absalom. Perhaps that possibility should not be disregarded. Finally, according to 14:1, "Joab son of Zeruiah perceived that the king's mind was on Absalom." What the text does not tell us is whether David was yearning, fearing, worrying, or simply reflecting. Chapter 14 will tell us where Joab's mind was; the king should "bring his banished one home again" (v. 13). It does not tell us if that is where David's heart was. It is what, in the story, David did; it appears that it was not where his heart was. Is David portrayed as ambivalent?

The story that follows is a story about Joab — [III]. He plays a more decisive role in ch. 14 than even Nathan played in ch. 12. He decides to influence the king; he sets up the parable to be acted out before the king; he acts on the order he has elicited from the king and brings Absalom to Jerusalem; he is the target of Absalom's resentful anger; he mediates with the king. As in ch. 20 to come, so here the story is about Joab. In due course, Joab will kill Absalom. In the narrative is that a confession that he has misjudged his man?

In the story, David might have been wise to seek counsel before sending Tamar to Amnon. He might have been wise to have sought counsel before sending Amnon to Absalom's shearing party. At this point in the story, he would have been wise to have sought counsel before sending Joab to bring Absalom back. In hindsight, the options are clear: bring Absalom back and forgive him; bring Absalom back and punish him; send a message to Geshur that Absalom is never to return. David did none of these and that may have been David's mistake.

The language of the story is worth observing. "David" does not occur once in ch. 14. "The king" occurs forty times. Joab gets fifteen references and Absalom thirteen. In ch. 13, reference to "the king" is far more frequent than to "David." This is in accord with the linguistic pattern of these Stories of David's Middle Years, but the preponderance of references to "the king" is higher here than in the surrounding text. The observation is minor but it raises the possibility of an originally independent story. The use of the mother's name, "Joab son of Zeruiah," in 14:1 may point in the same direction. In these Stories of David's Middle Years (2 Sam 11–20), this is the only reference to Joab in this fuller form. In the books of Samuel, it is used otherwise at 2 Sam 2:13, suggesting again the beginning of an originally independent story there, and at 2 Sam 8:16, the list of David's officials (but without the "patronymic" in the similar list in 2 Sam 20:23-26). In the texts of 1 Samuel, Joab does not figure (except as Abishai's brother, 1 Sam 26:6).

In 2 Sam 20, Joab operates at a distance from David. He goes out to Abel a subordinate; he returns to Jerusalem a chief. In this story, he operates close to his king. It is Joab's perception that the time has come to move his king to action (14:1). As we have noted above, the text does not tell us whether Joab moves to help the king make up his mind or whether, the king's mind being made up, Joab moves to help the king put his thoughts into action. Either is possible. Given that six years down the track Absalom will lead a rebellion against his father, this might be told as a cautionary tale reminding kings that power-brokers should not be allowed to preempt the role of counselors. As usual, the text leaves the questions unasked and the possibilities unexplored.

Joab sends for a wise woman (*'iššâ ḥăkāmâ*) from Tekoa — [III.A]. We do not know precisely what the role or position is that is designated as "a wise woman." We meet another, also involved with Joab, in 2 Sam 20:16, where in that story she has a leadership role in the town (cf. the different usage in Exod 35:25). Here, we can surmise two things about her. First, being from Tekoa she is an outsider whom David should not recognize. Tekoa is to the south of Bethlehem, but Joab probably knew more about the travels of the young David than we do; since joining Saul, David has had little time to visit distant towns. Second, she is a skilled actor and storyteller. She needs costume and make-up (14:2). To do what Joab wants, her storytelling skills and her ability to improvise have to be of the highest order; otherwise, she is likely to risk her life. It is likely she was a professional.

Like Nathan, she puts a parable before the king. She pleads for the life of her sole surviving son, the murderer of his brother. She pleads for her own survival ("my one remaining ember") and her husband's name and remnant (v. 7). Like Nathan's parable, this one too is different enough for David to fail to associate it with his experience of three years ago. So David grants her wish and is locked into it (vv. 8-11).

Then she turns her parable on David. Nathan had it easy; all he had to say was: "You are the man." Her task is more difficult. David has ordered the protection of her son. Now she applies this to David's son in exile. "Banished" is a little strong on her part; as we have the narrative, Absalom fled rather than being exiled or banished. Reality may be more important than words and David may not be yearning for his son. Joab may have grounds for knowing that Absalom is indeed banished. Joab wants Absalom home and has the woman implicate God in such plans. After this daring departure from her cause, her speech modulates back into the original case she placed before the king.

Some interpreters would like to rewrite her speech, placing vv. 15-17 immediately after v. 7 (so, for example, Budde, *Samuel,* 267; Mauchline, *1 and 2 Samuel,* 266-67; Ackroyd, *Second Book of Samuel,* 131-33). The temptation is to be resisted. Verse 15a is skillfully ambiguous; v. 16 returns attention to the parable, while the "heritage of God" can have national echoes; v. 17 has the courtly elegance needed for a graceful conclusion.

David is not fooled and asks: "Is the hand of Joab with you in all this?" (v. 19). The scene ends with the woman's exercise of exquisite diplomatic skill; she flatters the king. The narrative flatters Joab even more; "to change the course of affairs" (v. 20) is an aim granted elsewhere only to God (cf. 1 Kgs 12:15). Note: a different rendering of v. 20 is to be found in the NAB — "to approach the issue in a roundabout way."

Did David know what Joab wanted? — [III.B] We are not told. If David was moved to action by the woman's parable, what were his feelings toward Absalom? We are not told. Is David giving in to Joab, rather than following his own desires? We are not told, but v. 24 suggests that Joab is prevailing over David's better judgment. We are not told what that better judgment might have been. What we are told is that Absalom is brought back to Jerusalem and barred from appearing at court.

Again there is a transition, a passage of time (cf. Conroy, *Absalom,* 110). The condition imposed on Absalom's return is spelled out (v. 24). Then comes the transition. After it, the time that has passed is specified and the observance of the condition noted (v. 28). Almost as a distraction, to fill the two-year gap, we are treated to a description of Absalom's beauty and his luxuriant growth of hair and his children, three sons and a daughter — Tamar, a beautiful woman. We know nothing of what has happened to the other Tamar. We are reminded of her here. Later in the narrative, Absalom's claim to have no son is noted (18:18). Possibilities for harmonization can be surmised; we do not know.

The narrative resumes — [III.C]. Two full years have passed. Joab, who had engineered Absalom's return, appears to have gone cold on the project. We are not told why. Two approaches from Absalom are ignored. Drastic measures are needed — setting fire to Joab's field. Unresolved issues are latent in Absalom's "if there is guilt in me, let him kill me" (v. 32). The issue remains unresolved within this story. Joab confers with the king. Absalom is summoned to the king. "The king kissed Absalom" (v. 33). It is very formal. David's name has not been used throughout the chapter, so we should not expect it here. It would appear that father and son are reunited rather than reconciled. We are not told.

Genre

The genre is one of (→) story. There are potentially three stories here: of Amnon and the rape of Tamar; of Absalom and the murder of Amnon; of Joab and the return of Absalom. There are potentially three; in reality there is one — the story of the impact of David's folly on David's family. Even that is not quite accurate. For this story — made up of these three stories — is one in a collection of stories that are tightly enough interwoven that none can survive on its own, in its present form.

The tension of plot is unfolded as the story progresses. Amnon's lust is the stuff that energizes story. Will David's wisdom safeguard Tamar? Will the solidarity of the society in which she lives be her protection? Will her own integrity and intelligence be enough to keep her safe? When she is let down by all three, she is left a desolate woman. Her father is angry and does nothing. Her brother hates her violator. Hatred too energizes story. Once again the issue rises: Will David's wisdom safeguard his heir? Will Absalom's hatred be blocked? Amnon is left to his fate and meets his death. Absalom takes to flight, leaving the story uncertain as to its end. Will the man who is now heir remain in exile? Will he return? Will he be reconciled with the king, his father? For the third time, David does nothing, and it is Joab who pulls on the reins of power. And the outcome of the story: return, yes; reconciliation, no — not in the light of what is to come.

Setting

As with all the components of these Stories of David's Middle Years, the literary setting of the story is within the great collection. As already discussed, a possible, even probable, setting for the collection would be at the court of Jeroboam, at the beginning of the northern kingdom.

David's passivity contrasts with his decisive intervention in favor of Solomon in 1 Kgs 1. If versions of these three stories were to have been told in the courts of either David or Solomon, they would have needed to be radically different from the text we have before us. It is probable that this text, in its present form, would not have come to us independently of the collected Stories of David's Middle Years. It, or its three component stories, could well have circulated in the same setting as the later collection. There is a marked reciprocity between setting and story.

Meaning

These are well-told stories, abounding in unasked questions and devoid of easy answers. Meaning is more than usually elusive. The effects of David's sin within his own family and his own fate are there. The sowing of the seeds of rebellion within his kingdom is there (cf. Ackroyd, *Second Book of Samuel,* 123). What weight do we give to the context and complications within which these are told?

David's passivity portrayed in chs. 13–14 contrasts oddly with his activity in chs. 11–12. He takes Bathsheba; he eliminates Uriah; he intercedes with passion for his child. But in chs. 13–14, he sends an unprotected Tamar to an overheated Amnon; he sees rape in his palace and his family and he does nothing; he gives permission for Amnon to be where he will be murdered; he vacillates over reconciliation with his murdering son. In chs. 13–14, the active roles are taken by his senior sons (we hear nothing of Chileab), following in their father's footsteps with rape and murder. What is common within these contrasts for David is that he is not portrayed seeking any counsel. In the first story, he is portrayed acting energetically but without taking counsel. How different his actions might have been had he been wisely advised. In the second story, his passivity might have been moderated by the influence of good counsel. But none was taken. Meaning can be found in these instances where wise counsel might have induced far more benign outcomes.

Meaning can be seen in the power of modeling. The king acted on one impulse in his action with Bathsheba and was swept into a chain of impulsive acts. Even his attempt to influence God over his dying son smacks of the impulsive. Amnon needs only one thing: the opportunity to act on his overwhelming impulse. Absalom nurses his impulse while he waits for his opportunity to kill Amnon. David's impulses are swayed by Joab's manipulation; no modeling here — no wisdom either.

Very dark meaning might be seen in the passions of politics and power. David wanted Bathsheba, so he took her. Uriah proved a problem, so David had him killed. God seemed to be in David's way, and even there David tried to get his own way. Was David too obsessed with the politics of power to see what was under his nose and so delivered Tamar to her rapist? Could he possibly have wanted it that way? Macchiavelli might have thought so, but the odds are surely against it. Here, we should give David the benefit of the doubt. The story might well allow for the assumption that when David visited Amnon, presumably courtiers were around the crown prince; David could have expected — unwisely perhaps — that people's presence was all the protection Tamar needed. Later though, the narrative seems not to allow such excuses. Was David blind enough to the obvious that he allowed Amnon to walk into Absalom's trap? Did he want it that way? Did Joab have Absalom brought back, thinking king and heir could be reconciled — and realize he was wrong? Is that why Joab ultimately killed Absalom; or did David want it? The interplay of power between David and Joab is extremely subtle. The interplay of power around David's court may have been extremely subtle. If so, it was also very dark. Would wiser counsel have brought some light? Are the stories told the way they are so that such issues might be raised and discussed? Wise counselors explore the unthinkable.

Is meaning to be sought in reflection on the causes from which events flow and the influences that can be brought to bear on them? Modeling is, of course, part of this. Joab's intervention is another aspect of it. However 14:20 is understood, it is clear that Joab is attempting to direct the course of events. What might be the implications of this attempt? Had Joab left well alone, there might have been no rebellion. Had Joab made sure of David's readiness for a full and immediate reconciliation, there might have been no rebellion. Instead, in his effort to direct events, Joab may have contributed to Absalom's ultimate rebellion and so — to some degree — to his own killing of Absalom, his own demotion, his killing of Amasa, and even to his own death. David's need for support from Judah and Joab's error in backing Adonijah were contributory factors. An aspect of the meaning of this narrative may well be to invite reflection on the complexity of causation that unfolds in public affairs. 2 Sam 14 and 20, looking back to chs. 13–14 (and of course chs. 11–12) and bracketing chs. 15–19, situate Joab firmly within this web of complexity, woven so intricately round the figure of David.

Bibliography of Works Cited Above

Ackroyd, Peter R. *The Second Book of Samuel.* CBC. Cambridge: Cambridge University Press, 1977.

Campbell, Antony F. "The Storyteller's Role: Reported Story and Biblical Text." *CBQ* 64 (2002) 427-41.

Conroy, Charles. *Absalom Absalom!: Narrative and Language in 2 Sam 13–20.* AnBib 81. Rome: Biblical Institute, 1978.

Gray, Mark. "A Chip Off the Old Block? Rhetorical Strategy in 2 Samuel 13.7-15: The Rape of Tamar and the Humiliation of the Poor." *JSOT* 77 (1998) 39-54.

Gressmann, Hugo. "The Oldest History Writing in Israel." Pages 9-58 in *Narrative and Novella in Samuel: Studies by Hugo Gressmann and Other Scholars, 1906-1923.* Edited by D. M. Gunn. Sheffield: Almond, 1991. German original, 1921.

Mauchline, John. *1 and 2 Samuel.* NCB. London: Oliphants, 1971.

Smith, Henry Preserved. *Samuel.* ICC. Edinburgh: T.&T. Clark, 1898.

Wilson, E. O. "Religion and Evolutionary Theory." Pages 82-90 in *Religion, Science, and the Search for Wisdom: Proceedings of a Conference on Religion and Science, September 1986.* Edited by D. M. Byers. Washington, DC: National Conference of Catholic Bishops, 1987.

Chapter 8

DAVID'S RETREAT AND RETURN
(2 SAM 15–19)

2 Sam 15–19 is the indivisible core of the Stories of David's Middle Years. These five chapters, with their 165 verses, form an irreducible unity. David leaves Jerusalem, in flight from Absalom; Absalom is killed and his army routed; David returns to Jerusalem, making political moves during his return as he had in his flight. The plot is such that it cannot be subdivided into component stories. As we have noted, the surrounding stories are interwoven into a single whole by the absence of openings or conclusions. From the point of view of plot, they are susceptible of independent existence. This can be said, more or less, of chs. 11–12, of chs. 13–14, or even of the three component stories, suitably adjusted, of course, and of ch. 20. Episodes in chs. 15–19 could be shaped into independent stories; but in the present text, from the point of view of plot, they are not. Some interpreters have thought to identify a base narrative and a negative overlay, but without fragmenting the plot. As the present narrative proceeds, the plot is such that it cannot be reasonably divided into component stories. 2 Sam 15–19 is the indivisible core.

The interweaving within the elements across chs. 15–19 forms a tight web. Ten women of David's household ("concubines," secondary wives, *pîlagšîm*) are left behind to care for the palace; in the middle of the narrative, they are publicly violated by Absalom (16:22) and, at its end, they are secluded under guard by David (20:3). Ittai commits himself and his troops to David at the start. In the decisive battle, Ittai commands one of the three divisions of David's army (18:2). He and his men are not mentioned again. Zadok and Abiathar are sent back into Jerusalem with their sons. In the middle of the story, they will send a crucial message to David (17:15-21); after the battle, Ahimaaz, Zadok's son, takes a message to David (18:19-30); at the end, David uses Zadok and Abiathar to rally support in Judah (19:12-14 [Heb.; NRSV, 19:11-13]). On the Mount of Olives, David prays that Ahithophel's counsel be turned into foolishness. In 17:1-14, Hushai's counsel is preferred to Ahithophel's and Ahithophel commits suicide (17:23). Hushai is sent into Jerusalem to join Absalom and be David's informer; he achieves the goals that were set him. Also on the Mount of Olives, Ziba meets the king with supplies and negative news concerning Mephibosheth. At the Jordan, on his return, David is met by both Ziba and Mephibosheth (19:17-31 [Heb.; NRSV, 19:16-30]). At Bahurim, on the Mount of Olives, Shimei cursed David. At the Jordan, on David's return, Shimei arrives with Benjaminites to pledge his loyalty (19:17-24 [Heb.; NRSV, 19:16-23]). Finally, when David comes to Mahanaim, Barzillai is one of three who provide him with supplies. Again, at the end of the narrative, Barzillai's loyalty is recognized and rewarded (19:32-41 [Heb.; NRSV, 19:31-40]). The web is tight indeed (for reflection on the highly stylized literary composition, cf. Polzin, "Curses and Kings," 206-13).

There is a difference in these five chapters from their surroundings. The density of action is remarkable. In 2 Sam 11–12, two chapters are spent on two episodes: Bathsheba's violation and Uriah's murder. In 2 Sam 13–14, again two chapters arc spent on two episodes: Tamar's rape and Amnon's murder. In 2 Sam 20, one chapter suffices for Joab's return to power. In 2 Sam 15–19, to the contrary, action is packed on action. Jerusalem is to be abandoned. The "concubines" are to be left there. Ittai is to come with David. Zadok and Abiathar are to return with the ark to the city. Hushai is to collaborate with Absalom. Ziba curries favor with David. Shimei curses David. Absalom meets Hushai. The "concubines" are publicly violated. Ahithophel and Hushai trade counsel. Messengers are observed. Messengers inform David. And so on. The openness to question is constantly there. Counseling is central, as the story of Ahithophel and Hushai makes clear. The political lessons are there to be learned or at least discussed. The narrative does not dwell on them but moves inexorably to the next action. A minor stylistic observation highlights this aspect. The particle "behold" or "see" *(hinnēh)* — often not explicitly represented in the NRSV — occurs twenty-two times in these five chapters; it does not occur at all in chs. 11-14 and ch. 20. There is an almost visual immediacy to the narrative style. Nevertheless, the reflective issues are there.

There is a strange ambivalence in the stories of these chapters that has long been remarked. The narrative traces the path of a political craftsman, weaving alliances, cementing loyalties, assuring communications, and setting stratagems in place. Yet in the middle of it stand two sentences placing all of this within the directing will of God. David's prayer: "O LORD, I pray you, turn the counsel of Ahithophel into foolishness" (15:31). The narrator's comment: "For the LORD had ordained to defeat the good counsel of Ahithophel, so that the LORD might bring ruin on Absalom" (17:14). In all of this politicking, faith claimed that God's will was being achieved; but only one sentence, 17:14, declares it — without any reference to the royal prayer of 15:31.

Within this core story, two quite different issues can focus our attention. One is part of the overarching whole and we cannot answer it: why did David immediately take flight from Jerusalem to Transjordan? The second focus is the detail of each encounter as this consummate strategist leaves Jerusalem and returns there (cf. Conroy, *Absalom*, 89-90).

We do not know why David's response to the news of Absalom's rebellion was: "Get up! Let us flee, or there will be no escape for us from Absalom"

(15:14). Why should David abandon the reputedly impregnable Jerusalem? A possibly satisfactory answer would be that David had been kept informed all along of Absalom's preparations and of the strength and numbers supporting the conspiracy. In such a hypothesis, David could be expected to have laid his plans; he was ready to move to their immediate execution. Whether he was well informed or taken by surprise, we still do not know why the strategy adopted was appropriate. We do not know the depth of support for Absalom among the tribes west of the Jordan. We do not know what support existed for David across the Jordan to the east. Beyond the supplies provided by Shobi, Machir, and Barzillai, no troops are mentioned (17:27-29). David mustered "the men who were with him" (18:1); the battle was fought between "the men of Israel" and "the servants of David" (18:7). Did the territory east of the Jordan offer David a better opportunity for his mercenaries against Absalom's supporters? We are not told. Did a campaign across the Jordan, with the battle fought in the forest of Ephraim (18:6), have a better chance of sparing tribal lands from the ravages of war and its aftermath? We are not told. Were David's chances better on the open battlefield than cooped up defensively in a besieged city? We are not told. We do not know what drove David's strategic vision. We do know the details of his encounters along the way, and they are brilliantly told.

The overall structure can be represented as follows.

Modeling within the royal family: external impact 15:1–19:44 (NRSV, 43)

Textual Issues

15:7 Both the MT and the LXX have an unreal "forty" years. "Four" is closer to probability and is attested by some MS traditions, going back as far as LXX^L. It is adopted by most commentators. Possibilities exist as to how the "forty" might have come about.

    15:20 The MT is difficult (cf. Driver, 314); the LXX adds: "May the LORD show you," adopted by most commentators. Stoebe takes a different approach, understanding the Hebrew as a traditional salutation (p. 364).

    15:24 Both the MT and the LXX have something equivalent to "and Abiathar came up" in the middle of the verse, in conjunction with the setting down of the ark. Driver's puzzlement is evident (p. 315). Barthélemy suggests, with the medievals, that Abiathar may have stepped up out of the way (pp. 274-75). Stoebe suggests interpretation of the Greek "Baithar" should not be attempted (p. 365) and Anderson follows LXX^L in omitting the phrase (p. 201).

    15:27 Both the MT and the LXX agree on the text. Rather than "Are you a seer?" the MT can be understood with the LXX as the equivalent of "You see how things are" (cf. Barthélemy, 275-76). Abiathar is not mentioned, while clearly present in v. 29; the fact can be recognized without emending the text.

    16:12 The MT Kethib can be read as "on my iniquity"; the LXX has the equivalent of "upon my affliction." Driver, and most commentators, favor the LXX reading (cf. Driver, 318-19, preferring this to "the iniquity done to me"). Barthélemy adduces medieval evidence for reading the MT Kethib in the sense of the LXX (p. 277).

16:14 Both the MT and the LXX agree on the text, without reference to the Jordan. It is given in some LXX[L] manuscripts and elsewhere. While in the light of 15:28 it may not be needed (Barthélemy, 278), the location is right (cf. 17:21-22).

17:3 The MT is difficult. Most commentators favor the text of the LXX (cf. Driver, 320-21; McCarter, 381-82). Barthélemy (pp. 278-80) and Stoebe (p. 385) stay with the MT, despite its admitted difficulties. The overall sense remains clear.

17:9 LXX[L] has the equivalent of "the troops" without specifying whose (cf. McCarter, 382). Anderson (p. 211) and Stoebe (p. 386) retain the MT.

17:20 The key word of the MT's description of where the two boys went is totally opaque to us. McCarter lays out the issues carefully and qualifies his own view — "in the direction of the watercourse" — as "tentative" (p. 383); Anderson opts for another ancient view, "hurriedly" (p. 212). "Uncertain" is about as certain as one can get.

17:25 Two issues trouble this verse: Was Amasa's father Israelite (so MT and LXX) or Ishmaelite, and was Abigail the daughter of Nahash or of Jesse (cf. 1 Chr 2:13-17)? Most commentators opt for Amasa's father as an Ishmaelite (e.g., Driver, 326). On the other issue, Driver opts for uncertainty. On the first issue, Barthélemy opts for a northern Israelite; it sits uncomfortably with 2 Sam 19:14-15 (Heb.; NRSV, 19:13-14); 20:4. On the second (daughter of Nahash), McCarter comments: "this is an apparent error, but there is no reliable textual witness to contradict it. As Zeruiah's sister, Abigail was Jesse's daughter" (p. 392). The language describing their relationship is unusual (literally: who came to Abigail); it invites conjecture but does not communicate certainty.

18:3 In the middle of the verse, the LXX reads "you" ('attâ) instead of "now" ('attâ); it is adopted by Driver and most commentators (pp. 327-28).

18:9 The LXX uses the same word for what happened to Absalom's head and his hair. Apparently, 4QSam[a] supports "suspended" (Ulrich, 88; Barthélemy, 285); Stoebe points to support for understanding the MT appropriately (pp. 398-99). The meaning is clear.

18:12 In the quotation from David's appeal, the MT has the equivalent of "whoever you are": the LXX, the equivalent of "for me" or "for my sake" (cf. v. 5). Opinions are divided. McCarter outlines both options and introduces a third (p. 401).

18:29 Despite the witness of the LXX, since Wellhausen the verse has often been streamlined, omitting an apparent duplication (cf. Driver, 332). Barthélemy (pp. 287-88) and Stoebe (p. 410) argue for maintaining the MT.

19:11-13 (NRSV, 10-12) The complexity here is due to the parts of the verses being scattered in different order over the MT, LXX[B], and LXX[L]. Pisano (pp. 57-61) offers an overall presentation of the three verses involved. The key point is whether the clause, "and the talk of all Israel has come to the king," is to be located (with LXX) at the end of v. 11 (= NRSV, v. 10), where some consider it necessary to explain David's actions in the following verse (cf. McCarter, 415), or whether, alternatively, the clause remains where the MT has it and where it can be read as a pluperfect, "had come to the king" (see Stoebe, 416). To complicate matters, LXX^L repeats at the end of v. 13 (NRSV, v. 12) the phrase about the talk of all Israel coming to the king (using a different word for "talk"). Pisano may be right that we can see at the core of all this "an accidental dislocation of an entire clause in MT whose original position was maintained in LXX" (p. 61). Alternatively, we are seeing how different versions preferred to present a key issue.

19:18-19 (NRSV, 17-18)   Driver is helpful on these verses (p. 335; cf. McCarter, 416, 420; Stoebe, 420-21). Ziba's retinue provided help to the royal household in the business of its river crossing.

19:27 (NRSV, 26)   Most translate the verse as a command: "Saddle a donkey for me" (so LXX). Driver notes the possibility that the MT is reporting Mephibosheth's intentions (p. 336); so Stoebe, staying with the MT (pp. 420, 422 — your servant thought, "I'll have my ass saddled"). Similarly Barthélemy (p. 292).

Discussion

Often enough, the justification for a structure analysis emerges from the realization that it gives a shape to the text that accounts for its totality and that the junctions are legitimated by the syntax of the text itself. Sometimes this needs to be pointed out, sometimes it finds its place in the discussion, and sometimes it is too clear to need mention.

The structure of chs. 15–19 covers an extensive text. The major divisions are flight, conflict, and return. The divisions within these three probably need some attention to emphasize that they are grounded in the text itself; they are not the elaborated imaginings of a modern interpreter. At the same time, while the structure of chs. 15–19 has an autonomy of its own, the overall structure needs to be noted that eventuates when these chapters are brought together with the others to form the Stories of David's Middle Years, the present biblical text. Within this present text, reflecting multiple aspects of David's behavior that lurk in what precedes — his ruthlessness in achieving his aims, his carelessness of proper administration, his dependence on Joab — this narrative block reveals the external impact of David's behavior on the royal family, specifically on Absalom's posing a grave threat to David's rule. It is surely not the central message of the block; it is, however, appropriate as reflecting one role of the block within the present whole.

The first three episodes are clearly associated with Jerusalem. The decision to leave is taken in the city. The exchange with Ittai takes place as the troops are reviewed passing the last house, on the city's edge. Exactly where the exchange with Abiathar and Zadok happens is unclear. Verse 23 has the king crossing the Wadi Kidron, just outside the city; verse 24 has the ark put down until the last of the people had passed out of the city. Whether near the city boundary or across the wadi is unclear; the difference is not much.

A pointer to associating the first three episodes with the city is the statement in 15:30 that David began "the ascent of the Mount of Olives." What follows takes place on this mountain, just before the top (v. 31), at the summit (vv. 32-36), a little beyond the summit (16:1-4), at Bahurim (vv. 5-13). Finally, the royal party "arrived weary at the Jordan" (v. 14), the mountain behind them.

The shift of scene back to Jerusalem and Absalom and Ahithophel is signaled in 16:15. The battle of the counselors takes us through to 17:23. The narrative then takes up the battle of the armies. Its aftermath includes Absalom's death, the news brought to David, and the king's reaction.

With 19:10 (Heb.; NRSV, 19:9), the narrative's attention moves back across the Jordan to the context for what is to follow — whether the last clause of v. 9 (NRSV, v. 8) concludes what precedes (so: MT) or opens what follows (so: LXX and NRSV) is open to interpretation. "All the tribes of Israel" were arguing the appropriateness of "bringing the king back" (cf. 19:10). David's message, via Abiathar and Zadok, is aimed at ensuring that Judah is to the forefront in bringing back the king (vv. 11-15). The exchanges with Shimei, Mephibosheth, and Barzillai are all held at the Jordan, but on the east side. David's crossing of the Jordan is not reported until 19:40 (NRSV, 39); he comes to Gilgal, on the western bank, before the mountain, in v. 41a (NRSV, v. 40a).

The narrative's location for the final debate — headed here, "on the way to Jerusalem" — cannot be pinned down with precision. The NRSV has the people bring the king "on his way" (v. 40b; Heb., v. 41b) but, alas, the Hebrew does not guarantee that understanding. Sheba was "there," but "there" (20:1) could have been anywhere between the Jordan and Jerusalem. 20:2 insists that the people of Judah stuck with their king "from the Jordan to Jerusalem." The entire debate could have taken place at Gilgal, with Sheba's rebellion proclaimed there. The debate could have dragged on as the group climbed the mountain on the way to Jerusalem, with Sheba's rebellion proclaimed at some point along the way, probably at the summit. The text does not tell us. It would seem that the place does not matter; what matters is the fragility of David's hold on power that is so easily challenged again by rebellion. The narrative concern is with David's future in Jerusalem. "On the way to Jerusalem" may be geographically uncertain; as a narrative heading, it is satisfactory.

It is important to note how tightly interwoven these stories are. The story of Sheba's revolt has to begin in 20:1. The end of David's journey home is not reached until 20:2. 20:3 is concerned with David's activities in Jerusalem, providing for the ten women he had left behind in Jerusalem (15:16) and whom Absalom had publicly violated (16:22). While this is happening in Jerusalem, Sheba's rebellion is under way in the north.

It is time to return to the beginning and review the details that are significant for fully understanding chs. 15–19.

The preparations for Absalom's rebellion are the necessary prelude to the drama of the chapters that follow — [I]. 15:1 begins with one of the standard temporal clauses ("After this") that allow narratives to be linked together and assumes their sequence. Without the temporal clause, the beginning is rather too abrupt for an independent story in Hebrew narrative. If an independent story was needed, minor modifications could easily be made (cf. 1 Kgs 1:5a).

We do not know the exact significance of the "fifty men to run ahead of him" (15:1; cf. 1 Kgs 1:5b). For Adonijah, it is coupled with the statement of intention: "I will be king"; as a sign of rank and importance, it would have been the equivalent of a motorcycle escort in today's politics. Juxtaposed so closely with Absalom's reunion with "the king," David his father, the text has to expose the reunion as a failed reconciliation. Too little too late.

Two planks seem central to the platform for Absalom's rebellion: the promise of social justice and the issue of personal popularity. The demand for justice had kicked off one of the traditions of how kingship came about in Israel. As judges, the prophet Samuel's sons "took bribes and perverted justice" (1 Sam 8:3). As a result, the elders of Israel came to Samuel and asked for a king, for monarchy as their central government. The implication of Absalom's pitch is that David was not adequately providing justice for the people. No modern would trust a politician's attacks on his adversary; on the other hand, the claim appears to have mustered popular support. There is a sense of David's distance from his people in the charge leveled by Absalom. "There is no one deputed by the king to hear you" (v. 3b); gone are the days when appeal was made to the king in person. Absalom is portrayed taking an interest in the supplicants coming to the capital. Who are you? Where are you from? What are the details of your case? Verse 5 suggests that, when people treated him deferentially, he reached out to them and drew them into a personal embrace. Modern politicians kiss babies and press the flesh; Absalom is portrayed pressing the flesh and kissing the litigants. Over four years, it worked: "So Absalom stole the hearts of the people of Israel" (v. 6).

A further pointer to the popular nature of Absalom's movement is that the two hundred from Jerusalem — supposedly the elite — are portrayed knowing nothing of it, while the word had been spread through the countryside. The question that is not raised by the text, but that we can hardly avoid, is whether David knew of Absalom's preparations. We are not told. We are entitled to think that a competent king should have known what was going on in his kingdom — especially if it was spread over a period of time and extended through "all the tribes of Israel" (v. 10). Saul knew what David was up to and complained that he was being kept in the dark (1 Sam 22:7-8). Absalom's public moves — his chariot and escort and interviews — would hardly have passed unnoticed. So the question is there, unasked by the text and unanswered in it: What did David know?

Ahithophel is at Giloh, much nearer to Hebron than to Jerusalem. His role later marks a critical turning point in the rebellion (cf. 17:14). As David's counselor, was he innocent and ignorant, like the invited two hundred? The text does not say so. Given his advice later, it seems likely that he was privy to the conspiracy. Again, we have to ask ourselves the inevitable question: What was a man whose wisdom was considered almost divine (16:23) doing on the side of a revolutionary? We are not told.

Preparations for rebellion are one thing — [II.A.1.a]. The full drama of it all unfolds when the news is brought to David: "The hearts of the Israelites have gone after Absalom" (15:13). The oddness of David's reaction has to be noted. He opts to leave the city immediately. Some of the implications have been noted earlier. If David had advance intelligence of Absalom's moves, the absence of consultation can be accounted for; strategies were devised and plans were laid in advance. Why the strategy of flight we are not told. Presumably, there were advantages for David in moving across the Jordan; we are not told what they were. We can think of the horrors of a siege, of the loss of life among an attacking army against an impregnable city, of the wisdom of luring Absalom away from his base of popular tribal support. The reality is that we are not told and we do not know.

A tiny pointer may be given in the response to the king: "Your servants are ready to do whatever our lord the king decides" (v. 15). The NRSV's "decides" is a satisfactory rendering of the Hebrew "chooses" *(yibḥar)*. In the Hebrew Scriptures, this is the only place where this verb is used for a royal decision. God or the people choose kings; God chose Jerusalem. Only here does a king choose. Here the response to the king is not "whatever my lord says" or "whatever my lord commands," but "whatever my lord chooses." The implication appears to be that there are options that require the king to decide; they are not raised for discussion. When reading the text, we have to ask ourselves these questions. Counselors to kings have to ask themselves these sorts of questions. The text leaves us on our own with them.

The ten "concubines" left to look after the palace become the symbol of Absalom's definitive estrangement from his father (16:21-22). At the end, they remain secluded in David's Jerusalem until their deaths, a symbolic reminder of the fragility of the kingdom. Their special status is evident in 16:21; it is confirmed, for example, in 2 Sam 3:7 or 1 Kgs 2:22. The stories are told well after the event. With the mention of these unfortunate women, the whole narrative and its outcome are evoked.

More than that, a strong signal is being sent with the mention of these ten women. A king who leaves behind ten significant women of his household "to look after the house" is not abandoning his city; he is leaving it with intent to return. The narrative that reports this action is arousing an expectation in its hearers or readers. The question becomes all the more insistent: why did David flee from the city? The fate of these women is not a matter of cultural disparagement. That they were secluded in Jerusalem under guard until their deaths means that for a long time Jerusalem housed a reminder of Absalom's ability to rouse the people to revolt, of his having entered the abandoned city, and having shamed his father. Something in this narrative is calling for discernment.

The king and "all the people" left the city and halted at the last house — [II.A.1.b]. The identification of the participants is problematic. Verse 16, in a similar phrase, refers to all the royal household *(kol bêtô);* here the reference is to all the people *(kol hā'ām).* "The people" *(hā'ām)* is one of those words that has evolved through several phases; its meaning has included family, army, and people. These cannot be neatly compartmentalized; overlaps occur. The city's inhabitants seem appropriate here. The group with David halted at the edge of the city and apparently passed in review the standing army and the mercenaries. While the details of the scene may be a trifle unclear, there is no uncertainty over the general picture. The royal party — the king, his household, the people, and the armed forces — leave the city. A halt at the city's edge allows for the exchange with Ittai the Gittite. It is tempting to suggest that v. 17 reports the departure from the city and v. 18 introduces the exchange with Ittai; the syntax of v. 18, beginning with pronominal suffixes (his, him), does not support the suggestion. Verse 18 provides the occasion for the exchange; but it belongs with what precedes it, concluding the decision to leave the city.

Ittai and the six hundred men with him had only recently come from Gath, Goliath's town, to commit themselves to David's service. With the elegance of diplomatic language, David offers them their freedom and Ittai declines it. Two aspects of David's speech arouse interest. He refers to "the king": "Go back, and stay with the king" (v. 19). Absalom is not named but must be meant (cf. 15:34-35; 16:16). David declares himself a homeless refugee: "while I go wherever I can" (v. 20). Both play down David's determination to return; they sit uncomfortably with his leaving ten "concubines" to care for his palace. Equally diplomatic, Ittai is given a heroic response: "wherever my lord the king may be, whether for death or for life, there also your servant will be" (v. 21). The inevitable question for any diplomat or counselor is whether these statements are to be taken at face value or understood as courtly diplomacy. Ittai professes heroically unswerving loyalty; no reason is given why he should. Is his profession of loyalty backed by his political and military acumen? Does he expect David to emerge as winner from the confrontation ahead? Does the elegance of his language conceal shrewd judgment that backs a winner? We are not told. Ittai's speech favors loyalty; the narrative's context may be thought to favor shrewdness and acumen. It may have been both.

The "whole country" wept as "all the people" passed by (v. 23). Again, "all the people" are most likely to be the people of the city. The party crosses the Wadi Kidron and heads toward the wilderness.

The next scene is probably best thought of as not sequential — [II.A.1.c]. To be in sequence, it would have to take place between the Kidron and the ascent of the Mount of Olives. It is theoretically possible, but it would be odd to set the ark down across the wadi. The statement that the ark was set down "until the people had all passed out of the city" (v. 24) strongly suggests a place at the edge of the city, before crossing the Kidron. Naturally, all topographical allusions are complicated by our ignorance of the exact path followed by David's party. Further problems arise over the sequence within v. 24. According to the Hebrew sequence, Zadok and all the Levites with him, carrying the ark of the covenant of God, set down the ark of God. No location is specified. At this point in the Hebrew, and not before, it is said that "Abiathar came up." The verse goes on: "until the people had all passed out of the city." In vv. 25-28, Abiathar is not mentioned. In vv. 25-26, David addresses Zadok. In v. 27 he addresses "Zadok the priest" and refers to Zadok's son and Jonathan son of Abiathar. Only in v. 29 is Abiathar mentioned along with Zadok, but the verb (carry back) is singular; some highly regarded manuscripts have the final verb (remain there) in the singular also. The NRSV's sequence, with Abiathar to the fore, can be defended; it requires a reordering of the verse. The use of "Zadok the priest" in v. 27 suggests that varying fragments of tradition may be being collated here. The text's history is uncertain and it would be imprudent to either rearrange it or base conclusions on its sequence.

Two elements appear clear. First, David sends the ark back into the city, placing his own future in God's hands (vv. 25-26: "let him do to me what seems good to him"). Second, David sets up the necessary communications system to be informed of what transpires. The first might be another example of David's quasi-fatalistic faith and his trust in YHWH. It is then juxtaposed with careful strategic planning — the communications system. Exactly the same will recur in vv. 30-37. First, in vv. 30-31, David prays that Ahithophel's counsel will be turned into foolishness. Second, in vv. 32-37, David sets up the strategic planning that will give him a mole among Absalom's counselors who will defeat for him the counsel of Ahithophel.

None of this need be gainsaid. The leaving of the ten "concubines," however, suggests that David believed he would return, and the narrative imparts knowledge of that to us. We must decide for ourselves whether the belief portrayed for David was based on his planning, his prayer, or both. We are not told.

It is difficult for us to interpret David's action in sending the ark back to Jerusalem. Its coming to Jerusalem had been an important sign of God's favor earlier (2 Sam 6). What does it mean, narratively, that David sends it back to the city? Its importance in 2 Sam 6 goes against any attempt to downplay that importance now. Silence about it later in the narrative goes against any attempt to highlight its symbolic significance for David's return. Can it be that David wanted the ark back in Jerusalem because he wanted two allies, Abiathar and Zadok, safely positioned in the city? Certainly, beyond the use of their sons as runners, Zadok and Abiathar are entrusted later with the crucial task of rallying support for David among the people of Judah (19:12-14 [Heb.; NRSV, 19:11-13]). Certainly, too, even at this early point in the narrative, the episode shows the support of these significant priestly figures for David. As the royal procession leaves the city, three groups have been singled out showing their support for David: his court officials ("whatever . . . the king decides"), the recently arrived mercenaries, and the priests responsible for the ark. It is a powerful omen for the narrative to come.

The transition from the wadi to the ascent of the Mount of Olives is clearly enough marked in 15:30 — [II.A.2]. The scene is described with images that do not fit the notion of a military movement. Weeping and covered heads are singled out for the entire party; walking barefoot is added for the king. Covering heads is used elsewhere in a context of shame or mourning (cf. Jer 14:3-4; Esth 6:12); barefoot is used by Isaiah, along with nakedness, in the context of captives being led into exile (Isa 20:2-4; cf. Jer 2:25). The keynote seems to be one of shame. Why we are not told.

David's immediate decision to abandon Jerusalem is surprising ("Get up! Let us flee"). This portrayal of the emotional quality of the king's departure is surprising. The narrative offers no interpretation of either. The selective nature of the storytelling should be evident from the absence of any mention of David's wives and children. The "little ones" with Ittai are mentioned and the ten "concubines" left behind are mentioned; the women and children of the court are not mentioned — and later only by Joab in passing (19:6 [Heb.; NRSV, 19:5]; by way of contrast, compare the report of Jacob's behavior, Gen 33:1-2). It is noteworthy that the depths of David's dejection are imaged immediately before his prayer, and immediately after it comes the action that will prove to be the turning point of the entire narrative. It may be a matter of sheerest topography, but storytellers can turn topography to symbolic use; David's critical moves — his prayer and his mole — are made on the mountaintop, and their fruit is harvested in the city below.

As David is climbing the Mount of Olives, he is told of Ahithophel's presence among the conspirators — [II.A.2.a]. Nothing is said of the source of this information at this point. David's prayer is given six words in Hebrew ("Please frustrate Ahithophel's counsel, O LORD") and not mentioned again; yet it touches the core of the narrative.

It is typical of the portrayals of David that his prayer should be followed immediately by strategies aimed at achieving what has been entrusted to prayer — [II.A.2.b]. Meeting Hushai at the summit, "where God was worshiped" (v. 32), David proceeds at once to set him up as a mole among Absalom's counselors: "you will defeat for me the counsel of Ahithophel" (v. 34). The remarkable thing about the portrayal of this episode is that David is the sole speaker. Hushai is not given any profession of loyalty or even an acceptance of his commission. This is spare narrative at its sparest. The sharpest irony is that Hushai is being given the identical role that Ahithophel is playing; Ahithophel was David's servant in time past and now he is Absalom's servant — exactly what Hushai is to propose to Absalom (cf. v. 34). Hushai can count on support from Zadok and Abiathar and is told of the communications process that has been arranged. The story adds that Hushai came into the city at the same moment Absalom was entering it. In this story, nothing happens by chance.

David moves on a little from the summit — [II.A.2.c]. This narrative is indeed structured on the stages of the journey. Ziba meets him. He brings supplies. David's questions are sharp. First, "What do you expect from these?" (literally: what are these to you?). Then, "Where is your master's son?" After Ziba's reply, David gives him what presumably he came for: "All that belonged to Mephibosheth is now yours" (16:4). Two questions linger unanswered in the narrative. Did Mephibosheth really think that Israel would give him back Saul's kingdom and on what grounds could he have thought that? Second, what benefit was it to Ziba to have David, in full flight, transfer the estate to him? We can hazard suppositions; the hard politics escape us.

Ziba's supplies are miserly in comparison with Abigail's, also rustled up in haste (cf. 1 Sam 25:18; cf. also 1 Sam 17:17-18 and 2 Sam 17:28-29). He brings two donkeys, "for the king's household to ride"; is this, perhaps, the only allusion at this stage to the presence of the royal wives and children in the party? However, these are side issues. The two major questions are: What benefit did Absalom's rebellion hold out for Mephibosheth? What benefit was there for Ziba in having David's good will? We have no certain answers to either. The sincerity of Ziba's accusation has been doubted ("slanderous," Smith, *Samuel*, 347; "at once suspect," Mauchline, *1 and 2 Samuel*, 275); it is evidently not open to test, and the narrative does not provide us with grounds for improving on David's verdict (cf. 19:25-31 [Heb.; NRSV, 19:24-30]). Note that the accusation is elicited by David, not spontaneously offered by Ziba.

Again, David's next stage on the journey is noted — [II.A.2.d]. He has passed the summit of the Mount of Olives and now he comes to Bahurim. Shimei's pedigree is given at length. Son of Gera, he is of the family of the house of Saul. We may assume a blood connection to the house of Saul; we are not given any specifics.

The two episodes with Shimei ben Gera are unique in the Davidic traditions. Here and only here we are offered a glimpse of how David's enemies viewed his rise to power. It is fascinating to observe how it is handled in the narrative. Abishai's response to Shimei is simple and natural: he wants to take his head off (16:9). Later, he still wants Shimei's death (19:22 [Heb.; NRSV, 19:21]). David, on the other hand, exercises remarkable royal tolerance on both occasions (cf. 16:11-12; 19:23 [Heb.; NRSV, 22]). David's reaction is unusual, as it was to the death of his first child with Bathsheba (12:16-23) and as it was when he held Saul in his power (1 Sam 26:9-11, 18-19; also 1 Sam 24:6-15 [Heb.; NRSV, 7-16]). However, it is Shimei's later retraction that deserves most attention (cf. 19:19-24 [Heb.; NRSV, 19:18-23]). It is diplomatically ambiguous. He avows his iniquity *('āwon)* and that he has sinned *(ḥāṭā'tî);* he does not disavow his interpretation. To shout abuse at the king may be iniquity and sin; it may not be erroneous. It is clear that the text has Shimei apologize for his action; it does not have him clearly withdraw his accusation.

Shimei's view of David is sharply focused. Abigail, ever the diplomat, did not want David, when he will have become leader of Israel, to have any "cause of grief, or pangs of conscience, for having shed blood without cause" (1 Sam 25:31). Cause of grief and pangs of conscience are exactly what Shimei thinks David should have. No names are mentioned, no strategies denounced. We may wonder about the Amalekite (2 Sam 1:14-16) or about Ishbaal's captains (4:9-12) or about the seven sons of Saul of whose deaths we know almost nothing (21:7-9). Shimei is not bothered with such detail. We have texts that account for David's success "because the LORD was with him." Shimei has another accounting: David is a man of blood, and the LORD has brought back on him all the blood of the house of Saul, in whose place David has reigned (vv. 7-8). (The NRSV could be read as misleading; in v. 8, it has the LORD's vengeance "on all of you." The guilt could be understood to be shared. The Hebrew does not allow for this; as above, it has: "all the blood.") There is a strong echo of Israelite act-consequence thinking in v. 8. The kingdom David snatched from Saul has been snatched in turn by Absalom; the "evil" (NRSV, "disaster") in which David finds himself evokes both past and present, connoting the evil that David has done and in which he now finds himself enmeshed and trapped.

In so intensely ambiguous a narrative, we should not impose any single reason explaining the presence of this radical alternative understanding of David. The issue has nothing to do with what Shimei may or may not have said; the issue is why what is attributed to Shimei should be recorded here. Because it happened is an inadequate answer; many things have happened in the career of David that are not recorded. This is, so the question remains why it should be recorded here. A possible reason is as a testimony to David's faith and his trust in YHWH. Other possible reasons are as an example of royal wisdom, or as evidence of an alternative view of David that existed at the time, or because David needed Shimei's support, or because David was sure enough of his position not to need Shimei's support. We would be unwise to appeal to any single reason as the reason for the passage's presence.

The episode tells us three things that should not be overlooked. First, within ancient Israel a negative view of David's success could be found. Second, David knew that his son Absalom sought his life. Third, David can be portrayed asserting that the LORD may have instigated Shimei's cursing.

The biblical traditions from 1 Sam 9:1 to 2 Sam 18:18 portray David's rise to power as brought about by YHWH's support (the LORD was with him) and as being achieved without bloodshed on David's part. In vv. 7-8 here, Shimei gives utterance to a diametrically opposed view of David. He is a man of blood; he has killed his way to power; he is now paying for the blood of the house of Saul. If we focus on "the blood of the house of Saul," a number of possibilities can be brought under Shimei's accusation. David might be accused of having abandoned Saul and his sons to their death at the battle of Gilboa (1 Sam 28–31). David might be considered responsible for the death of Ishbaal (2 Sam 4). David could be accused of the death of seven of Saul's descendants (2 Sam 21:6-9). If we view Shimei's accusation more widely, it is an accusation that David clawed his way to power, aggregating superior military power to himself until he was finally in a position to force the house of Saul from the throne of Israel. It is a totally different picture from what we might call the authorized Davidic tradition. Where truth lies we are not told and do not know.

Verse 11 is the first allusion made to Absalom's wanting to kill David, for that is what "to seek his life" means. A little later, Absalom is depicted approving of Ahithophel's proposal to "strike down only the king" (17:2). But that is a little later. The later history of Israel's kings makes clear that rebels who seized power did not leave incumbents alive. Earlier, Abimelech wasted no time dispatching his brothers (Judg 9:1-6). Commonsense conviction may have been enough for David or he may have had inside information; we do not know. The text makes clear that the principal figures knew exactly what was at stake.

David's assertion that YHWH may have bidden Shimei to curse is no throwaway line. It is at the center of three verses (vv. 10-12). It may well be one further instance of that strange fatalism that has surfaced occasionally as an element in the make-up of Davidic faith. Deciding whether it reflects a reality in David's life or a reality in the view of David propagated by his supporters is out of our reach. In the narrative, Shimei is left alone to throw his stones, ready to reappear later when David is clearly victor.

David's journey on the mountain ends with the arrival at the Jordan — [II.A.2.e]. The narrative must turn back to Absalom. The conflict of the counselors, Ahithophel and Hushai, has to take place while David is still at the Jordan. Precise issues of time and distance do not matter; narrative verisimilitude does. Much remains to be settled before the narrative will be able to turn to a second journey, the bringing of the king back to Jerusalem (cf. 19:10-11 [Heb.; NRSV, 19:9-10]).

Hushai's integration into Absalom's advisory council is a matter that demands delicate handling — [II.B.1.a]. First, it has to seem plausible that Absalom should accept him. Second, it may be important that he is not implicated in the decision to violate David's "concubines." Hushai is given the initial move,

an affirmation of his loyalty to Absalom: "Long live the king!" (16:16). The
challenge by Absalom allows Hushai to unfold plausible grounds for his loyalty: a choice has been made by YHWH, by "this people" (the army?), and by all
Israel, and that is where Hushai's loyalty will be (v. 18). Hushai has a second
argument to support his case: he is doing exactly what Ahithophel has done. As
Ahithophel was, so was Hushai in David's service; what more appropriate than
that he should serve David's son — as Ahithophel was doing (v. 19). Those
who double-cross are vulnerable to the double-cross. Treachery can be out-
treasoned. Switching allegiances is always tricky.

The narrative concludes the scene without any decision made by Absalom. Tension is maintained until Hushai is summoned to give counsel (17:5).
Even then, we are not assured that Hushai has been fully accepted. Narrative
tension apart, the absence of any commitment by Absalom to Hushai here
means that Hushai is freed from any complicity in the violation of David's
"concubines." The advice is Ahithophel's alone; the action Absalom's alone.
Hushai, David's friend, is not involved.

The episode of the violation of these women, left to look after David's
palace, is terse in its telling, fearful in the action told. No comment is made on
Ahithophel's advice; it stands alone. Two reasons are offered for the action:
first, that you will have "made yourself odious to your father"; second, that "the
hands of all who are with you will be strengthened" (v. 21). It would seem that
fear of a reconciliation between Absalom and David was present among Absalom's supporters. The action Ahithophel advised would eliminate that fear and
enhance the level of support. We do not know the exact status of "concubines"
at the court of David but it is clearly significant (cf. 2 Sam 3:7; 21:11; also
1 Kgs 2:22). The action is juxtaposed in the narrative with Ahithophel's proposal that pleased Absalom: "I will strike down only the king, and I will bring
all the people back to you" (17:2-3). Rape and murder go hand in hand. To
make matters worse, the narrative moves from the rape of the "concubines" to
the comment that "in those days the counsel that Ahithopel gave was as if one
consulted the oracle of God" (16:23). The irony will not be lost on reader or listener; shortly, the narrative will add: "For the LORD had ordained to defeat the
good counsel of Ahithophel, so that the LORD might bring ruin *(hārā'â)* on Absalom" (17:14). Joab's killing of Absalom can be seen as an isolated incident in
the war; it can be seen as connected to Absalom's action here and the LORD's
will to bring evil upon him.

Immediately following 16:23's equating Ahithophel's counsel with the
inquiring of the word of God, 17:1 has Ahithophel counseling killing David —
[II.B.1.b]. This is the counsel the narrative describes as "good counsel" and the
counsel the LORD will defeat (17:14). This narrative excels at the art of irony.

Absalom has Hushai summoned; when Hushai has come, Absalom needs
to tell him what Ahithophel has proposed (17:5-6). Here is an indicator that
Hushai has not been fully accepted into Absalom's inner circle. It gives support
to the possibility that Hushai was dismissed from the meeting after giving his
counsel and before a decision was taken. The narrative does not say so, but it is
possible (cf. 17:13-14).

Ahithophel's counsel is described as "good" (17:14; contrast with 17:7);

in ordinary circumstances, it would be. But these are not ordinary circumstances; Hushai is a double agent for David. Ahithophel's counsel will be known to David well before Ahithophel and his troops could reach the Jordan. The best plans in the world are useless if they are betrayed. On the other hand, both Hushai's counsel and his message to David may tell us something of the state of David's forces. Hushai's counsel to Absalom suggests that he knew David needed time to regroup and organize reinforcements. His message points in the same direction. If David's troops were adequate, prior warning would have allowed them to ambush and destroy Ahithophel's elite force, wearied by a hurried pursuit and in part perhaps a night march. The background is not given to us; in all of this, something is known to Hushai that is kept from us. It is possible that the terrain was unsuitable for an ambush. It is even possible that an ambush could have exposed Hushai's role as double agent. We are not told, so we do not know.

Hushai's counsel is skillfully presented. It plays on two emotions: fear and pride. The fear is justified enough. David is known as an expert in war. He will have already taken appropriate dispositions. He himself will be well hidden. His warriors will have been assigned defensive positions. When the first attackers are killed, there might be a panic, and rumors of slaughter will be believed. Everyone knows David is a warrior. Having worked on Absalom's fear, Hushai works on his pride. To a proud and ambitious prince, the idea that he should in person lead a massive army representing all Israel would be almost irresistible — an army gathered from Dan to Beer-sheba, multitudinous as the sand by the sea. What newly anointed king could refuse such a challenge, could let slip such an opportunity? Absalom and his advisers (who have been transformed from "all the elders of Israel" [v. 4] to "all the men of Israel" [v. 14]) fall for it. The narrative tells us that Hushai's success was God's doing. Absalom's destiny is known to us already: it is ruin. Down the track, bad counsel will cost Rehoboam the bulk of his kingdom (also willed by the LORD, 1 Kgs 12:1-15); here, it will cost Absalom his life — and Ahithophel his.

Verses 15-23 have been grouped together as "Aftermath" — [II.B.1.c]. They describe the consequences flowing from the counsel session: David is told what was said, the Jordan is crossed during the night, and Ahithophel hangs himself. The last two are straightforward; the first is highly problematic. The message does not tally with Ahithophel's advice; the message does not tally with Hushai's victory; and, finally, the story of the messengers suffers from several major gaps.

Hushai follows the directions given him earlier (15:35-36). He reports to Zadok and Abiathar the counsel that Ahithophel gave and that he gave. He then formulates the message to be taken to David. His message raises two issues: it implies that Ahithophel's counsel has prevailed, not Hushai's; it misrepresents Ahithophel's counsel. The first can be accounted for in a couple of ways. As Hushai was called into the meeting after Ahithophel had spoken, it is not unlikely that Hushai was ushered from the meeting before a decision was taken. In this case, crossing the Jordan would be prudent. The text is silent on the issue of what Hushai knew. Alternatively, Hushai knew what had been decided but was urging prudence, lest there be a change of plan or lest Ahithophel take matters into his own hands. The misrepresentation of Ahithophel's counsel is a relatively minor matter, but this is not a narrative to gloss over minor matters. Ahithophel's strategy was to kill the king alone and "bring all the people back" to Absalom (17:2); that is a far cry from the message's fear that "the king and all the people who are with him will be swallowed up" (17:16). A wise commander might get his army across the river during the night; but that should be his decision, not Hushai's. To sharpen the issue, the first part of the verse uses singular verbs for the address to David ("do not lodge . . . cross over"); it is the second part that involves "all the people who are with him." Differing traditions are possible; Würthwein suggests later insertion of 16:21-23 and 17:5-14 (*Thronfolge Davids*, 40-41) — possible but not necessary, and unlikely given 17:15's claim that Hushai was present and gave counsel, coupled with the subsequent narrative's reflection on Hushai's counsel.

Verse 17 raises issues of its own, independently of the counsel and the message. The NRSV correctly reflects a frequentative usage ("used to go" etc.) and introduces a servant girl who has not been mentioned. Nothing is said to explain why Jonathan and Ahimaaz could not risk being seen entering the city and so needed the servant girl as intermediary. The possibility of a more extensive piece of storytelling lurks here. If attention is given to the frequentative aspect, two problems arise: the day hardly allows time for one message, certainly not more (despite McCarter's "while David was making his way towards the Jordan," p. 388); the news from the duel of counselors is presented as the first message for David. It is possible that a more expansive tradition is hinted at here. If so, this hint is almost all that we have of it.

The previous sentence has "almost all" because vv. 18-20 reflect more background than is provided in the present text; some of that background might relate to the "more expansive tradition" hinted at. According to v. 18, "a boy saw them." Presumably, he recognized the two young men, Jonathan and Ahimaaz, who could not risk being seen entering the city. This risk they could not run is from v. 17; in the present text, no indication has been given of any activity that would draw attention to them. Equally in v. 18, "both of them went away quickly," indicating that they knew they had been seen; there is more background to this than is being revealed. Finally, in vv. 18-20, they know to hide in a well at Bahurim, the woman of the house cooperates in their concealment, and Absalom's servants know where to go and whom to ask for. When the two emerge from the well and reach David, their message is akin to v. 16: cross now, for this is Ahithophel's counsel. But, contrary to Ahithophel's proposal, king and company are envisaged; the plural is used throughout the message (i.e., go, cross, against you). No mention is made of Hushai's counsel. There is a lot here that we are not being told. These may be traces from the more expansive tradition referred to. We are unable to reconstruct even an outline, especially if the message being carried now is to reach David on the first evening of Absalom's rebellion.

Verse 22 provides a formal report that the king and all those with him crossed the Jordan before daybreak. It could follow equally well on either v. 21 or v. 16. As a report of an action by David and those with him, it is complete in itself.

Verse 23 similarly reports Ahithophel's suicide; there are the cause, the return to his home, the death and burial. It is complete in itself. With Ahithophel's death, the narrative closes off the battle of counsel. What is next is the battle of armies. That is made clear by v. 24. Verse 23 ends with Ahithophel's burial in the tomb of his father. Verse 24 immediately reports David's move to Mahanaim and Absalom's move across the Jordan, "with all the men of Israel." Battle is to be joined.

In 17:24-29, information about the two sides is gathered in what can best be described as preliminaries — [II.B.2.a]. Verses 25-26 report on the commander of Absalom's army and the general location of its encampment. Verses 27-29 report on the support and supplies received by David and his troops at Mahanaim. The disposition of David's forces, prior to battle with Absalom's army, is begun in 18:1. In the text that follows, 18:1–19:9 (Heb.; NRSV, 19:8), the nature of the narrative is clear as to what it is not. It is not an account of the strategic struggle that gave David victory over Absalom and preserved David's rule over Israel. The battle itself is dealt with in one verse, 18:7. The section concerned with the organization of command brings to the fore two strategically subordinate issues: David's worth and David's desire to spare Absalom. The three verses devoted to the battle (18:6-8) are followed by the death of Absalom, the bringing of this news to David, and David's reaction to the news. Something more is running in this text than a chronicle of how David put down Absalom's rebellion.

We learn that Absalom's army is commanded by Amasa. This is his first appearance in the biblical text; his death will be noted in ch. 20. He is noted as having taken Joab's place in command of the army (17:25). By origin he is an Ishmaelite, son of Ithra (see above, under textual issues). By marriage he is connected with Joab's family; his father had married Joab's aunt, Abigal [Abigail], sister of Joab's mother, Zeruiah. For Chronicles, they were among the aristocracy of Judah (cf. 1 Chr 2:9-17). Absalom's camp is noted as "in the land of Gilead" (v. 26); no closer specification is given. The precise southern boundaries of Gilead at any time are unsure; it is certainly in northern Transjordan, and the Wadi Jabbok is probably its southern border (cf. Deut 2:36; 3:16). If so, the forces of Absalom and David would have been to the north and south of the wadi where tradition located Jacob/Israel's struggle for identity in his wrestling with God.

David's camp is at Mahanaim (traditionally named by Jacob, cf. Gen 32:3 [Heb.; NRSV, 32:2]), just south of the Jabbok; it had been where Abner had established Ishbaal (cf. 2 Sam 2:8, 12, 29). There David is given support (but not troops) from three rather surprising sources: Shobi, from Ammonite Rabbah (which David conquered in 2 Sam 11–12); Machir, from Lo-debar (who is reported to have housed Mephibosheth, cf. 2 Sam 9:4-5); and Barzillai, from Rogelim (unmentioned elsewhere). Barzillai's support is itemized: parched grain, wheat, barley, meal, lentils, honey, curds, cheese, and sheep, also beds, basins, and vessels (cf. vv. 28-29). Troops are not mentioned; nothing is mentioned in relation to Shobi and Machir. The significance of Mahanaim here is not given us; undoubtedly it has one. One aspect of the text, however, is not to be overlooked: conquered foes (Shobi) and former allies of the house of Saul (Machir) are now portrayed as solidly loyal to David.

The section that follows (18:1–19:9 [Heb.; NRSV, 19:8]) contains the core of the crushing of Absalom's rebellion — the defeat of the rebels and the death of the leader — [II.B.2.b]. Little attention is given to the defeat in battle; more attention is given to David's forces at the beginning and at the end of the chapter than in the scene of battle (18:6-8). Much attention is given to Absalom's death: the lead-up to it, the death and burial, and the bringing of the news to David. The section is carefully structured around this central event: the death of Absalom. While the structure analysis has proceeded from 1) to 3), it would be possible to organize the text chiastically, centered on Absalom's death, proceeding from 1) to 2) and then 1'). The envelope, or chiastic, structure is present in the text. At the same time, the text tells a story and reflects the movement of the narrative through time. It is a complex piece of storytelling and its complexity needs to be respected.

The opening verses of the section are devoted to the organization of command — [II.B.2.b.1)]. The commanders of thousands and of hundreds are appointed by David. A division into three battle groups puts one under Joab's command, one under his brother Abishai, and one under Ittai, the recently arrived Gittite. Strategic planning is not mentioned. It was significant before the battle with the Ammonites and their allies, where Joab's strategy is provided in detail (2 Sam 10:9-14); it was significant before the second battle against Ai, where Joshua's strategy is detailed in two versions (Josh 8:3-9 and 10-13). Nothing is noted in the narrative here.

Instead, there is the comparison of David's worth with that of his men (v. 3). Is this praise of David or invitation to reflection on what is to come? There is also David's plea for Absalom, an order given to all three commanders in the hearing of their troops (v. 5). Is this to exonerate David for doing ruthlessly what is politically right, or does it reflect a different side of the man who could order Uriah murdered? As usual, the text is silent.

The question has been asked before about David: Was he shortsighted or was he ruthless? It was asked on the occasion of Tamar's being sent unescorted to Amnon. It was asked again over David's permission for Amnon to accept the invitation to Absalom's feast. It has to be asked again here concerning Absalom. No farsighted king could allow an ambitious, murderous, and rebellious prince to live. So the question: Did Joab do what had to be done, or did Joab do what the king told him to do? The text clearly opts for the former view: David did not order what Joab did; quite the contrary. The unanswerable question then emerges: In opting for this position, is the text deliberately exonerating a guilty David or does the text express an honest viewpoint? Correlative with these questions is the earlier one: Was David shortsighted or ruthless? Does the text assert that David was shortsighted, blinded by his love for the son who was ready to kill him? From the text, questions abound; in the text, answers are few.

Where questions are concerned, there is at least one more option to be considered. The question above was whether Joab did what had to be done — for the sake of David's future. Another option asks the question whether Joab did what had to be done — for the sake of Joab's own future. It is likely that Joab had burned his boats with Absalom. He had been involved in Absalom's recall to Jerusalem and his long-delayed reconciliation with David. It had been a botched operation. Joab had no future under Absalom. In the long term, Joab could be considered to have a future with David. Was it in Joab's interest, therefore, to kill Absalom? If so, did Joab do the killing on his own account, for his own sake? We have no answers, but it must be considered possible (for a full and detailed study of the complex figure of Joab, see Bietenhard, *Königs General*).

The overall structure of the chapter can be indicated briefly. First, there is the concern for David's armed forces (vv. 1-4) and for Absalom (v. 5); at the end, the king receives the news of Absalom and weeps for him (18:19–19:1 [Heb.; NRSV, 18:19-33]), and Joab expresses concern for David's troops (19:2-9 [Heb.; NRSV, 19:1-8]). In the middle is the account of Absalom's death, introduced by the defeat and his being found in the oak and concluded by the end of the pursuit and Absalom's burial (vv. 6-18).

The simplicity of the structure belies the complexity of the crosscurrents within it. Ahithophel counseled killing the king alone, and his counsel was adjudged "good" by the narrative (17:14b). According to this counsel, David should order Absalom killed. He orders the exact opposite. Is his order "good"? David's men unconsciously take the side of Ahithophel; the king should be the primary target (v. 3). By analogy, Absalom should die; he is the primary target (cf. the strange story of 1 Kgs 22, where the Syrian king gives similar orders). David is caught in the narrative's web, flying in the face of what his own troops avow and what Ahithophel advised. Counselors have plenty to discern.

The battle and defeat cannot be ignored — [II.B.2.b.2)]. Armies have crossed the Jordan. Armies have been organized under commanders. Armies have gone out into the field. The morale of the troops is critical at the end of the section. For all that, the centerpiece of the action occurs following the defeat; it is the death of Absalom. The defeat is reported in vv. 6-8; the engagement is not ended until the pursuit has been called off and the Israelites have fled to their homes (vv. 16-17). Appropriately, Absalom's death is situated within the narrative of the pursuit of the defeated foe.

The battle was fought in the forest of Ephraim. This forest is mentioned only here. It must be located in Transjordan, presumably in southern Gilead; more than that we do not know. The outcome of the battle is given baldly: "the men of Israel were defeated there by the servants of David" (v. 7a). If "men of Israel" and "servants of David" are interpreted narrowly, this can be understood to say that the popular army raised by Absalom was defeated by the mercenary troops employed by David. It is not always wise to give a narrow interpretation to terms of this kind. On the other hand, such an interpretation would be consonant with the rest of the narrative; it could explain why David moved at once to Transjordan. If so, however, it suggests that, while dissatisfaction with David may have been relatively widespread, support for Absalom as successor to David was less than overwhelming. These are legitimate thoughts; they could not legitimately be considered as conclusions.

The observation is worth noting that "the forest claimed more victims that day than the sword" (v. 8). The rebellion has not been suppressed bloodlessly, but many of the deaths of Israelites will not be attributed to the swords of David's men. Joab's recall of the troops serves a similar purpose; he "restrained the troops" (v. 16b). It is important for a king who has lost power and needs to regain it not to alienate too many of his citizenry.

Joab's killing of Absalom is handled with kid gloves. The section (vv. 9-18) opens with what is practically speaking a headline; a near-literal rendering could be: "Absalom encounters David's men." As is often the case in Hebrew narrative, the details are then filled out. Absalom's mule passed under a large oak, Absalom's head got stuck in the oak, and the mule kept going. Nothing is said about how Absalom's head got stuck in the oak, but he is left there, dangling between heaven and earth, totally at the mercy of his enemies.

A soldier saw him and told Joab, with the narrative lingering on what they said to each other. It is instructive. For Joab, the question is automatic: Why didn't you kill him? (cf. v. 11). In Joab's eyes, it was the obvious thing to do and would have attracted an immediate reward. For the soldier, it was neither automatic nor obvious. In the hearing of the troops, the king had ordered his three commanders to spare Absalom. Had he acted treacherously (*šeqer,* v. 13), the king would have found out and Joab would have left the soldier to face the music (the Hebrew is dense, but this appears to be its trend). The narrative moves are to be noted: David's public position is reiterated, the action is described as treacherous, and Joab is named as unreliable (v. 13). Joab is portrayed terminating the exchange with no further explanation. He then initiates the action that has been described as treacherous (*šeqer,* v. 13). Three spears from Joab strike Absalom's heart; the ten armor-bearers finish him off. Actual responsibility for the death is muddied. Joab thrust three spears into his heart, "while he was still alive" (v. 14). Joab's ten armor-bearers then surrounded him and struck him — and the text adds only then "and they killed him" (v. 15). It is almost as if the text is observing the modern convention where it is known that at least one member of a firing squad will have been issued with a blank bullet.

The narrative does not linger on Absalom's death and makes no comment in relation to the rebellion, except perhaps obliquely. Joab calls off the pursuit, Absalom is buried then and there in the forest, and "all the Israelites fled to their homes" (v. 17). The battle is over; so is this rebellion.

Verse 18 follows appropriately on the report of Absalom's burial in the forest, under "a very great heap of stones." The verse notes that Absalom had set up a monument for himself, in the Valley of the King, that is there to the author's day. His body is in a pit in the forest; his monument is in the Valley of the King. The verse has Absalom say that he has no son; the tradition is in tension with the earlier notice that he had three sons and a daughter (14:27). There is an irony in this verse on Absalom's monument. Its function was to keep his name in memory (cf. v. 18), and it is noted at this point in the narrative. Absalom's rebellion is over; he is buried in a nameless pit, in Transjordan, in a forest, where he will be forgotten. Even David's tears in memory of his son will be prohibited by Joab.

The narrative moves to the final section in this central part of the text, devoted to David's conflict with Absalom: What will David's reaction be to the resolution of the conflict — [II.B.2.b.3)]? David's orders were explicit. He wanted the rebellion crushed and his son alive. The resolution he has got is a crushed rebellion and a dead son. Readers who believe that a resolution was impossible while Absalom remained alive have to face the question that the narrative leaves open at various points. Was David shortsighted, believing against all odds that a resolution was possible, even while Absalom remained alive? Or was David ruthless, believing that any resolution was indeed impossible while Absalom remained alive — so that David acted accordingly, but judged it desirable to maintain a different public persona? The narrative presents the public persona; readers and users are left to reflect.

The move to David's reaction is skillfully presented. It begins with the departure of the runners, going from Joab to carry the news to David. We may wonder why two runners feature in the narrative. We find out soon enough; narrative tension is built up as the two approach, but more is at stake than that. The focus has shifted to David, "sitting between the two gates." The news brought him is twofold: the fate of the rebellion and the fate of the son. Ahimaaz delivers the first and is mute on the second (vv. 28-29). The Cushite delivers the first and is diplomatic in his communication of the second (vv. 31-32). The first question David has for each runner indicates the focus of his concern: "Is it well with the young man Absalom?" (vv. 29a and 32a).

The news of Absalom's death is met with David's retirement from public view, his tears, and the explosion of his grief: "O my son Absalom, my son, my son Absalom! Would I had died instead of you, O Absalom, my son, my son!" (19:1 [Heb.; NRSV, 18:33]). The news of David's grief is met with Joab's views on the crushing of the rebellion and the morale of David's forces. Evidently, Joab was of the view that any resolution of the conflict arising out of the rebellion was impossible while Absalom remained alive.

The section dealing with the armed forces (19:2-9 [Heb.; NRSV, 19:1-8]) is a vintage example of the procedures of Hebrew narrative. The report of the basic information transmitted to Joab is given in 19:2 (Heb.; NRSV, 19:1). What follows spells out that basic information in detail. The turning of victory to mourning and the feelings of the troops occupy vv. 3-4 (Heb.; NRSV, vv. 2-3); the king's grief is portrayed again in v. 5 (Heb.; NRSV, v. 4). Then Joab, mentioned in v. 2 (Heb.; NRSV, v. 1), is portrayed moving into action in v. 6 (Heb.; NRSV, v. 5). As given in the text, Joab's words lack all diplomatic tact. Commanders do not usually address their kings with quite such brutal frankness: "this will be worse for you than any disaster that has come upon you from your youth until now" (v. 8 [Heb.; NRSV, v. 7]). And David did what Joab told him to.

Joab's speech repays close inspection. One important observation needs to be noted and then left aside. Almost in passing, Joab speaks of David's sons and daughters, of David's wives and "concubines." As was indicated earlier, this is the only reference in the narrative to the entourage that accompanied David. Up till now, not a word has been said about the presence of David's court in the retreat from Jerusalem, the crossing of the Jordan, and the establishment of camp at Mahanaim. This belated reference to their presence brings home just how selective the narrative is.

More important to the immediate context is the issue of the plausibility of Joab's speech. All the army is reported to have heard David order Joab, Abishai, and Ittai to "deal gently" with Absalom (18:5; cf. 18:12-13). We may assume that all the army was well aware that Joab and his bodyguard had done the killing. The text does not say it; we are entitled to assume it. Indirectly, it is confirmed by Joab's complaint, "for I perceive" (19:7 [Heb.; NRSV, 19:6]) — not the army ("they know"), but Joab himself ("I know"). The words given to the soldier in 18:10-14 suggest that his own anger would have been directed at Joab and his sympathy might have been extended to the king. How widely might that reflect the likely feelings of the army? We do not know, but the text does not give us grounds for portraying Joab as the army's hero. Yet here Joab claims to speak for the army. It would be in character for Joab to be speaking for himself. If so, why should Joab speak so frankly and bluntly to the king? If David does not already know, Joab is entitled to believe that David will very soon know the identify of Absalom's killer. Does the narrative want to portray Joab as in a position to be almost bullying his king? Is there a hint here that Joab knew more than the text reveals of the disjunction between David's public persona and David's private ruthlessness? If so, it is no more than a hint. It points again to the usefulness of such a text for those who one day will have to counsel kings. Here, the king's mourning is public; the narrative seldom addresses what is private.

Narrative works in ways that are wondrous to behold. This whole issue of David's reaction to his son's death may well be of great importance, but it impacts on a restricted circle, David's entourage and David's troops. Thanks to Joab, it is resolved within this circle; it therefore has no effect on the wider audience of all Israel. In the narrative, it is bracketed off between two repetitions of the same statement about that wider audience: "meanwhile, all the Israelites (had) fled to their homes" (18:17 and 19:9b [Heb.; NRSV, 19:8b]). Once this has been recognized, it is appropriate to treat the two statements as opening and closing parentheses isolating an important issue that, in itself, can be set apart from the story of the rebellion's end and David's return (so the Hebrew paragraphing in BHS). The paragraphing adopted in the NRSV, which has 19:9b [Heb.; NRSV, 19:8b]) as the start of a new paragraph, is possible but inappropriate. It points to resumptive repetition (German: *Wiederaufnahme*), an editorial technique used to resume a sequence after breaking off for an insertion. There is no indication that the material from 18:18 to 19:9a (Heb.; NRSV, 19:8a) is an insertion.

The issue of David's return to Jerusalem and his resumption of royal power there is begun in 19:10 (Heb.; NRSV, 19:9) — [II.C]. In its own way, it is a pointer to the fragility of David's hold on power. Absalom's death has deprived the rebellion of its leader; apparently, it has not deprived the rebellion of potential energy. As portrayed in the text, the debate rages "throughout all the tribes of Israel" (v. 10 [Heb.; NRSV, v. 9]). The debate: we anointed Absalom; he is dead; why do you say nothing about bringing the king back? (v. 11 [Heb.; NRSV, v. 10]) — [II.C.1]. An aside: if Absalom were not dead, what would they have been saying? We may allow ourselves to unfold the debate a little. They anointed Absalom; presumably they had good reason to do so. Now Absalom is dead. The question under debate: Do they have good reason to bring David back and restore the regime they had rebelled against? Hence, vv. 10-11 (Heb.; NRSV, 9-10) indicate the situation of political uncertainty that David has to deal with.

Once again, the narrative is structured on the stages of David's journey, this time of return — [II.C.2]. First, the preliminary note on the political situation: there is a debate in progress throughout Israel as to whether the king should return (vv. 10-11 [Heb.; NRSV, 9-10]). Then negotiations with Judah are needed to bring about an invitation to return and so trigger David's move back to the Jordan. At the Jordan, David's dealings with three figures are reported separately, and only then is the king's crossing of the Jordan definitively achieved. The move to Gilgal (v. 41 [Heb.; NRSV, v. 40]) begins the journey to Jerusalem. The political debate continues during the journey. One of the aspects of the sequence narrated here, that we should not overlook, is the presence of both military and political moves. The interplay between them is not discussed. Joab killed Absalom; that was a military move with political implications. David appointed Amasa to Joab's job; that too was a military move with political implications. The debates within Israel and Judah are political; beyond the death of Absalom, the military arguments within the debates are not raised.

The narrative has David move into the uncertainty of this political arena — [II.C.2.a] — with a message to Zadok and Abiathar. They are to energize Judah on David's behalf. Furthermore, they are to tell Amasa that David has given him Joab's job. According to the text, Amasa "swayed the hearts of all the people of Judah as one" (v. 15 [Heb.; NRSV, v. 14]). So Judah lined up as supporters of David and sent the message: "Return, both you and all your servants." So David came to the Jordan and Judah came to Gilgal — [II.C.2.a.1)]. There is a gap between them — between the Jordan and Gilgal, between David and Judah — a small gap, but a gap; the narrative will keep it open for twenty-five verses, until the king moves to Gilgal in v. 41 (Heb.; NRSV, v. 40). At that point, the political situation has shifted further in David's favor. At Gilgal are all the people of Judah "and also half the people of Israel."

Before the gap is closed, the text portrays David dealing with three different individuals: Shimei, who had cursed him on his flight from Jerusalem; Mephibosheth, who had stayed in Jerusalem; and Barzillai, who had supported him at Mahanaim — [II.C.2.a.2)].

Shimei is accorded the first interview. In his presentation, with his patronymic and his residence, it is noted that he came down with the people of Judah — and he had a thousand Benjaminites with him (v. 18 [Heb.; NRSV, v. 17]). Because Bahurim lay between Jerusalem and the Jordan, his presence might not seem remarkable. What is remarkable is that he had raised a thousand among the Benjaminites; that alone is reason for the narrative to note that he hurried. Ziba and his household are mentioned next; he is specified as "the servant of the house of Saul" (v. 18 [Heb.; NRSV, v. 17]); this specification may suggest his being associated in the text with the Benjaminites. The Hebrew text has "and they (plural) rushed down to the Jordan," allowing for the involvement of Shimei, Ziba, and their groups. The NRSV's presentation, beginning a new sentence, isolates Ziba, dependent of the house of Saul, his sons and servants, which is possible but may not be wise. This is a narrative where options need to be left open. That Shimei and his Benjaminite thousand were with the people of Judah who came to David at the Jordan before anyone else is significant. The presence of Shimei and these Benjaminite supporters is a pointer, early in the narrative of the return, that David will find support within the northern tribes of Israel. Shimei is not merely "of the family of the house of Saul" (16:5); he had expressed strong and negative views about David. His coming over to David's side is a clear indicator that David's return will be politically successful.

The speech given Shimei in his encounter with David makes two points: do not hold me guilty or remember what I did earlier; I know I did wrong and that is why I have come before any other northerners to pledge my support. There can be little doubt: Shimei is a smart operator. Abishai is not so smart. He wanted to take Shimei's head off at their first encounter (16:9); he still wants him dead (19:22 [Heb.; NRSV, 19:21]). Fortunately for Shimei, David is also a smart political operator. The words given David are: "Do I not know that I am this day king over Israel?" (v. 23 [Heb.; NRSV, v. 22]). The observation under-lines the seriousness of all that has been taking place. We tend to look at Da-vid's kingship with all the wisdom of hindsight. In the middle of the maelstrom, the realities of power looked very different. A politician — and David was a politician — would have expanded David's words, adding, "and I intend to stay that way, king over Israel." Maybe David added it too, but *sotto voce*. As noted earlier, Shimei's own words are ambiguous enough — as we might expect in this narrative. Shimei says: "For your servant knows that I have sinned" (v. 21 [Heb.; NRSV, v. 20]). This need go no further than the admission that Shimei made a mistake in cursing David; given that David will return to power, Shimei could be expected to realize that he had been most unwise. It is a further step to admit that the interpretation Shimei put on David's rise to power was a wrong interpretation. Shimei's words can be read to admit that; they can also be read to restrict his sin to the indiscretion of speaking his mind.

David's decision, "You shall not die," equally leaves the matter unde-cided. It responds to v. 20's plea (Heb.; NRSV, v. 19): "May my lord not hold me guilty or remember how your servant did wrong." David's sworn decision ac-quits Shimei of his wrong *('āwôn);* it is discreetly silent whether the wrong was what he said or that he said it. Shimei's support is needed; for a politically as-tute monarch, that is enough.

Mephibosheth is the one alleged to have been hoping that "today the house of Israel will give me back my grandfather's kingdom" (16:3). That hope has now vanished and Mephibosheth, who will plead his lameness for not hav-ing gone with David earlier, now arrives to meet the king at the Jordan. Imme-diately David asks: "Why did you not go with me?" (v. 26 [Heb.; NRSV, v. 25]). The question is an indication of the extent of the group that fled Jerusalem. No-body of moment had remained behind, except for the ten "concubines."

The text reports that Mephibosheth had neglected his own basic personal care while David was in danger (v. 25b [Heb.; NRSV, v. 24b]). The inclusion of these details suggests that the narrative may side with Mephibosheth against Ziba. David, on the other hand, does not seem impressed. Mephibosheth need not be lying; he might have learned his lesson, learned not to trust Ziba in a cri-sis, and have been better prepared this time. For all that, he did not leave Jerusa-lem or send a message to David, he knows that his estates have been awarded to Ziba, and his arrival at the Jordan is remarkably convenient; it is just as possible that he is lying.

David cut him off abruptly: "Why do you keep on talking?" (v. 30 [Heb.; NRSV, v. 29]). The NRSV is ambiguous. "Why speak any more of your affairs?" can be understood as "Why should we speak . . . ?" The Hebrew is specific with its second person singular: "Why do you speak . . . ?" "Affairs" or "words" is often a hard call; here, "words" is more probable. David has decided; the property will be divided. It is noteworthy that the narrative has David deciding the case without granting Ziba a hearing. This may be a pointer to what is at stake: not the issue of truth but the realities of political support. It would have been unwise for David to alienate Mephibosheth, a figure around whom supporters of Saul's cause might be rallied now that Absalom was dead. It would be wise for David to maintain Mephibosheth's dependence on him. It would have been equally unwise for David to alienate Ziba's support; as a former servant of the house of Saul, and now a substantial landholder, it would be better to keep him as an ally rather than have him as an embittered enemy. The decision to divide the land between the two suppliants meets David's political needs; it may have little to do with truth or its inaccessibility.

A point that was noted under 2 Sam 9 can bear repetition here. Mephibosheth's description of his dependence on David is in stark contrast with the situation portrayed in 2 Sam 9. The two can hardly belong in the same document. Mephibosheth's grateful words here would reflect badly on the David portrayed in 2 Sam 9 — not a likely outcome. For Mephibosheth, here, all Saul's ("my father's") house were doomed to death "before my lord the king"; that is, they were not yet dead and their fate depended on David. David set Mephibosheth among those at the royal table. In 2 Sam 9, to the contrary, David is portrayed asking whether there is still "anyone left of the house of Saul" (9:1). This is a different scenario. In 2 Sam 9, Mephibosheth is the sole survivor; here, in 2 Sam 19, he is the sole descendant of Saul's to be spared by David.

The narrative then comes to Barzillai. The text reflects what we know from 17:27-29. Barzillai is from Rogelim, he had come to David at Mahanaim, and he had provided supplies of food. The text here goes on to note that he was "a very aged man," an eighty-year-old, "a very wealthy man" (gādôl hû' mĕ'ōd), and that he had accompanied the king to the Jordan (19:32-33 [Heb.; NRSV, 19:31-32]). We do not know why Barzillai is singled out and Shobi from Rabbah and Machir from Lo-debar are left behind. David invites Barzillai to a place of honor in the court at Jerusalem. Barzillai declines, but offers his servant, Chimham, in his place. Chimham goes with David, and we do not hear of him again; nor are we told the nature of his position as "servant" of Barzillai. Wealth is seldom without power, so we may assume that "a very wealthy man" was also a very powerful one. It would be to David's advantage to have the powerful at his side. The episode brings home to us how much of the economic and political infrastructure of Davidic power escapes us.

Barzillai will cross the Jordan with the king, if only for a little while (v. 37a [Heb.; NRSV, v. 36a]). Probably, he will stay with David long enough for the news to reach the people assembled at Gilgal as to where Barzillai's support lies. That would be enough. Chimham's presence with David at Gilgal is noted (v. 41 [Heb.; NRSV, v. 40]).

In declining David's invitation to the Jerusalem court, Barzillai gives us a rare insight into the court life of the time. For Barzillai, the attractions of the court are summed up as food, drink, and listening to "the voice of singing men and singing women." These "singing men and singing women" of the court *(šārîm wĕšārôt)* are not to be confused with the male and female singers of the temple establishment, noted at both Ezra 2:65 and Neh 7:67 (paired and piel, *mĕšōrrîm ûmĕšōrrôt).* The term "singers" (qal, masculine, and unpaired, *šārîm)* is used for the temple (1 Kgs 10:12; Ezek 40:44; 2 Chr 9:11) and for liturgical singers (Ps 68:26 [Heb.; NRSV, 68:25]; 87:7). The pairing of "singing men and singing women" at the court is found in three places only: here (i.e., 2 Sam 19:36 [Heb.; NRSV, 19:35]); Qoh 2:8; and 2 Chr 35:25, in relation to King Josiah. If we assume that stories could be sung, we have evidence in these three references for the presence of male and female storytellers in ancient Israel.

These three special encounters are at an end. The movement of return to Jerusalem must be resumed — [II.C.2.a.3)]. So David crosses the Jordan, takes leave of Barzillai with a kiss and a blessing, and goes on to Gilgal. Chimham is with him. We had last heard of the people of Judah in v. 16 (Heb.; NRSV, v. 15), where they were at Gilgal "to meet the king and bring him over the Jordan." Now, in v. 41 (Heb.; NRSV, v. 40), they have been augmented by half the people of Israel, and they brought the king across. Exactly what is involved in this "bringing across" in either case is unclear. Obviously, though, it denotes support of David. Support will be the issue in what follows.

The drift of what follows is clear; the details are not — [II.C.2.b]. In v. 41 (Heb.; NRSV, v. 40), all the people (group) of Judah *(kol ʿam yĕhûdâ)* and half the people (group) of Israel *(ḥăṣî ʿam yiśrāʾēl)* are on hand. In the next verse, all the people (men) of Israel *(kol ʾîš yiśrāʾēl)* are talking to the king, and in the following verses all the people (men) of Israel *(kol ʾîš yiśrāʾēl)* are disputing with all the people (men) of Judah *(kol ʾîš yĕhûdâ).* The simplest understanding is that v. 41 (Heb.; NRSV, v. 40) is referring to the tribes as represented and vv. 42-44 (Heb.; NRSV, vv. 41-43) are referring to the representatives present on the spot. We know nothing about the degree of representation involved. An understanding related to representatives of half the people of Israel *(ḥăṣî ʿam yiśrāʾēl)* sits oddly with v. 44's (Heb.; NRSV, v. 43's) reference to "ten shares in the king." We are tempted to think automatically of the ten tribes, but the phrase occurs elsewhere only in Dan 1:20, where it has nothing to do with tribes. It may be highly idiomatic for something like: we are ten times better regarding loyalty to King David. Israel's claim to have been the first to advocate bringing back the king also lies outside the information offered us in the narrative.

The drift of the passage is clear: Israel and Judah disputed their support for the king and Judah prevailed. The way is prepared for Sheba ben Bichri's rebellion, but the details escape us.

Genre

The traditions brought together under 2 Sam 15–19 are complex and multiple. Presenting the events of David's retreat from Jerusalem and return to it, basically they constitute a complex (→) story. In the present text, the opening "After this" links back into what precedes. The link is one of those standard editorial procedures that does not necessarily indicate the original limits of a text. Certainly what precedes can be appropriately linked into the content of chs. 15–19. The behavior of David portrayed in chs. 11–12 has provided a pattern for what is to come. The happenings of chs. 13–14 offer a suitable seedbed for Absalom's alienation and bitterness. In what follows, Sheba's final rebellion sheds light on the fragility of David's return to power. But the trajectory of retreat and return is in itself complete, without needing the traditions that precede or follow.

The multiple scenes are welded together in a single story that begins with precipitous flight and ends with the uncertainty of return. The tension of an uncertain outcome is there from the beginning (see 15:25-26) and is maintained throughout. The events lead forward, preparing for the possibility of return; the return exploits some of the possibilities prepared for the return. The climactic battle and the death of Absalom occupy fifteen verses (18:1-15); the story is one of retreat and return.

Setting

While a single setting can hardly be determined for a story of this kind, certain pointers can be noted. Toward the end, viewpoints are presented that favor Israel over Judah. For example: the language of "stolen you away" (19:42 [Heb.; NRSV, 19:41]; root: *g-n b*); the imbalance, "we have ten shares in the king . . . more than you" (19:44 [Heb.; NRSV, 19:43]); the emotion, "Why then did you despise us?" (19:44 [Heb.; NRSV, 19:43]). A little earlier, the same issue is raised, again favoring the political inclinations of Israel over against Judah (19:12-13 Heb.; NRSV, 19:11-12]). The swaying of Judah's loyalty in David's favor is attributed to Amasa (19:15 [Heb.; NRSV, 19:14]), Amasa's hold on leadership and life was brief. He dies at the start of ch. 20. It is noteworthy that neither Bathsheba nor Solomon is mentioned.

Absalom had given Amasa Joab's job (17:25). Joab was last heard of in chs. 11–12 and 14; he has played no role in the retreat from Jerusalem. Now he is responsible for Absalom's death and David's reappearance in public. At the end of ch. 19, he is still out of a job. We are told nothing of Joab, beyond his being the son of Zeruiah and brother of Abishai and Asahel; we know more about Amasa (cf. 17:25). We know nothing of Joab's entourage (cf. 1 Chr 11:39 for his armor-bearer); he may have been a loner, but a family at least is likely. That such a story might have emanated from circles associated with Joab and/or Abiathar (banished by Solomon, 1 Kgs 2:26-27) is possible; it is not necessary.

If traditions such as these were to end up at the court of Jeroboam, first king of northern Israel (see ch. 10 below), an origin in Israel in the first place is not unlikely.

Meaning

At one level, the meaning of the story is clear: the combination of good faith, good politics, and God's good will maintained David's power as king over a united Israel, despite the ravages of his son's rebellion.

But there are many levels in this story. Rather than trying to identify them and discuss them in isolation, it may be better to realize how much storytelling of this kind takes account of the multiplicity of human motivations and the deviousness of so much human behavior. It may be significant that David was unaware of Absalom's long-term scheming against him — but was he? We are not told why David left Jerusalem in a hurry; the implications are adumbrated but not spelled out (cf. 15:14). Ittai the Gittite is loyal to David — but why? With Abiathar and Zadok, the priests of the ark, David is piously accepting of his fate and politically astute in influencing it — as throughout the narrative.

There is much to remember about these events. There is much to learn from them, much insight to be won. Political fragility threatened Israel in its beginnings. According to the text of Kings, the combination of political and religious fragility would destroy both Israel and Judah at the end.

Bibliography of Works Cited Above

Bietenhard, Sophia Katharina. *Des Königs General: Die Heerführertraditionen in der vorstaatlichen und frühen staatlichen Zeit und die Joabgestalt in 2 Sam 2–20; 1 Kön 1–2*. OBO 163. Freiburg, Switzerland: Universitätsverlag, 1998.

Conroy, Charles. *Absalom Absalom! Narrative and Language in 2 Sam 13–20*. AnBib 81. Rome: Biblical Institute, 1978.

Mauchline, John. *1 and 2 Samuel*. NCB. London: Oliphants, 1971.

Polzin, Robert. "Curses and Kings: A Reading of 2 Samuel 15–16." Pages 201-26 in *The New Literary Criticism and the Hebrew Bible*. Edited J. C. Exum and D. J. A. Clines. JSOTSup 143. Sheffield: Sheffield Academic Press, 1993.

Smith, Henry Preserved. *Samuel*. ICC. Edinburgh: T.&T. Clark, 1898.

Würthwein, Ernst. *Die Erzählung von der Thronfolge Davids — theologische oder politische Geschichtsschreibung?* TS 115. Zürich: Theologische Verlag, 1974.

Chapter 9

SHEBA'S REBELLION
(2 SAM 20)

Textual Issues

20:14   The town is Abel of Beth-maacah, however the syntax of the MT is to be understood (see Stoebe, 442). The Berites of the MT are unknown to us; "no place or people named הברים is known" (Driver, 344). Stoebe queries whether the space left in manuscripts after the word may have indicated lack of clarity or loss of text (p. 443). Barthélemy, noting the presence of both Joab and Sheba as possible subjects, opts for Joab as subject in v. 14 (pp. 296-97). Against this, the narrative has Sheba within the town and Joab besieging it; Barthélemy's suggestion leaves Sheba's arrival and entry into the town unmentioned. Sheba's clan, the Bichrites, has been conjectured; the Vulgate has "picked warriors" (cf. McCarter, 428). "Companions," "those associated with him" *(ḥăbērîm)* in the sense of Judg 20:11, may shed light. Stoebe passes over the word, as did Josephus and others (pp. 442-43). The narrative dilemma is evident: Sheba is portrayed as a serious threat to David (v. 6); the threat of Sheba's force inside Abel of Beth-maacah is outweighed with the townsfolk by the eloquence of one wise woman (v. 22). Given the uncertainty of the text, further emendation is unwise.

Discussion

2 Sam 20 offers remarkable insight into the fragility of David's kingdom. Without it, we might suspect; we could not be sure. With it, the recognition of the frailty of David's hold on power, both within Judah and Israel, is inescapable. It invites the reader to balance the Story of David's Rise with the Story of David's Fragility. As rulers know, once power has been attained there is only one danger to be feared: losing it. The stories explored so far have been marked by their ability to achieve neutrality and ambiguity. Any title should maintain that neutrality and ambiguity; that is the primary reason for advocating the title, The Stories of David's Middle Years.

All Judah and half Israel have been portrayed rallying to David and arguing over their loyalty to him. The dispute on the way back to Jerusalem ended with Judah having the upper hand (19:44 [Heb.; NRSV, 19:43]). The text follows that report immediately with Sheba ben Bichri's summons to rebellion. The language is substantially the same as Israel will use after the death of Solomon, David's son (1 Kgs 12:16). The key statements are repeated (the NRSV obscures this): "no portion *(ḥēleq)* in David," "no inheritance *(naḥălâ)* in the son of Jesse," and "to your tents, O Israel." What happens here for David will happen again for Rehoboam. Joab will restore the kingdom for David by force of arms; Shemaiah, the man of God, delivering God's word: "for this thing is from me" (1 Kgs 12:24), prevents Rehoboam from doing something similar.

Sheba's rebellion uncovers the fragility of David's kingdom. It also reveals the fragility of Sheba's revolt and the importance of the leader. When Sheba's head is thrown over the wall, his rebellion is at an end (2 Sam 20:22). Is it much the same with Jeroboam later? The biblical text indicates a key difference. The LORD is presumably with David still; "the LORD had ordained to defeat the good counsel of Ahithophel, so that the LORD might bring ruin on Absalom" (17:14). Nothing is said about Sheba. But later the LORD is with Jeroboam: "for this thing is from me" (1 Kgs 12:24).

Sheba ben Bichri is a Benjaminite — [I]. The Benjaminites were Saul's tribe. We can understand that David would not want to alienate Shimei and his troop of Benjaminites or Ziba and Mephibosheth with their links to Saul. The group that followed Sheba is the same that was arguing with the Judah group at the end of ch. 19. Technically, despite the NRSV, it is not "all the people" *(kol 'am)* but "all the men" *(kol 'îš)* who are portrayed defecting to Sheba, presumably the people of Israel's representatives on the scene. There is no indication later that Sheba's following was particularly extensive (cf. v. 14). At this point in the story, the men of Judah *('îš yĕhûdâ)* stay with "their king" from the Jordan to Jerusalem.

The narrative does not follow Sheba for the moment, but stays with David — [II.A]. Three moves are reported of David in Jerusalem. First, the ten violated women are put under protection, with an imposed isolation. They remain in this condition until they die. We have noted that their presence is a reminder to all Jerusalem of Absalom's revolt against his father; the text, however, says nothing. Second, the forces of Judah are to be called to arms. The king gives Amasa, the new army commander, a three-day period in which to achieve this. Third, with the passing of these three days (v. 5), David turns to Abishai, expressing anxiety that Sheba ben Bichri's rebellion may become more serious than Absalom's. So Abishai leads out the king's troops (vv. 6-7). The text has noted, without comment, that David gave Joab's job to Amasa (19:14 [Heb.; NRSV, 19:13]). There has been no mention of Abishai's appointment to the command of David's own troops. Nor is there any mention of Benaiah, who will figure immediately after Joab in the list of David's administration at the end of the chapter (cf. 20:23). It is worth noting, however, that Abishai is elsewhere listed as "chief of the Thirty," although he did not attain to the Three, the top leadership (2 Sam 23:18-19); interestingly, Joab does not rate a direct mention for himself in this text about the Three and the Thirty; obliquely, he is mentioned three times, once each as brother of Abishai and of Asahel, and once for his armor-bearer (see below).

Abishai's brief period in command here should not be resolved by adjusting the text, although the Syriac substitutes Joab for Abishai in v. 6. There is a powerplay in the background and we are not privy to it. The troops who leave with Abishai are an interesting lot: "Joab's men," given this description only here (cf. v. 11, Hebrew); "the Cherethites, the Pelethites," associated with Benaiah in 2 Sam 8:18; 20:23, but not in 15:18; and "all the warriors," troops loyal to David (cf. 2 Sam 16:6; 1 Kgs 1:8). These are regular troops, not the conscripts or volunteers who might called out by Amasa.

With the departure of the troops from Jerusalem, there are issues to be settled before the narrative can turn to the suppression of Sheba ben Bichri's rebellion — [II.B]. David had placed Amasa in command of the army, and Abishai had command of the royal troops. At Gibeon, not far north of Jerusalem, Joab makes light work of reordering this command structure to his own liking. He kills Amasa as he had Abner (2 Sam 3:27). The text has the note: "he

[Joab] did not strike a second blow." Swordplay is another area in which Joab proves himself decisive.

Here, once again, Baruch Halpern is overzealous. "The case of Amasa is perhaps the clearest assassination in which David is implicated" (*Secret Demons,* 90). In the text, Amasa shares Abner's fate. His suicidal folly was accepting Joab's job; David's only mistake was offering it to him. What the text points to but does not reveal is less a matter of David's murderous tendencies and much more the extent of Joab's power.

The reordered command is evident as the narrative moves forward. The pursuit of Sheba ben Bichri is led by "Joab and his brother Abishai" (v. 10); not a word of explanation is offered for this change at the top. The brothers understand each other. The episode of Amasa's body indicates a reluctance on the part of the soldiers to proceed. Whether this was a matter of human decency in the presence of a dead commander's body or whether it was a matter of loyalty to the commander appointed by David is not said. Joab's loyalist is allowed to confuse the issue skillfully: "whoever favors Joab, and whoever is for David, let him follow Joab" (v. 11). The pursuit of Sheba ben Bichri is continued.

The narrative can finally return to the suppression of Sheba ben Bichri's rebellion — [II.C]. As the long narrative in chs. 11–20 began, so it ends. The siege of Rabbah formed the frame around the story of David and Bathsheba; the siege of Abel of Beth-maacah forms the frame around Joab's exchange with the wise woman. Verse 14 is textually uncertain; however, Sheba's forces have entered the city and there is nothing to indicate that they were particularly numerous. Joab's siege operations are under way (v. 15), when the wise woman intervenes to open negotiations with Joab. She appeals to Abel's long tradition and pleads for the city, "a mother in Israel," to be spared. Joab points out that he only wants one rebellious Ephraimite given up. It is the woman who promises that his head will be thrown from the wall. In half a verse, the city's inhabitants yield to the woman's wisdom, Sheba's head is cut off, and the siege is lifted. The negotiations within the city are of no interest to the narrative. Of interest to us is the realization that a rebellion could depend on one leader. Absalom's rebellion ended with his death; Sheba's rebellion has gone the same way. In Ahithophel's view, David's kingdom would have succumbed with the king's death (17:2-3). Sheba's rebellion began with a trumpet blast (v. 1); it is ended with a trumpet blast (v. 22a), as was Absalom's (18:16).

The narrative ends dryly: "Joab returned to Jerusalem to the king" (v. 22b). Joab left Jerusalem in 11:1 in the service of his king. Joab did what was needed at Rabbah, played his role in Absalom's return, and was responsible for Absalom's death. Having gone out from Jerusalem subordinate to Amasa and Abishai, Joab now returns to Jerusalem in command and still in the service of his king. The narrative says nothing of David's reaction.

The list of David's administrators has been appended here (cf. also 2 Sam 8:16-18 and 1 Kgs 4:2-6). It is not in any way an integral part of the narrative. Outside this list, Benaiah, Adoram, Jehoshaphat, Sheva, and Ira are not mentioned in chs. 11–20. The changes from 2 Sam 8:16-18 are bedeviled by textual issues; whatever changes there are appear minor and not particularly significant, with the possible exception of Adoram's responsibility for forced labor.

Genre

The genre here is (→) story; it is succinct enough to be (→) reported story. What the story is about can be explored below, under the "Meaning" rubric. It opens with a call to rebellion; it concludes with the cause of the rebellion quite literally decapitated. The tension is heightened by David's comment that, the way things are going, "Sheba son of Bichri will do us more harm than Absalom" (20:6); this has the potential to be big. The plot follows Sheba's retreat north; with his death, the narrative moves south. Sub-plots nibble at the edges. Was Amasa given an impossible task or did he lose his time in treachery? Command of David's forces was given to Abishai; what understandings or rivalries existed between himself and his brother Joab we are not told. Joab brought the rebellion to a close — as he had with Absalom's — and returned to Jerusalem. Rather like Noah with his birds after the flood, David first sent out Amasa, who did not come back; then he sent out Abishai; at the end, it was Joab who "returned to Jerusalem to the king" — whether to David's joy or sorrow, the text does not say.

Setting

Assessing the issue of setting for this little piece is as complex as unraveling the many threads running through it. Circles interested in the realities of politics and the checks and balances of power have to be likely contenders. The role of Joab in it all means that those committed to him cannot be excluded as possible. The fragility of the kingdom is exposed and the credit for shoring it up goes to Joab; it is unlikely that Davidic circles were prime movers where this narrative was concerned. As in so many cases, certainty escapes us.

Meaning

The meaning of the piece is as multi-faceted as the potential of its plot. If emphasis is placed on the issue of modeling, then David's influence has gone beyond his family to have its effect on his kingdom, outside the royal circle. If emphasis is placed on this kingdom, then its fragility is to the fore. The frail union of Israel and Judah that was to come apart after Solomon is here prefigured. An unknown figure, Sheba ben Bichri, could threaten the kingdom of King David, anointed of YHWH. According to 1 Kgs 11:26-40, it was the will of God that took the kingdom away from David's son and would build for Jeroboam as enduring a dynasty as David's (cf. 11:38); according to 2 Sam 20, the fault-line was pretty much built into the fabric of the kingdom from the outset.

Amasa and Abishai are bit players on a bigger stage. Joab, however, is a leading player in the drama. Precise meaning is hardly to be pinned down. Joab's power is an evident theme. That kings are beholden to powerbrokers is also there. That Joab was a powerful figure in David's kingdom has been clear since ch. 11. All of this and more lies within the meaning of the story.

Bibliography of Work Cited Above

Halpern, Baruch. *David's Secret Demons: Messiah, Murderer, Traitor, King.* Grand Rapids: Eerdmans, 2001.

Chapter 10

THE STORIES OF DAVID'S MIDDLE YEARS: GENRE – SETTING – MEANING (2 SAM 11–20)

Genre for 2 Samuel 11–20

There is an irony in the attempt to isolate the generic in a text that by wide consensus is unique in biblical literature. Yet artistry is achieved by the unexpected interplay of the individual with the generic. Without the web of expectation woven by our experience of the generic, the particular individuality of any single piece would not emerge as it does. The generic background to the Stories of David's Middle Years has to be what the title claims: (→) story. What makes the Stories of David's Middle Years unique is not just the skill with which these traditions are told. There is more to it than that and part of the exploration of the genre of the piece is an exploration of these aspects that make it unique.

The literary work is unquestionably moving in the realm of (→) story. The story of David and Bathsheba is set within the siege and capture of Rabbah. It is a story of sexual violence, homicidal violence, political power, and divine intervention. It sets the tone for what is to come, not so much in its events as in the way that they are narrated. Options are left open; avenues are seldom closed.

The episodes with Amnon, Tamar, and Absalom are next. They affect the issue of succession within David's kingdom. Amnon will die; Absalom will be set on the path that leads to his death. Tamar is a stronger symbol of the kingdom. She remains "a desolate woman" (13:20). For all its model status later, at its core David's is a desolate kingdom. Violence has prevailed over innocence and life. What powerful figures want, powerful figures take. Fortunate are those who live at peace under their vines and fig trees (cf. 1 Kgs 5:5 [Heb.; NRSV, 4:25]).

The story of a rebellion follows, led by the king's son and leading to the flight of the king from his capital. It ends with the death of the king's son, the end of the rebellion, and the return of the king to Jerusalem. Another rebellion is stopped before it can really get under way. The king's reign is secured. There is material enough for a plot here. Will the rebellion succeed or will the status quo be restored? Yet the structures of the revolt are not explored. We know little of the extent of popular support or the reality of grievances generating that support. We know of Absalom as leader and Ahithophel as his chief counselor; more we do not know. The king returns to Jerusalem but — apart from providing for the violated "concubines" and arranging to suppress Sheba's revolt — we are not told of changes that might have made the monarchy more acceptable or more secure. The rebellion is hardly the primary focus of the storytelling.

There is the tension of a son who is happy to have his father dead and a father who desperately wants his son alive — and neither gets his way. There is too much drama that is incidental to this conflict for the conflict to be the primary focus of the storytelling. As the focus is thrown wider — bringing in the long-delayed meeting of David with Absalom, Absalom's murder of Amnon, Amnon's rape of Tamar, David's judicial murder of Uriah, and David's violation of Bathsheba — the difficulty of finding a primary focus for the storytelling increases.

Comparison with what are potentially other ancient biblical narratives is useful. The Ark Narrative (1 Sam 4–6; 2 Sam 6) has an external focus: the presence of the ark in Jerusalem and the significance of its coming there. The collection of largely story material that can be termed the Story of David's Rise (within 1 Sam 9:1–2 Sam 8:15) has an external focus: David's kingship in Jerusalem, brought about by God's will and without bloodshed. The hypothetical Prophetic Record (within 1 Sam 1:1–2 Kgs 10:28) has an external focus: the exercise of prophetic authority in relation to kings. The Josianic Deuteronomistic History (within Deut 1:1–2 Kgs 23:25a) has an external focus: traditional and theological underpinning for the Josianic reform. Even the revised Deuteronomistic History (Deut 1:1–2 Kgs 25:30) has an external focus: accounting for the failure of the reform. It is not possible to identify a similar external focus for the Stories of David's Middle Years (2 Sam 11–20). Their focus is internal; it does not lie outside the narrative.

The only candidate for an external focus for this narrative is the theme of succession to the throne; it is an unsatisfactory focus. The succession of Solomon to his father's throne is the theme of 1 Kgs 1–2; it is adequately dealt with there. If Amnon and Absalom are to be eliminated as potential successors, the text of 2 Sam 13–20 involves an enormous expenditure of literary energy simply to achieve two deaths. If YHWH's favor to Solomon in 2 Sam 12 was needed, it is totally absent from 1 Kgs 1–2. The aged David appeals to his own oath, sworn by the LORD the God of Israel (1 Kgs 1:13, 17, 30, 35), and not to any favor manifested by Nathan, predestining the infant Solomon (or: Jedidiah). Ancient Israel was far too theologically alert to confuse David's oath with YHWH's favor. As an external focus, the theme of succession to David's throne does not account satisfactorily for 2 Sam 11–20.

A similar conclusion emerges from the consideration of the status of these narratives as written documents. As we have them, all are of course written. It seems probable, though, that all except the Stories of David's Middle

Years, were written with a view to something beyond them; the Stories of David's Middle Years is the only text that seems to have been composed for itself. As written documents, all these stem from a time of limited literacy. As documents, they were not written for copying and wide distribution; they were written for preservation and for the use of what we can assume was a restricted few. What they sought to preserve was an understanding that gave meaning to the traditions that encapsulated Israel's experience.

The Ark Narrative took the traditions of the ark's departure from Shiloh, its sojourn at Kiriath-jearim, and its arrival in Jerusalem to promulgate an understanding of God's initiation of a new epoch in the history of Israel. The era of the old Israel, associated with Shiloh, had drawn to a close; a new era had opened under the monarchy of David, blessed by the coming of the ark to Jerusalem. The ark traditions were organized to express this understanding and committed to writing. The understanding needed dissemination among the people, achieved by word of mouth, not by distribution of the document. The document, then, preserved and organized traditions associated with the ark; its organization and interpretation of the traditions served as a base for communicating these convictions more widely.

The collection of traditional material we call the Story of David's Rise served a similar purpose in interpreting David's rise to power in Israel to a wider constituency. The traditions were presumably told and retold on many occasions and in many ways. The traditions in the written collection were structured and organized to bring out the role of God's spirit in David's success and to emphasize the claim that no blood was shed on David's way to the throne. The function of the document was to preserve this interpretation along with the traditions; both were to be enshrined together.

Similarly, the Prophetic Record put a particular stamp on traditions originating with Saul and David, with Jeroboam, Ahab, and Jehu. A pattern of divine action was made visible in the traditions associated with these figures. Where visibility was limited, literary action needed to be taken to be sure that God's action was recognized and given due weight. The prophetic authority to anoint kings and dismiss them was important. It went back to the legitimate origins of kingship in Israel, with Samuel, Saul, and David. The prophetic claim of authority to pronounce God's word, designating and rejecting kings, was important. It is at its most significant with Jeroboam, Ahab, and Jehu. The claim is that the rise and fall of these kings were not haphazard political events; God's guiding will, expressed through the prophets, could be seen in them all. The document put on record an expression of this interpretation. It was not for distribution to a readership; it was a base for communication to disciples and associates.

Much the same can be said for the Josianic Deuteronomistic History and the Revised Deuteronomistic History. The details do not need to be repeated. Instead, attention can turn to the question: Why were the Stories of David's Middle Years committed to writing? An external focus cannot be satisfactorily identified. The "something beyond" that might have stimulated their writing cannot be isolated. If the Stories of David's Middle Years is the only text that seems to have been written for itself, what purpose did it serve?

The issue is not one to be glossed over facilely. The text itself is dense and weighted toward ambiguity. It seldom takes sides but rather leaves questions open and offers little in the way of answers. If written for itself, what purpose did it serve?

The orientation toward David, the reigning monarch, is unhelpfully even-handed. David's treatment of Bathsheba and Uriah is shocking and attracts prophetic condemnation. David's immediate confession is met with forgiveness, he is portrayed in urgent prayer, and the child of his legitimate union with Bathsheba is favored of God. David can be seen as partly responsible for Tamar's rape, in sending her unescorted to his eldest son; on the other hand, he might be seen relying on the solidarity of those around his son. The text says nothing. Similarly, the exchange with Absalom over the sheep shearing at Baal-hazor could be seen again as highlighting David's responsibility in the lead-up to Amnon's death; on the other hand, it could be taken as distancing David from the murder. What might be described as the dithering over Absalom's return might also be called the exercise of appropriate distance from a murderous prince. Flight from Jerusalem can be called panicked folly or the height of strategic wisdom. And so on.

Clearly David is at the center of the stories, but the statistics provide both a surprise and a stimulus to thought. David is named some 94 times in 82 verses; "the king" is mentioned 382 times in 126 verses. The question is unavoidable: Is the narrative more concerned with the office of king than with its present incumbent? The question has to be left open, but it has to be left on the table (cf. Perdue, "Ambiguity," 183). It is not surprising that Absalom is named some 101 times in 82 verses; it is perhaps surprising that Joab is named some 67 times in 54 verses. These are the three leading characters in the narrative. Mention of others reach the twenties for a couple (Amnon and Uriah), some reach the teens (Tamar, Zadok and Abiathar, Sheba), others not even that (Ziba, Mephibosheth, Bathsheba). The role of Joab is surprisingly significant; he plays an important role in several major scenes (i.e., 2 Sam 11–12; 14; 18; 20).

None of this helps us identify a cause being advocated, a career being advanced, or anything that might give us access to the driving interest of this narrative. It may help, instead, to look to the possible sources of driving interest within the text.

In chs. 15–19, for example, there is a focus on what the king does in order to recover his royal power, threatened by rebellion. Confidence, prayer, and political strategy are all part of the mix presented. Confidence about his return to Jerusalem is expressed in David's leaving ten women there to care for his palace. It is also present in his decision to leave the ark there. That this may have been strategically desirable is a possibility to be entertained. That it is expressed in terms of religious faith and submission to God is evident. Prayer is explicit in David's plea that the counsel of Ahithophel be turned into foolishness. Trust in God is explicit in David's handling of the ark and his handling of the Shimei episode. Political strategy is present in much of what is recounted. The freedom given Ittai is a shrewd confirmation of his loyalty. The presence of Zadok and Abiathar in Jerusalem probably means a favorably placed political force and is certainly a sound base for communications. To have Hushai inside

Absalom's political circle is a stroke of genius — and luck. Potential allies are not to be alienated; so Ziba is believed and Shimei tolerated. When the military conflict has been won, the pot of popular support is to be stirred, future allies are to be welcomed and past allies rewarded. Overall, the construal is positive. The origins of such a picture need not be too far from Davidic loyalties.

The picture becomes more critical if the driving interest shifts from the question of how to regain power to the question of how not to lose it in the first place. This is latent in the portrayal of Absalom's successful rebellion; it is not developed in the narrative. Absalom's appeal is to the justice he would provide. This can be painted as fostering the inevitable sense of self-interest and personal grievance; or it can be painted as promising needed solutions to real problems. It is latent in the text. The picture of royal maneuvering that keeps Absalom at a distance for two years in Jerusalem, and three years before that in Geshur, is more easily seen as royal dithering than royal diplomacy. It opens up avenues to the origins of Absalom's spirit of rebellion. The action allowed Amnon (the rape of Tamar) and the failure to punish it, leading to his murder by Absalom, can also be portrayed as among the root causes that incited Absalom to his ultimate rebellion. For these aspects to be developed, some distance from David and the Davidic court seems desirable.

The interest driving the story of David and Bathsheba is harder to isolate. The twin crimes are bad enough. The judgment of God is clear. God's forgiveness may be asserted ("the LORD has put away your sin") but the telling of such sin shocks. David's prayer for the first child and YHWH's favor for the second may provide a balance; they hardly remove the shock of sin. Nathan's speech, unfolding God's judgment, articulates a clear case of modeling: what David has done, sexually and homicidally, will continue in his house. Even without Nathan's unfolding, the parallel to David's twin crimes of rape or violation and murder provided by Amnon's committing rape and Absalom's committing murder is evident. More tenuous, but present all the same, is the unbridled use of power by Absalom in his rebellion and by Joab in recovering his own position. It is unlikely that the portrayal of such negative modeling originated in sources close to David.

Common to all three of these focuses is a driving interest in the inner motivations of human behavior, especially at the level of the royal court and the kingdom. How to regain the kingdom: confidence, prayer, astute strategy, and luck. How to lose the kingdom in the first place: be indecisive, delaying and dithering. How to model the abuse of royal power: have sexual intercourse with the wife of one of your soldiers and have him killed when he fails to cover your tracks for you.

Despite the shock of sin, portraying David as violator and murderer, this document is not an anti-Davidic tract. The David of chs. 15–19 is portrayed as too skilled a monarch. The potential weaknesses of the king earlier are not exploited or emphasized. It is hard to see a polemicist refraining from making a lot more of such material. The text's treatment is stunning in its discretion. The primary issue is: What is this document? Secondary is: Where does it come from and what does it mean?

If, as we have been arguing, there is an inner focus to the document, one possible understanding of it — not excluding the likelihood of others — is as an invitation to profound reflection on the complexities of what powers human behavior. As such, it need not tell stories in their entirety, but allude to them. As such, it does not demand an external focus; its focus is on gaining access to the forces affecting human behavior, perhaps with a view to reflection on how such forces might be used or modified. As such, it is not the base for communication to a wider audience; it is enough that it is accessible to the few who need to think at this depth. As such, then, it is a (→) story of royal behavior, unfolded in such a way as to invite reflection on the forces that influence human behavior.

It is worth exploring this story of royal behavior a little further. While it is primarily a story of David's behavior, it is inextricably interwoven with the behavior of Joab. Kings exercise power; but power can be the domain of army commanders. The narrative holds the two and says nothing. Boiled down to its bare essentials, 2 Sam 11–20 is a narrative of two pairs of scandals (David with Bathsheba and Uriah; Amnon with Tamar and Absalom with Amnon), linked by the portrayal of a conflicted king to two rebellions (Absalom's and Sheba's). Joab is present at the start, involved in the siege of Rabbah. Joab is involved with the conflicted king; it is at Joab's manipulative insistence that Absalom is brought to Jerusalem and ultimately to the king. Joab is present at the end, killing Absalom, forcing the king to override his display of grief, and restoring himself to his place as military commander. Joab is a shadowy figure. He comes on the scene in 2 Sam 2–3, when the house of David is involved in a long war with the house of Saul (2 Sam 3:1). After 2 Sam 14, he is lost to the narrative's view, only to reappear in 2 Sam 18 and 20. Kings and commanders are inextricably linked to each other. David may replace Joab with Amasa and Abishai, but in the end it is Joab who dismisses the troops and who returns "to Jerusalem to the king" (2 Sam 20:22). On the figure of Joab, see Bietenhard, *Königs General.*

In its central block (chs. 15–19), it is a story told on multiple levels. The broad view holds in wide focus David's flight and return, as well as the military defeat of Absalom and his army. The middle view focuses on episodes significant to Absalom's defeat and David's return: Ittai's mercenaries; Hushai's counsel; Zadok and Abiathar's communications; Zadok and Abiathar's rallying of Judah; Amasa's support. The narrow view focuses in close-up on individuals: Ziba and Shimei. Almost too unknown to be inserted into these levels are the figures of Barzillai, Shobi, and Machir. Along with them is the question: Why Transjordan? Not to be overlooked are David's prayer in 15:31 and God's action in 17:14. It is a narrative of complexity and depth.

It is a narrative that can almost ignore the presence of David's wives and children in his flight and return, and yet that involves women at significant moments. On three occasions, women are victims: Bathsheba (most probably), Tamar (certainly, and left desolate), and the ten "concubines" (certainly, and left as if widows). On two occasions, wise women transform the potential trajectory of events (ch. 14 and Absalom's return; ch. 20 and Sheba's rebellion). Finally, Tamar, Amnon's victim, is the only figure in that story to act with integrity and intelligence. The story of royal behavior is a male-dominated one and women appear mostly as its victims. The narrative does not give their point of view; it does not consign them to silence either. The two wise women play roles that in a male-dominated portrayal can only be called unexpected.

It is a story of royal behavior, and it touches almost every aspect of life that a king can touch.

Setting for 2 Samuel 11–20

The question of a setting for a document such as 2 Sam 11–20 comes down to asking: Where might the few be found who needed to think at this depth and with minimal sacral overtones? There is nothing in the text to suggest attribution to official sources.

We know little of the wealthy families from around David's time who might have had the means, the leisure, and the interest to create a text of this kind. In the later Jerusalem of Josiah's time, we know of or may assume the existence of families like the house of Shaphan and the house of Hilkiah and others. Barzillai is witness that, in David's time even in distant Mahanaim, families were well off and presumably well established. Nearer to home, Nabal is described as "very rich" (1 Sam 25:2). Those described as "David's own warriors" (1 Kgs 1:8) may well have won renown for more than mere military exploits. Under Rehoboam, there were both "older men who had attended his father Solomon" and "the young men who had grown up with him" (1 Kgs 12:6, 8) who served as counselors. From all of this, it is likely that there were powerful families with assets enough to allow for leisure, an interest in the forces moving in their society, and either a literacy of their own or the ability to pay for needed scribal services. The possibility of the Stories of David's Middle Years having been put into writing within such a family, or group of families, has to be considered as a potential setting for the document.

While we may look for a single setting, it would be unwise to assume that the document we have now in 2 Sam 11–20 originated in a single creative effort. It may have. It may also have emerged over time and with contributions from more than one group. We have already taken cognizance of the different interests manifested in chs. 15–19 (20), chs. 13–14, and chs. 11–12, for example. Nothing can be alleged that requires one creative effort. There is, without question, a unity that reflects the uniqueness of the document. This unity may be adequately preserved by the inward-looking character of the piece, its inner focus; as such, it could be maintained over several stages of composition. The differing degrees of distance from David might be similarly accounted for.

As has been noted, these Stories of David's Middle Years have an evident interest in the role of counselors; there is also a noted absence of such consultation where it might have been most helpful. Reference to the role of counselors in the decision that led to the north's rebellion against Rehoboam — a rebellion closely paralleling those of Absalom and Sheba — points to an obvious fact and an associated possibility. The fact: with the new kingdom of northern Israel, Jeroboam would have needed royal counselors. The possibility: as suggested earlier, these Stories of David's Middle Years might have been useful in the preparation of such counselors. From that possibility, it is a short step to thinking that the document might have been committed to writing in such circles. As has been said, Jeroboam's court in the north is far enough away from Davidic influence to allow for criticism of David's actions. However, it would be highly surprising if counselors from Jerusalem had not migrated north with the division of the kingdom; Solomon's counselors would certainly not have been drawn solely from Judah. The young men's advice to Rehoboam was disastrously inappropriate. A document such as the Stories of David's Middle Years would have given younger counselors plenty of opportunity to test their innate wisdom.

Note that the narrative's comment on Rehoboam's choice of advice (1 Kgs 12:15) is revelatory of the same outlook as the comment on Absalom's choice of advice, when preferring Hushai to Ahithophel (2 Sam 17:14). Even if the comment on Rehoboam derives from the Deuteronomist, it reveals an awareness in ancient Israel of the similarity of the two situations. Access to good counsel was crucial; but even with wise counsel available, wisdom could be defeated. In the case of Ahithophel and Hushai, God intervened in order to "bring ruin on Absalom." In Rehoboam's case, God intervened in order to fulfill his word, spoken by Ahijah the prophet.

Meaning for 2 Samuel 11–20

This is a point where it is important to recognize the difference between function and meaning. As we have interpreted them, the function of these Stories of David's Rise is to explore the understanding of the forces that motivate human behavior at the top levels. It is achieved by carefully narrating the details of behavior that is often highly questionable and neither asking nor answering the questions that this mode of presentation raises. The function of the narrative is not to report; it goes well beyond what is needed for reporting. The function of the narrative is not to advocate a cause or support a position; it is too neutral for that. The function of the narrative of these stories is to expose the details of behavior in such a way to lay that behavior open to scrutiny.

The meaning of the narrative is what we derive from that scrutiny. If we do not enter into the scrutiny — as the narrative does not — then the meaning we must give the narrative is simply that the forces driving human behavior are complex and in need of scrutiny. Because nothing is said about the motivation of David or Bathsheba, the forces driving their behavior are opaque to us. Similarly for the behavior of Uriah. Amnon's motivation is specified; but David's behavior is left opaque. Absalom's motivation for the murder of his brother is apparent; again David's behavior is left opaque. When Joab manipulates Absalom's return, nothing is said of the motivation of any of the players. As David leaves Jerusalem, the narrative portrays aspects of his behavior in considerable detail. Of his motivation, almost nothing is said. What is said leaves us pondering whether it is for public consumption or is the truth of David's conviction. The wisdom of and the motivation for much of what David does are left open for reflection; the narrative remains neutral and refrains from comment. At this level, it is clear that the forces driving human behavior are complex and in need of careful scrutiny.

At another level, we are entitled to ask ourselves if there is a meaning in the portrayal that is significant for us. One point has already been touched on lightly at the end of the discussion of chs. 11–12. Fuller reflection here will not be out of place. The issue is whether the narrative presents what is happening as the direct outcome of God's will or as the working through of the inevitable consequences of human acts. Both understandings are present in Nathan's words to David. Nathan's first utterance reflects act-consequence thinking: "Now therefore the sword shall never depart from your house" (12:10). His second utterance invokes direct divine action: "Thus says the LORD: I will raise up trouble against you from within your own house" (12:11). As has been argued earlier, even without these explicit words of Nathan, the impact of David's behavior on his own house is particularly visible in the earlier stages of the narrative. David is guilty of violation/rape and murder; Amnon will commit rape and Absalom murder. Absalom's rebellion flows out of these actions and is not independent of them. It is Joab's actions in the killing of Absalom — as best we may guess because we are not told — that leave him with the need to reestablish his position of power under David. Even at this level, without Nathan's interpretation of the events, the narrative portrayal has this ambiguity of meaning.

In chs. 11–12, David's behavior is evil in God's sight. Nathan is sent to say so. This is a portrayal of direct divine intervention to name reality for what it is. David's prayer has no effect on the consequences for his illegitimate child. In chs. 13-14, there is no mention of divine action. Even prior to Nathan's interpretation, it may be assumed that God's displeasure is having its impact on David's house; it is not said by the text. In the next major segment, chs. 15–19, the text has David pray (15:31) and notes God's defeat of "the good counsel of Ahithophel" (17:14); nothing in the text associates the two, portraying the divine intervention as a response to David's prayer. Direct action by God is absent from ch. 20.

The narrative allows us to see God's displeasure at what David has done, clearly expressed in chs. 11–12, working itself out as divine punishment in the chapters to come. "I will raise up trouble against you from within your own house" (12:11). Equally, with the sole exception of 17:14, the narrative allows us to understand events as the working out of the consequences of what David has done. Every human act begets its consequences — and kings are no exceptions to this rule. God's displeasure is noted for David. God's action to defeat Ahithophel is noted. The two are not correlated; they appear to be in conflict. The claim of 17:14 is an option that can be taken; it is an option that need not be taken for the narrative sequence to be plausible. Hushai's advice has been proposed in terms that are seductive enough to have them accepted by a proud young king. There is more to the narrative than bringing evil on Absalom; the rest is left to unfold for itself, without any claim of divine direction.

Act-consequence or divine design? As to this realm of meaning, we are left to choose for ourselves. The narrative can be read as an unfolding in human history of God's design. David has sinned, is forgiven, and is punished — by the impact of his actions or by the justice of his God. God's role is in some cases evident, in others not. God is kept at a discreet distance from some of the more sordid acts (e.g., Tamar's rape and Amnon's murder), but not from others (e.g., the violation of the ten; cf. 2 Sam 12:12). Alternatively, the narrative can be read as an unfolding in human history of the consequences of human acts. The narrative is neutral and we are not told.

Nineteenth-century English historian Lord Acton's comment, reflecting on the Roman papacy, is well known: all power tends to corrupt and absolute power tends to corrupt absolutely. The conclusion he drew from this is not so often cited: therefore, great men are seldom good men. Are these Stories of David's Middle Years forerunners of Acton's cynicism? David's behavior with Bathsheba and Uriah is certainly not portrayed as that of a good man. Neither Amnon's act of rape nor Absalom's act of murder is categorized; neither is portrayed as good. Is the image of David as a good and great king the product of later legend? Great perhaps, but certainly not good. The portrayal in chs. 15–19 can be led as evidence for the defense. The great king is also portrayed as a good man. Ittai is offered his freedom. It is a good act; it may be politically shrewd, but the narrative leaves that untouched. Trust in God is a good act. It too may be politically shrewd, but again the narrative leaves that untouched. The setting up of communications, via Zadok and Abiathar, and the placing of Hushai within Absalom's advisers are shrewd acts; there is nothing to say they are not the acts of a good man. Trust in God recurs in the episode with Shimei. David's reaction to Absalom's death is portrayed as the honest grief of a good man. The politically shrewd may invite to closer examination; the narrative does not. The actions of the returning monarch may be politically astute; again, there is nothing to say they are not the acts of a good man. The narrative remains brilliantly neutral.

David sinned. Was he the victim of his sin or its beneficiary? The narrative does not say and we can never know. Had David not become involved with Bathsheba and had he not had her husband murdered, would the course of the campaign against Rabbah have changed? Probably not. Would David's relationship with Joab have been different? Probably. Would David's relationship with himself have been different? Almost certainly. Would Amnon or Absalom have been better kings than Solomon? We cannot know. All we do know is that ultimately Solomon was a very bad king; later text will lay at Solomon's door the total downfall of Israel (cf. 1 Kgs 9:1-9; 11:1-13). But this is later text. The Stories of David's Middle Years end with Joab's return to Jerusalem to the king. David loses two of his sons; he loses his kingdom and recovers it. Was he the victim of his sin or its beneficiary? Nathan is not neutral: what befalls David is punishment for what he has done. Beyond these words, the narrative is remarkably neutral. In the human experience portrayed in these stories, meaning is to be found. Its discovery is invited; it is not imposed.

Bibliography of Works Cited Above

Bietenhard, Sophia Katharina. *Des Königs General: Die Heerführertraditionen in der vorstaatlichen und frühen staatlichen Zeit und die Joabgestalt in 2 Sam 2–20; 1 Kön 1–2.* OBO 163. Freiburg, Switzerland: Universitätsverlag, 1998.

Chadwick, H. Munro, and N. Kirshaw Chadwick. *The Growth of Literature.* Vols. 1-3. Cambridge: Cambridge University Press, 1932, 1936, 1940.

Delekat, L. "Tendenz und Theologie der David-Salomo-Erzählung." Pages 26-36 in *Das Ferne und Nahe Wort;* Fs. L. Rost. Edited by F. Maass. Berlin: Töpelmann, 1967.

Flanagan, James W. "Court History or Succession Document? A Study of 2 Samuel 9–20 and 1 Kings 1–2." *JBL* 91 (1972) 172-81.

Gunn, D. M. *The Story of King David: Genre and Interpretation.* JSOTSup 6. Sheffield: JSOT, 1978.

Josephus, Flavius. *Jewish Antiquities.* Books V-VIII. The Loeb Classical Library. London: Heinemann, 1934.

Lessing, Doris. *The Diaries of Jane Somers.* London: Penguin, 1985.

Noll, K. L. *The Faces of David.* JSOTSup 242. Sheffield: Sheffield Academic Press, 1997.

Perdue, Leo G. "'Is there Anyone Left of the House of Saul . . . ?' Ambiguity and the Characterization of David in the Succession Narrative." Pages 167-83 in *The Historical Books: A Sheffield Reader.* Edited by J. Cheryl Exum. Sheffield: Sheffield Academic Press, 1997. Original: *JSOT* 30 (1984) 67-84.

Rad, Gerhard von. *Old Testament Theology.* 2 vols. Edinburgh: Oliver and Boyd, 1962-65.

Rost, Leonhard. *The Succession to the Throne of David.* Sheffield: Almond, 1982. German original: 1926.

Würthwein, Ernst. *Die Erzählung von der Thronfolge Davids — theologische oder politische Geschichtsschreibung?* TS 115. Zürich: Theologische Verlag, 1974.

Chapter 11

THE SPECIAL COLLECTION
(2 SAM 21–24)

With forty or so chapters in 1–2 Samuel devoted to the activities of David, we might think we had a fairly clear picture of this great figure. The value of these four chapters at the end of 2 Sam is to make clear to us how wrong we would be. In that sense, the collection is particularly special. Its first and last stories (of atonement: famine/plague incurred and averted) refer to a period later in David's life; one assumes Saul's death and the other the possession of Jerusalem. The two groups of traditions about warriors and war refer to a period earlier in David's military career. From this point of view, the first of the two songs is problematic. "Saul" in 22:1 suggests the earlier part of David's career; "all his enemies" (also 22:1) suggests a period in the middle or toward the end of David's career. If McCarter's rendering is followed, "all his enemies, including Saul" (p. 452), the reference is rather more global, allowing for a period toward the end of David's career. In this it would cohere well with the final song (23:1-7), "the last words of David," referring to the end of what might have been thought of as David's activity as singer and poet. These questions of potential reference are not to be confused, of course, with the quite separate issue of the date of composition for each item.

The organizing structure of the total collection can be represented as follows.

The Special Collection	2 Sam 21:1–24:25
I. Of atonement: famine incurred and averted	21:1-14
II. Of warriors and war: the giant-killers collection	21:15-22
III. Of song	22:1–23:7
A. David's deliverance song	22:1-51
B. David's final song	23:1-7
IV. Of warriors and war: the names and exploits collection	23:8-39
V. Of atonement: plague incurred and averted	24:1-25

Once this organizing structure has been recognized, component elements can be analyzed in greater detail. It is important, though, to see the wood first before looking at the trees. The impact of the collection as such needs to be seen before attention can be given to the components. Brueggemann: "It is commonly thought that this arrangement [the chiastic or concentric pattern] cannot be accidental" (p. 335). Two points need to be made about this special collection; it is a collection and it is special.

There is a sense in which this special collection can be described as the third wave of Davidic tradition. It is different from the stories of David's rise to power and it is different from the stories of David's middle years. It forms a third group. The stories of David's rise to power are for the most part formulated in such a way as to be favorable to David; "all Israel and Judah loved David" (1 Sam 18:16). The stories of David's middle years (2 Sam 11–20) linger over human behavior, leaving questions to be asked and answering none. The traditions in 2 Sam 21–24, poetry perhaps apart, are not particularly favorable to David and are hardly explored for human behavioral motivation. There is a neutrality to them that could be interpreted as observing a certain distance from the story of King David (cf. Brueggemann, "2 Samuel 21–24," 385-94).

Its unity derives from the combination of three elements. First, its concentric pattern of organization (A-B-C/C'-B'-A'). Second, its concern throughout with David. Third, its status as "third wave," with its unexpected traditions and its unusual neutrality. There is no thematic unity, no sense of historical progression, no mention of the prophet Samuel. If anything holds the material together — apart from its concentric organization — it would be that nothing in it is known to us from the other Davidic traditions and some of it is in surprising contrast with what is given us in these other traditions.

No consensus exists as to the process, if any, by which the collection came into being; its date and origin, as a collection, are unknown. It cannot be shown that it was put together as a single artifact; it can be seen that the final product presents as a structured whole. Its component elements could have been composed at various times; a process of growth that preceded the final product cannot be excluded. All in all, the chapters are a substantial puzzle — in more ways than one, as we shall see.

The Gibeonite atonement tradition (21:1-14) refers to an episode under Saul that is otherwise unknown to us, although Rizpah, the secondary wife (concubine) involved, features in the Abner episode of 2 Sam 3:6-11. A three-year famine is reported "in the days of David," without any specification of its extent or areas affected. We have not heard of it elsewhere in Samuel or Chronicles. David's understanding is that its origin comes from the LORD (21:1); atonement required the ritual elimination of Saul's descendants. David's enemies would say, "How convenient!" David's actions are reported neutrally enough. The portrayal of the sparing of Mephibosheth (v. 7) contrasts with 2 Sam 9 and differs in details of oath and table with 2 Sam 19:29 [Heb.; NRSV, 19:28]. The noble act of the episode is given to Rizpah, who protected the corpses from desecration. Her example leads to David's giving proper burial to Saul and Jonathan and those who had been impaled. (Note: in 1 Sam 31:12, "the body of Saul and the bodies of his sons" were taken to Jabesh; here, attention is paid only to the bones of Saul and Jonathan.)

In the traditions that follow (2 Sam 21:15-22), David's life was apparently saved by Abishai (vv. 15-17); when "a man of great size" taunted Israel, David's nephew killed him (vv. 20-21). According to the text, "these four . . . fell by the hands of David and his servants"; in the reality of the tradition, the "servants" slew all four, and David, if anything, while leader was also something of a liability. The little collection may be neutral; it is not an exaltation of David.

The two songs we may leave aside for the present. Both are otherwise unknown in the Davidic traditions of Samuel (but see Noll, *Faces of David,* 118-82).

The next collection of military traditions is particularly surprising (2 Sam 23:8-39). It contains information that is not given to us in the earlier Samuel texts, where it would be expected. The information, with some additions, is to be found in 1 Chr 11:10-47, following David's coronation as king over all Israel. Oddities in the collection include the existence of the two groups, the Three and the Thirty, which we have not heard of elsewhere in Samuel; the names of the Three, whom we have not heard of in Samuel (or elsewhere outside 1 Chr 11); finally, the prominence of Abishai and Benaiah and the low profile of Joab. David, the guerrilla leader of 1 Samuel, is a different figure from David, the leader of a tightly organized military command structure. We may note the neutrality; we may be puzzled by the contrast.

The final atonement tradition, the tradition in 2 Sam 24 of the purchase of Araunah's threshing floor and the building of an altar there is, of course, reported in 1 Chr 21, with a couple of well-known differences. The Samuel formulation may be considered neutral, but it is certainly not favorable to David. Incited by YHWH, he overruled his army commanders and ordered the census. Offered a choice between three punishments, David chose the shortest (out of three years' famine, three months' flight, and three days' pestilence), while piously intoning, "Let us fall into the hand of the LORD . . . but let me not fall into human hands" (v. 14). Hearers and readers would have known well that all three — famine certainly and flight probably — came from the LORD, not from human hands. There is something odd here. Finally, in the Samuel version, David's purchase of Araunah's threshing floor for an altar is not explicitly correlated with the later Jerusalem temple, as it is in 1 Chr 22:1.

All of this heightens the mystery of the collection: Where did it come from and how much more is there about David that we do not know? The text does not tell us and we do not know. What this special collection does point up for us is the limited state of our knowledge about King David. For that alone, it is indeed special. Its position at the end of the books of Samuel is not an afterthought; without being broken up, it can hardly be placed anywhere else. Chapter 24 requires a more energetic monarch than the bed-bound David of 1 Kgs 1:1-4, even though preceded by the "last words" of David (23:1-7). Especially in the light of our emphasis here on the unity of 2 Sam 11–20 as the Stories of David's Middle Years, the position of this special collection at the end of these Davidic traditions is appropriate. Its differences of emphasis remain puzzling (a detailed study of the chapters is offered by Simon, *Identity and Identification*).

Genre

These four chapters constitute a collection; technically, a collection is not a literary genre. To anticipate what is said below, we probably have two (→) accounts, encompassing two (→) reports, in turn encompassing two (→) songs. The chiastic structure suggests that these traditions were arranged and preserved as a unity. As such, they do constitute a collection; they do not constitute a new literary genre.

Setting

Such a collection, however, while it may not be a literary genre does have a location within society, and it is necessary to reflect on what that location might have been. The traditions are not wholly favorable to David, even though at the beginning it is YHWH who interprets the famine for David and David who finally does the right thing, while at the end it is YHWH who has incited David against Israel and it is David who brings the episode to a successful conclusion. The warriors in the traditions are David's men, but the exploits are theirs not his. All six traditions are markedly different from the "received" Davidic traditions that have been enshrined in the preceding text of 1–2 Samuel. More than that, to a degree they do not fit very comfortably with the "received" David traditions.

A setting and a date for the collection as a whole are extremely difficult to determine. There is no consensus about the dates of the various elements; without this, there can be no consensus on the date of the collection. In some cases, the component traditions seem likely to be old. A certain distancing from David may be accounted for in several ways. All in all, the collection is both special and puzzling. For a helpful evaluation of proposals and a brief history of research for these chapters, see Stoebe, 36-38.

Meaning

We can offer at least a twofold meaning for this collection. At one level, it clearly preserves traditions about David that are not preserved elsewhere. We might expand that to say: that otherwise would not have been preserved. The collection suggests that it was important for these traditions to be preserved. At another level, the contrast between what this collection preserves and the traditions preserved earlier in 1–2 Samuel is a reminder to listeners and readers that the story of King David is far from an open book for us. Without this collection, we might justifiably believe that we were well informed on the life and times of King David. With this collection in the sacred books, we know that there is more to be known about David than the "received" traditions have preserved for us. We would be naive to think that this collection in chs. 21–24 has filled out for us all that the "received" traditions did not preserve. We are left aware that, after forty chapters, we have been given a plurality of approaches to the story of King David — and no more.

It is time to turn to a closer examination of the collection's individual components.

Textual Issues

21:6 Reading with the MT is possible; the mountain of 21:9 can be understood in v. 6 without emendation (Barthélemy, 300). The great majority of commentators emend in the sense adopted by the NRSV.

Discussion

The episode recounted in this passage is one that anyone with some sensitivity to David's reputation as king would have needed to handle with immense care. That David should have eliminated any threat from the descendants of Saul might have been politically prudent but it is not acknowledged in other Davidic traditions (cf. 2 Sam 9:1; 19:29 [Heb.; NRSV, 19:28]). Appalling parallels are available in the fate of the seventy sons of Jerubbaal at the hands of their brother Abimelech (Judg 9:1-5) and the seventy sons of Ahab at the hands of Jehu (2 Kgs 10:1-11). Other Davidic traditions have been careful not to stain David's reputation in this way. This episode, therefore, needs — and receives — careful handling.

The passage begins with a statement of uncontestable experience: there was a famine for three years — [I]. It was "in the days of David," after the death of Saul and therefore necessarily the responsibility of David. The interpretation of experience is usually an uncertain affair. Here the interpretation comes from God. We are not told how. Usually, inquiries of the LORD are framed to be able to receive a Yes or No answer. In this case, the answer goes well beyond that. The phrase translated "David inquired of the LORD" is unprecedented in Samuel for this meaning. It is used for Saul's seeking David (1 Sam 24:3 [Heb.; NRSV, 24:2]; 26:2; cf. 2 Sam 3:17; 5:17). The closest equivalent in Samuel is David pleading with YHWH (2 Sam 12:16; cf. also Zeph 1:6). The famine is a result of bloodguilt, on Saul and his house, the result of killings among the Gibeonites (v. 1b). Two aspects are notable. First, there are no details about the famine and we know nothing of it. Second, in the text it is David who unsolicited inquires of the LORD, and the response is to his benefit. This is neutrally formulated; it could conceivably be made favorable to David but the text does not do so.

David convenes a meeting with the Gibeonites — [II]. The text adds a note about the Gibeonites, recalling something of the tradition that is now Josh 9:3-27. That it is probably an insertion in the text can be seen from the phrases that precede and follow it. Preceding it: "and spoke to them"; following it: "David said to the Gibeonites." The resumptive repetition makes the procedure clear. Once a meeting has been convened and the audience is aware of who the Gibeonites are, the exchange that is at the heart of the meeting can be reported.

Two things are made clear in the opening section of the exchange. First, the issue is a matter of atonement or expiation. David's question establishes this (v. 3). Second, it is not a matter that can be settled by monetary compensation. The Gibeonites do not have the right to put anyone to death in Israel, but death — life for life — is what the atonement requires. The Gibeonites' demand can be addressed once David has accepted to act on their request: "What do you say that I should do for you?" (v. 4b). The Gibeonite request is specific: "let seven men from his sons be given to us" for impalement before YHWH (v. 6a). Two observations to be noted here. First, the Gibeonites specify the sacral number seven men from his sons (NRSV: "seven of his sons"); they do not ask for the death of all his sons, only the sacral seven. Second, if the famine is from YHWH, implied in the inquiry and response, impalement "before YHWH" is an appropriate action. The exchange is concluded when David acquiesces to the Gibeonite request.

At this point, it may be helpful to stand back and observe what has been established from the point of view of David's reputation as king. The event is described as a response to the experience of famine, interpreted by YHWH. The famine has lasted three years; three years have passed, therefore, during which David has taken no action against the survivors of Saul's house. That is not the behavior of a vengeful or insecure king. Furthermore, the request for the death of seven substitutes has come from the Gibeonites; it has not been initiated by David. Finally, the Gibeonites have been portrayed requesting the death of "seven of his sons" — a demand in the sacral realm, not meeting the political exigency of exterminating all his sons. From this presentation of the tradition, no charge can be laid against David. However, while the seven may not comprise all Saul's descendants, it does eliminate all his sons.

The king has said: "I will hand them over" (v. 6) — [III]. The first action then reported of the king, indeed the first verb *(wayyaḥmōl),* is the sparing of Mephibosheth, prior to handing over the victims; the reason given is the oath between David and Jonathan. The seven sons are then identified; two from Rizpah, Saul's "concubine" (cf. 2 Sam 3:7), and five from Merab, Saul's elder daughter (the Hebrew has Michal, but Adriel the Meholathite was the husband of Merab, cf. 1 Sam 18:19). There is tragic history associated with both women. Rizpah was alleged as the source of Abner's quarrel with Ishbaal and his readiness to transfer allegiance to David. Merab was promised by Saul to David, according to the text as a bait to have David killed by the Philistines; in the event, she was given to Adriel (1 Sam 18:17-19). The NRSV specifies the mode of execution as impalement; the Hebrew verb is rare and uncertain, occurring three times in this form (twice here and Num 25:4).

The precise picture of what follows is not given us. The seven men were executed "before the LORD," "on the mountain." "Before the LORD" suggests a sanctuary; execution by the Gibeonites "on the mountain" suggests the great sanctuary at Gibeon (cf., for example, 1 Kgs 3:4). We are not told what was done with the bodies, and the issue of expiation (v. 3) adds complexity to the possibilities. What we are told is that Rizpah, mother of two of the men, protected the bodies from birds by day and beasts by night. David is told of Rizpah's respect for the dead, and the text has him move to the formal burial of Saul, Jonathan, and the seven. The text is surprising on two points. First, in a tradition concerning the execution of seven of Saul's descendants, the emphasis in this burial material is quite clearly on Saul and Jonathan; the seven are almost an appendage in v. 13b, preceded and followed by emphasis on Saul and Jonathan. Second, there is some tension between 2 Sam 21:12, here, and 1 Sam 31:10-13. Here, the rescue was from the public square *(rĕḥōb)* at Beth-shan; there, the bodies were fastened to the wall *(ḥômâ)* at Beth-shan, brought to Jabesh, burned, and buried under the tamarisk tree (but see Stoebe, 455: "no contradiction with 1 Sam 31:10"). In David's response to this act, nothing is said of a need for reburial (cf. 2 Sam 2:4b-7). As noted above, in 1 Sam 31:12 the reference is to "the body of Saul and the bodies of his sons" ("his three sons," v. 8); here, the reference is to Saul and Jonathan alone. To balance this, we should note that, in 2 Sam 2:4b-7, the reference is to Saul alone. The reference to bodies before the burning and to bones afterwards may suggest the legitimacy of some harmonization.

The episode is brought to an end with the statement that afterward "God heeded supplications for the land" (v. 14b). The verb is relatively rare; in Samuel–Kings, it occurs only in this collection's two "atonement" passages, here and in 2 Sam 24:25.

Genre

While the potential for storytelling is clearly present, it is not exploited. The passage is best described as an (→) account. There is no tension developed between the experience of famine (v. 1) and God's heeding supplication for the land (v. 14). It may be said to go beyond a neutral (→) report in three areas. First, the responsibility for the expiatory killing is placed on the Gibeonites, but after consultation of the LORD by David. Second, situating the sparing of Mephibosheth in this context, with explicit reference to David's oath with Jonathan, gives a certain, if limited, nobility to David's action. Third, the nobility of Rizpah's action in protecting the bodies of the dead provides the stimulus for David's giving a formal burial to the remains of Saul, Jonathan, and the seven. In all this, the ugliness of seven (politically expedient) deaths is clothed with a sense of legitimacy.

Setting

The setting for this tradition is probably one neutral to David. At the same time, we need to ask why no mention has been made earlier of a three-year famine and the execution of Saul's distant descendants. It is implicitly denied in 2 Sam 9; it is not explicitly mentioned in 2 Sam 19:29 (Heb.; NRSV, 19:28). The formal burial in the family tomb is probably something that David ought to have done; it is unmentioned in 2 Sam 2:6-7. Perhaps Rizpah's respect for the bodies of the dead is a pointer to behavior that should have been David's. The account is likely to have been preserved in circles somewhat distanced from what we might call the Davidic establishment. More cannot prudently be said.

Meaning

There is meaning in this account at two distinct levels. At one level, it communicates a series of events we did not know about: the famine, the Gibeonite request for expiation, David's honoring of his oath with Jonathan, Rizpah's act of piety, and the formal burial of Saul, Jonathan, and the descendants. At another level, there is a side of David revealed that might have been guessed at but that lacked this attestation. David had not wiped out all the descendants of the house of Saul; it took a three-year famine and a Gibeonite request to bring this about. David honored his oath to Jonathan. David allowed himself to be inspired by Rizpah's piety to procure the formal burial of Saul and Jonathan and the victims of the expiation. There is an openness to nobility here, but also to critique. Neutrality is dominant in the formulation.

Discussion

The central topic of these traditions is expressed in the summary, v. 22; each of the four traditions deals with the death of a descendant of the giants in Gath, killed by David and his troops. Such descendants of the giants *(yĕlîdê hārāpâ)* are so named nowhere else in the Hebrew Bible. McCarter refers to recent studies and opts for the translation "votaries of Rapha," an elite group of warriors (pp. 449-50; see also Stoebe, 462). McCarter is right to refer to the warriors as Philistine champions; he is not right to refer to the collection as "a miscellany of unrelated items at the end of the story of Abishalom's revolt, awaiting integration into the book" (p. 451; similarly, Anderson, 248).

Of these four traditions, only the first involves David directly and it is the most extensive. In the other three, the warriors involved — Sibbecai the Hushathite, Elhanan ben Jaare-oregim, and Jonathan ben Shimei — are otherwise unknown to us. An Elhanan ben Dodo is listed in 2 Sam 23:24; while both men are from Bethlehem, the unknown quality of the other two cautions against any attempt at an identification here. A Hushathite is also listed in 23:27; his name is Mebunnai. The second and third encounters are located at Gob, otherwise unknown. The fourth of the descendants of the giants is nameless. What holds this collection together is its focus on the killing of these descendants of the giants.

All four are set within the context of war with the Philistines. Even the first tradition in the collection has an "again" *('ôd);* an earlier setting in association with the Philistine wars seems likely. The information that David grew weary, that Ishbi-benob saw his chance to kill David, and that Abishai saved David's life and killed the Philistine is used to motivate the decision of David's men: "You shall not go out with us to battle any longer, so that you do not quench the lamp of Israel" (v. 17). We do not hear of this decision again; the reference to quenching the lamp of Israel is unique. Conceivably it could have its bearing on interpretations of 2 Sam 11:1. It appears to belong relatively early in the Davidic traditions; it is mirrored later in different circumstances in 2 Sam 18:3.

The third tradition has Elhanan killing Goliath the Gittite. This has caused problems for those who want to bring it into harmony with the story of 1 Sam 17. As we have noted in treating that text the name of Goliath occurs only twice, once in each tradition (vv. 4 and 23), with some suggestion of being a later insertion. Apart from these two verses, the text is concerned to describe combat between David and "the Philistine." Given the paradigm status of this encounter, such generalized usage as David and the Philistine is to be expected. It is David's performance against a champion of the feared Philistines that is alleged to have singled him out in Israel. It is not surprising — and not unlikely — that at some stage the name of the legendary Goliath the Gittite was attached to the opponent vanquished by David in this legendary combat.

Interestingly enough, the parallel reporting in Chronicles (1 Chr 20:4-8), situated there after the fall of Amman (cf. 2 Sam 12), omits the first episode represented in 2 Sam 21:15-17. Perhaps David's weariness and near escape from death were not judged a fitting remembrance of the founder of the future temple. Whether discreetly or not, Chronicles omits the total of four in its summary (v. 8). So totally different a location, however, tends to further muddy our access to Israel's past.

Genre

We have a collection of four (→) reports. They are brief narratives, telling what happened, without trying to arouse interest by creating tension leading to resolution.

Setting

As noted, these traditions seem to refer to a period relatively early in David's career. Certainly, they are located within the Philistine wars. The tradition concerning David does not refer to him as king. That is not decisive, but it offers tentative support for an association with David's early days. Also as noted, each tradition begins with the phrase "there was again *('ôd)* war" — twice "war" and twice "the war." The likelihood of an earlier setting in association with the Philistine wars complicates the establishment of a setting here. Some association with the collection in 2 Sam 23:8-39 has to be considered.

Meaning

The memory of the deaths of these four descendants of the giants at the hands of David and his troops has been preserved. David's value as the "lamp of Israel" that should not be quenched has been emphasized. No feat of David's is narrated; his only achievement in the text is to grow weary. Yet, as the final verse inaccurately claims, these four giant Philistine fighters fell "by the hands of David and his servants" (v. 22). It is one more trophy achievement chalked up to David in the necessary task of subduing the Philistines.

Textual Issues

22:33   Reading *wayyattēr* as a hifil from the root *n-t-r* (to be free, loose), Barthélemy understands the second verset metaphorically in the sense of the NRSV, he "has opened wide my path" (pp. 306-7).

     22:36   4QSam^a has the text rendered "your help" (Ulrich, 140). The MT is understood as "your answering" (with the LXX); in the Davidic context it is intelligible (Stoebe, 475).

     22:44   "With my people" is attested by the MT and Vulgate; "with the peoples" (or equivalent) is attested by the LXX. For McCarter, "my people" could have emerged "by 'actualisation' towards the events of David's life" (p. 461). For Barthélemy, "people" (without the suffix) has the best chance to be original (p. 308). Anderson and Stoebe retain the "my," Stoebe noting the possible influence of David's situation.

Discussion

The superscription describes the text as a song and claims its words were sung by David when saved by YHWH from all his enemies (delicately general) and from Saul (in second place) — [I]. Like all such superscriptions, little or no trust can be put in its historical value. The general nature of the occasion invoked — saved from all his enemies and from Saul — is a pointer to the absence of historical value. One can debate whether, out of respect to the superscription, reference throughout the analysis should be to the singer as "David" or whether, out of respect for the text's distance from Davidic specifics, reference should rather be to the singer — leaving readers to be aware that the superscription attributes the singing of the song to David. Here, the text is reflected throughout rather than the superscription alone; those who choose otherwise may prefer to substitute "David" as needed.

As appropriate, because YHWH is acclaimed as the singer's savior, the song is focused on YHWH — [II]. YHWH's relationship to the singer is primary — [II.A]; it is David who is purported to be singer of the song. The relationship is expressed first in metaphor, then in the narrated experience of deliverance. Only then does the song broaden into praise of YHWH, first in more general terms of loyalty to the loyal but then again in direct association with the singer, as the source of political and military strength.

The metaphors are military, as befits the deliverance to come; they are summed up in the final clause: "you save me from violence" (v. 3). Places, powers, and persons are pressed into play. Places: rock and fortress (v. 2), stronghold and refuge (v. 3). Powers: shield and horn of salvation (v. 3). Persons: deliverer (v. 2), God as rock and refuge, savior (v. 3). No pattern is apparent informing their use.

For the deliverance aspect of the relationship, the song moves into narrative mode. First the appeal: confronted by death, the singer cries to YHWH. The response is portrayed in two stages: first, God's coming and God's deliverance; second, the singer's reflection on the deliverance.

In the appeal, the cry to God is accompanied by the affirmation of salvation (v. 4). The two lines that follow image the reason for the cry and the need for salvation, modulating into the affirmations of threatening death. Two pairs of metaphors evoke the threat of death: waves and torrents, cords and snares.

The first stage of the response opens with a restatement of the singer's cry to the LORD, "my God," and an affirmation that the cry has been heard (v. 7). In this coupling of the cry and its being heard, v. 7 echoes the cry and the salvation of v. 4. Verse 7a belongs with what follows; otherwise, there is no point of reference for the third person singular pronouns and suffixes until v. 14.

The impact of God's hearing is unfolded for earth and heaven, with two verbs each — only then is the cause noted: "because he was angry" (v. 8). The imagery of God's anger is then unfolded in terms of fiery heat: smoke, fire, and glowing coals (v. 9). Movement on God's part is clear from the verb "and came down" (v. 10); in this context, what exactly is the image conjured up by "he bowed the heavens" escapes us (cf. Ps 144:5), but the power of the creator is likely since the usual context is one of "stretching out" the heavens in association with creation. God's "descent" is expressed in terms of a mythic thunderstorm, with the thick darkness of rain-heavy clouds contrasting with the bright flashes of lightning. The mythic character of what is happening is expressed in the laying bare of the channels of the sea and the foundations of the earth; even the storm wind responsible comes from "the blast of the breath of his nostrils" (v. 16).

Third person pronouns and suffixes continue in vv. 17-20 (with only one reference to YHWH, in v. 19) associating the portrayal of God's movement with the portrayal of God's deliverance. God has come down, but competent theology is careful to maintain God's distance; so God reached "from on high" (v. 17). The description of deliverance modulates swiftly from the metaphoric (mighty waters) to the military (mighty enemy). The "broad place" of v. 20 contrasts with the "narrow" concept within the distress of v. 7. A cry has been uttered and a response has been received.

The second stage of the response to the appeal may strike a modern reader as intolerably smug. The deliverance is affirmed as correlative with the singer's righteousness and the cleanness of his hands (cf. NRSV: "according to" twice each in vv. 21 and 25). These affirmations enclose two *kî*-clauses (NRSV: "for" twice, vv. 22-23) detailing what is involved in such righteousness and cleanness of hands. Verse 24 summarizes: "I was blameless before him [YHWH], and I kept myself from guilt" — compatible with the trend of traditions about David's struggle with Saul. While distasteful to many modern ears, the verses are in keeping with the mainstream of the wisdom tradition. Within the structure of the song, they prepare the way for the modulation into praise of YHWH, who is loyal to the loyal (vv. 26-31).

Those troubled by the affirmation of righteousness, here or elsewhere, may take comfort from the difference in modern legal language between "not guilty" and "innocent." "You are righteous" can mean merely that the person addressed has observed the required rules; as such, it is an external observation. Similarly, in the language of much modern law, the verdict of "not guilty" means that a case has not been proven; it does not affirm innocence.

Verses 24-25 have the singer clearly in view: "I was blameless before him . . . according to my cleanness in his sight." The move to YHWH's praise — [II.B] — is achieved by three verses that focus on God alone (vv. 26-28), followed by a further three verses that unfold the implications for life of what is said in vv. 26-28 (i.e., vv. 29-31). The two lines of vv. 26-27 have four versets in all, each beginning with *'im* (NRSV, "with the"). The tone is set by the first: "With the loyal you show yourself loyal." The third line changes in form. A similar pattern is present in vv. 29-31, with two lines beginning with *kî* (not reflected in the NRSV) and the third line changing in form. God's loyalty to the loyal is unfolded in terms of its impact on the singer: "the LORD lightens my darkness" (v. 29). The last clause facilitates the modulation to the praise of God as a source of military strength: "he is a shield for all who take refuge in him" (v. 31). It picks up echoes of vv. 2-3 (shield and refuge).

The focus of vv. 32-43 is on God as the source of military strength for the singer of the song. The affirmation of God as "rock" continues the echo of the beginning of the song (v. 2). The thrust of these verses can be summed up in the following: "He trains my hands for war. . . . I pursued my enemies and destroyed them" (vv. 35, 38).

The focus of vv. 44-49 shifts from the overtly military to an emphasis on power over nations and peoples. As v. 49 shows, nations and peoples can be categorized as enemies and adversaries, but the shift is from an emphasis on military prowess to an emphasis on the political achievements of that prowess in foreign affairs (cf. vv. 45-46).

The song ends with a couplet promising praise — [III]. It opens with an address to God: "I will extol you, O LORD" (v. 50). It concludes with a three-verset line summarizing why God is to be extolled, moving through three terms for the monarch: king, anointed, David and his descendants (v. 51).

Genre

The literary genre is precisely what the text describes itself as: a (→) song. It is a combination of (→) thanksgiving song and (→) hymn of praise. The first is described as a jubilant cultic song to celebrate victory, divine help, and all sorts of joyful occasions. The hymn has been described as a "joyful song of choir or community extolling the greatness and kindness of Yahweh and his dwelling place. . . . The hymns intoned vary in contents: They praise creation and creator . . . , and Yahweh's glorious deeds in history. . . . They admire Mount Zion, his abode . . . , and jubilate at his just reign . . ." (Gerstenberger, *Psalms,* 1.249). Hymns tend to celebrate who God is and what God does. The hymn, or more specifically the hymn of praise, is a psalm or song that extols and glorifies YHWH.

These two sets of characteristics run through 2 Sam 22:1-51. There is the jubilant song of divine help and victory: "to my God I called" (v. 7); "he delivered me from my strong enemy" (v. 18). There is the celebration of who God is and what God does: "the LORD is my rock" (v. 2); "with the loyal you show yourself loyal" (v. 26).

Setting

The association of the song with David is explicit only in vv. 1 and 51. Both are third person references; the reference to "David and his descendants" (v. 51) tends to distance the song from the historical figure of David.

That it might have been prayed by David and then reused is possible but unlikely. The mass of 1st person references in vv. 2-50 is hardly determined by the envelope of third person references in vv. 1 and 51.

That it might have been prayed by a Davidic king is also possible but again unlikely. There is no explicit reference to present need or divine response that goes beyond the vaguely general and almost universal.

That it might have been prayed by a third person (not excluding a Davidic king, naturally) is both possible and likely. That it represents an invocation of the God of David in a time of personal need is unlikely, for the reason just noted — there is no explicit reference to present need or divine response that goes beyond the vaguely general and almost universal. With its opening verse, the song certainly celebrates David and the God of David. The occasions when this would have been appropriate are numerous. "If David were the author of this psalm, we might have expected some more specific allusions or references to David's past experiences. As it is, the descriptions are very general and would suit very well a recurrent cultic setting" (Anderson, 261). A preexilic date might have been less of a challenge to the theological imagination, but exilic or postexilic dating cannot be denied. Precisely the qualities of "the vaguely general and almost universal" render any precision on date out of the question.

Commenting on Psalm 18, Gerstenberger remarks: "its reflective air and communal liturgical orientation, the influences of wisdom and universalistic hope, and its linguistic peculiarities all make Psalm 18 a song of early Jewish congregations, although older traditions also have clearly been worked into the text" (*Psalms,* 1.99-100). While this description is certainly possible and points in valuable directions, it is suggestive rather than demonstrative. The "communal liturgical orientation" is not demonstrably evident; the "influences of wisdom and universalistic hope" are a possible interpretation of parts of the song, but not a necessary one. So Gerstenberger's designation of the psalm as "a messianic thanksgiving song of the Jewish community" is to be regarded as possible rather than necessary.

For McCarter, the deuteronomistic language in vv. 21-25 probably does not allow the song as a whole to predate the seventh century (p. 474). However, "one or both of the major parts of the psalm [vv. 2-20 and vv. 29-51] may have been composed as early as the time of David, and it is unlikely that either postdates the ninth century" (p. 475). The argument is "that the poetry of the psalm is consistently archaic, as shown by comparison to Ugaritic poetry, early biblical poetry, and (by contrast) later biblical poetry with sporadic archaizing features" (p. 474). The pioneer study in this regard was, of course, by Cross and Freedman in 1953. Judgments vary and certainty remains out of reach.

Meaning

The song's meaning is a celebration of YHWH, a God who answers the cry of the distressed and who displays power. This is unfolded both in the evocation of who God is: rock, fortress, shield, stronghold, refuge, etc., and in the evocation of what God does: deliverer, enabler, source of strength and victory, showing steadfast love, etc.

David's final song	**23:1-7**
I. Superscription	1a
II. Last words of David	1b-7
A. Identification of speech and speaker	1b
1. Speech: oracle	
2. Speaker: David — exalted, anointed, favorite	
B. Oracular image of a ruler	2-4
1. Origin of the words: God	2-3a
2. The words: image of a ruler	3b-4
C. Affirmation of status of David's house	5-7
1. Rhetorical question concerning his own house	5
2. Contrast: status of the wicked	6-7

Textual Issues

23:1 The MT has "raised up on high" (cf. Driver, 356). 4QSam^a and LXX^L have "whom God exalted" (cf. Ulrich, 113). See the discussion in Barthélemy (p. 310) and McCarter (p. 477).

23:3 The MT and LXX^B have "God of Israel"; LXX^L has "God of Jacob." As Stoebe notes, many follow the LXX^L reading, on analogy with v. 1 (p. 485).

Discussion

The superscription to the passage describes these as David's last words. There is, naturally, no evidence for this.

The opening has strong echoes of the beginning of Balaam's third and fourth oracle (Num 24:3-4, 15-16). Perhaps the echo is not surprising given the climax of Balaam's fourth oracle in the vision of David afar (cf. Num 24:17-18). What is to come is described as "the oracle of David" *(ně'ūm dāwīd),* a term favored of the prophets (among 376 occurrences: 1 is in Genesis, 7 in Numbers [all Balaam], 2 each in 1 and 2 Samuel, 4 in 2 Kings, 4 in Hosea, 21 in Amos, 25 in Isaiah, 176 in Jeremiah, 85 in Ezekiel, etc.). The description of David could not laud him more highly: exalted of God, anointed of the God of Jacob, favorite of the Strong One of Israel. Higher praise than this is not to be found in biblical text.

The prophetic mode continues. The oracle images the just king (vv. 3-4). First, though, its origin is given. The prophets claimed to have God speak through them. So David's oracle is attributed to the spirit of the LORD, the God of Israel and Rock of Israel. The oracle itself is in two parts: one is theological, paralleling a ruler's justice with the fear of God; the other is purest poetry, likening a just ruler to the light of morning, to sunrise, to a cloudless morning, to the gleaming of rain on grass. The imagery of morning light would do credit to the Sun King (Louis XIV, le roi soleil).

What follows would be an extraordinary claim — "Is not my house like this with God?" (v. 5) — were it not more of a faith statement for the future. The final verb is one of growth and sprouting, much beloved of Isaiah. It leads beautifully into the comparison with the worthless: thorns, untouchable, consumed by fire (vv. 6-7).

Two aspects, at least, are to be noted about this passage. First, David, God's anointed, is cast in the prophetic role. The interplay of prophet and king is marked in the texts of the Deuteronomistic History. Samuel anointed and rejected Saul; he anointed David. Ahijah designated and rejected Jeroboam; the prophet Jehu ben Hanani rejected Baasha; Elijah rejected Ahab; Elisha's disciple anointed Jehu, who eliminated the house of Ahab; Nathan confirmed David, Isaiah Hezekiah, and Huldah Josiah. That David should here be portrayed in the role of prophet is remarkable. Second, the imagery used for the ruler is exclusively pastoral: morning light, glistening grass. It is unparalleled in biblical text.

Genre

The genre is what the piece says it is: an (→) oracle. The oracle itself is given in vv. 3-4. What precedes is an expansion of it and what follows an application of it. The expansion indicates the speaker and the origin of the oracle. The application identifies David's house with the imagery of the oracle and contrasts the future of David's house with the fate of the worthless, the thorns.

Setting

The setting for an oracle would be expected to be prophetic. The contrast with the fate of the wicked is common in wisdom literature, but the term "thorns" *(qôṣ)* is not found in Israel's wisdom books, but is common enough in the prophets (cf. Isa 32:13; 33:12; Jer 4:3; 12:13; Ezek 28:24; Hos 10:8).

What the passage does is put the concept of a just ruler into the highly poetic language of a divine oracle and attribute its utterance to David. Instinct suggests that such high praise has to be relatively late, when the Davidic monarchy has moved into the realm of the legendary and the injustice asserted by Absalom and the abuse hurled by Shimei have long been forgotten. Prudence, on the other hand, would be loath to deny such high praise to Davidic followers at any time. Sycophancy has seldom been constrained by reality or humility.

Meaning

The meaning can be seen as twofold: the abstract image of the just ruler and the individual portrayal of David ben Jesse.

A right relationship with God is essential for just rule. We cannot be sure of the precise parameters of "the fear of God"; a right relationship with God is a safe paraphrase. The sentiment is endorsed in Ps 82:2-4; what is true of the gods is undoubtedly true of kings, their earthly representatives. The association of justice with the imagery of the shining of rain-freshened grass is a subtle association of the royal maintenance of justice with the fertility of the kingdom.

The portrayal of David is pitched at the level of highest praise. Here David has been moved from the harsh world of politics to the exalted world of legend. Here is the model of a just ruler; here is the opposite of all that is evil.

It is the distance between these two songs and the life of David that leaves one wondering about the purposes for which this collection was put together. Perhaps it is best simply to wonder.

Of warriors and war: the names and exploits collection   **23:8-39**
  I. Concerning David's warriors: names and exploits   8-39a
      A. The superscription   8a
      B. The names and exploits   8b-39a

Textual Issues

23:8 There is an overwhelming consensus among scholars that these verses deal with two groups within David's troops, the Three and the Thirty. Beyond this consensus, the textual issues are complex and the consensus does not extend to how to deal with them. Stoebe notes that the complexity may be less a text-critical than a transmission-of-traditions issue ("weniger ein textkritisches als ein überlieferungsmässiges Problem," p. 495). McCarter opts for emendation ("the context, however, requires . . . ," p. 489); Barthélemy, after close analysis, resists emendation (pp. 312-13). Confusion certainly holds sway over the details, both in the ancient versions and in the present day; while there is room for speculation, the overall picture may be clearer.

Barthélemy stays with the MT in both v. 8 and v. 18, understanding the Rosh-Shalish *(rō'š haššālošî)* as "the elite of the guard," with the apposition then meaning "belonging to the elite of the guard" (p. 313). Among the moderns, McCarter (pp. 489, 491) and Anderson (p. 273) have "chief of the Three" in v. 8 and "chief of the Thirty" in v. 18, while Stoebe has chief of the Three in v. 8 (p. 497) and (p. 503) opts for chief of an unspecified group in v. 18 (the NJPS has "head of another three").

23:13 The MT Kethib has "thirty of the thirty"; the Qere has "three" and moderns agree. Driver qualifies this Kethib "thirty" as "an evident error" and goes on to point out that these three warriors are not to be confused with the Three — although that confusion may have accounted for the place here of vv. 13-17 (pp. 365-66).

23:18 See on 23:8. On the ranking involved in vv. 18-23, between the Three and the Thirty, see McCarter, 499-500 (also Stoebe, 505-6).

23:19 The MT and most other ancient witnesses have "the Three"; in the light of the second verset, emendation to "the Thirty" is almost universal.

Discussion

No text in 1–2 Samuel brings home so starkly how little is known of the histori- cal David and the forces bearing on these traditions. The structural organization of the passage is looser than we might expect; Stoebe, for example, sees four independent units put together here (i.e., vv. 8-12, 13-17, 18-23, 24-39; cf. pp. 495-512). The structure analysis of the present text (above) is derived from two observations.

First, contrary to expectations, there are no superscriptions for what might be expected to be the lists of the Three and the Thirty, just a superscrip- tion for the whole collection. This opening superscription concerns the names of David's warriors — [I.A]. As a descriptor, "David's warriors" *(gibbōrîm)* could connote more than the top three (cf. for example, 1 Sam 14:52; 2 Sam 20:7). Whether it does in this text is uncertain. A great deal depends on the ori- gins of the text (or collection); these origins remain uncertain. Verse 9 suggests it applies here to the Three, but it is lacking for Shammah (vv. 11-12). It occurs in vv. 16-17, describing three warriors. Their inclusion may have been on the assumption that they were the Three; the assumption need not be correct (cf. McCarter, 495). Verse 22 points to a clear association of "the warriors" with "the Three." There is no superscription for Abishai, Benaiah, and none for those that follow (the NRSV adjusts the Hebrew word order of v. 24, resulting in a certain emphasis for the Thirty; the Hebrew has: "Asahel, brother of Joab, was among the Thirty" — certainly not a superscription). The superscription in v. 8a has to suffice for the collection.

Second, the final note gives a total of thirty-seven — [II]. Allowing for one name in the textually uncertain v. 32b, there are thirty-one names in vv. 24-39a. If we add to these the names of Abishai and Benaiah, renowned mem- bers of the Thirty, and the three members of the Three, and of course David himself, the total is thirty-seven. This may be sheerest chance. It may reflect the overall command structure of David's guerrilla forces. It may also reflect the structural organization of the passage, providing a list of the names and some of the exploits from David's early days, when he was a guerrilla leader.

Among the Thirty, Asahel is named; he was killed by Abner in the struggles after Saul's death (2 Sam 2:18-23). In the light of this, these names have to come from the early years of David's rise to power. Benaiah occurs in the list (23:20, 22 [v. 30: same name, different person]), as also in the lists of David's officials (8:16-18; 20:23-26); otherwise, Benaiah has no role to play until 1 Kings.

What is so starkly surprising is that, among all the traditions we have of David's forces and with two lists of David's administrations, we have no trace of a group called the Three, nor have we heard of the names of its members. Of the Thirty, five names only are known to us. Of the exploits reported, none are known to us. Traditions have been reported selectively. Perhaps selectivity is to be expected; nevertheless, it comes as a surprise.

Equally surprising is the realization that this is unlikely to reflect merely the preservation of variant traditions. Variant traditions from World War II are inevitable. It would be most unlikely, however, for an account of the war in Europe to make no mention of command structures such as the Chiefs of Staff, or field commanders such as Montgomery (UK) and Eisenhower (US), or elite troops such as airborne divisions and commando units. Yet that is precisely what the text here reveals has happened in the mainstream Davidic traditions of 1 and 2 Samuel — and we do not know the reason. It is quite understandable that circles allied with David would play up his role and downplay the role of others. What we do not know is who might have had an interest in emphasizing the military organizational structures. As we have seen, within the four chapters of this Special Collection, David is not given an overwhelmingly glamorous role. The situation is complicated by Chronicles, where these particular traditions are placed together, situated immediately after David is made king over all Israel (1 Chr 11:10-47). Variations exist, but they are relatively minor. Noteworthy exceptions are: (i) Chronicles gives two names in the next chapter as leaders of the Thirty (Ishmaiah, 12:4; Amasai, 12:19 [Heb.; NRSV, 12:18]) — both are totally unknown to us; (ii) Chronicles adds at the end of the list, after Uriah the Hittite, some sixteen more names as well as a reference to another thirty (11:42). The collection is a reminder of how much is concealed in what is revealed.

The precise phrase used in the superscription ("warriors who were to David") is found only here and in 1 Kgs 1:8 — as well as 1 Chr 11:10-11, where v. 10 goes beyond what is noted in 1–2 Samuel. It would seem a common enough expression, but its occurrence is restricted. Possibly, the use in 1 Kgs 1:8 denotes the commanders among those warriors loyal to David. Shimei (also in 1 Kgs 1:8) is a common enough name; at the same time, the individual could be David's brother (cf. 2 Sam 21:21). Rei, of course, is otherwise unheard of.

The names of the Three are unknown — [I.B.1]: Josheb-basshebeth, a Tahchemonite (an identification mentioned only here); Eleazar ben Dodo ben Ahohi (cf. 2 Sam 23:28; 1 Chr 24:4); and Shammah ben Agee, the Hararite (cf. 2 Sam 23:25). The exploits of the last two are situated within the Philistine wars; we may assume the same for the eight hundred killed by Josheb-basshebeth, but it is not said.

It is said of Abishai ben Zeruiah and Benaiah ben Jehoiada (both well known to us) that they "did not attain to the Three" (23:19, 23) — [I.B.3.a]. Abishai is noted as the commander of the Thirty (23:19); Benaiah is noted as "renowned among the Thirty" and in charge of David's bodyguard (23:23). The Three, therefore, appear as elite warriors at the very top of the military structure. Even the commander of the Thirty does not make it into the Three. Without this collection, their existence and their names would be unknown.

The exploits reported for Abishai and Benaiah are akin to those of the Three. However, an association is not made with the Philistine wars. The more expansive notice about David's thirst is associated with Philistine forces (vv. 13-17). It is tempting to attribute this exploit to the Three (cf. v. 17b). The statement, even if textually troubled, that three from the Thirty did it (v. 13) cautions against yielding to the temptation — nameless though the three warriors remain. David's reaction to the deed is the sort of thing that maddens pragmatic folks; it is also the sort of reaction that generates undying loyalty and admiration. There is a similarity with the tradition of 1 Sam 26; again, three warriors (David, Ahimelech, and Abishai) are named in relation to the proposal to penetrate a Philistine camp. Ahimelech the Hittite is mentioned in 26:6 and nowhere else.

The final element in the collection adds the names of others among the Thirty — [I.B.3.b]. There are no conjunctions between the names, a feature shared with the list of kings in Josh 12:9-24. Contrast the linking for the Three (vv. 9, 11; NRSV, "next to him") and the conjunctions for Abishai and Benaiah (vv. 19, 20). It is a small matter, but it fosters a sense of unity for the names in vv. 24-39 and suggests some separation between them and what precedes. Asahel, brother of Abishai and Joab, is listed first; Uriah the Hittite is listed last. Only five of the members are known to us: Abishai, Benaiah, Asahel, Eliam, and Uriah. Both Abishai and Asahel are listed as "brother of Joab" (vv. 18, 24). Joab is not listed.

Genre

The collection comprises a motley group of traditions. First there are five names with associated brief (→) reports of the individual's exploit or exploits. Then there are some thirty-one names of those who belonged in the Thirty. Between the names of the Three and names of the Thirty, there is a (→) report of the daring action of three of the Thirty, who risked their lives to bring drinking water for David, and his action in pouring it out to the LORD rather than drinking it. The overall genre involved is the (→) list. Its perspective is a listing of those warriors associated with David. A heading is actually given in v. 8a and a total count in v. 39b. However, the text goes beyond a simple list of names to give brief reports of the exploits of the Three as well as of Abishai and Benaiah. It is not surprising that such a collection should attract the report in vv. 13-17.

Setting

The plethora of otherwise unknown warriors, the association with Philistine fighting, and the similarities of the exploits all tend to associate 2 Sam 21:15-22 and 23:8-39. The setting for such a collection — with its emphasis on command and organization and exploits other than David's — may be assumed to have been among military circles interested in the preservation of their traditions. While this may be a sound assumption, we need to keep in mind that any single individual might have had reason or interest enough to preserve such traditions.

Meaning

Potentially, there is a twofold meaning in the collection. First there is the preservation of the traditions for posterity: the structures, the exploits, and the names. Second, there is the association of the exploits with the individuals and their leader. David was served by and held the loyalty of warriors of this high caliber, warriors able to perform the prodigious deeds reported. Tradition is preserved; high esteem for David is preserved as well. The possibility remains that the reporting of leadership and organization (the Three and the Thirty) redresses an imbalance created by their omission from earlier traditions.

Of atonement: plague incurred and averted	24:1-25
I. The sin	1-9
A. Incitement by YHWH	1
1. General: concerning Israel	1a
2. Specific: involving David	1b
B. Census of Israel by David	2-9
1. The order	2-3
a. King's order to Joab	2
b. Joab's remonstration	3
c. King's order maintained	4a
2. The census taken	4b-8
3. The report by Joab to the king	9
II. Confession and punishment	10-15
A. Confession of sin by David	10
1. David's remorse	10a
2. David's confession of sin to YHWH	10b
B. Punishment to be chosen	11-14
1. Options presented by Gad	11-13
a. Word of God to Gad	11-12
b. Word of God by Gad to David: 7 years, 3 months, 3 days	13
2. David's decision: "the hand of the LORD"	14
C. Punishment administered: pestilence and death in Israel	15
III. Termination of the punishment	16-25
A. By YHWH directly: pestilence stopped	16
B. By YHWH indirectly: mediated by David's action	17-25
1. David's assumption of responsibility	17
2. Concerning the altar to the LORD	18-25a
a. Order to erect an altar: from Gad to David	18
b. Compliance with the order	19-25a

Textual Issues

24:2 The MT, LXX[B], and Vulgate have David speak to "Joab, the commander of the army"; LXX[L] and 1 Chr 21:2 have to "Joab and the commanders of the army." The MT is not of great help with both a singular and a plural imperative later in v. 2 (so the Vulgate too); Driver emends with LXX[L] to make both plural (p. 373), while LXX[B] has both singular. According to v. 4, both Joab and the army commanders were present at the audience with the king; this need not prevent the text from having David's address in v. 2 single out Joab, his army chief. Chronicles speaks of the commanders (plural) at the outset, but then has Joab alone carry out the census (vv. 4-6). Emendation of the MT here would be incautious.

24:5 Most moderns emend with LXX[L] to replace "encamped south" with "began from" (e.g., Driver, 373; Hertzberg, 409; McCarter, 504; Barthélemy, 323-24; Anderson, 281).

24:13 The MT, Josephus, and the Vulgate have "seven" years; Chronicles and the LXX have three. Years to months to days creates a descending sequence; three of each is attractive. Certainty is elusive. Driver emends with caution (three is "probably the original number," p. 376); Barthélemy is equally cautious (given the complex and uncertain situation, assimilation to 1 Chr 21:12 is to be avoided, p. 326). The MT appears to have the *lectio difficilior.*

24:20 The ancient versions vary, with the MT, LXX, and Vulgate in agreement and 4QSam[a], Chronicles (Heb. and Gk.), and Josephus providing more detail (see Ulrich, 157-59). McCarter discusses the differences and comments: "The short text of MT in II Sam 24:20, however, evidently arose from an expanded text of the type of 4QSam[a]" (p. 507). Pisano, after an equally full discussion, concludes: "The text of MT is the shortest. . . . MT is to be preferred as the more primitive state of the text, to which the additional information was appended" (p. 116). Both Stoebe (p. 528) and Anderson (p. 280) retain the MT.

Discussion

The passage begins with two statements both of which express remarkably odd views — [I.A]. They are: "Again the anger of the LORD was kindled against Israel" and the LORD "incited David against them" (24:1). There is nothing odd in the LORD's anger being kindled against Israel; that happens often enough in biblical texts. What is odd is the absence of any reason and also the verb indicating that this was not an isolated occurrence (NRSV, "again"; Hebrew root: *y-s-p,* not in 1 Chr 21:1). We have no context for it as well as no reason for it. Even stranger is the punitive action attributed to God: he incited David against Israel — odd enough that Chronicles assigns the blame to Satan (possibly the only occurrence in the Hebrew Bible where Satan may be understood as a proper name). At a later stage in the text, David is allowed to take full and total responsibility for what he has done: "I alone have sinned, and I alone have done wickedly" (v. 17). No court of law would accept such a confession in the light of v. 1. All the more amazing when we consider that this is in the context of establishing an altar that will be claimed as the place for the future temple (implicit here; explicit in 1 Chr 22:1).

The situation becomes more curious when David moves to comply with the LORD's order (v. 1b; Chronicles discreetly omits the order). The king gives an order to Joab to take a census of Israel and Judah. Joab questions the order (esp. v. 3b). No reason is given for Joab's dissent; simply the question: Why do this? Army commanders receive orders; they do not question kings. Joab is portrayed changing his orders (cf. Uriah) or disobeying them (cf. Absalom); he has not been portrayed openly questioning the king's orders. The impact of his action is to heighten awareness of God's incitement of David to do wrong as a result of God's anger against Israel. Very strange theology.

According to the text, David's order prevails and the census is taken — [I.B]. It comprises Transjordan, from Aroer north, and from northern Galilee (Dan) down to the Negeb of Judah (Beer-sheba). It took almost ten months. It reported totals of eight hundred thousand arms-bearing troops in Israel and five hundred thousand in Judah.

Chronicles intensifies Joab's question (why bring guilt on Israel?), does not have the description of the territory covered, reports different numbers (eleven hundred thousand troops for Israel and four hundred and seventy thousand for Judah), and excludes Levi and Benjamin from the count "for the king's command was abhorrent to Joab" (21:3-6).

David's confession of sin is fulsome in comparison with 2 Sam 12:13a — [II.A]. It is also surprising in the light of v. 1b. Within the narrative, David's sin — for example, "I have done very foolishly" — consists in having obeyed God's order, when incited by God against Israel. It does not speak well of God. Very strange theology. Chronicles, which had Satan do the inciting, now has God displeased and taking action against Israel (21:7): in so doing, it provides an appropriate prelude to David's confession.

David's confession is followed by an offer from God, communicated by Gad — [II.B]. Its formulation requires attention: "choose one of them, and I will do it to you" (v. 12). There are three; all three are to be God's doing. Gad spells out the three for David: famine, defeat, or pestilence. The Greek follows Chronicles (21:12) and has three years' famine, three months' defeat, or three days' pestilence; the Hebrew has seven years' famine (echoing Joseph and Egypt, surely) and three for the months of defeat and the days of pestilence. David's response can be read as one of deep piety or as remarkably shrewd theology. His reply includes: "let us fall into the hand of the LORD, for his mercy is great" (v. 14). Why shrewd? Because, as formulated in the text, all three options are from God. The text is elliptical, with the option there to understand that David is portrayed diplomatically placing the choice in God's hands (cf. Klein, "David," 110). If so, he did wisely, for God moves to the shortest option, the three-day pestilence (v. 15). There would be a delightful irony: God incited David to the sin; David invited God to choose among the punishments on offer. Smart move.

At this point, an interesting set of moves occurs within the text. With v. 16, the pestilence is stopped: "It is enough; now stay your hand" — [III.A]. The location of the angel is noted: by the threshing floor of Araunah. With v. 17, the narrative goes on to have David see the destruction, take sole responsibility for the sin, buy Araunah's threshing floor, build an altar there, and offer sacrifices — [III.B]. According to v. 25, the LORD granted David's supplication "and the plague was averted from Israel." Two endings to the tradition are possible: one with the LORD relenting spontaneously; the other with David offering sacrifices on the newly built altar, following prophetic instructions. Equally possible is the forging of a unity from the two. The basic statement: the LORD relented and stayed the angel's hand. The unfolding of this basic statement: David built an altar and made supplication and so the Lord relented and the plague was averted. We can argue for one or the other; nothing says we cannot have both. Storytellers are offered options.

David's assumption of responsibility (v. 17) can be seen as a duplication of his confession (v. 10). On the other hand, the contexts are different. The first follows on completion of the census and is precisely a confession of sin: "I have sinned greatly" (v. 10). The second follows on the destruction among the people and is an assumption of responsibility: "I alone have sinned . . . these sheep, what have they done?" (v. 17).

David's moves are initiated by instructions from Gad. Appropriately, there is nothing in the text to say where Gad got these instructions from; in Chronicles, the instructions originate with the angel of the LORD. Classic bargaining takes place between David and Araunah (cf. Gen 23:8-16). David: I will buy it and build an altar to avert the plague (v. 21b). Araunah: I give you all you need (vv. 22-23). David: No, I will buy them from you (v. 24). The transaction is significant; properly negotiated transfer of the site is important. The altar is built, the sacrifices offered, and the plague averted. The threshing floor belonged to a Jebusite, in close proximity to Jerusalem (cf. v. 16). It is surprising that nothing more is made of this in the text of 2 Sam 24; it is left to 1 Chr 21:28–22:1 to be specific.

Genre

The strangeness of this passage is particularly evident at its beginning and its end. At the beginning, as noted, the Hebrew text has YHWH angry with Israel and inciting David against them. While emphasis is attached to the threshing floor of Araunah, at the end the Hebrew text has no etiological note concerning the future significance of this location.

Again as noted, the Chronicles text differs from the Hebrew in both areas. At the beginning, it is Satan who "stood up" against Israel and incited David to take a census (21:1). At the end, the threshing floor is the location of the future temple (22:1).

From the point of view of genre, it is probably best described as (→) story, although it is not far from an extended (→) account. The potential for a story is certainly there. The initial tension of God's inciting David against Israel is heightened by the opposition of the army commanders to the census proposal. The equilibrium of ancient Israel is moved into imbalance. How will the balance be restored? The balance is restored by royal repentance (v. 10) and royal assumption of responsibility (v. 17), coupled with either an unmotivated change of heart on God's part (v. 16) or the appropriate purchase of a site, building of an altar, and offering of sacrifice (vv. 18-25) or a combination of both.

What brings the passage close to an (→) account is that this tension can hardly be said to be exploited at any point. The text is very matter-of-fact. While there are areas that cry out for expansion, nothing is absent that is essential to the narrative. Given this completeness, a designation as (→) reported story would be dubious.

Setting

The setting for such a story is probably to be sought in pro-Davidic circles. At first sight, this may not be evident; after all, it is a story in which David admits to having done "very foolishly" (v. 10). On the other hand, there are David's confession of sin, assumption of responsibility, and appropriate reparation in obedience to Gad's instructions. Add to this the tradition that the threshing floor is the site of the future temple (cf. 1 Chr 22:1; 2 Chr 3:1) and the text can certainly derive from circles favorable to David.

Setting is one thing; dating is another. A text like this is very difficult to date. The only other references to the Jebusite's threshing floor are in Chronicles. In 1 Kgs 8, Solomon correlates the temple with God's promise to David (2 Sam 7). Nothing is said about the site. Appropriate discretion about David's folly is a possible motive. The focus on David, apparent in Chronicles, could suggest a later origin for the text; but the later the text, the more surprising the silence over the temple site. Any dating has to remain uncertain. This text is associated, at least to some degree, with 2 Sam 21:1-14; both are concerned with averting divine disfavor: "after that, God heeded supplications for the land" (21:14) and "so the LORD answered his supplication for the land" (24:25; the concern with supplication is absent from the Chronicles text). In the Samuel text, both passages belong in this apparent addition to the Deuteronomistic History (i.e., 2 Sam 21–24). The threshing floor as temple site is unmentioned in

209

the deuteronomistic traditions about the temple. For whatever reasons, these passages do not seem to have been part of the deuteronomistic armory of traditions. This observation may tell us nothing of their date; it may have something to do with the time when they came to be part of Israel's scriptural holdings.

The LORD's inciting of David against Israel (v. 1) can be seen as shifting the blame for what happened away from David. According to the text, "the anger of the LORD was kindled against Israel." David, therefore, is not the one responsible; it is Israel that has angered the LORD. The LORD has then incited David against Israel. By David's later admission, he should have known better. But anyone who has been incited by YHWH can surely plead diminished responsibility. The text of Chronicles gives less scope for this Davidic evasion; but even there, Satan's stance is taken "against Israel" (21:1), diminishing something of the blame for David.

Meaning

The etiological aspect is subjacent in the Hebrew text; it is not made explicit at any point. The pestilence is stopped with the angel "by the threshing floor of Araunah the Jebusite" (v. 16). The threshing floor is purchased by David and an altar is built there. The Hebrew text says nothing about the future of this threshing floor and its altar. The narrative has lingered over it; it passes over its significance. As noted above, it is left to Chronicles to make this aspect explicit (cf. 1 Chr 22:1; 2 Chr 3:1).

If the narrative is ended at v. 16, the etiological aspect would be greatly muted. The emphasis then falls more on David's wisdom in relying on God's mercy, the goodness of God in selecting the shortest punishment, and the favor of God in sparing Jerusalem. With vv. 17-25, the emphasis on the threshing floor is much greater. Yet in the text of 2 Sam 24, nothing is done with it. The aspects of Davidic wisdom (balancing Davidic folly, v. 10), divine mercy, and Jerusalem's special status remain; they are not negligible.

Bibliography of Works Cited Above

Brueggemann, Walter. "2 Samuel 21–24: An Appendix of Deconstruction?" *CBQ* 50 (1988) 383-97.

Cross, Frank Moore, and David Noel Freedman. "A Royal Song of Thanksgiving: 2 Samuel 22 = Psalm 18." *JBL* 72 (1953) 15-34.

Gerstenberger, Erhard S. *Psalms.* Part 1. FOTL 14. Grand Rapids: Eerdmans, 1988.

Klein, Ralph W. "David: Sinner and Saint in Samuel and Chronicles." *CurTM* 26 (1999) 104-16.

Noll, K. L. *The Faces of David.* JSOTSup 242. Sheffield: Sheffield Academic Press, 1997.

Simon, László T. *Identity and Identification: An Exegetical and Theological Study of 2 Sam 21–24.* Rome: Pontificia Università Gregoriana, 2000.

Chapter 12

DIACHRONIC DIMENSION:
FROM PAST TEXTS TO PRESENT TEXT

The Diachronic Dimension for 1–2 Samuel has been fully treated in the 1 Samuel volume (FOTL 7); it is not desirable to repeat it here. However, a few words are needed to indicate the traditions that can be discerned in 2 Samuel and to sketch both what is needed for an understanding of the text of 2 Samuel and what is available in the diachronic section of 1 Samuel for fuller reflection.

Ark Narrative

Of the four chapters constituting or associated with the Ark Narrative, three are in 1 Samuel (1 Sam 4–6) and one in 2 Samuel (2 Sam 6). Two points are worth noting with regard to 2 Sam 6.

The first relates to the role of YHWH in the ark's coming to Jerusalem. As narrated in the text, it was the action of YHWH in striking Uzzah dead that prevented the ark being brought by David to Jerusalem. "David was angry. . . . David was afraid. . . . David was unwilling to take the ark of the LORD into his care in the city of David" (vv. 8-10). As narrated in the text, it was again the action of YHWH in blessing Obed-edom and all his household that encouraged David to bring the ark into Jerusalem (vv. 11-12). The ark is indeed brought to Jerusalem by David, but the narrative makes clear that this happens under YHWH's patronage and with YHWH's approval. It may have been a stroke of political and religious genius on David's part. The move to Jerusalem is presented in the narrative as sanctioned and blessed by YHWH.

The second relates to the history of Israel's literature. The narrative ends with the ark's installation "in its place, inside the tent that David had pitched for it" (v. 17). There is no note to the effect that the temple had not yet been built (cf., for example, 1 Kgs 3:2). No text providing a continuation to the installation of the ark in the Jerusalem temple can be identified as part of any ark narrative. The relevant text in 1 Kgs 8 is notably different; it is not suitable as a continuation and cannot be detached from where it is without damaging the narrative of the temple's consecration. This ending with the ark in the tent argues against the origins of the Ark Narrative being late, at least as regards the composition of 2 Sam 6. At the same time, the recognition that the transfer of the ark to the Jerusalem temple is not reported within the Ark Narrative makes it evident that the focus of the Ark Narrative has to be on something other than the reporting of the ark's movements. 2 Sam 6 is where the narrative ends, not where the ark ends up; the ark ends up in the temple. If the focus of the Ark Narrative is on the transition from the era of Shiloh to a new epoch in Jerusalem, the move to the temple is not needed. The ark's coming to Jerusalem is enough. A late date for the composition of 2 Sam 6 is problematic.

Looked at from the point of view of the diachronic, it is important to recognize the remarkable diversity of titles for the ark used within the short space of four chapters. The details cannot be rehearsed here; they have been treated fully in *1 Samuel* (FOTL 7). They were examined in 1971 in a study by Georg Fohrer ("Ladeerzählung"). The significance for 2 Sam 6 is the possibility — and it is no more than that — that an older version may have preexisted the present text. If one gives weight to the distribution of the titles for the ark between "ark of God" and "ark of YHWH," there is the possibility of a text centering around the verses 2, 3, 4, 6, 7, 12 ("ark of God") and a later expansion of that text centering around the verses 9, 10, 11, 13, 15, 16, 17 ("ark of YHWH").

As noted in *1 Samuel* (FOTL 7), "two assumptions are required for the reconstruction to be considered adequate. First, that 1 Sam 6:1–7:1 has replaced an earlier account of the transfer of the ark from Philistine territory (1 Sam 5:12) to the house of Abinadab (2 Sam 6:3). Second, that 2 Sam 6:10-11 has replaced an earlier mention of a sojourn in the house of Obed-edom" (p. 305). These two assumptions are grounds for serious reserves with regard to such a reconstruction. Nevertheless, there is a text in 2 Sam 6:2-7, 12 that gets the ark to Jerusalem under the effective auspices of YHWH. The emphasis on God's power and purpose is heightened by the "ark of YHWH" verses (vv. 9-11, 13-17). They are conceivable as a faith-enhancing expansion of the earlier text. In such a hypothesis, however, the transfer of the ark to the house of Obed-edom in an earlier version has been completely replaced by vv. 10-11. The possibility can be entertained; it can hardly be affirmed.

Stories of David's Achieving Power

The point was emphasized throughout the 1 Samuel volume that the so-called Story of David's Rise could not be considered a monolithic composition. It is of the nature of the traditions that, although they often constitute sequences, they have an independence of their own. Whether as independent units or as shorter sequences, they could have been combined to offer a variety of versions as to how David achieved power in Israel. They could have begun as early as 1 Sam 9:1 and ended as late as 2 Sam 8:15 or 8:18. They could have begun and ended at a variety of places in between. They could have varied considerably in content. In short, even restricted to the traditions available to us, there could have been several versions of how David rose to power.

However, the clustering of these traditions, available for forming a story of David's rise to power, would not extend beyond the establishment of that power and its consolidation reported in 2 Sam 8. The tail end of these traditions overlaps with and is in sharp contrast with the traditions in Chronicles for the same period. According to Chronicles, Saul died on Gilboa, all Israel made David king at Hebron, and David and all Israel took Jerusalem and made it David's capital (1 Chr 10:13–11:8; for those reputedly joining David, see 1 Chr 12). The Chronicler might quite justifiably be accused of covering up the sordid aspects of civil war associated with David's acquisition of power. On the other hand, the traditions in 2 Sam 1–4 account for about four days out of the alleged total of some seven years. No one familiar with 1–2 Samuel would be surprised if the text were found to be covering up the more brutal aspects associated with David's acquisition of power. Historically, uncertainty is the order of the day.

It is worth noting that what has been said of the independence of many of the stories in the Davidic traditions can be exemplified in 2 Sam 1–5. The story of David's lament for Saul, for example, could have been begun comfortably enough within 2 Sam 1:2, passing over the first three or four words (Hebrew) to begin: "A man came from Saul's camp. . . ." All that is needed as background is that the Philistines met Israel in battle and Saul and his sons were slain. The story would then end with David's lament (vv. 19-27). The retro-reference to Ziklag (1:1-2a*) would be part of the compositional activity, combining the various independent traditions.

Similarly, the story of the battle at Gibeon and the subsequent death of Abner could have been wholly independent. A beginning at 2:8 is convenient for the composition and the overall picture of two warring kingdoms; but it can be relegated to useful background. What was noted earlier on the text itself (see above, in the discussion of 2:8-11) holds true for the composition; the issues are less significant for a shorter and independent story. A beginning with 2:12 is possible. An ending with 3:39 is clearly possible. The status of 3:1-6a is then worth reflection; it will be discussed below.

A third candidate for independence is the story of Ishbaal's assassination. The two killers are identified adequately in 4:2. Oddly, the LXX and 4QSam[a] add the personal name "Mephibosheth" to "Saul's son" in v. 2 (cf. Ulrich, 43-45, with a discussion of the error); again, both versions have Mephibosheth in v. 1a, where a personal name is also lacking in the MT (supplied by the NRSV as Ishbaal, naturally). The ending of the story in 4:12 is satisfactory. The status of 4:3-4 may, of course, be compositional.

Finally, it is also to be noted in this context that David's crowning at Hebron, perhaps together with the capture of Jerusalem and the victories over the Philistines, could have formed an independent account. Naturally, this is equally true of the traditions of 2 Sam 6, 7, 8. These points are noted in contradistinction to the stories of David's middle years (2 Sam 11–20) where independence is perfectly possible in theory but is not possible within the syntax of the present text.

At this point we need to return to the beginning of ch. 3. Verses 1 and 6a are the only witness we have to the existence of "a long war"; without them, we have stories of battles and killings, but nothing about a long period of time. As has been noted, the list of sons in vv. 2-5 is an odd one. Technically, the six sons could have been conceived within a week; narratively, that is not the impression that is given. What must be recognized is that if the witness of vv. 1-6a is relegated to the compositional, the "seven years and six months" of 5:5 for David's reign in Hebron is bereft of any early external support. This would mean that a reconciliation between the traditions of Samuel and of Chronicles would become much easier. These considerations do not affect the issue of historical accuracy; they have to do with the possible reconciling of traditions. As any historian should know, traditions can flourish independently of what may be termed historically recoverable. This is certainly not an invitation to reconstruct texts or traditions or past history; quite the contrary. It is a reminder of the impassable chasm that sometimes exists between what might have happened and what has in fact entered into story.

What we are exploring here is not so much a question of our becoming aware of the development within the text. It is rather a matter of our developing an awareness of how much of the political and social context of both the events and the narratives reflecting them is hidden from us. It is important, too, to be aware that these traditions have not come down to us in documents that we can reconstruct. They were crystallized in the Prophetic Record (or, if one prefers, whatever may be assumed in its place) which, if it was selective — and it probably was — operates primarily from its own point of view and not that of the collections of traditions it presents.

Stories of David's Middle Years: Recent Research

As was noted in *1 Samuel* (FOTL 7), the traditions in the stories of David's middle years (= 2 Sam 11–20) are both too disparaging of David and at the same time too laudatory of David to be late compositions. Among the elements disparaging David, we may note his ordering Uriah killed, his sending Tamar to Amnon without an escort, his allowing Amnon to go to his death, and his handling of Absalom (including his death). Among the elements laudatory of David, we may note the portrayal of his faith (15:24-26), his capacity to inspire loyalty (15:19-23), his political decision-making (16:1-4 and 19:25-31 [Heb.; NRSV, 19:24-30]), his political and religious wisdom (16:5-13 and 19:17-24 [Heb.; NRSV, 19:16-23]), and his reputation for military leadership (17:8-10; 18:2-4).

The disparaging of David can hardly have been too close to the Davidic or Solomonic court. It does not sit comfortably with the later, almost messianic, image of David either. The laudatory elements do not have the stamp of later invention and are coherent enough with the traditions of David's rise to power. Interestingly, they are associated with David's time in the field, as military strategist. As sovereign, in the capital, David is either foolish or coldly ruthless.

A setting at the court of Jeroboam I, where such stories might have served in the formation of royal counselors, has been suggested above and in *1 Samuel.*

These chapters, 2 Sam 11–20, which we are calling the Stories of David's Middle Years, form one of the most sustained and highly regarded pieces of prose narrative in the Hebrew Bible. It would not be helpful to attempt a developmental or diachronic analysis of the traditions; of necessity, it would be speculative and unlikely to add much to meaning (see the analyses discussed by Seiler, *Geschichte von der Thronfolge,* 13-19). What I believe will be helpful is to provide an outline of the trajectory taken in recent studies of this text. An exhaustive survey is not possible within the present scope. What follows is much more a schematic outline.

A major source of confusion in the interpretation of these stories has been the interplay of extent and intent for the overall narrative. The extent generally given in scholarship is 2 Sam 9–20 and 1 Kgs 1–2. But for Leonhard Rost, the piece began much earlier than that in 1 Samuel; for many, it ends before 1 Kgs 1–2. The intent attributed to the narrative can be gauged by the name frequently given it, the "Succession Narrative"; dissatisfaction with this assessment of its intent can be seen in alternative names, such as the "Court History," and suggestions that 1–2 Kgs be dropped from the end of the narrative.

As was noted in the discussion of the text itself, the understanding of these chapters has been bedeviled by the intrusive issue of succession. The dispute with Michal (2 Sam 6) reflected the change of dynasties. Her barrenness was symbolic of this; David's dynasty had heirs in plenty. The characteristics which give a sense of unity to these Stories of David's Middle Years are clustered in 2 Sam 11–20. They are not typical of earlier chapters. While 2 Sam 11–20 has the birth of Solomon and eliminates Amnon and Absalom from leadership contention, its focus is different from that of 1 Kgs 1–2. With 2 Sam 20, a narrative can find closure; the list of officials is witness to that judgment in antiquity (20:23-26). The account of Solomon's accession, given in 1 Kgs 1–2, can stand as a text in its own right. It begins with King David "old and advanced in years" (1 Kgs 1:1); it ends with the kingdom "established in the hand of Solomon" (2:46).

In 1926, in a study that achieved "quasi-canonical status in Biblical studies for the best part of forty years" (Conroy, *Absalom,* 1), Rost investigated four pieces of early Israelite writing: the Ark Narrative, the Prophecy of Nathan, the Account of the Ammonite War, and the Succession Story *(Succession).* For Rost, the Succession Story began with 2 Sam 6:16, 20-23, followed by a core of 2 Sam 7:11b, 16, and culminated in the question, "Who shall sit on David's throne?" *(Succession,* 85-86). With understandable embarrassment, Rost attached this beginning to the very different Ark Narrative *(Succession,* 87-90). Along with the selection from 2 Sam 7 and the account of the Ammonite war, it formed "a convenient way into" the biblical author's own story, the Succession Narrative *(Succession,* 89).

For the rest of the narrative, Rost had adopted a different approach, deeming it "a better strategy to start from the end and then work backwards to the beginning" *(Succession,* 67). So 1 Kgs 1 becomes "the key to understanding the whole work" *(Succession,* 68). Unfortunately, determining the meaning of a narrative from one verse (in this case, 1 Kgs 1:48) is not a particularly appropriate methodological approach. Equally unfortunately perhaps, Seiler too begins at the end and proceeds toward the beginning (cf. *Geschichte von der Thronfolge,* 26). Instead, it is necessary to approach the narrative as a whole, determine whether there is a central theme or organizing structure, and ascertain the extent of text that comes under this. One verse chosen from the end of the narrative may not be a satisfactory point of departure.

Scholarship's tendency to refer to the narrative as 2 Sam 9–20 and 1 Kgs 1–2 points to dissatisfaction with Rost's suggestion for its beginning. As noted, even stalwart supporters have abandoned the claim (so, Whybray: it is "probable that the beginning is missing," *Succession Narrative,* 8; Seiler: "its beginning is lost," *Geschichte von der Thronfolge,* 324, n. 8). The presumption of an ending in 1 Kgs 1–2 has also provoked resistance. In 1963, Mowinckel expressed the view that "an original literary connexion between 2 Sam 20 and 1 Kings 1–2" was "very doubtful" ("Israelite Historiography," 11). "The latter chapters in no wise give the impression of having been conceived as a continuation of 2 Sam 9–20. . . . 1 Kings 1–2 gives the impression of having been written as the beginning of a history rather than as a finale" (ibid.). In 1972, James Flanagan expressed a preference for the name "Court History," dispensing with 1 Kgs 1–2. In 1978, Conroy expressed similar dissatisfaction with the alleged ending: "there is no reason why the relatively independent narrative unit 2 Sam 13–20 should not be read on its own without extrapolation from 1 Kgs 1–2" (*Absalom,* 101; cf. pp. 101-5). These are issues of extent.

Gerhard von Rad supported Rost's position (originally: "Beginnings of Historical Writing" [1944]; now: *Theology,* 1.312-17). Both accepted the extent of the narrative from 2 Sam 6 to 1 Kgs 2; both saw its movement from a barren woman (Michal) to a promised heir (Solomon). For Rost, it was written for the greater glory of Solomon ("in majorem gloriam Salomonis," *Succession,* 105; cf. pp. 85-86); for von Rad, "it deals with the anointed and his throne, and so with the messianic problem . . . the anointed who suffers!" (*Theology,* 1.316-17) — more nuanced, but favorable to the anointed. Here there is agreement on intent.

In due course, a contrary view was expressed by Lienhard Delekat and Ernst Würthwein who both viewed the so-called Succession Narrative as oriented negatively toward the monarchy of David and Solomon. For Delekat, it advocated Solomon's overthrow ("Tendenz," 31). For Würthwein, the position of Rost and von Rad was being uncritically repeated (*Thronfolge Davids,* 10). Würthwein — in a semi-popular piece valuable for its expression of conviction rather than intensive critical analysis — introduced the issue of later additions countering the thematic coherence of the original (the arguments adduced by Rost and von Rad are based on texts that were added later ["spätere Zutaten bzw. Überarbeitungen"]; cf., by way of summary, *Thronfolge Davids,* 49-59).

In 1972, Flanagan, apparently unaware of Mowinckel's comments, opened the way to separating 1 Kgs 1–2 from the preceding narrative ("Court History"). "If the Solomonic sections are set aside there remains a history of the difficulties and challenges that David faced in maintaining his control over the kingdoms of Judah and Israel. The most severe threat to his sovereignty was raised by his own son, Absalom. His rebellion is recognized as the central feature of the narrative because it is the longest single episode, and it holds the narrative together" ("Court History," 177). Flanagan argues for an intentional, balanced structure that once seen "confirms the removal of the Solomonic sections in 2 Samuel 11–12 and 1 Kings 1–2" (ibid.). His conclusion: "the structure and content of the Court History verify it as a record of how David maintained the powers of office and continued to be the legitimate king of Israel and Judah. Only later was the narrative used as a basis for the story of Solomon's accession . . ." ("Court History," 181). Here the issue of extent ("if the Solomonic sections are set aside") affects the question of intent ("a record . . ." etc.).

Charles Conroy's 1978 work was a literary study of 2 Sam 13–20. Reflecting on the justification for the limit to 2 Sam 13–20, he writes: "Should not one take into account all the material commonly included in the Succession Narrative (at least 2 Sam 9–20; 1 Kgs 1–2)? Here one must recall the doubts and problems which have recently arisen concerning the Succession Narrative hypothesis. The extent of the literary unity to which 2 Sam 13–20 belongs is no longer clear . . ." (*Absalom,* 5). Earlier, after a brief review of much of the literature, Conroy had concluded: "the current state of research no longer justifies an automatic and uncritical acceptance of 2 Sam 9–20; 1 Kgs 1–2 as a fully rounded literary unity with a clearly defined theme" (*Absalom,* 3). He argues emphatically that 2 Sam 13–20 can be read as a thematic unity without 1 Kgs 1–2. "2 Sam 13–20 for all its complexity is a recognizable narrative unity centred on Absalom and David" (*Absalom,* 101).

With this background, an aspect of the recent discussion can be introduced. The richness of the narrative's many-sided ambiguity looms deliciously large on the interpretative horizon. Symbolic of this vaunted ambiguity is the messianic and anti-messianic understanding proposed respectively by Gerhard von Rad ("Beginnings of Historical Writing") and some four decades later by John Van Seters *(In Search of History).* The debate here is over the intent of the narrative.

More than a difference of message separates von Rad and Van Seters; there is a huge difference in time. For Rost, von Rad, Würthwein, and others, the narrative belongs around the time of David or Solomon. For Van Seters, it is much later, "from the post-exilic period" (*In Search of History,* 290). The enormous debt that biblical scholarship owes John Van Seters in this regard is the recognition of the impact of reading 2 Sam 11–20 in the exile and later, given the model status accorded to David in the DH. It is clear that the narrative had the potential to ground the image of David in the earthy and sometimes sordid reality of his behavior. It is not at all clear that the various scenes and episodes of the author's work "may all be contrived" (ibid.). The nature of the text — including its roughnesses and inconcinnities — does not favor the idea of a late author's free composition.

Extensive treatment of Van Seters's groundbreaking views is not possible here; a brief reflection is in order. If David's status as "model king" is to include "complete obedience to *all* of the laws, statutes, and commandments" ("Court History and DtrH," 72), there can be no doubt that David's behavior portrayed in 2 Sam 11–20 is in flagrant contrast with the model status. Whether such "complete obedience" is envisaged is open to doubt. Jehu is given good marks in 2 Kgs 10:30; yet the man is portrayed as a murderous thug. The exception noted in 10:31 does not relate to the murder and bloodshed Jehu committed, but to his failure in cultic fidelity, "following the sins of Jeroboam." There are half a dozen kings of Judah who "did what was right in the sight of the LORD. . . . Nevertheless the high places were not taken away" (cf. 1 Kgs 15:11a and 14a; 22:43-44; 2 Kgs 12:3a and 4 [Heb.; NRSV, 12:2a and 3]; 14:3a and 4; 15:3a and 4; 15:34a and 35a). If these six exercised "complete obedience to *all* of the laws," except for the high places, they set standards that royalty before and since has not lived up to. The differing patterns in these royal judgment formulas make it far from clear that they come from a single theologian (cf. the tables in Campbell and O'Brien, *Unfolding,* 478-85). As Van Seters himself remarks of this (for him, postexilic) Court History: "It was integrated into that earlier DtrH with much 'redactional' skill so that the two works had to be read together" ("Court History and DtrH," 92). With the meaning and authorship of the judgment formulas to be resolved, what can be skillfully integrated after the exile can be skillfully integrated before the exile, without prejudice to precisely when. The issue is fascinating; it remains open.

It is important to keep separate the issues of composition and incorporation. In my judgment, a time of composition for the narrative as a whole makes sense around the early royal court of northern Israel. The incorporation of this polyvalent narrative into the sweep of Israel's story is another issue altogether. It deserves to be intensely debated; its theological implications are of major proportions. Given the nature of the beast, hard evidence is not available; as might be expected, consensus is unlikely.

The ending of one narrative with 2 Sam 20 and the beginning of another narrative in 1 Kgs 1 depends on a number of factors and is not concerned with avoiding difficulties in 1 Kgs 1–2. Apart from thematic issues, a primary concern is that in 2 Sam 20 David is not an old and feeble man; in 1 Kgs 1 he is. The narrative of 2 Sam 11–20 is not the Story of David's Later Years; it is the Story of David's Middle Years.

Stefan Seiler is concerned with the conflicting positions of Rost and Würthwein *(Geschichte von der Thronfolge).* He gives a comprehensive survey of the relevant literature and a close study of the text; his conclusion comes down in favor of a pro-Davidic narrative from the Solomonic period. Although various proposals for the ending and beginning of the narrative are discussed, the impression remains that the centrality of thematic focus on the succession to David dominates the study, leaving its literary delimitation unchallenged (as 2 Sam 9–20* and 1 Kgs 1–2*).

Seiler's painstaking downsizing of Würthwein's analyses invites reflection on Martin Noth's comment "a literary-critical possibility is not a literary-critical necessity" ("eine literarkritische Möglichkeit ist jedoch noch keine literarkritische Notwendigkeit," *Könige,* 246). What is possible is not necessary. Had Noth had time to explore this, he might have regretted writing it; but it remains true. The possible generates the optional which an interpretation can ignore and still be responsible. The necessary generates the obligatory which an interpretation cannot ignore and be responsible. If we assume editors to have been intelligent — which here we do — the final text as a necessary given must always be explored if an interpretation is to be responsible. A "literary-critical necessity" reveals conditions that must be addressed if an interpretation is to be responsible. A "literary-critical possibility" allows for options that need not be exploited for an interpretation to be responsible — not to be exhaustive, but to be responsible.

In other words, "the possible" generates options for interpretation that *may* be exploited if occasion arises. Possibilities may or may not be exploited. An interpretation can remain responsible even if the possible is not explored. "The necessary" generates obligations that *must* be met for interpretation to be responsible. The final text is invariably necessary. Seiler's study has considerably reduced the negative impact of Würthwein's little monograph; in my judgment, Seiler's analyses remain an exploration of the possible, rather than a discovery of the necessary. In this regard, the present or final text can be read without undue reservation.

It is symptomatic of the polyvalence of this narrative that the five members of a 1997 seminar on the text were summarized as having four different positions as to its dating. For W. Dietrich, a limited base (2 Sam 11–12* and 1 Kgs 1–2*) might have been Solomonic. O. Kaiser and T. Naumann considered a "Court History" improbable before the end of the eighth century. S. McKenzie attributed it to an early-exilic Deuteronomist. For J. Van Seters, the whole "Court History" was exilic or postexilic (de Pury and Römer, *Die sogennante Thronfolgegeschichte Davids,* 2).

To round off this account, we may note that to be added to the list of those opting for the composition of the Succession Narrative within the lifetime of Solomon are both Erhard Blum (OBO 176) and Stefan Seiler (BZAW 267). Gillian Keys, in her comprehensive study noted earlier, is discreetly cautious: "The only conclusion that can be drawn is that it was written some time between the last years of David's reign and the incorporation of the books of Samuel into the Deuteronomistic History" (*Wages of Sin,* 215).

If a number of recent studies suggest that 1 Kgs 1–2 should be treated as a separate unit (e.g., Flanagan, Conroy, McCarter, Keys), it would be dishonest not to note that the possibility has also been raised of regarding 2 Sam 11–12 as potentially separate from chs. 13–20. The Solomonic aspect should not be over-emphasized. Solomon is scarcely central to chs. 11–12; he is conceived, born, and loved by the LORD — all in one verse at the end (12:24). It is to be hoped that the interpretation given in the body of this book shows clearly the relevance of 2 Sam 11–12 to what follows in chs. 13–20. Von Rad claims that "the idea of a nemesis, which dominates the whole presentation of this history, reaches its culmination in the word of a prophet" (*Theology,* 1.314). Würthwein, commenting on an earlier version of von Rad's views (reflecting on 2 Sam 12:11-12 as possibly later but appropriate), almost sputters in print about neutering the results of critical scholarship in this way ("Aber darf man in dieser Weise eine literarkritische Erkenntnis verharmlosen?" *Thronfolge Davids,* 20, n. 23). The issue of diachronic and synchronic approaches, of process and product, is at its sharpest here (on the general issue, see further Dietrich and Naumann, "David-Saul Narrative," 276-91). When a later addition is claimed, the appropriateness of its being added needs exploration. In the case of 2 Sam 11–12, evidence for a later origin is severely restricted.

2 Samuel 21–24

2 Samuel 21–24 was not treated as such in the diachronic chapter of *1 Samuel* (FOTL 7). That this material formed a single collection is highly likely, as has been noted in the commentary. The time of composition is extremely difficult to pin down, whether of the composition as a whole or of its component elements. The military traditions appear to date from David's time in the wilderness; the plague traditions, at the beginning and end of the composition, are situated relatively late in David's life. Of the two poems, one would be appropriate early and the other late in the life of David. Dating is therefore uncertain. Apart from the two poems, the content is surprising and unexpected. Other things apart, one service these chapters render is to reveal how incomplete our knowledge is of David's time.

Prophetic Record

The Prophetic Record has been fully discussed in *1 Samuel;* the discussion will not be recapitulated here. It features in only the first third of 2 Samuel (chs. 1–8). The principal data identifying a Prophetic Record are the private anointings of kings by prophets (Saul and David by Samuel, Jehu by Elisha's disciple) and the prophetic discourses commissioning or dismissing kings. If the hypothesis of a PR cannot be endorsed, something equivalent is needed to account for the phenomena in the text of Samuel and Kings. There is a commonality of understanding and specific expression associated with Samuel and later Ahijah and Elijah that has to be accounted for. Past scholars have spoken of cycles of prophetic stories. I do not believe that this concept is adequate to account for the phenomena. In the text that we have, Saul has been anointed and dismissed; David has been anointed. It is in the interests of the Prophetic Record to follow through to the establishment of David's kingship and its consolidation.

While Nathan's discourse (2 Sam 12:7-14) has some of the characteristics evoking concerns of the Prophetic Record, it is neither the commissioning nor the dismissal of a king, and the characteristics do not extend beyond the discourse itself (see further, Campbell, *Of Prophets and Kings,* 82-83; Campbell and O'Brien, *Unfolding,* 295-96). After 2 Sam 8, sure evidence for the Prophetic Record does not reemerge until at least after the report of David's death (see Campbell and O'Brien, *Unfolding,* 330).

What is important here, within the context of diachronic discussion, is the realization that the PR is significantly later (at least a century or so) than the events it purports to record. The rewriting is inescapably evident in 1 Sam 9:1–10:16; it is equally present in 1 Sam 15. The activity of PR editors is present in 2 Sam 7 (esp. vv. 8-10). The portrayal of Samuel and Nathan is extremely important for an understanding of Israelite history and the theology and activity of preexilic prophets. Modern interpreters should not be blind to the possibility that the full image of this portrayal may have originated a century or so after the time of Samuel and Nathan.

It is not desirable to explore the detailed implications here; it is important to be aware that the traditions of a significant period in Israel's past have come down to us in the form given them by the PR. Specifically, we may not have a Story of David's Rise. Instead, we may have the Davidic traditions that were gathered and crystallized in the PR. Potentially, this may not be significant; it should not be lost to awareness.

Josianic Deuteronomistic History

The Josianic Deuteronomistic History (JDH) is built in part on the Prophetic Record (PR); the Prophetic Record is built in part on the stories of David's rise to power. The traditions associated with that rise to power provide a favorable portrayal of David's political moves in becoming king of Israel. These are taken over by the PR, with little need to do much more than put its own stamp on 2 Sam 7 and expand the promise of a dynasty to David to include in the dynasty specific and unconditional mention of Solomon, by comparison with the rejected Saul (see Campbell and O'Brien, *Unfolding*, 290-91).

Little was left to be added in the JDH. The chronological details were added for Ishbaal (2 Sam 2:10a) and for David at Hebron (2:11) and more generally (5:4-5). Beyond a couple of details in 2 Sam 8, the JDH emphasizes three elements in 2 Sam 7: (i) the dtr issue of "rest"; (ii) the building of a temple "for my name"; and (iii) the unconditional promise of the establishment of Solomon's throne "forever" (vv. 1b, 11a, 13). The Davidic inheritance will therefore be available for Josiah. David is a model figure in the JDH; after all, he is remembered as king of all Israel, as the lord of Jerusalem, and as the king who remained faithful to YHWH (two of Saul's sons, it will be remembered, had suspect names — Ishbaal > Ishbosheth and Meribaal > Mephibosheth; Solomon turned apostate in his old age; the less said about most of the subsequent kings the better). It is fair to say that "the text of 2 Sam 11-20 holds much to fuel" admiration for David (see Campbell and O'Brien, *Unfolding*, 296).

Assuming the inclusion of chs. 11-20 in the JDH, therefore, even if only on the grounds that they were too good to do without, it is probable that in the context of support for the Josianic reform these chapters were read with emphasis on what was favorable to the king. Despite the evils of the past, and their ongoing consequences, thanks to adroit politics and commitment to YHWH the king was in the end triumphant.

Without chs. 11-20, either 2 Sam 21-24 or 1 Kgs 1-2 (or indeed 1 Kgs 3!) would have needed to follow directly on 2 Sam 8:18 — in the first two cases, reasonably possible but certainly not necessary. The "anticipatory appendices," 2 Sam 9 and 10 are hardly likely to have featured without chs. 11-20. When 2 Sam 21-24 came into the text is a very good question and very hard to answer.

Revised Deuteronomistic History

David remains a model figure; his image is not in need of revision. Royal failure was not directly alleged of David in 2 Samuel; nor was the people's failure to the fore. The attribution of 2 Sam 7:22-24 to the revision's national focus is not based on its evocation of national failure but on its similarity to Deut 4:7-8, 34-39.

Assuming the presence of chs. 11–20 in the RDH, again if only on the grounds that they were too good to do without, it is probable that in the changed context of the failure of the Josianic reform these chapters were read with emphasis on what was unfavorable to the king. Despite adroit politics and royal commitment to YHWH, the evil of the past and its ongoing consequences were in the end triumphant, with the king obliged to flee his capital and, at the end of it all, the kingdom left overwhelmingly fragile. Without chs. 11–20, the implication for the placement of 2 Sam 21–24 and 1 Kgs 1–2 remains the same.

Bibliography of Works Cited Above

Campbell, Antony F. *Of Prophets and Kings: A Late Ninth-Century Document (1 Samuel 1–2 Kings 10)*. CBQMS 17. Washington: Catholic Biblical Association of America, 1986.

––––––. *1 Samuel*. FOTL 7. Grand Rapids: Eerdmans, 2003.

––––––. *Joshua to Chronicles: An Introduction*. Louisville: Westminster John Knox, 2004.

Campbell, Antony F., and Mark A. O'Brien. *Unfolding the Deuteronomistic History: Origins, Upgrades, Present Text*. Minneapolis: Fortress, 2000.

Conroy, Charles. *Absalom! Absalom! Narrative and Language in 2 Samuel 13–20*. AnBib 81. Rome: Biblical Institute, 1978.

Delekat, Lienhard. "Tendenz und Theologie der David-Salomo-Erzählung." Pages 26-36 in *Das ferne und nahe Wort: Festschrift Leonhard Rost*. Edited by F. Maass. Berlin: Töpelmann, 1967.

Dietrich, Walter, and Thomas Naumann. "The David-Saul Narrative." Pages 276-318 in *Reconsidering Israel and Judah: Recent Studies on the Deuteronomistic History*. Edited by G. N. Knoppers and J. G. McConville. Winona Lake, IN: Eisenbrauns, 2000.

Flanagan, James W. "Court History or Succession Document? A Study of 2 Samuel 9–20 and 1 Kings 1–2." *JBL* 91 (1972) 172-81.

Fohrer, Georg. "Die alttestamentliche Ladeerzählung." *Journal of Northwest Semitic Languages* 1 (1971) 23-31.

Keys, Gillian. *The Wages of Sin: A Reappraisal of the 'Succession Narrative.'* JSOTSup 221. Sheffield: Sheffield Academic Press, 1996.

McKenzie, Steven L., and Thomas Römer (eds.). *Rethinking the Foundations: Historiography in the Ancient World and in the Bible. Essays in Honour of John Van Seters*. BZAW 294. Berlin: de Gruyter, 2000.

Mowinckel, Sigmund. "Israelite Historiography." *ASTI* 2 (1963) 4-26.

Noth, Martin. *Könige 1. 1 Könige 1–16*. BKAT IX/1. Neukirchen: Neukirchener Verlag, 1968/1983.

Pury, Albert de, and Thomas Römer (eds.). *Die sogennante Thronfolgegeschichte Davids: Neue Einsichten und Anfragen*. OBO 176. Freiburg, Switzerland: Universitätsverlag, 2000.

Rad, Gerhard von. *Old Testament Theology*. Volume I: *The Theology of Israel's Historical Traditions*. Edinburgh: Oliver and Boyd, 1962. German original, 1957.

―――."The Beginnings of Historical Writing in Ancient Israel." Pages 166-204 in *The Problem of the Hexateuch and Other Essays*. Edinburgh: Oliver & Boyd, 1966.

Rost, Leonhard. *The Succession to the Throne of David*. Translated by M. D. Rutter and D. M. Gunn. Sheffield: Almond, 1982. German original, 1926.

Seiler, Stefan. *Die Geschichte von der Thronfolge Davids (2 Sam 9–20; 1 Kön 1–2)*. BZAW 267. Berlin: de Gruyter, 1998.

Van Seters, John. *In Search of History: Historiography in the Ancient World and the Origins of Biblical History*. New Haven: Yale University Press, 1983.

―――. "The Court History and DtrII." Pages 70-93 in *Die sogenannte Thronfolgegeschichte Davids: Neue Einsichten und Anfragen*. OBO 176. Freiburg, Switzerland: Universitätsverlag, 2000.

Whybray, R. N. *The Succession Narrative: A Study of II Samuel 9–20; I Kings 1 and 2*. SBT 2/9. London: SCM, 1968.

Würthwein, Ernst. *Die Erzählung von der Thronfolge Davids — theologische oder politische Geschichtsschreibung?* ThSt 115. Zurich: Theologischer Verlag, 1974.

GLOSSARY

ACCESSION FORMULA (Einführungs, Thronbesteigungs Formel). The term may be used for the introductory part of the regnal resumé (see below). The full introductory resumé may contain as many as five elements. For Saul, at 1 Sam 13:1, two are noted: his age at accession and the length of his reign. The numbers involved are contested and difficult: one-year-old and a two-year reign (for discussion, see the commentary). The age at accession is given here, unusual since Saul is a Benjaminite; the note of age is usual only for kings of Judah, but occasionally is missing in the resumé (cf. Long, *1 Kings,* 264).

ACCOUNT (Bericht). Account is one of the literary genres coming under the overarching concept of (→) narrative. It is used where there is concern for the communication of information without any need for plot, raising tension and reaching resolution. It is often found practically as a synonym for (→) report. For some, account is felt to be rather more extensive and explanatory in nature; for others, it is felt to be rather less impersonal; for others again, account is the more general non-plot term, with report being rather more restricted. Precision in definition and use is unlikely to be achieved. Readers will need to be sensitive to context. An allied genre is (→) notice, usually implying greater brevity.

G. Coats (with R. Knierim) characterizes account as relating additional information that brings some particular light to bear on what might otherwise be reported more neutrally; the aspect of accountability is given weight (*Exodus 1–18,* 155-56). The emphasis on accounting for something, rather than neutrally reporting it, is attractive. However, it cannot be taken for granted as a usage among scholars. Readers must exercise judgment.

ANECDOTE (Anekdote). A short narrative of an interesting or amusing or otherwise memorable episode, often told to illustrate a point. See Holman, *Handbook to Literature,* 25.

ASIDE (Neben Bemerkung). One way of describing an editorial insertion that breaks the flow of a text in order to provide information judged helpful at that point. Cf. 2 Sam 21:2b.

BATTLE REPORT See REPORT OF BATTLE.

COLLECTION (Sammlung). Collection as used here — not to be confused with what is taken up in church and other holy places (cf. Exod 25:2) — is not strictly a literary genre. It is a grouping of various items that has been given a certain unity. It is not the same as a list, where items are assembled under a certain perspective or heading; the component elements in a collection usually have generic identities of their own. The unity may be internal and thematic. For example, the traditions comprising the Story of David's Rise could be called a collection of stories and other materials brought into the service of the portrayal of David's rise to power through God's favor and without bloodshed. The unity may be external and compositional. For example, the traditions comprising the Special Collection at the end of 2 Samuel form a collection in the light of the tight chiastic organization of otherwise quite disparate traditions.

COMMENT (Kommentierende Bemerkung). Comment is the general term used to describe a narrator's activity in stepping outside the narrative to express an opinion on what is taking place. Comment is a part of narrative: the activity that occurs when the narrator steps back from the narrative itself and communicates directly with the narrative's audience. It may be purely secular, as in the comment on the lying prophet: "he lied to him" (1 Kgs 13:18). It may express belief, indicating God's action within apparently human affairs: "it was a turn of affairs brought about by the LORD" (1 Kgs 12:15).

HISTORICAL STORY (Geschichtserzählung). The term was used by Rolf Rendtorff to describe stories where historical rather than heroic elements were to the fore ("Beobachtungen," 431-32). For 2 Samuel, he had in mind 2:12-32. He considered the designation particularly appropriate where there was no central individual figure involved (e.g., 1 Sam 21:2-10; 22:6-23).

HYMN OF PRAISE (Hymnus, Loblied). According to E. Gerstenberger (*Psalms Part 1* [FOTL 14], 249) the hymn is a "joyful song of choir or community extolling the greatness and kindness of Yahweh and his dwelling place. Seasonal and ad hoc festivals for the ancient Israelite give ample occasion to get together at holy places. Sacrifices and celebrations extend over several days. The hymns intoned vary in contents: They praise creation and creator (cf. Psalms 8; 19; 104), and Yahweh's glorious deeds in history (cf. Psalms 68; 105). They admire Mount Zion, his abode (cf. Psalms 46; 48; 76), and jubilate at his just reign (cf. Psalms 24; 47; 93; 96). Hymn-singing always has been a vital part of Jewish-Christian worship services. . . ."

Hymns tend to celebrate who God is and what God does. The hymn, or more specifically the hymn of praise, is a psalm or song that extols and glorifies YHWH. Typical elements are: a call to praise or worship; praise of YHWH; blessings or petitions. The opening call to praise may be resumed at the conclusion of the hymn. The blessings and petitions play a minor role; the focal point is the descriptive or narrative praise. Modes of expression vary, ranging from solemn measured stanzas to a free narrative style. The Hebrew use of the participle (hymnic participle) is a feature of many hymns of praise; it functions to describe or recall the great deeds of YHWH in creation or salvation (e.g., 1 Sam 2:6-8; Pss 33; 103; 104; 135; 145; 146; Job 5:9-16; Amos 4:13; Isa 40:22-23). Even when hymns seem to glorify intermediate things, YHWH is usually the real subject of praise. Praise is closely associated with thanksgiving.

Reading:
F. Crüsemann, *Studien.*
E. S. Gerstenberger, *Psalms.* Part 1 (FOTL 14), 249-50.
H. Gunkel and J. Begrich, *Introduction.*
S. Mowinckel, *Israel's Worship.*

LAMENT (Klagelied). A funeral song bewailing the death of the deceased, describing his merits (eulogy), and calling for further mourning. The typical meter is *qînâ* (3 +2). The most characteristic formulas used are *'êk* (or *'êkâ*), "how" or "alas," and imperatives which call for mourning (e.g., "weep," "mourn," etc.). The description of the merits of the deceased may be termed eulogy, a particular type of speech designed to praise a given person, whether living or dead.

The lament or dirge was ordinarily performed by hired women or gifted individuals after a death and was usually sung in the presence of the corpse as part of the funeral preparations. The communal lament has a quite different setting from the lament over an individual (as is the case for 2 Sam 1:19-27; 3:33-34).

Adapted from: E. S. Gerstenberger, Form-critical project files, Institute for Antiquity and Christianity, Claremont.

LEGEND (Legende). A (→) narrative primarily concerned with the wonderful and aimed at edification. See Campbell, *1 Samuel,* 343.

LIST (Liste). A simple recounting in writing of names of items assembled under a certain perspective or heading. In an elementary form of list, the names or items may be assembled regardless of any ordering system. In a developed form, elements are logically or explicitly linked together in successive order, providing an artistic form. Adapted from an entry in the FOTL project files by R. Knierim.

NARRATIVE (Erzählung). Narrative is information about action communicated directly. Narrative is an overarching concept; it does not itself constitute a literary genre. It is characterized as information: it is not primarily concerned with moving an audience to action or creating an attitude. It is characterized as about action: its subject is event or movement; even if the action is emotional or intellectual, it will involve the development of interplay of emotions or ideas in action, not their simple description or logical progression. It is characterized as direct communication: it is addressed to its audience rather than acted out before a group which "overhears" it.

OT narrative takes many different forms. From the point of view of technique: (→) story which moves from created tension to its resolution, (→) report which simply describes events with no overt effort to create tensions and resolution, and (→) legend which seeks to edify. From the point of view of situation: narrative may be historical or non-historical. The first is bound to time and space in ways that are plausible within ordinary or remembered experience (e.g., legend, novella, story). The second moves in a parameter of space or time that transcends, precedes, or follows ordinary experience (e.g., fable, märchen, myth). (→) Anecdote and märchen are other types of narrative with special techniques and content. For further reading, see Scholes and Kellog, *Nature of Narrative.* Adapted from entries in the FOTL project files by D. J. McCarthy.

NOTICE (Notiz). A brief account noting for the record either traditions/information or opinions/views.

ORACLE (Orakel). "A communication from the deity, often through an intermediary such as priest or prophet, especially in response to an inquiry" (from Knierim, in Coats, *Exod 1–18,* 166). The occurrence here: 2 Sam 23:1-7.

PRAYER OF THANKSGIVING (Danklied). The prayer of thanksgiving is an adaptation of the thanksgiving song of the individual, with a view to reporting private prayer. The thanksgiving song is described as a "jubilant cultic song to celebrate victory, divine help, good harvests, and all sorts of joyful occasions" (Gerstenberger, *Psalms,* 1.256-57). In the case of David's prayer (2 Sam 7:18-29), the "jubilant cultic song" has been adapted to become a respectful outpouring of gratitude for a particular form of divine help, the promise of a dynasty.

PROPHETIC ANNOUNCEMENT (CONCERNING ROYAL DESTINY) (Prophetische Ankündigung [des Schicksals eines Königs oder einer königlichen Dynastie]). A prophetic announcement is described as "a broad collecting generic term for an unsolicited . . . announcement of a prophet concerning future events or future actions of YHWH" (Sweeney, *Isaiah,* 529). The qualification "concerning royal destiny" is largely a matter of content. Cases in point would be: 2 Sam 7:1-17; cf. 1 Sam 10:1; 13:13-14; 15:26; 1 Kgs 11:31-39; 14:7-16; 21:17-24; 2 Kgs 9:6-10. "Royal destiny" points in two directions: the equivalents of elevation to kingship or rejection from kingship. The promise of a dynasty is a commitment to the long-term elevation to kingship of a specific king's heirs.

PROPHETIC JUDGMENT SPEECH (Prophetische Gerichtsrede). A passage in which the prophet speaks on behalf of YHWH to announce judgment against an individual, group, or nation. Examples include: 1 Sam 2:27-36; Isa 22:16-24; Amos 7:14-17; Jer 20:1-6 (individual); Jer 23:9-12; 23:13-15; Mic 3:9-12 (group); Isa 8:5-8; Jer 11:9-12 (nation). The main elements of the genre are: (i) a statement of the reasons for judgment; (ii) a logical transition ("therefore" or equivalent), usually with the messenger formula; (iii) the announcement of punishment. Associated elements may include a call to attention or the oracle formula. The reasons for judgment are presented often but not always in the prophet's own words; the prophet then reports the announcement of punishment by YHWH. Sweeney distinguishes a "Prophetic Announcement of Punishment against an Individual" as employing "a more direct form of the accusation against the individual" (*Isaiah,* 530), probably reflecting judicial proceedings in Israel or Judah.

Adapted from Marvin A. Sweeney, *Isaiah 1–39,* 533-34 (cf. 530).

Sources:
Gene M. Tucker, *Form Criticism.*
C. Westermann, *Basic Forms.*
H. W. Wolff, "Begründungen."

REGNAL RESUMÉ (Abriss einer königlichen Regierungszeit). A formulaic summary, above all in the books of Kings, which provides information about the kings of Israel and Judah. The regnal resumé normally appears in two parts, as an introductory and a concluding summary, forming a framework around the account of a particular reign. The introductory part typically includes: (1) name of the king and date of accession; (2) the age of the king at accession (for Judah only); (3) the length of reign and the capital city where he reigned (one or both sometimes given in the concluding summary); (4) the name of the queen mother (for Judah only); and (5) a theological evaluation, usually stylized and stereotyped. Occasionally some elements, or even the entire resumé, may be omitted. The concluding part of the regnal resumé, also sometimes omitted, usually includes: (1) a citation formula, referring the reader to other sources for information about the reign; (2) a notice of death and burial of the king; and (3) a notice of succession, i.e., who succeeded him. Examples are 2 Kgs 13:10-13 (both parts); 1 Kgs 15:1-5, 33-34 (introductory part); 1 Kgs 14:19-20; 2 Kgs 10:34-35 (concluding part). See also: ACCESSION FORMULA.

Adapted from Long, *1 Kings,* 259.

REPORT (Bericht). A usually brief (→) narrative, which tells what happened without trying openly to arouse interest by creating tension leading to resolution — by contrast with (→) story. Alternative terms used are (→) account and (→) notice. They may have the same definition; for some authors, account may imply a less impersonal tone than report, with notice tending to imply greater brevity.

REPORT OF BATTLE (Kampfbericht). A short (→) narrative of a battle, providing the basic information about a battle and its outcome. It does not attempt to describe the battle; on the other hand, it is more than a bare notice of the fact of a battle or its result. See Campbell, *1 Samuel,* 345-46.

REPORTED STORY (Berichtete Erzählung). As a genre, reported story is used of narrative texts that stand in only an indirect relationship to the performance of storytelling. Instead, they look in two directions: rearward, back to the storytelling tradition that they report; forward, to the stories to be told in the future.

The rearward glance is the report of storytelling tradition. We know the texts we have and the high quality of their literary style; it is tribute to the quality of ancient Israel's storytelling. Those who told the stories told them well; those who reported the stories reported them well. The plot structure is there. The gems of dialogue are there. The details that go to make a good story are there. There is enough stuff there to hold a report together. The trimmings that any good storyteller can generate are not there. Variant versions are there, even if only briefly noted. A storyteller may choose to use one; no good storyteller would actualize conflicting ones. Contradictory traditions are sometimes noted. Good storytellers knew how to handle them. Fundamentally, a good report preserved whatever possibilities the tradition contained. The aim of a reported story is to recapitulate the story — not to retell it.

The reported story also looks forward as a base for the storyteller whose task is to retell the story. Choices may be made from that base: which variants to tell, which details to include. A good storyteller knows, on any given occasion, which details to provide and which to withhold, which gaps to fill and which to leave as gaps. A good storyteller knows when to extend a story and when to shorten it. The base may contain several variants; the good storyteller will actualize only one and will know which is the right one to actualize for the particular audience. It is not a matter of being bound to a text but bound to a story — to the opportunities that a text offered and limited for the telling of a story. To be more nuanced for later generations: canonically, it is a matter of being bound to a text; aesthetically, it may be a matter of being bound to a story, which in its own appropriate fashion is duly bound to the text.

The reported story preserves a past tradition, rehearsed in the telling of the story, and prepares for a future rehearsal of the tradition, in the retelling of the story. There is a structured move from the oral into the written with a view to returning to the oral. We have no certainty that such reported stories functioned as bases for storytelling; it is an assumption, based on respectable grounds. The description given is fully compatible with the processes described in the field studies reported by Culley, *Structure of Hebrew Narrative,* 4-20, and by Long, "Recent Field Studies."

How Israel's traditions, preserved in some instances as reported stories, can be woven into Israel's longer narratives is adequately illustrated in 1 Samuel. Clearly, it is possible for a longer report to be condensed for the sake of an extended narrative. Clearly, it is equally possible for a terse report to be expanded during its incorporation into another narrative. We cannot identify where such possibilities may have been actualized. What we can affirm is this: some texts bear characteristics that point to the reporting of stories rather than the performing of stories. Such characteristics do not affect any canonical aspects of a text, which are unchanged. Instead, they point to the possibility of a text's addressing both readers and also storytellers — which can change matters quite significantly.

For the purposes of this volume, reported story will be suggested as genre when the text appears to require a storyteller's choice, clarification, or expansion; where such development is not required by the text but is merely possible, the genre will be given as the more conventional (→) story. Alternative terms used are STORY OUTLINE and STORY SUMMARY.

229

Reading:
Campbell, "Reported Story"; "Storyteller's Role."
Campbell and O'Brien, *Sources,* 19; "1–2 Samuel," 580-81; *Unfolding,* 7.
Culley, "Oral Tradition," 1-33, esp. 9; *Structure of Hebrew Narrative,* 1-32, esp. 15-16.
Long, "Recent Field Studies."
Rofé, "Prophetical Stories," 432-33.
Wilcoxen, "Narrative," 65-66.

SHORT COMMUNICATION (Kurze Mitteilung). These are not fully fledged narratives or stories, nor do they appear to stem from annals or chronicles. Rather, they are pieces of information which, in themselves, are unlikely to have been important enough to find their way into official annals or chronicles and which are hardly substantial enough to have existed as independent traditions or stories. But they are necessary for the telling of a story, and they are collected by the compiler or storyteller in order to provide the proper setting for the story. In the case of the story of David's rise to power, for example, we find such short communications interspersed with the stories, which are viable enough to have had a literary independence of their own, and with the data that might be culled from royal chronicles and other records. These short notices contribute background and a certain framework to the whole narrative; they may be traditions which were personally known to the narrator; they may be the result of his inquiries. They are largely details that would be of little interest outside the larger perspective of the narrative.

Reading:
Rendtorff, "Beobachtungen."

SHORT NOTICE (Kurze Notiz). An alternative term for SHORT COMMUNICATION.

SONG (Gesang, Lied). A poetic composition performed by an individual or group. See also HYMN OF PRAISE and THANKSGIVING SONG.

STORY (Geschichte). A ($\rightarrow$) narrative that creates interest by arousing tension and resolving it. A story's structure is controlled by plot, moving from exposition and the initial introduction of characters through forms of complication to resolution and conclusion. Plot is understood in the Aristotelian sense of the arrangement of the incidents of an action. See Campbell, *1 Samuel,* 348.

STORY OUTLINE/STORY SUMMARY (Erzählungsskizze, -zusammenfassung). Alternative terms for REPORTED STORY.

THANKSGIVING SONG (Danklied). A jubilant cultic song to celebrate victory, divine help, and all sorts of joyful occasions. There are personal thanksgiving songs and communal ones.
Adapted from E. S. Gerstenberger, *Psalms,* Part 1 (FOTL 14), 256-57.

THEOLOGICAL NARRATIVE (Theologische Erzählung). The term is used to describe those cases where the (→) narrative has acquired a new function: the shaping of theological questions and affirmations. Its function is to grapple with theological problems and assertions through the medium of narrative. The same can, of course, be said of a theologically told (→) story. While the terms narrative and story might sometimes seem interchangeable, there are occasions when the mingling of (→) account and (→) comment, (→) report and story, within a single text make it advisable to use the overarching term of narrative.

Bibliography of Works Cited Above

Campbell, Antony F. "The Reported Story: Midway between Oral Performance and Literary Art." *Semeia* 46 (1989) 77-85.

———. "The Storyteller's Role: Reported Story and Biblical Text." *CBQ* 64 (2002) 427-41.

———. *1 Samuel.* FOTL 7. Grand Rapids: Eerdmans, 2003.

Campbell, Antony F., and Mark A. O'Brien. *Sources of the Pentateuch: Texts, Introductions, Annotations.* Minneapolis: Fortress, 1993.

———. "1–2 Samuel." Pp. 572-607 in *The International Bible Commentary: A Catholic and Ecumenical Commentary for the Twenty-First Century.* Edited by W. R. Farmer. Collegeville: Liturgical Press, 1998.

———. *Unfolding the Deuteronomistic History: Origins, Upgrades, Present Text.* Minneapolis: Fortress, 2000.

Coats, George W. *Exodus 1–18.* FOTL 2A (completed and edited by R. Knierim et al.). Grand Rapids: Eerdmans, 1999.

Crüsemann, Frank. *Studien zur Formgeschichte von Hymnus und Danklied in Israel.* WMANT 32. Neukirchen: Neukirchener Verlag, 1969.

Culley, Robert C. "Oral Tradition and the OT: Some Recent Discussion." *Semeia* 5 (1976) 1-33.

———, *Studies in the Structure of Hebrew Narrative.* Philadelphia: Fortress, 1976.

Gerstenberger, Erhard S. *Psalms: With an Introduction to Cultic Poetry.* Part 1. FOTL 14. Grand Rapids: Eerdmans, 1988.

Gunkel, H., and J. Begrich. *Introduction to Psalms: The Genres of the Religious Lyric of Israel.* Macon, GA: Macon University Press, 1998. German original, 1933.

Holman, C. Hugh. *A Handbook to Literature.* 3rd ed. Indianapolis, IN: Bobbs-Merrill, 1972.

Long, Burke O. "Recent Field Studies in Oral Literature and Their Bearing on OT Criticism." *VT* 26 (1976) 187-98.

———. *1 Kings: With an Introduction to Historical Literature.* FOTL 9. Grand Rapids: Eerdmans, 1984.

Mowinckel, Sigmund. *The Psalms in Israel's Worship.* 2 vols. Oxford: Blackwell, 1962.

Rendtorff, Rolf. "Beobachtungen zur altisraelitischen Geschichtsschreibung anhand der Geschichte vom Aufstieg Davids." Pp. 428-39 in *Probleme biblischer Theologie.* Edited by H. W. Wolff. Munich: Chr. Kaiser, 1971.

Rofé, Alexander. "The Classification of the Prophetical Stories." *JBL* 89 (1970) 427-40.

Scholes, Robert, and Robert Kellog. *The Nature of Narrative.* London: Oxford University Press, 1966.

Sweeney, Marvin A. *Isaiah 1–39: With an Introduction to Prophetic Literature.* FOTL 16. Grand Rapids: Eerdmans, 1996.

Tucker, Gene M. *Form Criticism of the Old Testament.* Philadelphia: Fortress, 1971.

Westermann, Claus. *Basic Forms of Prophetic Speech.* Philadelphia: Westminster, 1967.

Wilcoxen, Jay A. "Narrative." Pp. 57-98 in *Old Testament Form Criticism,* edited by J. H. Hayes. San Antonio, TX: Trinity University Press, 1974.

Wolff, Hans Walter. "Die Begründungen der prophetischen Heils- und Unheilssprüche." Pages 9-35 in *Gesammelte Studien zum Alten Testament.* Munich: Kaiser, 1964.

Afterword

THE BIBLE'S BASIC ROLE

The Bible has many roles to play in support of the life of faith and in fanning the flame of spirit.

For some, the well-supported avowal that 1–2 Samuel is not the best authenticated, near-contemporary record of aspects of the history of Israel comes as a matter of relief and liberation; for others, such distancing from history is a cause for sorrow. For some, the realization that 1–2 Samuel contains optional variants and conflicting, on occasion contradictory, traditions comes as no surprise; for others, the fact that it is not a reliable source of information, to be trusted once academically sifted, comes with a feeling of great loss.

Text-based biblical scholarship is primarily concerned with the interpretation of text, an activity that is fundamentally different from the recovery of event. Form criticism of its nature is text-based. Within the subtlety of text, as opposed to the potential simplicity of event, we are obliged to recognize, as inherent in human effort, the presence of advocacy and opposition, of insight and inadequacy, of partisanship and prejudice, which divine concurrence — however understood — has not excluded. For some, this recognition is a source of relief; for others, it is a source of pain.

It may help to put these two books of Samuel in context, so that the Bible as a whole speaks for itself. The Bible may not be a mine of information and instruction; instead, as text, it may be an invitation to reflection and response.

Beyond this, it is important — if we are to take the Bible's account of itself seriously — that we become aware of the full justification of our own interest in the Bible and our study of it. Form criticism has always taken the Bible seriously; as form critics, academically we must justify that seriousness. For all of its brevity, that is the purpose of this Afterword. (An earlier version of these reflections appeared in *ABR* 50 [2002] 1-9; see also Campbell, *Authority of Scripture*.)

It will help to list from the outset two triads that, for many, sum up their main reasons for turning to the Bible.

- For a spiritual approach: usually reading rather than study — looking primarily to spirituality, prayer, preaching, etc.
  — To arouse feeling
  — To fuel faith
  — To fire imagination
- For a critical approach: usually study rather than reading — also available for the service of spirituality, prayer, preaching, etc.
  — To explore the incarnational, a God almost concealed in the human
  — To probe the foundational, the base of our faith-identity
  — To risk the interpretational, the challenge of self-discovery

The first triad deserves more space than can be allotted here; it is better to prescind. The second needs our closer exploration. Somewhere in the middle of these, there is also the well-informed and highly knowledgeable reading that is not necessarily critical; it can be most important to the life of faith and to bringing the fire of spirit to a blaze.

The base for any initial discussion here is well known, whether we speak of it as the options offered in the Bible, the multiplicity of vantage points available, the complementarity of views expressed, or the contradictions presented. What concerns us is the conclusion drawn from these observations. Is the basic role of the biblical text to provide something (e.g., information), impose something (e.g., ideas), witness to something (e.g., God's action), or invite to something (e.g., reflection)? Experience of the text leads me to the last, to invitation.

The implications are there for those who read or pray the Bible, for those who teach in relation to the Bible, and for those who are leaders in communities of biblical faith. The elaboration of these implications will not be undertaken here. Of course, there are challenge, encouragement, energizing, etc. — another story.

A saying that I have not heard contested or queried over the years sharpens the issue. It is not an axiom; it is a matter of observation.

> We do not believe something because we can quote it from the Bible; we quote something from the Bible because we believe it.

This confronts us with two questions: (i) By what process and for what reasons do we come to believe something of relevance to our faith, if it is not on the authority of the Bible? (ii) Why then do we quote from the Bible in support of what we believe? What need is operative in us?

I find the metaphor of signposts useful. Signposts may be vital to travelers on a journey. A signpost pointing in a single direction is helpful, if the direction is the right one. Several signposts, pointing in different directions to the same destination, invite reflection. They may be misleading, having been tampered with by vandals, for example, but maybe not. Several routes can lead to the same goal; sometimes, the longest way round (in distance) is the shortest way there (in time or effort). Further exploration may be needed; reflection is invited. Many readers will find that the Bible often offers conflicting signposts (i.e., competing YHWH faith claims), from extensive texts — about creation, flood, deliverance at the sea, sojourn in the desert, occupation of the land, emergence of monarchy, and even divine providence — to matters that can be compassed in a verse or two. In such cases, readers are invited to reflection; the signposts point in differing directions. The biblical text tends not to adjudicate, but to amalgamate.

The decision about what is predominantly the nature of biblical text and how it functions is one that needs to be remade out of the experience of the text by each generation of its readers. Any other way risks dogmatism or superstition. Each generation must study its Bible. These considerations should not deflect attention from the complementary roles of the biblical text: to arouse feeling, fire imagination, and fuel faith. The task here is to explore the biblical text and reflect on its signposts.

Biblical Text

Creation

The Bible offers us manifold allusions to creation, whether lengthy descriptions or shorter references. Psalm 104 moves magnificently from the earth on its foundations and the deep as its cover to the ocean with ships sailing on it and Leviathan sporting in it. Proverbs 8 has a marvelous image of creation, with wisdom's primacy over everything else, "the first of God's acts of long ago" (v. 22) through to rejoicing in the world and delight in the human race (v. 31). Job 38, opening God's discourse out of the whirlwind, has a wonderful series of questions about the laying of the foundation of the earth, the shutting in of the sea with doors, the origins of morning and the dwelling of light, the storehouses of the snow and the channels for the rain. Genesis 2 has the forming of a man and God's search for human completeness, achieved in the forming of a woman. Genesis 1 has the creation of our visible world, majestically segmented into days, finding its completeness in the hallowing of the seventh day, the creator God's observance of later Israel's Sabbath.

Alongside these, in the sophistication of Isaiah, Job, and Psalms, we have allusions to creation by combat and the dismembering of the primeval sea monsters — with Rahab cut in pieces in Isa 51:9; with the dragon (Tannin), Rahab, the Sea, and the serpent (Nahash) all featured in various parts of Job (e.g., 7:12; 9:13-14; 26:12-14); with Leviathan being crushed in Ps 74:14 and Rahab crushed in Ps 89:10. When, in its times of distress, Israel needed a God with grunt, the awesome power of the conqueror in creation was available.

In all of these, God creates. Nothing else is common. We have witness to faith in God as creator. As to the "how" of creation, we are invited to reflection.

Flood

We know well that there are at least two traditions of the Flood. They are inter-woven because both end with God's solemn commitment never to destroy sin-ful humankind again (Gen 8:21-22; 9:1-17). Arranged differently, one would subvert the other.

In one set of traditions, the flood is portrayed in 40-day blocks, comes from a great rainstorm, and with the preservation of seven pairs of clean ani-mals as well as one pair of each of the unclean has surplus enough for a great sacrifice. In another set of traditions, the flood is portrayed in 150-day blocks, comes from the bursting forth of the fountains of the great deep and the opening of the windows of the heavens, and with the preservation of only one pair of all animals fortunately does not end in a sacrifice.

We may be comforted by faith in a God who will not destroy or reject us because of innate human evil. If we wish to know more detail, we are invited to reflection.

Sea

The deliverance at the Sea (Exod 13:17–14:31), whether Red Sea or Reed Sea, is one of the great images in Israel's experience of salvation worked by God (cf. Deut 11:1-7; Josh 2:10; 4:23; 24:6; Ps 106:7-12, 22; 136:13-15).

The classic image is clear: at the gesture of Moses' hand, the waters were parted to left and right, Israel marched across, followed by the Egyptians who were then swamped. But also, in the same text, there is a tradition of deliver-ance but no crossing. The pillar of cloud moves from in front of Israel to take up station between Israel and the Egyptians all night (14:19-20*); God's wind drives the sea back all night (14:21*); at the end of the night, near dawn, from the pillar of cloud God causes panic among the Egyptians so that they retreat across the dry seabed and are swamped by the returning waters (14:24, 25b, 27*), assuming that God's "all-night" wind stopped with the dawn. Since, at the start of it all, the Israelites were told to turn back and camp by the sea (14:2), they had already gone past it. Crossing the sea was not the problem; escaping the Egyptian pursuit was. (Note: the asterisk [*] indicates "only relevant por-tions" of the verse or text given.)

Israel believed they had been delivered. As to how, at best reflection is in-vited. To quote from Campbell and O'Brien:

> The maintenance of duality within this carefully combined text can only be understood as witness to the conviction in ancient Israel that Israel's history did not declare God to Israel without interpretation. Rather Israel's theolo-gians and people of faith read and interpreted their experience of history and declared God from it. The unity achieved in the text attests a faith that the passage from Egypt to the wilderness, from slavery to freedom, a passage symbolic of Israel's emergence from the womb of history, was a moment of such significance to Israel it needed to be focused in the uniqueness of a sin-

gle story, in which Israel expressed their confession of deliverance by the God who was the source and center of their being. (*Sources of the Pentateuch,* 256)

Israel's authors were professing and celebrating faith; they were not reporting details of fact, not informing the people of the present of precisely what had occurred in the past. Deliverance is reported; as to the processes, reflection is invited.

Wilderness

In the pentateuchal texts of Israel's sojourn in the wilderness, it — the wilderness — is the classic location for Israel's rejection of their God. If we forget for a moment Israel's longing for the fleshpots of Egypt and their fill of bread (Exod 16:3), along with the fish, the cucumbers, the melons, the leeks, the onions, and the garlic (Num 11:5), we can hear God's angry complaint to Moses, "How long will this people despise me? And how long will they refuse to believe in me, in spite of all the signs that I have done among them? I will strike them with pestilence and disinherit them, and I will make of you a nation greater and mightier than they" (Num 14:11-12), followed by God's characterization of the people who "have tested me these ten times and have not obeyed my voice" (Num 14:22).

For Jeremiah and Hosea, the wilderness is a time and place for honeymoon fidelity. For Jeremiah: "I remember the devotion of your youth, your love as a bride, how you followed me in the wilderness, in a land not sown" (2:2). For Hosea: "I will now allure her, and bring her into the wilderness, and speak tenderly to her. . . . There she shall respond as in the days of her youth, as at the time when she came out of the land of Egypt" (NRSV, 2:14-15).

Infidelity and fidelity are marvelously mingled. If we seek for understanding, we are invited to reflect.

Occupation

Israel's occupation of its land is as complex an issue as any in the biblical tradition. For our purposes, we can set aside recent scholarly reconstructions involving infiltration, peasant revolt, social upheaval, and all that sort of thing; what we need is already in the biblical portrayal. Three traditions dominate the picture; two are enough for us here. In one, Israel wages a military campaign, with God's help. Kings and their soldiers are handed over to the Israelites (cf. Josh 6:2; 8:1-2; 10:1, 16-27; 24:11). In the other, the work is entirely God's, with Israel having little more role than that of being there — i.e., the stories of the Jordan crossing, the capture of Jericho, and the failed attack on Ai. The capture of Jericho is a good example. To march around a besieged city once a day for six days and finally seven times on the seventh day may be brilliant psychological warfare, unnerving the defenders. But a shout, no matter how fierce, does not cause the walls to collapse. Only God can do that.

If we want to look back to Israel's occupation of the land and reflect on its meaning for Israel's life in the land, we cannot go beyond speculation as to what took place. There is an invitation to thought; there is no imposition.

Monarchy

At least three traditions are preserved about the origins of monarchy in Israel. One reflects Israel's need for defense against its external enemies. Another reflects Israel's need for internal justice. A third regards the request for a king as apostasy, the rejection of God. (For details, see Campbell and O'Brien, *Unfolding the Deuteronomistic History,* 217-19, 230-49.)

Should we want to think about it, we are not told what to think. We are invited to reflection.

Providence

In much of the wisdom literature, providence and God's relationship to goodness and wickedness is clear. Psalm 1 puts it well: "Happy are those . . . [whose] delight is in the law of the LORD. . . . In all that they do, they prosper. The wicked are not so . . . the way of the wicked will perish."

Job's verdict is equally clear: What rubbish! "Have you not asked those who travel the roads, and do you not accept their testimony, that the wicked are spared in the day of calamity, and are rescued in the day of wrath?" (Job 21:29-30).

Conclusions

In all of this, it seems clear that the biblical text does not impose thought on us from outside. It invites us inside ourselves and calls us to reflection. I have nothing against thought and reflection, but I am not alone in needing something more to account for my particular passion for the Older Testament.

Three areas at least catch something of what fires that passion and excites my critical interest in the Bible. They can be named the incarnational, the foundational, and the interpretational (as noted rather densely in the Introduction to *1 Samuel*).

The *incarnational* is important to me (it may well be different for others). For me, it is not restricted to God's becoming one of us, but expanded to reflect our experience of God as unobtrusive and intangible, almost concealed from us in the ordinariness of life. It speaks of God who is not distant from us, but deeply involved with us. The imagery is intense: "as the bridegroom rejoices over the bride, so shall your God rejoice over you" (Isa 62:5); "as the loincloth clings to one's loins, so I made the whole house Israel and the whole house Judah cling to me, says the LORD" (Jer 13:11). At first sight, God as unobtrusive and intangible, the ordinariness of God, may not seem evidently applicable to the Bible. Many long to escape the ambiguity and uncertainty of so much human living, and the Bible often seems to offer a way into the certainty and clarity of the divine. Closer acquaintance with it calls us back to explore, be reconciled with, perhaps rejoice in the incarnational (involvement-in-the-human) uncertainty and ambiguity we find in the Bible as well as in ourselves — an invitation to compassion.

The *foundational* is for me at the base of faith-identity. It arises where we quest for what is of ultimate concern to us in our lives. We need to know about the wellsprings in our past that are vital to our present. We yearn for foundations that rest in bedrock. We may need to examine the nature and the quality of the foundations on which major aspects of our faith-identity are built — just as people buying a house run checks on foundations and structural soundness, plumbing, roofing, and wiring, etc., or financial institutions contemplating takeovers run due diligence checks. In such a situation, adherents of biblical faith need to explore the Bible.

The *interpretational* relates to that risky activity of exploring our present beings, of self-discovery, when we need to make meaning for ourselves of our living, when we need to interpret our lives to ourselves. For many, the exploration of the Bible — probing in the foundations of faith and even discovering there roots and something of the incarnational — is an indispensable aid in interpreting life.

To simplify, the attraction exciting much critical engagement with the Bible can be spelled out in terms of three activities: being at home with God, being at home with one's faith, and being at home with oneself.

Incarnational

The God I experience in my faith is a God who engages with the human rather than bypassing it, a God experienced as unobtrusive and intangible, almost concealed from us in the ordinariness of life. I would be suspicious if the God of the Bible were much different.

It is true, of course, that Exodus 14 has the Sea parted to left and right; but the same chapter records wholly other actions by God. It is true that the Jordan is portrayed as parted and the walls of Jericho as collapsed; it is equally true that factors in the text point to the role of liturgy. It is true that the text has the ark dispense death in the Philistine cities, at Beth-shemesh, and on the way to Jerusalem; theology is not unlikely. The issue is not whether Older Testament traditions can be demythologized, whether by the text or by its interpreters. The issue is not whether some of the Newer Testament miracles can be conveniently explained. The reality is that these play a relatively small part in the traditions of either Testament, as do wonders and miracles today. The God of the Bible was scarcely more demonstrably evident in the life of the community than is God today. I am grateful.

I do not want neon lights, but the soft uncertain illumination that filters through so much of human living and allows for the occasional insight.

I believe I am a modern, well-informed, and questioning human being, with a pleasantly broad critical streak. I have a very strong religious faith; I have very deep doubts. I do not find the fact of doubt to be in conflict with the act of faith. What I look for in biblical texts is not in conflict with what I learn from recent science. I do not look for modern science in biblical texts; I do not look for insights into the meaning of life in recent science.

When I look into biblical texts, I can find faith and doubt there. I can find prayer and politics there. The faith I find there is occasionally expressed in terms I would today describe as grossly unscientific. What I find in the wide range of biblical texts is a struggle to find meaning in human existence. That struggle is not denied; it is not always successful. It is there. Recent science does not for me deny the struggle for meaning; it does not resolve it either. The struggle is there. Biblical text that neither denies nor always resolves the struggle for meaning is for me text that is deeply steeped in the mystery of human experience. It is incarnational and I am at home with that. On occasion, biblical text can offer meaning that I do not find helpful; on occasion, it can offer meaning that helps me in making sense of my life, meaning that I can build on and enlarge — and I am at home with that.

Foundational

Once upon a time, it was said that a career in the Church was the bolthole for the fool of the family. I would be disappointed and uncomfortable to find too many of the family fools among the pillars of the Bible.

I would not want the core documents of my faith to be substantially the work of those who might be characterized as credulous, gullible, and unsophisticated. Fortunately for me, the evidence suggests quite the opposite.

As should be clear from these commentaries on 1–2 Samuel — and as is equally evident for me in close study of the Pentateuch and the Deuteronomistic History — those responsible for our biblical text, whether in its beginnings, in the process of its development, or in its final form, were highly intelligent, highly skilled, and insightful thinkers and theologians.

Interpretational

There can be joy in encountering text that challenges one's understanding of life and self. Jeremiah puts it well:

> They have forsaken me, the fountain of living water,
> and dug out cisterns for themselves,
> cracked cisterns that can hold no water. (Jer 2:13)

We need the challenge of living water; all too easily we can lapse into making cisterns for ourselves that can hold no water — cannot generate life and cannot sustain it or nourish it.

For me, that "fountain of living water" involves awareness of what is named "spirit" and acceptance of "commitment to faith in God." The idea of God is not, I hope, the product of need, the preserver of privilege, the opiate that anesthetizes by holding out a hope beyond injustice and oppression. Commitment to faith in God is at bottom a giving weight and worth to the whisper of spirit at the deep core of human life. Yearning for the spirit has been an issue across all human history: whether to seek it, spurn it, or ignore it. Often, the options are fundamental and basic, involving the meaning or absurdity of life lived at depth. For some, Christian faith may be chosen because it gives most meaning (for example, acceptance of God's reality). Again, of the absurdities on offer, Christian faith may be the least absurd (for example, acceptance of God's love). For such faith, the reality of God, incarnation, eucharist, and resurrection are too vital to be lost in the turmoil of Church politics or institutional change. (I speak of "Christian faith" because it is the faith I know and live; I dare not speak of the "meaning or absurdity" of other faiths that I do not know from within.)

Spirit can impact on us in many ways. It may be extraordinary, erupting into our lives powerfully, overwhelming us. We may have to be careful; it can be risky. It may be very ordinary, quietly and unobtrusively present. We may have to be attentive; it can be elusive. A biblical example of the extraordinary might be Elijah's great wind, or earthquake, or fire (1 Kgs 19:11-12a); since the LORD was not in these — but could have been — another example nearby is Elijah's long-distance run in front of Ahab, halfway across Israel (1 Kgs 18:46). In our lives, it could be a passionate love affair, at its best, or the cataclysmic encounter with nature or great art. The prime biblical example of the ordinary is surely Elijah's "sound of sheer silence" (1 Kgs 19:12b). In our lives, there is the stillness of intimacy, the quiet of contemplation, the wonder of fidelity — and so much more.

The awareness of spirit is often coupled with an awareness of ourselves and our world as insufficient — inexplicable to the best of our understanding. The discoveries and theories of science are fascinating and illuminating. They open avenues to new universes of the mind. They do not diminish our sense that we and our universe are insufficient. So we seek a cause that is sufficient; the sense of spirit validates our search. The outcome of the search is not factual and certain knowledge; it is chosen belief — commitment to a point of view, while recognizing that it might not be right. C. S. Lewis's biographer refers to the whole European philosophical tradition since Plato as attempting to account for "our sense that we do not belong in this world, that we are pilgrims and strangers here, homesick for another place where one day we shall be truly ourselves" (Wilson, *Lewis,* x). We might never use such language — for we do indeed belong in this world as well as beyond it — but is that "sense" (what Karl Rahner calls the transcendental experience of God) romantic rot or does it touch on ultimate truth? Awareness of spirit leans toward the latter. At the core of it all is a mystery that says Yes — a mystery whom we name God.

241

Postscript

Responses are now possible to the two questions raised at the beginning.

To the first: Why do we believe something that is of relevance to biblical faith, if not on the authority of the Bible?

We believe it because it has its proper place within the *interpretation* of ourselves, our lives, and our world that we have shaped — from our experience of ourselves and the various levels of community within which we have been shaped — based on an insight into ourselves and our world to which we are committed and which gives meaning to our lives.

To the second: Why do we quote from the Bible in support of what we believe, if it is not the authority for our belief?

We quote from the Bible because of *foundations*. It is important to us that our faith-identity and our present belief are in substantial conformity with some aspect of the experience we find articulated within the Bible, in substantial conformity with some aspect of our foundations.

Bibliography of Works Cited Above

Campbell, Antony F. *The Authority of Scripture: Canon as Invitation.* Occasional Paper No. 37. Claremont, CA: Institute for Antiquity and Christianity, Claremont Graduate School, 1996.

———. "Invitation or . . . ?: The Bible's Role." *Australian Biblical Review* 50 (2002) 1-9.

Campbell, Antony F., and Mark A. O'Brien. *Sources of the Pentateuch: Texts, Introductions, Annotations.* Minneapolis: Fortress, 1993.

———. *Unfolding the Deuteronomistic History: Origins, Upgrades, Present Text.* Minneapolis: Fortress, 2000.

Wilson, A. N. *C. S. Lewis: A Biography.* London: Collins, 1990; paperback, Flamingo, 1991.